National Infrastructure Planning Handbook 2015

National Infrastructure Planning Handbook 2015

General Editor

Michael Humphries QC
Barrister, Francis Taylor Building

Assistant Editors

Douglas Edwards QC
Barrister, Francis Taylor Building

Gregory Jones QC
Barrister, Francis Taylor Building

James Pereira QC
Barrister, Francis Taylor Building

Hereward Phillpot QC
Barrister, Francis Taylor Building

Authors

Alexander Booth
Barrister, Francis Taylor Building

Richard Honey
Barrister, Francis Taylor Building

Mark Westmoreland Smith
Barrister, Francis Taylor Building

Rebecca Clutten
Barrister, Francis Taylor Building

Isabella Tafur
Barrister, Francis Taylor Building

Guest Contributors

Sarah Merritt
Solicitor, Pinsent Masons LLP

Emma Cottam
Solicitor, Pinsent Masons LLP

Bloomsbury Professional

Bloomsbury Professional Ltd, Maxwelton House, 41–43 Boltro Road, Haywards Heath, West Sussex, RH16 1BJ

Bloomsbury Professional is an imprint of Bloomsbury Publishing plc

A CIP Catalogue record for this book is available from the British Library.

ISBN 978 1 78043 881 8

Typeset by Phoenix Photosetting, Chatham, Kent
Printed and bound in Great Britain by CPI Group (UK) Ltd, Croydon, CR0 4YY

Preface

The Planning Act 2008 represented a fundamental change in the approach to consenting major infrastructure projects in England and Wales. Born out of a sense of frustration arising from the experience of long planning inquiries during the 1980s and 1990s, Government commissioned a number of reviews of the planning system, including the Barker Review of Land Use Planning (2006). It was Kate Barker who outlined what became many of the themes for reform that found their way into the Government White Paper 'Planning for a Sustainable Future' (2007) and ultimately into the 2008 Act. They include:

- Government policy to be set out in National Policy Statements;
- a requirement for pre-application consultation;
- the creation of an Infrastructure Planning Commission (the IPC);
- a greater emphasis on written procedures; and
- a move towards a single consenting process.

Whilst the IPC was abolished by the Localism Act 2011, the new regime otherwise survived a change of Government almost intact and has flourished. The Planning Inspectorate has had to adapt rapidly to an entirely new set of procedures, but has risen to the challenge and maintained its very high standards of decision making. The 2008 Act has also required a new approach by practitioners and a willingness to identify new forms of 'best practice'.

It was with this latter point in mind that in 2011 I came up with the idea for an 'on-line' National Infrastructure Planning Service (NIPS), being a hyperlinked and searchable series of articles and primary materials on the new regime. The idea was to create a single reference point for busy practitioners where they could search articles and materials on a wide range of practical issues arising under the Planning Act 2008. I then recruited a number of experienced fellow practitioners in chambers at Francis Taylor Buildings (ftb) to write articles on a range of 2008 Act issues; for my part, I had the (enjoyable) task of writing some of the articles and editing all the others! I have also been fortunate in having external contributors who have submitted articles for inclusion in the work, and I am always on the lookout for more. More articles are being added to the on-line service as new issues arise.

NIPS launched in late 2012 and its success has led to demands for a paper version of the articles and the Act itself; to distinguish it from the 'on-line' work we have called this the National Infrastructure Planning Handbook. Clearly a paper version cannot have the hyperlinks and searchability of the 'on-line' service, and nor can it have the full range of materials; it does, however, provide an accessible, and I hope helpful, guide to practice and procedure under the Planning Act 2008.

It would not be right for me to end this preface without expressing my gratitude to those who have helped in producing the work. I am, of course, enormously indebted to all the assistant editors, authors and other contributors who have written articles; they are identified on the title page to this book. They have produced a high quality body of work that has certainly revealed new insights into the law for me and, I hope, will be of interest and assistance to readers generally. A constant source of help, encouragement and ideas has been my in-house Bloomsbury editor, Leanne Barrett. Leanne was instrumental in turning my initial proposal into a coherent project and I could not have been better assisted along the way. Finally, I must thank my wife, Juliet, without whose love and support so few of the things of which I am most proud would ever have come to pass.

Michael Humphries QC
Francis Taylor Building
January 2015

Contents

Contributors

General editor

Michael Humphries QC

Barrister, Francis Taylor Building

Michael Humphries specialises in all aspects of property development law, but is particularly well known for his major infrastructure planning and compulsory purchase work, where he has acted in relation to some of the largest and most important projects in recent years. Michael has promoted and advised on a large number of nationally significant infrastructure projects under the Planning Act 2008, including the Preesall Underground Gas Storage project, the Thames Tideway Tunnel project, the A30 Improvement project and the Hinkley Point Connection project. Michael has also promoted major infrastructure schemes under the Transport and Works Act 1992, the Town and Country Planning Act 1990, the Electricity Act 1989, the Highways Act 1980, the Gas Act 1965, and the Pipelines Act 1962.

In *Chambers & Partners 2015* Michael was identified as one of the six 'star individuals' at the Planning Bar. He was both *Chambers & Partners* and *Legal 500* planning silk of the year in 2013 and also appeared in *Planning Magazine's* 'Power 100' list as one of the most influential people in the UK planning system. In 2013 Michael was appointed a Visiting Fellow in the University of Cambridge Land Economy Department where he delivers an annual lecture on infrastructure planning.

Published comments about Michael have been consistently complimentary and include: 'increasingly *the* name in large infrastructure projects' (*Chambers & Partners 2013*); 'He is a brilliant advocate whose analysis of legal points cannot be faulted. He is a pleasure to work with however much pressure he is put under' (*Chambers & Partners 2014*); and 'Renowned for his expertise in infrastructure law', 'An extremely intelligent operator, with laser-like focus on the issues' (*Chambers & Partners 2015*).

Michael helped to found the National Infrastructure Planning Association (NIPA) and is its current Treasurer.

Assistant editors

Douglas Edwards QC

Barrister, Francis Taylor Building

Douglas Edwards practices in the fields of planning, compulsory purchase environment, administrative and local government, highway law and property law. He also has particular expertise in the law relating to common land and greens. He appears regularly for both appellants and local planning and other authorities at inquiries and in the courts. Douglas has advised on a number of nationally significant infrastructure schemes, including the A30 Improvement project.

Chambers & Partners 2015 described Douglas as 'Efficient and commercial in his approach' and 'Very capable, approachable and able to assimilate complex technical issues quickly'.

Gregory Jones QC

Barrister, Francis Taylor Building

Gregory's practice covers all aspects of administrative law including judicial review and statutory challenges, town planning, compulsory purchase, environmental law, EU law and public procurement, education, local government, administrative law. Regularly appearing in both public inquiries and the higher courts, Gregory acts on behalf of developers, local planning authorities and third parties.

Gregory has advised on a number of nationally significant infrastructure projects and successfully promoted the Able Marine Energy Park project.

Legal 500 2015 describes Gregory as 'A superb advocate' and *Chambers & Partners 2015* states that Gregory 'gets to grips with complex intellectual issues very quickly and is '[a]n authority on environmental impact assessment, habitats directives and wider planning and environment issues. He is also renowned for his expertise in matters involving CPOs. A likeable, quick-thinking advocate who is always fun to work with and who shows a deep understanding of the implications of EU environmental law on the UK planning system' and that 'He has a very calm and reassuring approach, and his expertise in environmental impact assessment matters is invaluable.'

James Pereira QC

Barrister, Francis Taylor Building

James specialises in all aspects of planning, environmental, local government and administrative law, compulsory purchase and compensation, and has considerable experience in national infrastructure planning. James promoted both the Galloper Offshore Wind Farm project and the Willington cross-country gas pipeline project.

Before taking silk James was in the highest rank of junior barristers in both environmental law and planning law in the *Legal 500 2012* and *Chambers & Partners 2012*, who list him as one of only four 'star individuals' at the junior planning bar. He is also ranked as a leading junior in Administrative Law in both directories. *Chambers & Partners 2015* says that 'He's just got it all – he's approachable, easy to work with, very bright, knows his stuff and clients like him.'

James was appointed Queen's Counsel in 2014.

Hereward Phillpot QC

Barrister, Francis Taylor Building

Hereward has an extensive practice in nationally significant infrastructure planning and has promoted a number of major nationally significant infrastructure projects including the Hinkley Point C nuclear power station, the East Anglia One and Navitus Bay offshore wind farms, Thames Tideway Tunnel and the National Grid Carbon Capture and Storage scheme.

Hereward was named 'Junior Barrister of the Year' in environment and planning by *Chambers & Partners 2012*, which also ranks him as one of only four 'star Individuals' in the field of planning. *Legal 500* similarly ranked him as one of the top four juniors in planning, and the RTPI *Planning Magazine* Law Survey ranks him as one of the top three.

Published comments about Hereward include: 'He is our go-to barrister. He is very efficient, really gets to the problem quickly, is very good at thinking around the issues, gives clear advice and guidance, and is just a really nice guy to work with. He's definitely our number-one choice.' *Chambers and Partners 2015*.

Hereward was appointed Queen's Counsel in 2015.

Authors

Alexander Booth

Barrister, Francis Taylor Building

Alex Booth has a practice which encompasses all aspects of planning, compulsory purchase and environmental law. He regularly appears at Public Inquiries, in the Upper Tribunal (Lands Chamber) and in the High Court, and has also appeared in both the Court of Appeal and the Supreme Court.

He has wide experience of infrastructure development generally, and of nationally significant infrastructure projects promoted pursuant to the 2008 Act in particular. As regards the latter, he promoted the Rookery South Resource Recovery Facility on behalf of Covanta, and acted on behalf of Associated British Ports to oppose the Able Marine Energy Park promoted on the south bank of the Humber Estuary. He also acted for Thames Water in the legal challenges to the Thames Tideway Tunnel development consent. Other experience includes the promotion of LNG pipelines in South Wales on behalf of National Grid, opposing the expansion of Coventry Airport and advising statutory undertakers regarding the laying of high voltage electricity cabling in Central London, required in connection with Crossrail.

Richard Honey

Barrister, Francis Taylor Building

Richard Honey practises as a barrister in public and environmental law, with particular specialisms in judicial review and statutory High Court challenges, infrastructure projects, and compulsory purchase and compensation.

Richard's infrastructure experience includes schemes under the Transport and Works Act and the Electricity Act, and parliamentary work including appearances before the Crossrail and HS2 Bill committees for various objectors. Recent infrastructure work includes the Olympics, Thameslink, Crossrail, highway schemes, wind farms and airports (Stansted, Southend, Lydd). Richard advised Natural England on the examinations into Hinkley Point C nuclear power station and the Able Marine Energy Park.

Richard is ranked as a leading barrister by *Chambers & Partners* for planning and environmental law and was also ranked in the top 10 highest rated planning junior barristers in the 2013 *Planning Magazine* survey.

Mark Westmoreland Smith

Barrister, Francis Taylor Building

Mark has been described as 'a tenacious advocate', 'rapidly scaling the ranks', 'particularly well regarded', having 'a bright future' and 'practical, experienced, down to earth and always gives clear advice' (*Chambers & Partners*). He was consistently recognised as one of the leading planning barristers under the age of 35.

He has particular experience in infrastructure planning and has recently been working on development consent orders for electrical infrastructure, power stations, ports, waste management facilities as well as roads.

He is a member of the National Infrastructure Planning Association, the Compulsory Purchase Association and is a former Assistant Secretary to the Planning and Environmental Bar Association.

Rebecca Clutten

Barrister, Francis Taylor Building

Rebecca Clutten was called to the Bar in 2008 and is currently ranked third in the top planning juniors under 35 (*Planning Magazine* Survey, 2014), having been rated consistently highly since joining ftb in 2010.

Rebecca has substantial experience in infrastructure planning, having advised and appeared for promoters of DCOs and Transport and Works Act Orders at the application and examination stages, both being led and in her own right. Her experience also includes Parliamentary work, and she recently appeared before the House of Commons Select Committee on High Speed 2. Rebecca's practice extends to include general town planning matters and compulsory purchase and compensation. Her clients include major utilities providers, developers and local authorities, as well as private individuals.

Rebecca is a member of the National Infrastructure Planning Association and is an elected member of the committees of the Planning and Environmental Bar Association and the Compulsory Purchase Association.

Isabella Tafur

Barrister, Francis Taylor Building

Isabella has gained considerable experience of national infrastructure planning through her involvement in a number of DCO applications.

She has worked for National Grid in relation to its application for development consent for an innovative carbon capture and storage project, as well as for the promoters of the Walney Extension offshore windfarm application in the Irish Sea, the A30 trunk road improvement in Cornwall and the Able Marine Energy Park on the Humber estuary. In these cases she has been involved in the preparation and review of documents both prior to, and after the submission of the application. She has attended preliminary meetings and issue specific hearings and prepared written submissions during the examination period.

Guest contributors

Sarah Merritt

Solicitor, Pinsent Masons LLP

Sarah is a senior associate at Pinsent Masons LLP, specialising in major infrastructure planning and regulatory matters.

Sarah advises utility companies, distribution network operators, developers, local authorities and government agencies on a variety of matters, both national and international.

Sarah's practice focuses on the energy and natural resources, waste and infrastructure sectors. She has experience of advising on obtaining regulatory consents for nationally significant infrastructure projects, including development consent orders under the Planning Act 2008, planning permission under the Town and Country Planning Act 1990, Electricity Act 1989 consents and nuclear site licences. These projects include biomass, nuclear and gas-fired power stations, energy from waste facilities, electricity distribution infrastructure, proposals for a nuclear waste repository, non-nuclear waste facilities and road schemes.

Emma Cottam

Solicitor, Pinsent Masons LLP

Emma is a Solicitor in the Planning & Environment and Energy & Infrastructure team based in the Pinsent Masons' London office. Emma has experience in consenting major infrastructure projects in England and Wales and has advised on a number of energy schemes at various stages in the Planning Act 2008 process.

Table of Cases

[*References are to pages numbers*]

P

R

S

T

W

Table of Statutes

[*References are to page numbers*]

Table of Statutory Instruments

[*References are to page numbers*]

Part 1

The Examining Authority and the Secretary of State

The Major Applications and Plans Directorate of the Planning Inspectorate

Written by: Richard Honey, ftb
Edited by: Michael Humphries QC, ftb

On 1 April 2012 the Planning Inspectorate (also known as PINS) became responsible for operating the planning process for nationally significant infrastructure projects. Before that date applications for nationally significant infrastructure projects were handled by the Infrastructure Planning Commission (IPC). The IPC was, however, abolished under the Localism Act 2011 and its functions transferred to the Inspectorate. The Major Applications and Plans Directorate (MAPD) now discharges the former functions of the IPC. MAPD is a department within the Planning Inspectorate that was formed in March 2013 following an internal reorganisation of the Planning Inspectorate that saw the merger of the National Infrastructure Directorate and the Development Plans Directorate.

MAPD has responsibility for the administration of major applications under the Planning Act 2008, local plans and the measures for major planning applications under the Growth and Infrastructure Act 2013 where developers opt to apply direct to the Inspectorate.

MAPD handles major applications and discharges many of the procedural functions of the Secretary of State under the Planning Act 2008, the Infrastructure Planning (Applications: Prescribed Forms and Procedure) Regulations 2009 and the Infrastructure Planning (Examination Procedure) Rules 2010. This includes the pre-application process, submission of an application, acceptance, pre-examination, examination and reporting.

The Secretary of State has established a formal framework of delegation, delegating nationally significant infrastructure projects actions to the Inspectorate's Chief Executive, who in turn has sub-delegated functions to the Director of Major Applications and Plans and the Chief Planning Inspector (as reported in the Inspectorate's 2012/13 annual report published on 27 June 2013).

MAPD is based at Temple Quay House in Bristol. It currently has a staff of around 70, including both salaried and non-salaried inspectors. The current Director of Major Applications and Plans is Mark Southgate, a chartered town planner with over 20 years' experience. Prior to his appointment he was Director of Casework and Plans at the Inspectorate.

The Planning Inspectorate's 2012/13 annual report shows that the Inspectorate received over £3m in fee income for national infrastructure work, against an operating cost of almost £6m.

Further information about the MAP and the Planning Inspectorate can be found at: http://infrastructure.planningportal.gov.uk.

MAP works with the Consents Service Unit (CSU). The CSU was launched in April 2013 to help provide a 'one-stop-shop' approach to non-planning consents for nationally significant infrastructure projects that are required in addition to any development consent order. The purpose of the CSU is to improve the coordination between the developer, relevant consenting bodies and the Inspectorate, to seek to make the overall consenting process more efficient. The CSU published a 'Prospectus for Developers' that sets out the unit's objectives.

During 2012 the Major Infrastructure Environment Unit (MIEU) was established within Defra to work on matters relating to the Habitats and Wild Birds Directives and infrastructure projects. MIEU was set up to support progress on individual infrastructure projects and improve processes for infrastructure projects by:

- playing a key early risk management role to identify issues associated with the Habitats and Wild Birds Directives for projects
- ensuring collaboration between all parties to support resolution of issues as necessary
- introducing and overseeing a new process for agreeing evidence requirements
- providing greater clarity to developers on requirements

Further information on MIEU can be found at: http://www.defra.gov.uk/habitats-review/implementation/infrastructure-projects/.

The Appointment and Composition of the Examining Authority

Written by: Isabella Tafur, ftb
Edited by: Michael Humphries QC, ftb

Introduction

Pursuant to section 86 of the Planning Act 2008 (PA 2008), the Examining Authority is defined as either a Panel or a single appointed person appointed by the Secretary of State to examine an application for a development consent order. It is for the Secretary of State to determine whether the application should be handled by a Panel (under Chapter 2 of PA 2008) or by a single appointed person (under Chapter 3 of PA 2008). That decision will be made after an application has been accepted by the Secretary of State and a certificate has been received from the applicant confirming that it has complied with the notice and publicity requirements contained in PA 2008, s 56 (and, where applicable, a notice of the persons interested in land to which a compulsory acquisition request relates) (PA 2008, s 61).

Rule 2(1) of the Infrastructure Planning (Examination Procedure) Rules 2010 (as amended) ('the 2010 Rules') defines the Examining Authority as follows:

> '(a) the Panel or single appointed person appointed under section 62 (appointment of members, and lead member, of a Panel) or section 79 (appointment of a single appointed person), and may include one or more members of the Panel allocated a function of the Panel in accordance with section 76 (allocation within Panel or Panel's functions); or
>
> (b) the Secretary of State, in respect of those matters which are the subject of a direction by the Secretary of State under section 95A(2).'

Section 95A was inserted into the PA 2008 by the Localism Act 2011. It enables the Secretary of State to direct that representations of a type specified in his direction may only be made to persons of a specified description (rather than being made in public). It applies where part or all of the examination procedure will take the form of a meeting or hearing and the Secretary of State is satisfied that the making of oral representations at such a meeting or hearing would be likely to result in the disclosure of information as to defence or national security, and that public disclosure of that information would be contrary to the national interest.

Criteria for determining how an application should be handled

PA 2008, s 61 requires the Secretary of State to publish the criteria that are to be applied in determining whether an application is to be handled by a Panel or a single appointed person. The criteria are currently set out in the consultation draft of DCLG's non-statutory 'Guidance for the examination of applications for development consent for nationally significant infrastructure projects'. The main criteria which the Secretary of State will consider are: (a) the complexity of the case; and (b) the level of public interest in the outcome (paragraph 12). When looking at the complexity of the case the Secretary of State will consider whether the application raises novel issues for development, raises complex legal or technical considerations, proposes associated development which would require consideration of policy contained in more than a single National Policy Statement (NPS), or involves analysis of policy issues because, for example, there is no relevant NPS. In considering the level of public interest the Secretary of State will have particular regard to the likelihood of the examination requiring hearings so that parties can make oral representations about the application. Of the 15 applications which had been, or were being, examined by the end of 2012, seven were handled by Panels.[1] All of those Panels were made up of three members, with the exception of the Hinkley Point C nuclear generating station application, where a fourth member was subsequently appointed. The remaining eight applications were handled by single appointed persons[2].

Transfer of the application from a single appointed person to a Panel

Where the Secretary of State has appointed a single appointed person to examine the application, he may at any time decide that the application should be handled by a Panel instead (s 62). He must publish the criteria to be applied when making such a decision. DCLG's consultation Guidance explains that the Secretary of State will be able to transfer the application to a Panel if he considers the application is more complex than the original assessment indicated and that it requires a wider range of expertise (paragraph 14). The Guidance does not, however, suggest that the Secretary of State can make a decision to transfer the application to a Panel on the basis that it has generated a greater level of public interest than originally anticipated.

Where an application is transferred from a single appointed person to a Panel, the single appointed person may be appointed as a member of that Panel, and may also be appointed as chair of the Panel (s 71). Where such a transfer is effected, it will not always be necessary for the examination procedure to start again. Pursuant to s 71 the Panel may, so far as it thinks appropriate, decide to treat things done by or in relation to the appointed person on the application as done by or in relation to the Panel. In these circumstances it will be the duty of the lead member to ensure that the members of the Panel have the necessary knowledge of the proceedings which took place under the appointed person.

Notifying the parties

The Secretary of State must, before the preliminary meeting, notify all those who have been notified of the accepted application that the Examining Authority has been appointed, and give details of who has been appointed (r 4 of the 2010 Rules).

1 Rookery South; Hinkley Point Power Station; Galloper Offshore Windfarm; Preesall Saltfield Underground Gas Storage; Able Marine Energy Park; Triton Knoll Offshore Windfarm; and Roosecote Biomass Power Station (which was subsequently withdrawn by the applicant).

2 North Doncaster Chord; Ipswich Chord; Kentish Flats Extension; Brechfa Forest Wind Farm; Heysham to M6 Link Road; East Northants Resource Management Facility; Port Blythe New Biomass Plant; M1 Junction 10a Grade Separation.

Where the Secretary of State had originally appointed a single appointed person and subsequently decides that the Examining Authority should be a Panel, he must notify all interested parties of this decision. He must also notify interested parties of any change in the membership of the Panel or appointment of any replacement appointed person, or any direction made under PA 2008, s 95A.

Appointment and replacement of Panels and single appointed persons

The Panel procedure is set out in Chapter 2 of the PA 2008, and the single appointed person procedure in Chapter 3 of the PA 2008. The Secretary of State may appoint a Panel of either 3, 4 or 5 members, with one of those members (the 'lead member') appointed as chair.

A Panel may, instead of undertaking a part of the examination, allocate the undertaking of that part to one or more of its members (PA 2008, s 76). Where it makes such an allocation, anything which is required or authorised to be done by the Panel under Chapter 4 of the PA 2008 in connection with the allocated part of the examination, may be done by or to the member(s) concerned. The findings and conclusions of the member(s) concerned in respect of the matters allocated will be taken to be those of the Panel as a whole, provided the Panel so agreed at the time of making the allocation (or before the allocation was made). Where there is an allocation to two or more members, the making of a decision by the members concerned requires the agreement of all of them. Procedural powers conferred on the Panel for the purposes of its examination of the application can be exercised by the Panel itself and by any one or more of its members (unless the Panel has decided to restrict or prohibit the exercise of procedural powers other than by the Panel itself) (PA 2008, s 77).

Members of the Panel and single appointed persons can resign their positions by giving notice in writing to the Secretary of State, and they can also be removed by the Secretary of State if he is satisfied that they are unable, unwilling or unfit to perform their duties (sections 66 and 80).

In a Panel, the lead member can be removed from that office without being removed from the Panel altogether. In such circumstances the Secretary of State must appoint another lead member (either from amongst the other members of the Panel or be appointing a new member) (PA 2008, s 69). New members may be appointed by the Secretary of State at any time after the initial appointment of the members (provided the total number does not exceed five), and he must do so if the membership of the Panel falls below three (PA 2008, s 68). He cannot, however, use this power to appoint new members where the Panel ceases to have any members (PA 2008, s 72(5)).

If the Panel ceases to have any members at all, a new Panel must be constituted (PA 2008, s 72). Where a new Panel is constituted, it may decide to treat things done by or in relation to the previous Panel (or treated by the previous Panel as being done by or in relation to that Panel, under PA 2008, s 71(3)) as done by or in relation to the new Panel. The lead member will be responsible for ensuring that the members have the necessary knowledge of the proceedings up until the reconstitution of the Panel.

PA 2008, s 73 makes it clear that the Panel's continuing identity is not affected by any change in its membership; the Panel coming to have only two members or a single member; any change in the lead member; or a vacancy in the office of lead member.

Where a person ceases to be the single appointed person, the Secretary of State must make a new appointment (PA 2008, s 82). Where this happens the new single appointed person may, so far as may be appropriate, decide to treat things done by or in relation to any previous single appointed person as done by or in relation to the new single appointed person (PA 2008, s 82(2)). Where he does so, the single appointed person is under a duty to acquire the necessary knowledge of the previous proceedings on the application.

The functions of the Examining Authority

Regardless of whether it is a Panel or a single appointed person, the functions of the Examining Authority are to: (1) examine the application; and (2) make a report to the Secretary of State on the application setting out: (i) its findings and conclusions in respect of the application; and (ii) its recommendation as to the decision to be made on the application. Its functions must be carried out in accordance with Chapter 4 of the PA 2008 (Examination of applications under Chapter 2 or 3 of PA 2008).

Where the Examining Authority is a Panel, the making of a decision requires the agreement of a majority of its members. The lead member has a casting vote, in the event that the vote is tied.

Appointment of assessors and advisors

Pursuant to PA 2008, s 100, the Secretary of State may, at the request of the Examining Authority, appoint a person to act as an assessor to assist the Examining Authority in its examination of the application. The Secretary of State may only appoint an assessor if it appears to him that the person has the expertise that makes him suitable to provide assistance to the Examining Authority.

The Secretary of State may also appoint, at the request of the Examining Authority, a barrister, solicitor or advocate to provide legal assistance to the Examining Authority in connection with its examination of the application, including carrying out any oral questioning at a hearing on behalf of the Examining Authority.

The role of assessors and legal advisors is to assist the Examining Authority, but those persons do not form part of the Examining Authority.

Where an assessor or a barrister, solicitor or advocate is appointed, the Examining Authority must notify all interested parties of the name of the assessor and/or the details of the legal advisor and, in the case of an assessor, must notify the parties of the particular matters on which the assessor is to assist the Examining Authority (rr 11 and 12 of the 2010 Rules).

DCLG's consultation draft Guidance explains (paragraphs 65–66) that in most cases the appointment of an assessor is likely to take place at the pre-examination stage, because the initial assessment of the application would usually have identified to the Examining Authority the issues that required further examination with the assistance of an assessor.

DCLG's consultation draft Guidance also explains (paragraph 67) that the Examining Authority may sometimes need to appoint a professional advocate to ensure evidence is 'tested in the most effective and revealing way'.

The Role of the Examining Authority

Written by: Isabella Tafur, ftb
Edited by: Michael Humphries QC, ftb

Introduction

Once the Secretary of State has appointed either a single appointed person or a Panel as the Examining Authority (see Article 3.2.2 for further details on the appointment and composition of the Examining Authority) its role in relation to the application for development consent is governed by the PA 2008, ss 74–77 and 83.

One of the principal changes introduced by the Localism Act 2011 is that all decisions on development consent applications are now made by the Secretary of State. The role of the Examining Authority is, therefore, limited to examining the application and reporting to the relevant Secretary of State.

Panel

Where the Examining Authority is a Panel, its role is set out in PA 2008, ss 74–77. It must examine the application and prepare a report for the Secretary of State, setting out its findings and conclusions in respect of the application, and its recommendation as to the decision to be made (PA 2008, s 74).

Decisions made by the Panel require the agreement of a majority of its members, and the lead member has a casting vote in the event of a tied vote (PA 2008, s 75). However, the Panel may choose to allocate parts of the examination to one or more members of the Panel (PA 2008, s 76). Where they do so, the findings or conclusions of that member (or those members) will be taken to be the findings and conclusions of the Panel in relation to the allocated matter. If a matter has been allocated to two or more members of the Panel, their decision on that matter requires their unanimous agreement.

Single appointed person

Where the Examining Authority is a single appointed person, its role in relation to the application is governed by PA 2008, s 83. Its functions mirror those set out in s 74 in relation to a Panel: it is to examine the application and prepare a report to the relevant Secretary of State setting out its findings and conclusions in respect of the application and its recommendation as to the decision to be made.

Examination of the application

The functions of the Examining Authority must be carried out in accordance with Chapter 4 of the PA 2008, which governs the manner in which an application should be examined (see PA 2008, ss 74(3) and 83(3)). The Infrastructure Planning (Examination Procedure) Rules 2010 also contain provisions relating to the examination of applications. Later articles consider the 'examination' process in detail.

The Legal Status of the Secretary of State in Litigation

Written by: Richard Honey, ftb
Edited by: Michael Humphries QC, ftb

Although any Secretary of State or other Minister acts formally on behalf of the Crown, it is important to understand the legal distinction between the Queen and her Ministers. Whilst the Crown retains certain prerogatives and indeed public immunity in litigation (subject to the Crown Proceedings Act 1947), Parliament will normally confer administrative powers and duties on 'the Secretary of State' or 'the Minister' and no such prerogatives or immunity attach to such a Minister acting on the Crown's behalf. This greatly assists the operation of administrative law as it means that all legal remedies are potentially available against a Minister.

It is a well-established principle of constitutional law that powers given to Ministers are normally exercised not by the Ministers themselves but by their officers and, further, that a Minister is not obliged to take an action himself but can act through an officer. In *R v Secretary of State for the Home Department, ex p Oladehinde* [1991] 1 AC 254 at 300–B Lord Griffiths held that 'It is obvious that the Secretary of State cannot personally take every decision ... The decision must be taken by a person of suitable seniority in the [Department] for whom the [Secretary of State] accepts responsibility. This devolution of responsibility was recognised as a practical necessity in the administration of government by the Court of Appeal in *Carltona Ltd v Works Commissioners* [1943] 2 All ER 560 and has become known as the *Carltona* principle.' Thus it can be said that an act of a duly authorised civil servant is an act of the Minister and, furthermore, that the Minister is legally responsible for the acts of such a civil servant taken in the Minister's name.

It also needs to be recognised that the titles and functions of Ministers and their departments are frequently changed. This is usually effected under the Ministers of the Crown Act 1975. This Act allows the Queen, by Order in Council, to transfer the functions of Ministers and, furthermore, to make changes in departments of the office of Secretary of State. In this regard, such Order in Council may also make a Secretary of State a 'corporation sole' and transfer property etc to a named Secretary of State.

It is in this context that the PA 2008 confers various powers and duties on 'the Secretary of State'. The Act does not, however, identify the particular 'Secretary of State' to which any particular power or duty relates. It is clear, however, from Schedule 1 to the Interpretation Act 1978 that references to 'the Secretary of State' should be taken to mean 'one of Her Majesty's Principal Secretaries of State'. Thus the powers and duties of the Secretary of State are in theory conferred on all the Secretaries of State in existence at the time. This arises because, constitutionally, there is only a single office of Secretary of State although that office may be performed by a number of named Secretaries of State as determined by the Queen in Council.

In practice, however, an application for development consent under the Planning Act 2008 is determined by whichever Secretary of State, or Secretaries of State, have responsibility for the field of activity in relation to which the application relates. Thus, the Secretary of State for Transport in practice determines applications for consent for transport projects. This would include road, rail and port projects. Similarly, the Secretary of State for Energy and Climate Change makes decisions on energy infrastructure applications.

There may be other roles for a Secretary of State in the DCO process. For example, the power in PA 2008, s 127 (statutory undertakers' land) would be exercised by the Secretary of State who is responsible for the particular affected statutory undertaker's activity (for example, the Secretary of State for Environment, Food and Rural Affairs in relation to a water company).

Legal challenges relating to applications for orders granting development consent are to be brought by judicial review under PA 2008, s 118. In litigation connected with an application for a development consent order, it will be the Secretary of State responsible for the decision on that application who would, in practice, be the defendant in any judicial review proceedings. So, for example, the Secretary of State for Energy and Climate Change was the defendant in the judicial review challenges to the decisions on the Hinkley Point C generating station application and the Preesall underground gas storage facility application, as it was that Secretary of State who had taken the decisions challenged.

In practice, it is usual for the Treasury Solicitor's Department (TSol) to act on behalf of a Secretary of State in litigation. The TSol website states that the Litigation Group within TSol acts for over 800 different clients spread across 180 Government Departments and public bodies and that they handle over 20,000 cases each year in a wide range of courts and tribunals. The TSol operates from its headquarters at: Treasury Solicitor's Department, One Kemble Street, London, WC2B 4TS (www.tsol.gov.uk).

Part 2

National Policy Statements

Context for the Identification of Need in National Policy Statements

Written by: Rebecca Clutten, ftb
Edited by: Michael Humphries QC, ftb

Introduction

The Government's stated aim in *Planning for a sustainable future*, the White Paper that preceded the PA 2008, was to create a system for determining applications for nationally significant infrastructure projects that was 'timely, efficient and predictable'.

One of the perceived major obstacles to bringing forward such projects was the absence of clear policy frameworks for all types of nationally significant infrastructure. This resulted in a lack of certainty for promoters and communities, and significant time being spent at public inquiries debating high-level issues including need.

In order to address this problem, the Government proposed the introduction of the national policy statements ('NPSs'), which would 'set out the national need for infrastructure and explain how this fits with other policies such as those relating to economic development, international competitiveness, climate change, energy conservation/efficiency and protection of the historic and natural environment'.

NPSs were subsequently introduced through Part 2 of the PA 2008.

The legislative framework relating to the identification of need

Need in NPSs

The legislative basis for NPSs is found in Part 2 of the PA 2008. By virtue of the PA 2008, s 5, the Secretary of State has power to designate a statement that sets national policy in respect of one or more specified descriptions of development.

PA 2008, s 5(5)(a) specifically provides that the Secretary of State may, in particular,

> 'set out, in relation to a specified description of development, the amount, type or size of development of that description which is appropriate nationally or for a specified area'.

PA 2008, s 5(5)(c) empowers the Secretary of State to set out in the NPS 'the relative weight to be given to specified criteria'.

PA 2008, s 5(1) and (5) taken together therefore permit the Secretary of State to identify through NPSs both the need for national infrastructure, and the weight to be attached to that need.

How need is taken into account in determining applications for development consent

The primary provision identifying how national policy on need is to be taken into account when determining applications for development consent is section 104 of the

PA 2008. Section 104 requires that, where there is a designated NPS having effect in relation to development of the description to which the application relates, the Secretary of State must in deciding the application:

- Have regard to that NPS (PA 2008, s 104(2)); and
- Determine the application in accordance with it, unless one of the situations identified in PA 2008, s 104(4)–(8) apply (PA 2008, s 104(3)).

The effect of PA 2008, s 104 is therefore to require the Secretary of State to have regard to the national policy position on need, including the weight that it has been determined should to be attached to it, and to determine the application so as to accord with that policy position (including by attaching any prescribed weight to the need for that type of development), save in one of the cases identified in PA 2008, s 104(4)–(8).

Also noteworthy are PA 2008, ss 87 and 106. PA 2008, s 106 entitles the Secretary of State, when determining an application for development consent, to disregard any representations made to him or her relating to the merits of a policy set out in a NPS. PA 2008, s 87 makes similar provision for the Examining Authority.

As a result of these enactments, where the need for infrastructure (and any weight to be attached to the same) has been identified in a NPS, promoters of, and objectors to, schemes will, in effect, be precluded from taking issue with the need as identified.

Designated National Policy Statements

A number of NPSs have now been designated under PA 2008, s 5, as follows:

- Overarching National Policy Statement for Energy (EN-1) (DECC July 2011);
- National Policy Statement for Fossil Fuel Electricity Generating Infrastructure (EN-2) (DECC July 2011);
- National Policy Statement for Renewable Energy Infrastructure (EN-3) (DECC July 2011);
- National Policy Statement for Gas Supply Infrastructure and Gas and Oil Pipelines (EN-4) (DECC July 2011);
- National Policy Statement for Electricity Networks Infrastructure (EN-5) (DECC July 2011);
- National Policy Statement for Nuclear Power Generation (2 volumes) (EN-6) (DECC July 2011);
- National Policy Statement for Ports (DfT January 2012);
- National Policy Statement for Waste Water: A framework document for planning decisions on nationally significant waste water infrastructure (Defra March 2012);
- National Policy Statement for Hazardous Waste: A framework document for planning decisions on nationally significant hazardous waste infrastructure (Defra June 2013); and
- National Policy Statement for National Networks (DfT January 2015).

In addition DfT has also produced an interim policy document entitled 'Strategic Rail Freight Interchange Policy Guidance' (DfT November 2011) that it proposes will be replaced by the National road and rail networks NPS.

Other NPSs are anticipated in relation to:

- Aviation (DfT); and
- Water Supply (Defra).

The Identification of Need in the Energy National Policy Statements

Written by: Rebecca Clutten, ftb
Edited by: Michael Humphries QC, ftb

Introduction

DECC has designated the following NPSs under the PA 2008, s 5 in relation to Energy Infrastructure:

- Overarching National Policy Statement for Energy (EN-1) (DECC July 2011);
- National Policy Statement for Fossil Fuel Electricity Generating Infrastructure (EN-2) (DECC July 2011);
- National Policy Statement for Renewable Energy Infrastructure (EN-3) (DECC July 2011)
- National Policy Statement for Gas Supply Infrastructure and Gas and Oil Pipelines (EN-4) (DECC July 2011);
- National Policy Statement for Electricity Networks Infrastructure (EN-5) (DECC July 2011); and
- National Policy Statement for Nuclear Power Generation (2 volumes) (EN-6) (DECC July 2011).

The Overarching Energy NPS (EN-1) together with the relevant technology-specific NPSs (EN2 – EN-6) are intended to set out national policy for energy infrastructure, including that on national need.

Applicants are informed in EN-1 that they should 'ensure that their applications, and any accompanying supporting documents, are consistent with the instructions and guidance in this NPS, the relevant technology NPS and any other NPSs that are relevant to the application in question' (paragraph 1.1.3).

EN-1: Overarching Energy

EN-1 first sets out the overarching need for energy infrastructure. The Government emphasises that significant new infrastructure will be required not only to meet and secure energy demands in the right location, but also to contribute to the mitigation of climate change (paragraph 2.1.2). The security of supply will be dependent upon factors including having sufficient electricity capacity to meet demand at all times, and having available energy from a diverse mix of technologies (paragraph 2.2.20). Developers are thereby encouraged to bring forward applications for a wide range of energy infrastructure projects.

EN-1 also sets out, in Chapter 3, the Government's position on need in relation to each of the energy infrastructure types for which there is a technology-specific NPS. A summary of the need for each is given below.

Need for electricity infrastructure NSIPs

Adopting prudent assumptions as to likely levels of electricity demand, the Government considers that the UK will need at least 113GW of total generating capacity by 2025, some 28GW over and above current capacity. 59GW is anticipated to come from new-build electricity infrastructure. Of that 59GW, 33GW is to come from renewable sources (to meet committed targets), with the remaining 26GW (of which 8GW is already under construction) coming from elsewhere, in a mix to be determined by industry. The Government is supportive of nuclear contributions that that remaining 18GW (paragraph 3.3.22).

Need for renewables NSIPs

There is an urgent need for large-scale renewable generation (from sources including onshore and offshore wind, biomass, energy from waste and wave and tidal power), in order to meet the target of sourcing 15% of energy from renewables by 2020, and to facilitate de-carbonisation of the power sector by 2030 (section 3.4).

Need for nuclear electricity generation

Nuclear power is one of the key elements of the Government's de-carbonisation strategy, being capable of large-scale deployment and the least expensive source of low-carbon energy (paragraphs 3.5.7–3.5.8). It is also needed to ensure energy security, as uranium prices are less subject to fluctuation than gas and other fossil fuels. The Government therefore seeks the early construction and operation of new stations, in any case before 2025 (paragraph 3.5.9).

Need for fossil fuel generation

Fossil fuel generating stations are more flexible than many renewable technologies (which produce energy intermittently) and are considered to remain necessary in order to ensure security of energy supply (paragraphs 3.6.2–3.6.3).

A reduction of emissions from this kind of infrastructure is, however, needed in order to meet carbon reduction targets. The Government considers that carbon capture and storage ('CCS') offers a potential means of achieving such reductions. The Government is therefore seeking to support four commercial-scale demonstration projects for the full CCS chain, and the IPC is directed to take account of the importance placed on these projects in considering applications for CCS projects and infrastructure (paragraphs 3.6.4–3.6.5).

Pending demonstration of the viability of CCS, combustion power stations (300MW or greater) will however need to be carbon-capture ready (ie CCS will be adoptable at a later stage) and coal-fired stations will need to demonstrate CCS on up to 300MW of capacity (paragraph 3.6.6).

The need for these CCR fossil fuel stations, and the CCS demonstration projects, is regarded as urgent, as existing capacity will go offline by the end of 2015 (paragraph 3.6.8).

Need for electricity networks infrastructure

The urgent need for additional transmission infrastructure reflects the 'similar' urgent need for new generating capacity to be provided (paragraph 3.7.7). It is recognised that much new generating capacity (particularly wind farms) will be sited in locations where there is little or no existing electricity infrastructure, and it will have to be provided (paragraph 3.7.1).

Need also arises as a result of increasing demands for electricity, which will require a sufficiently robust network to prevent interruptions. A sufficiently robust network will be achieved through making existing infrastructure 'evolve and adapt' and through expansion of the network through new lines (paragraph 3.7.2). The scale of need can be appreciated through consideration of the increases in generation and net electricity flows to 2020 set out in EN-1 (paragraph 3.7.6). Whilst there is an urgent need for transmission and distribution infrastructure generally, it is considered that there is a particular need for new lines of 132kV upwards (paragraph 3.7.10).

The IPC is directed to consider need as demonstrated if it: (a) represents an 'efficient and economical means' of connecting a new generating station; or is (b) reinforcing the network. The cost/benefit of achieving these aims (eg by overhead line or underground cable) and alternatives must however be considered before consent is granted (paragraph 3.7.10).

Need for gas NSIPs

Gas infrastructure will continue to be required to meet both domestic (household and industrial) needs, including peaks in demand, and export demand (paragraphs 3.8.2 and 3.8.7). The Government's current assessment is that in order to ensure security of supply, without consumer price risks, additional infrastructure, over and above that which is existing and under-construction, is needed (paragraph 3.8.8).

Particular emphasis is placed on the need for gas (gaseous and liquid) import and storage infrastructure, as the UK's gas production and reserves decline (paragraph 3.8.9). Decisions as to the nature, location, capacity and specification of gas infrastructure are, however, commercial ones for the industry (paragraphs 3.8.13 and 3.8.20).

Need for oil NSIPs

The Government considers that the need for oil products will continue to increase in the short-medium term as a result of transport sector dependency, notwithstanding a predicted fall in petrol consumption (paragraph 3.9.2). The need to ensure the security of this supply, and protect against excessive costs, means that new infrastructure for the importation, production, storage and distribution is required (paragraph 3.9.3).

There is a particular focus on the need for pipeline infrastructure, and works associated with the same, the 'significant need' for which the IPC is to take as its starting point in considering applications coming forward (paragraphs 3.9.6–3.9.8).

As a result of the identified need for energy infrastructure, the IPC (now the Examining Authority and/or Secretary of State, but referred to as the IPC for consistency with the original text) is directed to start its consideration of applications with a 'presumption in favour of granting consent to applications for energy NSIPs', the application of such presumption being subject to any more specific and relevant policies set out in the technology-specific NPSs which 'clearly indicate that consent should be refused', and to section 104 of the 2008 Act (paragraph 4.1.2). Need is also a factor which the IPC is directed to take into account in its consideration of where the balance of favour lies on any given application (paragraph 4.1.3).

The weight to be attached to the need for energy infrastructure of all types is also set out in EN-1. Such weight should be 'substantial' but 'proportionate to the anticipated extent of a project's actual contribution to satisfying the need for a particular type of infrastructure' (paragraph 3.2.3).

As in other, non-energy NPSs, the section of EN-1 dealing with Assessment Principles sets out a number of specific policies which require the IPC to weigh in the balance the benefits of the proposed development, which expressly include the stated need for the same (including national need), against various harms which might arise.

These harms include, after mitigation, likely harm to the notified special interest features of a Site of Special Scientific Interest ('SSSI'), in which case the benefits including need should 'clearly outweigh' the harm if consent is to be granted (paragraph 5.3.11). They also include harm to species or sites of principal conservation importance, ancient woodland (by reason of loss or deterioration), and dynamic shorelines (by reason of impacts on sediment flow or other coastal processes) in which case the benefits would need simply to 'outweigh' the harm (paragraphs 5.3.17, 5.3.14 and 5.5.11 respectively).

In the case of designated sites, consent should be granted on sites with national designations (such as Areas of Outstanding Natural Beauty) only in 'exceptional circumstances', where development has been shown to be in the public interest, including by reference to the need for it (paragraph 5.9.9). Regional and local designations should not be used to refuse consent without more (paragraph 5.3.13), and where local landscape impacts arise, the IPC is required to consider whether any adverse impacts are 'so damaging' as to outweigh the benefits, including the need for development of that type (paragraph 5.9.15).

Need is also a factor in decisions as to whether or not to grant consent for development proposals on existing open space, sports and recreational buildings and land. Such proposals should not be consented unless, amongst other things, the decision-maker determines that the benefits of the project (including need) outweigh the potential loss of such facilities (paragraph 5.10.14).

Finally, because of the need for energy infrastructure, the Government's policy is that the IPC is entitled to give little weight to 'speculative assertions of [adverse] socioeconomic impacts [arising from energy development] not supported by evidence' (paragraph 5.12.7).

Whilst no specific reference is made to the weight attaching to the need for the proposed infrastructure, the presumption in favour of consent, and repeated reference to it as benefit of the proposals that must be weighed in the balance, it is clear enough that the weight attached to need by decision-makers is likely to be substantial.

EN-2 – EN-6: the technology-specific energy NPSs

EN-2 - EN-5 inclusive are the technology specific NPSs for energy, providing detailed policy for each of the different kinds of energy infrastructure within the 2008 Act regime.

The majority of the technology-specific energy NPSs do not contain a discrete chapter addressing the need for energy deriving from the technology with which those documents are concerned. EN-2 – EN-6 inclusive (Fossil fuels, Renewables, Gas, Electricity Networks and Nuclear respectively) each cross-refer back to the need identified in Chapter 1.3 of EN-1.

In each case, the need for the energy infrastructure identified in EN-1 is also then reiterated and the IPC is directed, when determining applications for development consent, to 'act on the basis that the need for the infrastructure covered by this NPS [ie the technology-specific NPS in which the statement appears] has been demonstrated' (2.1.2).

A number of the technology-specific NPSs do provide either further commentary on the need that had been identified in EN-1 (for example, emphasising the role a particular technology has to play), or further guidance as to how the need for particular energy infrastructure is to be taken into account by the Secretary of State where particular issues (for example, environmental impacts) arise on any given application. These policies are identified, by NPS, below. NPSs not referred to do not contain any such comment or guidance.

EN-3: Renewable Energy Infrastructure

In addition to the cross-reference to EN-1, EN-3 sets out the principles guiding assessments of applications for each specific type of renewable energy infrastructure covered by the NPS (Biomass and Waste Combustion, Offshore Wind, and Onshore Wind).

There are just two technology-specific references to the need for energy infrastructure. First is the reference, made in Chapter 2.5, to the increasingly important role that energy from waste is anticipated to play in meeting the UK's energy needs.

Second is the reference to balancing the need for offshore wind infrastructure with the impact that the presence of that infrastructure has on recreational craft. It is stated that the IPC should be satisfied that offshore wind schemes have been designed to minimise impacts on such craft. However, in cases where adverse impacts are identified, and no reasonable mitigation is feasible, the IPC is required, 'in view of the level of need for energy infrastructure', to 'weigh the harm caused with the benefits of the scheme', instead of simply refusing the scheme on the basis of that residual harm (paragraph 2.6.166).

EN-4: Gas Supply Infrastructure and Gas and Oil Pipelines

In addition to the cross-reference to EN-1, and in spite of the emphasis on low-carbon energy resources, the continued importance of, and need for, gas and oil energy infrastructure is made clear at the outset of EN-4, which states:

'The efficient import, storage and transmission of natural gas and oil products is crucial to meeting our energy needs during the transition to a low carbon economy. We cannot achieve national objectives relating to security of supply without enabling investment in new infrastructure' (paragraph 1.1.1).

EN-5: Electricity Networks Infrastructure

In addition to the cross-reference to EN-1, EN-5 also emphasises the continued need for electricity networks infrastructure, notwithstanding the emphasis on low carbon resources. It states that:

'The new electricity generating infrastructure that the UK needs to move to a low carbon economy while maintaining security of supply will be heavily dependent on the availability of a fit for purpose and robust electricity network. That network will need to be able to support a more complex system of supply and demand than currently and cope with generation occurring in more diverse locations' (paragraph 1.1.1).

Chapter 2.3 of EN-5 gives specific guidance on circumstances in which the need for electricity infrastructure will have to be weighed in the balance against other factors. It addresses the general assessment principles for electricity networks, and states *inter alia* that, in view of the need for planning to take a holistic approach to the impacts of energy infrastructure development, applications for new generating stations and related infrastructure should, wherever reasonably be possible, be contained in a single application (paragraph 2.3.1).

Where this is not possible or appropriate, and an application for network infrastructure is brought forward in isolation, the IPC will have to have regard to both the need for the network infrastructure identified in EN-1 and the indirect, secondary and cumulative effects that the proposed development is likely to have, and be satisfied that there are no obvious reasons why the necessary approvals for the other element are likely to be refused (paragraph 2.3.3).

Chapter 2.3 goes on to identify two circumstances in which the IPC might consider it appropriate to consider a network infrastructure-only application. One is the situation where 'the project is based on reasonably anticipated future requirements' (also paragraph 2.3.3). It therefore appears that promoters of network infrastructure-only schemes may be required to demonstrate a more specific need for their project, over and above the general need for electricity network infrastructure, which the IPC is directed in Chapter 2.1 to treat as established.

EN-6: Nuclear Power Generation

Whilst EN-6 cross-refers to EN-1, it also contains additional policy relating to need, including the need for early deployment of nuclear technology, if policy ambitions in relation to the de-carbonisation of the energy industry are to be met (paragraphs 2.1.1–2.1.2).

EN-6 provides that the number of sites identified gives the IPC sufficient flexibility to meet that need, but also to refuse consent on any of those sites, if it considers it appropriate to do so (paragraph 2.4.4). This tends to suggest that the level of national need for nuclear power is not as great as the output from eight stations.

EN-6 also addresses the relationship between the stated urgent need for nuclear power stations to come forward, and the consideration of alternatives. The guiding principle for the IPC in the consideration of alternatives is,

'Whether there is a realistic prospect of the proposed alternative being able to generate a comparable amount of low carbon electricity on a comparable timescale' (paragraph 2.5.2).

This guiding principle applies to both alternative sites and alternative proposals (paragraph 2.5.1).

In relation to flood risk assessments, the IPC is advised that part of the Exception Test applying to developments in flood risk zones does not apply to new nuclear development, in view of *inter alia* the need for that development to come forward (paragraph 3.6.13). It appears that, in view of the continued application of the Exception Test in relation to other development, the need for nuclear development is considered particularly pressing, though it is acknowledged that the policy may also be recognising the greater physical constraints upon the provision of new nuclear facilities (such as the need to be near the sea).

The Identification of Need in the Non-Energy National Policy Statements

Written by: Rebecca Clutten, ftb
Edited by: Michael Humphries QC, ftb

Introduction

Defra and DfT have designated the following NPSs under section 5 of the Planning Act 2008 (PA 2008) in relation to non-Energy Infrastructure:

- National Policy Statement for Ports (DfT January 2012);
- National Policy Statement for Waste Water: A framework document for planning decisions on nationally significant waste water infrastructure (Defra March 2012);
- National Policy Statement for Hazardous Waste: A framework document for planning decisions on nationally significant hazardous waste infrastructure (Defra June 2013); and
- National Policy Statement for National Networks (DfT January 2015).

In addition DfT has also produced an interim policy document entitled 'Strategic Rail Freight Interchange Policy Guidance' (DfT November 2011) that it proposes will be replaced by the National road and rail networks NPS.

Other NPSs are anticipated in relation to:

- Aviation (DfT); and
- Water Supply (Defra).

Ports NPS

The need for new ports infrastructure is set out in Chapter 3 of the Ports NPS, in particular in Chapters 3.4 and 3.5.

The headline in relation to need is that there is a 'compelling need for substantial additional port capacity' in all areas, over the 20–30 year period from 2012 (paragraph 3.4.16). This is based on a number of factors including:

- Demand forecasting, which at 2007 indicated a need for substantial increases in capacity for containers and ro-ro traffic (182% and 101% respectively), and 4% in non-unitised traffic (paragraphs 3.4.2–3.4.3).
- The need to support the offshore wind industry, both in respect of the shipment of parts, and in respect of installation, operation and maintenance facilities (paragraph 3.4.5).
- The need to provide sufficient capacity to facilitate genuine choice and competition for ports users. This may mean capacity in excess of forecast demand. Such capacity also contributes to the resilience of the UK's ports infrastructure (paragraphs 3.4.13–3.4.15).

- To meet growth in the coastal shipping sector, as an alternative to inland freight (paragraph 3.4.14).

There is no specific policy on where such growth should be located. The Government recognises the merit in the provision of a wide range of facilities at a wide range of locations, such as will enable changing market demands and shipping patterns to be met (paragraph 3.4.11).

As for energy infrastructure, the need described is considered to be of a level and urgency that the IPC should 'start with a presumption in favour of granting consent to applications for ports development', subject to PA 2008, s 104 and any other, more specific policies within the NPSs, which 'clearly indicate' that consent should be refused (paragraph 3.5.2).

There are also number of specific policies identified within the Assessment Principles set out in the Ports NPS which require the IPC to weigh in the balance benefits of proposed development, which expressly include the stated need (including national need), against various harms which might arise. The approach is broadly reflective of that taken in relation to energy, and the situations contemplated include where there would, after mitigation, be harm to a SSSI interest or other sites of principal conservation importance, in which case the benefits would need to 'clearly outweigh' the harm (paragraph 5.1.12 and footnote 37, and paragraph 5.5.18), or where open space, sports and recreation facilities would be lost, save where they are surplus to requirements (paragraph 5.13.13).

The impact of national, regional and local land designations, and whether these are capable of outweighing the identified need, is also addressed. Current policy is that regional and local designations should not, of themselves, be a reason for refusing consent (paragraph 5.1.14). In the case of land subject to national designations (National Parks, AONB and the Broads), the IPC is guided that it may grant consent for development in these areas in exceptional circumstances, which expressly include the need for the development (paragraph 5.11.8).

In respect of harm to ancient woodlands (by loss or deterioration) and dynamic shorelines (through impact on sediment flows or coastal processes), permission should only be granted where the benefits, again including national and local need, outweigh those adverse impacts (paragraphs 5.1.15 and 5.1.39 respectively).

Waste Water NPS

The need for new waste water infrastructure is set out in Chapter 2 of the waste water NPS. Policy objectives and demand drivers are set out in sections 2.2 and 2.3. The waste water infrastructure considered to meet that need is set out in section 2.6.

It remains Government policy to reduce the need for waste water capacity, through reductions in water use, increasing use of sustainable drainage systems, separation of surface and waste water sewers, and through decentralisation of waste water treatment infrastructure (ie encouraging more local treatment) (section 2.4). However, even with these measures in place, more and better waste water infrastructure will be required to:

- meet the requirements of European and domestic legislation in relation to water body management, waste water and freshwater (paragraphs 2.3.1–2.3.4);

- adapt to the increased pressure on infrastructure resulting from climate change generated events, such as intense rainfall events and reduced river flows (paragraphs 2.3.5–2.3.7);
- meet the additional capacity requirements generated by the expected increase in population growth (paragraph 2.3.8) and also the increase in urbanisation (and corresponding reduction in permeable surfaces) (paragraph 2.3.9); and
- to ensure that existing, dated infrastructure remains fit for purpose or is replaced (paragraph 2.3.10)

Waste water infrastructure projects and improvements required to meet legislative and environmental objectives (which typically overlap) are currently identified by the Environment Agency ('EA') in their National Environment Plan (NEP), which is subject to confirmation by the Secretary of State, and which is scrutinised by OFWAT through water undertakers' business plans (paragraphs 2.5.1–2.5.2).

The NEP currently identifies two projects for which there is a need: improvements at Deephams Sewage Treatment Works ('STW') and the Thames Tideway Tunnel (section 2.6). The need for these, and other projects included in the NEP and said by the EA to be necessary for environmental reasons, is considered to be established (paragraphs 2.5.3-2.5.4).

The urgent need for such infrastructure means that the decision-maker should start with a presumption in favour of granting consent to applications for waste water NSIPs, subject to any more specific and relevant policies in the NPS that 'clearly indicate that consent should be refused', and the requirements of the Planning Act 2008 (paragraph 3.1.2). Further, need is a particular factor which must be taken into account when weighing the benefits and adverse impacts of any proposed NSIP (paragraph 3.1.3).

As for the other NPSs, the Assessment Principles require the decision-maker to weigh in the balance benefits of proposed development, which expressly include the stated need (including national need), against various harms that might arise. These include where there would, after mitigation, be likely to be harm to a SSSI's notified special interest features, to sites or species of principal conservation importance, or ancient woodland, in which case the benefits would need to 'clearly outweigh' the harm (paragraphs 4.5.10, 4.5.13 and 4.5.16).

The impact of national, regional and local land designations, and whether these are capable of outweighing the identified need, is also addressed. Current policy is that regional and local designations should not, of themselves, be a reason for refusing consent (paragraph 4.5.12). In the case of land subject to national designations (National Parks, AONB and the Broads), development should be demonstrated to be in the public interest and consideration of such applications should include an assessment of, amongst other things, 'the need for the development, including in terms of any national considerations [covering both national need and impacts upon the national economy] and the impact of consenting, or not consenting it, upon the local economy' (paragraph 4.7.8).

Need is also a factor in decisions as to whether or not to grant consent for development proposals on existing open space, sports and recreational buildings and land. Such proposals should not be consented unless, amongst other things, the decision-maker determines that the benefits of the project (including need) outweigh the potential loss of such facilities (paragraph 4.8.13).

The need for waste water infrastructure is also a factor which has resulted in a policy that the Secretary of State may reasonably conclude that:

> 'speculative assertions of [adverse] socioeconomic impacts [arising from waste water development] not supported by evidence should be given little weight' (paragraph 4.15.10).

Hazardous Waste NPS

The need for new hazardous waste infrastructure is set out in Chapter 3 of the Hazardous Waste NPS, in particular in sections 3.2 and 3.5.

The headline in relation to need is that there is a need for a 'small number of large facilities' for nationally significant hazardous waste, to deal with a range of hazardous waste arisings (paragraphs 3.3.7 and 3.4.1).

The need for increasing numbers of hazardous waste facilities is a result of:

- the trend toward increased hazardous waste arisings (deriving from both the continuing demand for consumer goods producing such waste, as well as from more waste being classified as hazardous) (section 3.2); and
- the need to meet European and domestic legislative requirements in relation to disposal of waste, in particular the requirements of the Waste Framework Directive (2008/98/EC) for pushing waste up the waste hierarchy (ie improved levels of recycling and re-use) (paragraphs 1.5.3, 3.2.3–3.2.6 and 3.3.5) and for national self-sufficiency in terms of capacity to dispose of hazardous waste (paragraph 3.3.3–3.3.4).

The need for a large number of small facilities arises because of the economies of scale which operate in the waste disposal sector, and in order to avoid cumulative impacts which might be generated by the operation of multiple, smaller sites (paragraph 3.3.6). The author notes that smaller facilities may still come forward through the Town and Country Planning regime.

The Government has not sought to identify particular technologies which should be used, or to identify locations for development, it being considered ill-advised to be too prescriptive when technologies are evolving (paragraph 3.4.1), and because it considers the industry best placed to know where facilities should be located (paragraph 2.4.2). This provides significant flexibility to applicants for hazardous waste developments, as compared to applicants for some other NSIPs.

Broad types of facilities required are however identified, drawing on the 2007 Strategy for Hazardous Waste Management in England (paragraph 3.3.6). The types of facility for which there is an identified need are:

- Waste electrical and electronic equipment plants – a small number of larger facilities (paragraph 3.4.3);
- Oil regeneration plants – a requirement of at least one new plant already existing at July 2011 (paragraph 3.4.3);
- Treatment plants for air pollution control residues;
- Facilities to treat oily washes and oily sludges;

- Bioremediation/soil washing facilities;
- Ship recycling facilities (which covers oil and gas platform recycling) – a mixture of new facilities with capacity to manage both above and below 30,000t of ship(s) pa within the next 10 years (paragraph 3.4.12); and
- Hazardous waste landfill sites.

The Examining Authority is directed to examine applications for facilities falling within these categories on the basis that the need for them has been demonstrated (paragraph 3.4.14). Moreover, there is a presumption in favour of granting consent for applications for such facilities where they clearly meet the need for infrastructure identified in the NPS (paragraph 4.1.2). This presumption is subject, as in other NPSs, to the other policies of the Hazardous Waste NSP and also PA 2008, s 104. The need for types of hazardous waste facilities not included on the above list is to be considered on a case-by-case basis, following consultation by the applicant with Defra (paragraph 3.4.1).

The Assessment Principles require the decision-maker to weigh in the balance benefits of proposed development, which expressly include the stated need (including national need), against various harms that might arise. These include where there would, after mitigation, be harm to species or sites of principal conservation importance, or ancient woodland, in which case the benefits would need to 'clearly outweigh' the harm (paragraphs 5.3.14 and 5.3.17).

The impact of national, regional and local land designations, and whether these are capable of outweighing the identified need, is also addressed. Current policy is that regional and local designations should not, of themselves, be a reason for refusing consent (paragraph 5.1.13).

In the case of land subject to national designations (National Parks, AONB and the Broads), development should be demonstrated to be in the public interest and consideration of such applications should include an assessment of, amongst other things, 'the need for the development, including in terms of any national considerations [covering both national need and impacts upon the national economy] and the impact of consenting, or not consenting it, upon the local economy' (paragraph 5.9.7).

The need for hazardous waste infrastructure is also a factor that has led the Government to include guidance that the Secretary of State may reasonably conclude that:

> 'speculative assertions of [adverse] socioeconomic impacts [arising from hazardous waste development] not supported by evidence should be given little weight'.

National Networks NPS

This NPS was designated in January 2015, as this publication was going to press. This article will, therefore, be updated online as part of the National Infrastructure Planning Service.

The Status and Role of NPSs within the Planning Act 2008 Regime

Written by: Rebecca Clutten, ftb
Edited by: Michael Humphries QC, ftb

Introduction

National Policy Statements ('NPSs') are the statutory planning policy statements for nationally significant infrastructure projects in England and Wales. They derive from PA 2008, Part 2.

This article explains the status that NPSs have within the PA 2008 regime. Any references to NPSs herein are references to NPSs which have been designated in accordance with PA 2008, s 5. Further information on the requirements for designation can be found in other parts of this Service.

PA 2008, s 104: the primacy of the NPS

The primary effect of NPSs is set out in PA 2008, s 104 (decisions in cases where national policy statement applies).

PA 2008, s 104 will apply in respect of any application for a development consent order (DCO) for development in relation to which there is an extant NPS: see PA 2008, s 104(1). Where section 104 applies, the Secretary of State must, when determining an application for a DCO, have regard to *inter alia* that relevant NPS: see PA 2008, s 104(2). Although there are other specified documents and matters to which the Secretary of State must have regard, the PA 2008 goes on to provide that, save in specified circumstances (that is, where the circumstances set out in PA 2008, s 104(4)–(8) apply), the DCO application must be decided in accordance with the relevant NPS.

The NPS therefore has a comparable status in the decision making process to the statutory development plan in the determination of applications for planning permission under the Town and Country Planning regime. It is important to note, however, that Planning and Compulsory Purchase Act 2004, s 38(6) which requires planning applications to be determined in accordance with the development plan unless other material considerations indicate otherwise, does not apply to applications for development consent under the PA 2008. There is, therefore, no conflict between the requirements of the two regimes.

The circumstances in which an application for a DCO can be determined otherwise than in accordance with the relevant NPS are as follows (PA 2008, s 104(4)–(8)):

- the SoS is satisfied that to do so would lead to the UK being in breach of any of its international obligations;
- the SoS is satisfied that to do so would lead to him being in breach of any duty imposed on him by or under any enactment;

- the SoS is satisfied that to do so would be unlawful by virtue of any enactment;
- the SoS is satisfied that the benefits of doing so would outweigh the adverse impacts; and
- the SoS is satisfied that to do so would meet any prescribed condition for determining an application otherwise than in accordance with the relevant NPS.

At the time of writing, there are no prescribed conditions as referred to in the last exception.

Again, a comparison can be drawn between these exceptions to the primacy of the NPSs, and in particular the exception at PA 2008, s 104(7) (benefits outweigh adverse impacts), and the ability for applications for planning permission under the Town and Country Planning regime to be determined other than in accordance with the development plan where 'material considerations indicate otherwise'.

In light of the primacy afforded to NPSs, it is vital that applicants explain in detail how their proposals relate to and comply with the NPS and, insofar as that is not so, make the case for consent being granted in any event by reference to the exceptions identified. For a decision in which the Examining Authority and Secretary of State did not consider that an NSIP was in accordance with the NPS see the *Preesall* underground gas storage report and decision.

Thus promoters will need to consider carefully and establish that:

- the NSIP is 'in accordance with' any material NPS; and
- the exceptions in PA 2008, s 104(4)–(8) to not outweigh the policy support in the NSIP and the benefits of the project.

Section 106: restricted challenge to NPS policy

A further effect of the NPSs is set out in PA 2008, s 106, which provides that in determining an application for a DCO the Secretary of State may disregard representations which he considers 'relate to the merits of policy set out in a national policy statement': see PA 2008, s 106. In this regard, clearly, the Examining Authority and Secretary of State must act with *Wednesbury* reasonableness. The practical effect of this is preclude challenges to the merits of a national policy other than through the NPS consultation process, or at the Secretary of State's discretion.

A similar provision is contained in PA 2008, s 94(8), which allows the Examining Authority to refuse to allow representations at any hearings relating to a DCO application where it considers those representations to relate to the merits of a policy contained in a NPS. Again this power must be exercised reasonably.

Suspension

Effect of suspension of the NPS

It is possible for the Secretary of State to suspend the operation of all or part of an NPS if an unexpected change in circumstances arises that would have led to the policy in the NPS being materially different had that change of circumstances been anticipated at the time: see PA 2008, s 11.

Where such suspension occurs the designation of all or part of the NPS (as the case may be) is treated as withdrawn and, until such time as designation is reinstated, the NPS will not be treated as extant and relevant for the purposes of the duty to determine in accordance with the NPS (PA 2008, s 104) nor, indeed, to the blight provisions referred to further below.

Suspension of the determination of an application

If the SoS considers that a NPS should be suspended and reviewed as a result of an unexpected change in circumstances, and that such review should take place before any given application for a DCO is determined, he has a further power to direct that the examination of the application (if not already completed) be suspended pending that review: see PA 2008, s 108.

NPSs can therefore be a potential source of delay for applicants in the DCO process.

A cause of statutory blight

Amendments to the Town and Country Planning Act 1990 brought about by the PA 2008 also mean that land which is 'in a location identified in a national policy statement as suitable (or potentially suitable) for a specified description of development' is now 'blighted land' for the purposes of the submission by an affected party of a statutory blight notice pursuant to s 150 of and Sch 13 to the TCPA 1990. A new s 165A of the TCPA 1990 gives the Secretary of State power to compulsorily acquire such blighted land where a statutory blight notice is served.

Legal Challenges to National Policy Statements

Written by: Rebecca Clutten, ftb
Edited by: Michael Humphries QC, ftb

Introduction

Section 13 of the Planning Act 2008 ('PA 2008') prescribes the means by which legal challenges to National Policy Statements ('NPSs') can be brought, and restricts the time period within which prospective claimants have to lodge their claims.

This article provides information on:

- the circumstances in which PA 2008, s 13 applies;
- the effect of PA 2008, s 13 upon: the mode by which challenges to NPSs and decisions related to them can be brought, the time limit applicable to such challenges, and the date from which time runs in each case;
- the effect of a legal challenge on the status of a NPS; and
- challenges brought to date.

When does PA 2008, s 13 apply?

Broadly speaking, PA 2008, s 13 applies where a person seeks either to challenge a NPS or a decision of the relevant Secretary of State ('SoS') relating to a NPS.

PA 2008, s 13, however, identifies six specific circumstances where a challenge may be brought. Thus a court may entertain proceedings questioning:

- a NPS or anything done, or omitted to be done, by the SoS in the course of preparing a NPS (PA 2008, s 13(1));
- a decision of the SoS not to carry out a review of all or part of a NPS pursuant to PA 2008, s 6 (PA 2008, s 13(2));
- a decision of the SoS to carry out a review of all or part of a NPS pursuant to PA 2008, s 6 (PA 2008, s 13(3));
- anything done, or omitted to be done, by the SoS in the course of carrying out a review of all or part of a NPS pursuant to PA 2008, s 6 (PA 2008, s 13(4));
- anything done by the SoS under PA 2008, s 6(5) after completing a review of all or part of a NPS (that is, amending or doing nothing to an NPS, or withdrawing its designation) (PA 2008, s 13(5)); and
- questioning a decision of the SoS as to whether or not to suspend the operation of all or part of a NPS under PA 2008, s 11 (PA 2008, s 13(6)).

Whilst it is envisaged that that the six circumstances described cover all decisions relating to the designation and subsequent review of NPSs, PA 2008, s 13 is not phrased in such a way as to preclude challenges to other decisions relating to NPSs, should they arise. It contains no drafting comparable to, for example, section 284 of the Town and Country Planning Act 1990 (as amended), precluding any challenge to the validity of development plans etc, except as provided for in that Part.

It is considered that, in the event that a claimant wished to challenge a decision of the SoS relating to a NPS, but which did not fall within any of the six circumstances referred to in PA 2008, s 13(1)–(6) inclusive, that decision would be treated in the same way as any other decision of a Minister not subject to any statutory provision relating to challenge, that is, ordinary judicial review principles and procedure would apply.

The effect of PA 2008, s 13

Where it applies, PA 2008, s 13 has three main effects:

- it requires a person wishing to bring a challenge to do so by way of judicial review;
- it imposes a time limit of six weeks, within which any application for judicial review must be lodged; and
- it identifies the day from which that time limit runs in each circumstance described.

Challenge by way of judicial review only

The requirement that any challenge to a NPS be brought by way of judicial review has a number of implications for prospective claimants. It requires them to have standing to bring a claim (presently, a 'sufficient interest'), to obtain the permission of the court to bring a claim, and it limits them to challenging the decision on traditional judicial review grounds (ie broadly, irrationality, illegality and procedural impropriety). In other words, there is no direct opportunity to challenge the merit of Government policy in an NPS, as opposed to the legality of such policy.

Furthermore, PA 2008, s 106 provides that, when determining applications for development consent for Nationally Significant Infrastructure Projects, the Secretary of State is entitled to disregard any representations he or she receives relating to the merits of policy set out in a NPS. A similar power to disregard applies to the Examining Authority (section 87).

When read together with PA 2008, s 106, the effect of PA 2008, s 13 is, therefore, to preclude the public at large from challenging the merits of planning policy that has been set at national level, other than through the instigation of the review procedure provided for by PA 2008, s 6.

Date from which time runs

Readers are referred to section 13 for details of the date from which the six week time limit runs in each given circumstance (see PA 2008, s 13(1)–(6) inclusive). It should, however, be noted that in each case, time begins to run on the date described in the subsection, and not on the following day. The words 'beginning with' in PA 2008, s 13 contrast with the word 'from' which is used in r 54.5 of the Civil Procedure Rules (CPR) for judicial review challenges generally. Time for a s 13 challenge begins to run 'on' the date described in the section, and not 'from' the following day: see *Hinde v Rugby BC* [2011] EWHC 3684 (Admin) and *Barker v Hambleton DC* [2012] EWCA Civ 610. Furthermore, the period of six weeks is to be calculated as 6 × 7 days (ie 42 days): see *Okolo v Secretary of State for the Environment* [1997] 4 All ER 242.

For example: if a NPS is designated and published on 1 January (the circumstance identified in PA 2008, s 13(1)), the first day of the six weeks will also be 1 January, and the time for challenge will expire on 12 February.

Accuracy is vital bearing in mind the inability of the court to extend the time limit in cases of error (see below).

The time limit of six weeks is set by statute

The time limit of six weeks for challenges to is one set by statute (ie by the terms of s 13 and not by the Civil Procedure Rules) and thus it is important to note that the court has no power or discretion to extend it: see *Mucelli v Government of Albania* [2009] 1 WLR 276.

Effect of a challenge

The filing of a claim for judicial review of a NPS has no impact upon its status. The NPS remains extant and valid for the duration of any challenge.

In principle it seems possible that, in appropriate circumstances, the court might exercise its discretion grant to a claimant injunctive relief, preventing decisions being taken in accordance with a NPS the subject matter of a current application for judicial review.

Such a course of action would require the court to balance the harm caused by any policy vacuum that would be created, with any harm caused by determining an application for development consent in accordance with a potentially flawed or unlawful policy. The outcome of any such balancing exercise would represent a judgment on the facts of the given case.

Challenges to date

At January 2015, ten of the twelve currently proposed NPSs had been designated and published; the most recent (the National Networks NPS) on 14 January 2015. These designations resulted in just one application for permission to apply for a judicial review.

The application, made by Greenpeace in August 2011, related to the designation of the Nuclear Power NPS ('the Nuclear NPS'). In short, Greenpeace alleged that, in designating the Nuclear NPS at that time, the Government had acted prematurely and had failed to take into account the implications of the nuclear disaster at Fukushima, Japan, which had occurred earlier that year.

Permission was refused in December 2011. Although his reasons for refusing permission have not been published, it was reported in the legal press that Ouseley J considered that the matters upon which Greenpeace argued further evidence was required before a decision could be taken on potentially suitable sites through the NPS – flood risk, off-site electricity supply and on-site emergency controls – were matters upon which evidence would be considered by the (then) Infrastructure Planning Commission and the Office of Nuclear Regulation when determining whether development consent and/or an operating license should be granted at any site for which an application ultimately came forward.

There have been no reported challenges to decisions relating to the review of the NPSs.

Part 3

Nationally Significant Infrastructure Projects

General Characteristics of an NSIP

Written by: Alex Booth, ftb
Edited by: Michael Humphries QC, ftb

Nature of Development

There is no single, over-arching definition of a 'nationally significant infrastructure project' ('NSIP') contained in PA 2008. The closest that the legislation comes to providing such definition is at PA 2008, s 14, of which subsection 14(1) provides a list of 16 types of development which may potentially comprise a NSIP.

The spectrum of development identified in PA 2008, s 14(1) is diverse. It ranges from highways and harbours to reservoirs and railway infrastructure. Further, whilst the list provided at PA 2008, s 14(1) is expressed in exhaustive terms, the 2008 Act confers on the Secretary of State an express power both to add new types of development to that list, and to remove existing ones from it: see PA 2008, s 14(3).

When seeking to understand the scope of development which may currently be classified as an NSIP, one can at least note that the various developments cited all fall within one of five categories, namely: energy, transport, water, waste water and waste. Indeed, even the Secretary of State's power to identify a new form of development as comprising an NSIP is subject to this same restriction, since only development falling within these five categories of infrastructure may be newly classified as an NSIP.

Currently, the 16 types of NSIP project identified in PA 2008 comprise:

- generating stations (PA 2008, s 15);
- electric lines (PA 2008, s 16);
- underground gas storage facilities (PA 2008, s 17);
- LNG facilities (PA 2008, s 18);
- gas reception facilities (PA 2008, s 19);
- gas transported pipelines (PA 2008, s 20);
- other pipelines (PA 2008, s 21);
- highways (PA 2008, s 22);
- airports (PA 2008, s 23);
- harbour facilities (PA 2008, s 24);
- railways (PA 2008, s 25);
- rail freight interchanges (PA 2008, s 26);
- dams and reservoirs (PA 2008, s 27);
- transfer of water resources (PA 2008, s 28);

- waste water treatment plans (PA 2008, s 29); and
- hazardous waste facilities (PA 2008, s 30).

In addition, The Infrastructure Planning (Waste Water Transfer and Storage) Order 2012, made under PA 2008, s 14(3), extended the 16 types of NSIP project to include a further type being, infrastructure for the transfer and storage of waste water with a capacity of over 350,000 cubic metres.

Note also, that the effect of s 26 of the Growth and Infrastructure Act 2013 was to amend PA 2008, s 35 to allow the Secretary of State to direct that certain business and commercial projects be treated as development for which development consent is required.

Scale of Development

Whilst only development relating to the five categories identified may comprise an NSIP, it goes without saying that not all development within those categories will do so. The question of whether a development will comprise an NSIP turns largely on the scale of development in question. That is to say, it is only in circumstances where the development comprises infrastructure of a particular scale that the consenting procedure of the 2008 Act will be engaged.

As to whether development is of sufficient scale to merit classification as an NSIP, it is necessary to consider whichever is applicable of the various statutory thresholds contained in ss 15–30 of the PA 2008 (and, indeed, the Waste Water Transfer and Storage Order, as above). These provisions, which are the subject of separate articles in this Service, provide in respect of each of the various (now) 17 types of development, a threshold couched in terms of scale or capacity that is used to determine whether or not the development proposed must be regarded as an NSIP or not.

Although all NSIPs are, by definition, 'nationally significant' it would not be right to conclude that they will all necessarily comprise development on a 'grand' scale; indeed, this has been one of the issues that taxed Government and practitioners alike in the early years of the new regime. An obvious example relates to 'electric lines'. The definition in PA 2006, s 16, as originally drafted, was such that an electric line of 132 kilovolts and above was 'nationally significant' even if it only comprised a single tower and span. The thresholds in s 16 were amended by The Planning Act 2008 (Nationally Significant Infrastructure Projects) (Electric Lines) Order 2013 to exclude, for example, a project where the length of the line (when installed) will be less than two kilometres in length. Other changes to the original thresholds may be anticipated over time as the new regime beds down.

A further threshold issue relates to 'extensions'. Many of the types of NSIP in PA 2008, ss 15–30 are defined by a threshold that relates to both 'construction' or 'extension' of a project. By way of example, the construction or extension of a generating station is an NSIP where its capacity is more than 50 megawatts. This may, however, appear a relatively modest 'extension' to an existing (say) 1,500 megawatt combined cycle gas turbine generating station (circa 3%). Again, this may be an issue that the Government will need to tackle as the regime matures.

Highway Related Development

Written by: James Pereira QC, ftb
Edited by: Michael Humphries QC, ftb

Introduction

Section 14(1)(h) of the PA 2008 includes within the list of NSIPs the category 'highway related development'. However, it is only highway related development that satisfies the relevant criteria set out in PA 2008, s 22 that will require a DCO. It is important to note that section 22, as originally enacted, was replaced with a new PA 2008, s 22 with effect from 24 July 2013. The new PA 2008, s 22 was introduced by article 3 of the Highway and Railway (Nationally Significant Infrastructure Project) Order 2013 ('the 2013 Order'). The replacement PA 2008, s 22 was introduced because of concerns that the thresholds in the original version were too low, so that the PA 2008 procedures were being imposed upon highway related development that was not truly of national significance. In addition, it was recognised that the original version of PA 2008, s 22 lacked clarity, which was giving rise to uncertainty as to whether a DCO was required and hence delays in progressing important infrastructure proposals (see, generally, the Government's consultation documents on the draft 2013 Order, 'Nationally significant road and railway schemes: changes to the Planning Act 2008 definitions' (DoT, 18 December 2012 (the consultation) and 3 June 2013 (the response to consultation)).

The current PA 2008, s 22 seeks to overcome these concerns by providing clearer criteria, including size thresholds, which must be satisfied before highway related development will require a DCO.

Construction, alteration and improvement of highways: definitions

For highway related development to require a DCO it must comprise one of three categories of development, and meet certain criteria applicable to each of the three categories. The categories are the construction, alteration and improvement of the highway. Relevant definitions are found in PA 2008, s 235(1).

The term 'highway' is defined in PA 2008, s 235(1) as having the same meaning as it has under section 328 of the Highways Act 1980. By PA 2008, s 328(1), 'highway' means the whole or part of any highway other than a ferry or a waterway. By PA 2008, s 328(2), where a highway passes over a bridge or through a tunnel, that bridge or tunnel is to be taken as part of the highway.

It will be noted that the definition of highway is tautologous, since it includes the word 'highway' within the definition. It is relevant to consider the common law definition of highway. At common law, a highway is 'a way over which there exists a public right of passage, that is to say a right for all of Her Majesty's subjects at all seasons of the year freely and at their will to pass and re-pass without let or hindrance' (*ex p Lewis* (1888) 21 QBD 191 at 197). This definition will be of relevance under the PA 2008.

The term 'Highway Authority' is defined under PA 2008, s 235 as having the same meaning as it has under sections 1 to 3 of the Highways Act 1980. Sections 1 to 3 set out in detail the different highway authorities that may exist in law and the highways to which they relate. Reference should be made to those sections of the Highways Act 1980 in relation to the facts of any particular case. Only general guidance can be given here. Generally, though not always, a Unitary Authority will be the highway authority for roads within its area, a county council of a district will be the highway authority for roads within its county area, Transport for London is the highway authority for certain roads within London, and the Secretary of State will be the highway authority for certain major roads, such as motorways and trunk roads.

The term 'construction' is not given a specific definition (in this context) under section 235(1). It should therefore be given its ordinary meaning. So 'construction' would usually be concerned with the physical making or laying out of a new highway.

The term 'alteration' is defined under PA 2008, s 235 as including stopping up, diverting, improving, raising or lowering the highway. The definition is not, however, exhaustive and other kinds of works to an existing highway, which can properly be termed an alteration to that highway, are likely to fall within this expression.

The term 'improvement' in relation to a highway is defined under section 235 as having the same meaning as it has under the Highways Act 1980. Section 329(1) of the Highways Act 1980 defines 'improvement' as 'The doing of any act under powers conferred by part V of this Act, and includes the erection, maintenance, alteration and removal of traffic signs, and the freeing of a highway or road-ferry from tolls.'

Part V of the Highways Act 1980 sets out specific acts that are deemed to be highway improvements. There is a general power of improvement given by section 62(2) of the Highways Act 1980 in respect of highways maintainable by the highway authority carrying out the improvements. This power is then subject to specific kinds of improvement that are excluded from the general power and for which specific powers must be found. The specific powers are set out in the rest of part V of the Highways Act 1980.

It is important to note that highway improvements which are carried out by a highway authority within the boundaries of a road may be exempt from the definition of development under section 55 of the Town and Country Planning Act 1990. The exemption does not apply where they are likely to have significant adverse environmental effects: see section 55(2)(b) of the Town and Country Planning Act 1990. This proviso seeks to give effect to obligations arising out of the Environmental Impact Assessment Directive.

Relevant criteria for the construction, alteration or improvement of highways

PA 2008, s 22 contains detailed criteria in relation to each of the three categories of highway related development. Reference should be made to its provisions in relation to any particular case. The text below considers certain issues that arise on the wording of the section.

The location of the highway and the requirement for the Secretary of State to be the highway authority

None of the three categories of development (construction, alteration or improvement of a highway) will require a DCO unless the highway falls entirely within England

and the Secretary of State is or will be (in the case of a newly constructed highway) the highway authority for the highway: see PA 2008, s 22(2)(a) and (b), (3)(a) and (b), and (5)(a) and (b).

A question arises as to whether this criterion is satisfied by highway related development where the Secretary of State is or will be the highway authority for part only of the highway. The drafting of PA 2008, s 22 does not clearly identify whether such a highway will be caught by PA 2008, s 22 or not. However, since the definition of highway includes the whole or part of any highway (see section 328(1) of the Highways Act 1980), this criterion can be read as being met where the Secretary of State is or will be the highway authority for at least part of the highway as constructed, altered or improved.

The application of size thresholds to development consisting of the construction and alteration of highways

The construction or alteration of a highway will not be highway related development falling within PA 2008, s 14(1)(h) unless the area of development is greater than the relevant limit set out under PA 2008, s 22(4) (PA 2008, s 22(2)(c) and (3)(c)).

The limits under PA 2008, s 22(4) are as follows:

(a) in relation to the construction or alteration of a motorway, is 15 hectares;

(b) in relation to the construction or alteration of a highway, other than a motorway, where the speed limit for any class of vehicle is expected to be 50 miles per hour or greater, is 12.5 hectares; and

(c) in relation to the construction or alteration of any other highway is 7.5 hectares.

The 'area of development' is then defined under PA 2008, s 22(9) as follows:

(a) in relation to construction of a highway, it means the land on which the highway is to be constructed and any adjoining land expected to be used in connection with its construction;

(b) in relation to alteration of a highway, it means the land on which the part of the highway to be altered is situated and any adjoining land expected to be used in connection with its alteration.

In relation to the definition of 'area of development', a number of points arise.

First, 'in connection with [the] construction' of the highway is not defined in the PA 2008. The words should therefore be given their natural meaning. The land to be included is therefore land that the developer expects to use in connection with the works of construction or alteration (as the case may be), rather than land which may be needed for other development that is part of the scheme, such as associated development. The land to be included would normally comprise construction and works compounds and the like. This approach is supported by the fact that the size thresholds were based upon the size of the works areas required to construct or alter a single junction on the various categories of road that make up the Secretary of State's network (see page 6 of the Government's response to the consultation on the changes proposed in the draft 2013 Order (June 2013)).

Secondly, to be included within the 'area of development' such land must be 'expected to be used' in connection with the construction and also be 'adjoining' the highway. The legislation therefore expects that all land that the developer expects to use in connection with the construction or alteration will be included within the application for the DCO (since otherwise the thresholds could be circumvented). However, the use of the word 'adjoining' suggests that construction compounds which are remote from the land on which the highway is to be constructed are not to be included in the calculation of the threshold.

Thirdly, what approach should be taken in cases where part but not all of the highway being constructed or altered is (or will) be a highway for which the Secretary of State is (or will) be the highway authority. In such a case, should the area of development only include those works areas expected to be used in connection with the Secretary of State's part of the highway, or should it include works areas expected to be used in connection with the construction or alteration of the entire highway? The position is unclear. However, it may be thought that limiting the area of development to that expected to be used in connection with the Secretary of State's highway was more in keeping with the underlying objective of the changes to PA 2008, s 22, and with the basis upon which the sizes of the thresholds were chosen.

The need for significant environmental effects for development consisting of the improvement of a highway

In addition to the criteria already referred to, the improvement of a highway will not be highway related development falling within PA 2008, s 14(1)(h) unless the improvement is likely to have a significant effect on the environment (PA 2008, s 22(5)). This should be read as having the same meaning as the equivalent term under the Environmental Impact Assessment Regulations and Directive. For guidance on the approach to be taken to the assessment of whether development has significant environmental effects, see *R (Loader) v Secretary of State* [2012] EWCA Civ 869.

Alteration of a highway that is necessary as a result of development with planning permission

In certain circumstances the alteration of a highway is necessary as a result of a development that already has the benefit of a grant of planning permission. Such alterations will not be highway related development falling within PA 2008, s 14(1)(h) if the developer has asked for the alteration to be made to the highway: see PA 2008, s 22(7). Note however that the alteration must be 'necessary' as a result of the development that has planning permission. This would appear to be an objective test. It would not be satisfied where the alteration were merely desirable.

Effect of requirement for development consent on certain statutory orders under the Highways Act 1980 and New Roads and Street Works Act 1991

PA 2008, s 33(4) provides a list of statutory orders under the Highways Act 1980 and the New Roads and Street Works Act 1991 that may neither be made nor confirmed in relation to a highway or in connection with its construction, improvement or alteration, where development consent is required for that construction, improvement or alteration. Reference should be made to PA 2008, s 33(4) for the list of orders in question.

Limited exemption from the requirement for Development Consent where certain statutory orders under the Highways Act 1980 or the New Roads and Street Works Act 1991 have already been made

However, where an order listed under PA 2008, s 33(4) has *already* been made, the construction, improvement or alteration of the highway may be exempt from the requirement for development consent by reason of either PA 2008, s 22(6) or 22(8). Reference should be made to the detailed wording of those provisions in relation to any particular case.

Associated development

Some highway related development may include associated development. The Guidance on associated development applications for major infrastructure projects (DCLG, April 2013), lists the following as examples:

- replacement roadside facilities where this becomes necessary due to the elimination of an existing facility by highway improvement;
- infrastructure associated with cycle/pedestrian access;
- off-site landscaping, habitat creation and other environmental works;
- off-site drainage works;
- alteration/diversion/stopping up of local roads, accesses and other rights of way; and
- off-site diversion of statutory undertakers' equipment

The Infrastructure Planning Commission's Interim Guidance Advice 134/10 included as examples of associated development Motorway Service Areas, Rest Areas and Truck Stops. Associated development may therefore include reasonably significant forms of development.

Note that some highways works will comprise associated development for other kinds of NSIPs. The Guidance on associated development applications for major infrastructure projects (DCLG, April 2013), lists access arrangements and demand management measures as examples.

Highway related NSIPs awaiting examination

Highway related development that is currently awaiting examination includes the following projects: A30 Temple to Higher Carblake Improvement, Morpeth Northern Bypass, Woodside Connection Houghton Regis Bedfordshire, A556 Knutsford to Bowdon Scheme.

Construction or Alteration of a Hazardous Waste Facility

Written by: Mark Westmoreland Smith, ftb
Edited by: Michael Humphries QC, ftb

Introduction

Section 14 of the PA 2008 identifies those 'types' of project that are 'nationally significant infrastructure projects' ('NSIPs') for the purposes of the PA 2008 regime; subject to the thresholds set by PA 2008, ss 15–30. PA 2008, s 14(1)(q) states that a project consisting of 'the construction or alteration of a hazardous waste facility' is an NSIP; this is subject to the thresholds set out in PA 2008, s 30.

This article considers the scope and effect of these provisions.

Commencement

Section 14(1)(p) came into effect on 26 November 2008 for the purposes of making orders (other than development consent orders) regulations or rules relating to its exercise, but for all other purposes that section and s 30 came into effect on 1 October 2011.

Thresholds and geographical issues

The effect of PA 2008, ss 14(1)(p) and 30 together is that:

- The 'construction' of a hazardous waste facility is a nationally significant infrastructure project where:
  - The facility (when constructed) will be in England;
  - The main purpose of the facility is expected to be the final disposal or recovery of hazardous waste; and
  - It is expected to have the capacity of, in the case of the disposal of hazardous waste by landfill or in a deep storage facility, more than 100,000 tonnes per year and, in any other case, more than 30,000 tonnes per year; and
- The 'alteration' of a hazardous waste facility is a nationally significant infrastructure project where:
  - The facility is in England;
  - The main purpose of the facility is expected to be the final disposal or recovery of hazardous waste; and
  - The alteration is expected to have the effect, in the case of the disposal of hazardous waste by landfill or in a deep storage facility, to increase by more

than 100,000 tonnes per year the capacity of the facility and, in any other case, to increase the capacity of the facility by more than 30,000 tonnes per year (irrespective of whether the capacity of the original facility exceeded the thresholds).

PA 2008, s 14(1)(q) relates, therefore, to hazardous waste facilities in England only. In Scotland, Wales and Northern Ireland, planning consents for all hazardous waste projects are devolved to the Scottish Government, Welsh Government and Northern Ireland Executive respectively.

Development consent for development that is 'associated' with the construction or alteration of a hazardous waste facility within PA 2008, s 14(1)(q) (ie 'associated development' under PA 2008, s 115) is also restricted to England.

It is worth noting that the thresholds for both 'construction' and 'alteration' are set by reference to the 'capacity' or 'increased capacity' of the facility, and not its intended or likely throughput; this is important.

Where a proposed hazardous waste development in England does fall below the thresholds in s 30, the applicant may request the Secretary of State to issue a s 35 Direction to the effect that the project should be treated as an NSIP such that an application for development consent could be considered under the PA 2008 regime.

Definitions within PA 2008, s 30

PA 2008, s 30 contains a number of defined terms, some of which are defined in other legislation.

PA 2008, s 30(5) defines the terms:

- 'disposal',
- 'hazardous waste', and
- 'recovery'

by reference to the Hazardous Waste (England and Wales) Regulations 2005 and, in particular, regulation 5 of those regulations.

Regulation 5(2) defines 'disposal' to mean 'any operation which is not recovery even where the operation has as a secondary consequence the reclamation of substances or energy (Annex I of the Waste Directive sets out a non-exhaustive list of disposal operations)'.

Regulation 5(2) defines 'recovery' to mean 'any operation the principal result of which is waste serving a useful purpose by replacing other materials which would otherwise have been used to fulfil a particular function, or waste being prepared to fulfil that function, in the plant or in the wider economy (Annex II of the Waste Directive sets out a non-exhaustive list of recovery operations)'.

In both cases 'the Waste Directive' means Directive 2008/98/EC of the European Parliament and of the Council on waste.

Regulation 5(2) defines 'hazardous waste' by reference to regulation 6, which states that

'Subject to regulation 9, a waste is a hazardous waste if it is—

(a) listed as a hazardous waste in the List of Wastes;

(b) listed in regulations made under section 62A(1) of the 1990 Act; or

(c) a specific batch of waste which is determined pursuant to regulation 8 to be a hazardous

waste, and the term 'hazardous' and cognate expressions shall be construed accordingly.'

Regulation 9 identifies specific waste to be treated as non-hazardous and the term 'List of Wastes' is refined in regulation 4.

Essentially, 'hazardous waste' is waste that contains one or more hazardous properties that may cause harm to human health or the environment. It does not include waste classified as radioactive waste under the Environmental Permitting (England and Wales) Regulations 2010 (except in the limited circumstances where such waste does not require a permit because it falls under an exemption provision), such that facilities for the disposal or recovery of radioactive waste do not fall to be considered as an NSIP under PA 2008, s 14(1)(p) and 30.

Note, however, the National Policy Statement for Hazardous Waste (June 2013) (see below and paragraph 2.2.1 of the NPS) states that proposals for hazardous waste facilities that handle a relatively small proportion of low level radioactive waste ('LLW') alongside hazardous waste may fall within the scope of the NPS and PA 2008, ss 14(1)(p) and 30.

The term 'Deep storage facility' in PA 2008, s 30 is defined by sub-s (6) to mean a facility for the storage of waste underground in a deep geological cavity.

The National Policy Statement for Hazardous Waste

The National Policy Statement for Hazardous Waste was published in June 2013 and will be used by the Secretary of State as the 'primary basis' for decision on development consent applications for hazardous waste infrastructure falling within the 2008 Act regime in England (para 1.1.1).

The NPS sets out a summary of the Government's policy on Hazardous Waste, the main objectives of which are (section 2.1 summary):

- To protect human health and the environment – stringent legislative controls are in place to control the management of waste with hazardous properties;
- Implementation of the waste hierarchy – to produce less hazardous waste, using it as a resource where possible and only disposing of it as a last resort;
- Self-sufficiency and proximity – to ensure that sufficient disposal facilities are provided in the country as a whole to match expected arisings of all hazardous wastes, except those produced in very small quantities, and to enable hazardous waste to be disposed of in one of the nearest appropriate installations;
- Climate change – to minimise greenhouse gas emissions and maximise opportunities for climate change adaptation and resilience.

The NPS concludes that a small number of large facilities (ie with a capacity above the NSIP thresholds) are likely to be needed to meet the expected increase in arisings in hazardous waste (para 3.3.7 and see section 3.1 Summary of Need).

Having set out Government policy on hazardous waste (Part 2) and the need for large scale hazardous waste infrastructure (Part 3), the NPS then sets out in detail:

- the Assessment Principles for hazardous waste infrastructure (Part 4), and
- the Generic Impacts to be considered by the Planning Inspectorate when examining an application for hazardous waste infrastructure (Part 5).

The King's Cliffe application

To date there has been a single application under PA 2008, ss 14(1)(p) and 30 for the alteration of existing and the construction of new facilities for the recovery and disposal of hazardous waste and disposal of low level radioactive waste at the East Northants Resource Management Facility, Stamford Road, Northamptonshire, known as 'King's Cliffe'.

During the examination itself and at the time the Examining Authority came to report (22 April 2013), only the draft NPS (July 2011) was available. As a result the Examining Authority's Report was based on the approach set down in PA 2008, s 105 ('Decisions in cases where no national policy statement has effect'). The NPS was, however, adopted on 6 June 2013 about five weeks before the Secretary of State's decision letter (11 July 2013). The Secretary of State, therefore, determined the application under PA 2008, s 104 ('decisions in cases where national policy statement has effect'). He did not, however, consider the changes between the draft and the final versions of the NPS significant enough to warrant further consultation.

A further interesting feature of this case was a jurisdictional point. As can be seen from the description of development above, that the application included the disposal of low level (radioactive) waste ('LLW'). Given that the definition of hazardous waste does not include radioactive waste, the Examining Authority asked the applicant (Augean) to set out how LLW fell within PA 2008, ss 14(1)(p) and 30.

Paragraphs 2.2.4–2.2.7 of the Examining Authority's Report states as follows:

> 'LLW is not included in the definition of hazardous waste specified in section 30(5) of PA 2008 and I therefore asked Augean to provide a legal submission setting out why, and on what basis, it considered it appropriate to include the disposal of low level waste in the draft DCO when this is not hazardous waste as defined in PA 2008. In its response Augean referred to section 115 of PA 2008.20 This states in subsection (1) that "development consent may be granted for development which is (a) development for which development consent is required: and (b) associated development." Augean considered that disposal of LLW in the hazardous landfill facility can fall within either of these categories. Section 31 states that "consent under this Act (development consent) is required for development to the extent that the development is or forms part of a nationally significant infrastructure project." In Augean's view use of the words "forms part of" demonstrates that the development does not itself have to constitute an NSIP but also that

> the development can form part of an NSIP. In addition section 30 which defines hazardous waste NSIPs states that "the main purpose of the facility is expected to be the final disposal or recovery of hazardous waste." Augean argued that the facility would continue to be an NSIP notwithstanding that activities subsidiary to the main purpose of disposal of hazardous waste are carried on. Such subsidiary activities could for example include the disposal of other appropriate waste types.
>
> Augean concluded on this point that "It is considered that Sections 30 and 31 of the Act allow for the disposal of LLW in the hazardous landfill facility NSIP provided that it is subsidiary/subordinate to the main purpose of the NSIP which requires development consent. It is therefore development for which development consent is required and it is correct to characterise it as integral."
>
> Augean considered whether the disposal of LLW might also be regarded as associated development and be included in the DCO on that basis. Drawing on revised guidance on associated development put out for consultation by DCLG in April 2012 Augean concluded that the Secretary of State would have sufficient flexibility to make his decision on a case by case basis and that""the disposal of LLW would fit well within the tenor of the proposed amended core principles."
>
> The draft DCO submitted by Augean with the application does not identify LLW as associated development and in this report I have considered it as an integral part of the development for which consent is sought not as associated development. Consideration is given later in this report to whether the inclusion of LLW as part of the waste to be disposed of at the site has any implications in terms of this proposed development remaining an NSIP.'

On this issue the Examining authority concluded at paragraph 5.134 that

> 'A hazardous waste facility is classified as an NSIP if, inter alia, "the main purpose of the facility is expected to be the final disposal or recovery of hazardous waste" (s30(1)(b) PA 2008). That leaves scope for some other activity to form part of the facility. In my view it is reasonable, as considered earlier at paragraphs 2.24 to 2.27, for disposal of LLW to be included as part of the proposed development for which development consent is being sought as long as that does not prevent the NSIP from being used for it "main purpose".'

The Secretary of State considered this issue and agreed with the Examining Authority's conclusion (para 24). A total limit on the amount of LLW was imposed, however, to ensure that the disposal of hazardous waste remains the main purpose of the NSIP.

Part 4

Requirement for Development Consent

When Development Consent is required

Written by: Mark Westmoreland Smith, ftb
Edited by: Michael Humphries QC, ftb

Introduction

Although brief, Part 4 of the PA 2008 is pivotal to the entire regime, as it sets out when development consent is required. It is this Part of the PA 2008 that also ensures various other consents are not required for NSIPs, which was one of the principal objectives behind the new regime. As a result, there is much cross-referencing to other Acts in order to dis-apply the need for consents other than development consent for NSIPs. This makes the navigation of this Part somewhat difficult.

The requirement for development consent

PA 2008, s 31 is the key provision and provides as follows:

> 'Consent under this Act ('development consent') is required for development to the extent that the development is or forms part of a nationally significant infrastructure project.'

Two concepts require consideration, being:

- 'development', and
- 'is or forms part of a nationally significant infrastructure project'.

'Development'

PA 2008, s 32 defines the term 'development' for the purposes of the PA 2008. It provides that, subject to PA 2008, s.32(2) and (3), 'development' has the same meaning as in Town and Country Planning Act 1990 ('TCPA1990').

'Development' is defined by s 55 of the TCPA1990 as being 'the carrying out of building, engineering, mining or other operations in, on, over or under land, or the making of any material change in the use of any buildings or other land', subject to further definitions and exclusions set out in that section.

The construction or alteration of nationally significant infrastructure projects will almost always involve some form of operational development (ie building, engineering, mining or other operations) and so clearly fall within the PA 2008, s 32 definition for the purposes of the PA 2008. Perhaps less clear, however, is that development comprising a 'material change of use' and for that reason the Act provides some clarification in s 32.

The effect of PA 2008, s 55(2) is that:

- the conversion of a generating station with a view to it using crude liquid petroleum, a petroleum product or natural gas as a fuel source (s 32(2)(a));

- starting to use a cavity or strata for the underground storage of gas (s 32(2)(b)); and
- an increase in the permitted use of an airport (s 32(2)(c));

are all treated as a 'material change of use' and therefore fall within the meaning of 'development' for the purposes of the development consent regime. This clarification is helpful.

The conversion of generating stations

The effect of the provision relating to generating stations makes clear that the conversion of such a station with a view to its using certain fossil fuel types is a material change of use and, therefore, 'development' for the purposes of the PA 2008. Interestingly, the conversion of such a station to the use of non-fossil biofuels is not so brought within the definition of development; although such a conversion could still require consent under s 36 of the Electricity Act 1989 depending on the particular circumstances.

Until June 2013, the provision relating to the conversion of generating stations to the use of certain fossil fuels had to be understood in the context of s 14 of the Energy Act 1976 under which the Secretary of State was able to control the fuelling of new or converted power stations. However, s 14 has been repealed by the s 18 of the Growth and Infrastructure Act 2013 (effective June 25, 2013). Section 14 of the 1976 Act implemented EU Directive 75/404/EEC on the restriction on the use of natural gas in power stations and Directive 75/405/EEC concerning the restriction on the use of petroleum products in power stations. Both Directives have since been repealed (EC/75/404 in 1991 and EC/75/405 in 1997) and the policy objectives behind s 14 (arising in response to market conditions for gas and petroleum products in the 1970s) no longer exist.

Although the conversion of a generating station to the use of certain fossil fuel is a material change of use, and therefore 'development for the purposes of the PA 2008, such development will only be an NSIP requiring development consent, however, if the 'construction' or 'extension' of that generating station exceeds the thresholds in PA 2008, s 15.

Thus the conversion of a generating station to the use of fossil fuels that was *not* (i) the construction or extension of a generating station in England or Wales with a capacity of more than 50MW, or (ii) the construction or extension of an offshore generating station of more than 100MW, would not be an NSIP for the purposes of the PA 2008 and would not, therefore, require development consent.

The use of natural porous strata for underground gas storage

There are broadly two forms of underground gas storage development being (i) the creation of gas storage caverns in underground salt deposits by solution mining, and (ii) the use of natural porous strata (eg depleted gas production fields). The first of these clearly involves 'operational' development, whilst the second may simply amount to a change of use. What PA 2008, s 32(2)(b) makes clear, however, is that such a change of use is a 'material' change of use for the purposes of the PA 2008 regime.

Again, although such a use of porous natural strata may amount to a 'material change of use' and therefore comprise 'development' for the purposes of the PA 2008, it will only be an NSIP requiring development to the extent that such development 'is starting to use underground gas storage facilities' in England or Wales above the relevant 'working capacity' or 'maximum flow rate' threshold in PA 2008, s 17.

Increase in permitted use of an airport

Clearly operational development comprising the 'construction' or 'alteration' of an airport will be an NSIP, subject to the thresholds in PA 2008, s 23. The effect of s 32(2)(c), however, is to make an increase in the permitted use of an airport a 'material change of use'. Such a change of use could, potentially, involve no operational development, but still be an NSIP by virtue of s 23(1)(1)(c) and (7).

PA 2008, s 23(1)(c) relates to 'an increase in the permitted use of an airport in a case within subsection (7)'; which sets an annual passenger or air transport movement threshold. The words in s 23(1)(c) reflect those in s 32(2)(c). The important words here are 'permitted use'. The term 'permitted' is defined in s 32(4) and s 23(9) are meaning permitted by planning permission or development consent. At present no airport has been permitted by development consent and so, for all practical purposes, this means permitted by planning permission.

More important, however, is that, currently, very few UK airports have a level of 'use' – in terms of annual passenger numbers or air transport movements – that is controlled by the terms of any planning permission. Heathrow and Stansted airports do have planning conditions limiting the use of the airport, but most do not. Thus the application of the 'material change of use' in PA 2008, s 32(2)(c) may be of relatively limited scope.

PA 2008, s 32(3) further clarifies the meaning of 'development' for the purpose of the PA 2008 by making it clear that the following is development (to the extent that they would not be otherwise):

- Works for the demolition of a listed building or its alteration or extension in a manner which would affect its character as a building of special architectural or historic interest;
- Demolition of a building in a conservation area;
- Works resulting in the demolition or destruction of or any damage to a scheduled monument;
- Works for the purpose of removing or repairing a scheduled monument or any part of it;
- Works for the purpose of making any alterations or additions to a scheduled monument; and
- Flooding or tipping operations on land in, on or under which there is a scheduled monument.

In short, this provision ensures that the development consent regime is aligned with the Planning (Listed Buildings and Conservation Areas) Act 1990 and the Ancient Monuments and Archaeological Areas Act 1979. Where development consent is required for development, PA 2008, s 33(1)(f), (g), (i) and (j) then removes the requirements for consent under those other Acts and thereby removes the need for multiple consents for the same development.

'Is or forms part of a nationally significant infrastructure project'

Development consent is only required for development under PA 2008, s 31 to the extent that it is, or forms part of, a nationally significant infrastructure project. The determination of what is, or forms part of, an NSIP needs to be considered by reference to s 14 in combination with the thresholds in ss 15–30.

Section 31 required development consent for two broad types of development, being;

- development that is an NSIP; and
- development that forms part of an NSIP.

Different issues arise in relation to each.

Development that is an NSIP

A consideration of PA 2008, ss 14 and 15–30 reveal three aspects that need to be considered, namely:

- an action;
- a type of project; and
- a relevant threshold.

The various types of project identified in PA 2008, ss 14 and 15–30 are usually preceded by what might be described as an 'action'; for example, the 'construction or extension' of a generating station, or the 'construction or alteration' of a waste water treatment plant. Even those types of development that do not have an associated 'action' in the various sub-categories within s 14(1), and there are four of them, still have such 'actions' in their corresponding threshold section (ie ss15–30). So, for example, s 14(1)(h) is simply 'highway-related development', but s 20 makes it clear that the NSIP must be the 'construction', 'improvement' or 'alteration' of a highway.

PINS has made it clear that it will expect an applicant to specify, to use the example above, whether PA 2008, s 20 development is the 'construction', 'improvement' or 'alteration' of a highway; that is, to specify what 'action' is engaged. It is worth noting that an 'action', so called, is not the same as the limb of operational development, in that, extending the example, the 'construction', 'improvement' or 'alteration' of a highway may all be classified as 'engineering operations'.

The various terms to describe what this article has referred to as an 'action' are often derived from the predecessor legislation and are, no doubt, maintained as development below the relevant threshold would still be determined under that predecessor legislation. Thus PA 2008, ss 14(1)(b) and 16 refer to the 'installation' of an electric line above ground, echoing the language in s 37 of the Electricity Act 1989.

The next aspect to consider is the 'type of project' identified in PA 2008, ss 14 and 15–30. In some cases the threshold section does further define the type of development, but often it doesn't. So, for example, s 18(3) defines what is meant by an 'LNG facility', but s 24 does not define the term 'harbour facility'.

Even where a type of project is further defined, however, there still seems to be considerable scope as to what is properly described as being, for example, a 'hazardous waste facility': see the Examining Authority's Report (paras 2.24-2.27 and 5.134) and

Secretary of State's decision (para 24) on the East Northants Resource Management Facility (aka 'King's Cliffe') DCO application.

This raises wider the issue as to whether development normally constructed together with a particular form of infrastructure (for example, a generating station) can properly be described as being 'part of' that type of development', as opposed to 'associated development' within PA 2008, s 115. This issue is particularly relevant in Wales where, subject to the exception in s 115(4), a development consent order cannot include 'associated development'. In this regard the Examining Authority's comments in its report into the Brechfa Forest West wind farm DCO application are interesting (see paras 4.139-4.146).

The final aspect to consider is the relevant threshold. For the most part these are quantitative and set by reference to an aspect of the scale or capacity of the particular development. These thresholds are considered in more detail in other parts of this work.

Development that forms part of an NSIP

Clearly many of the above considerations relate to development that forms 'part of' an NSIP, but additional points are also potentially relevant.

Clearly, a development may form 'part of' an NSIP because it is a phase of a larger project. Thus, for example, an early phase of an offshore generating station that was itself below the threshold in s 15(3), would nevertheless require development consent under s 31 if it was 'part of' a larger offshore generating station that was above that threshold. The words 'part of' in this context is clearly intended to prevent the 'salami slicing' of projects to bring them under a relevant threshold.

Issues do then arise as to whether a development below the relevant threshold would be within the PA 2008 regime if it was an early phase of a much larger project that was not expected to be promoted for some years. In other words, when does a phase of a project become a separate project? At the moment no clear guidance exists and the issue will have to be approached on its own facts, if and when it arises.

Commercial and Business Development

Written by: Michael Humphries QC, ftb

Introduction

Whilst the Planning Act 2008 (PA 2008) was originally conceived as a means of improving the process for delivering major infrastructure projects, its success has attracted the attention of those seeking to provide the same benefits for other forms of development and, in particular, major business and commercial development.

The PA 2008 regime has a number of features that may be attractive to major business and commercial developers including:

- a (largely) single consenting regime;
- a single application across local authority area boundaries;
- determination by the Secretary of State;
- fixed timetables; and
- the ability for private developers to promote the compulsory purchase of land.

Whilst some of these benefits may be available to developers with the support of a host local planning authority, such support is not always forthcoming. In consequence, during 2012 the Government decided to extend the PA 2008 regime to include business and commercial projects.

The timetable for the amendments

On 6 December 2012 the Government announced, by written Ministerial statement, a series of reforms to the PA 2008, including a commitment to extend the development consent regime to business and commercial projects.

On 22 November 2012 a consultation paper was published seeking views on the form of any extension of the PA 2008 to business and commercial development.

On 23 April 2013 the Growth and Infrastructure Act 2013 was enacted giving effect to the Government's proposals as refined following consultation. Section 26 of the 2013 Act made amendments to the PA 2008 by substituting PA 2008, s 35 with a replacement s 35 and inserting a new PA 2008, s 35ZA.

The Infrastructure Planning (Business or Commercial Projects) Regulations 2013 (SI 2013/3221) ('the BCP Regs') were made on 17 December 2013 and came into force the following day. It was the coming into force of the BCP Regs that effectively 'switched on' the PA 2008 regime for business and commercial development.

On 29 October 2013 DCLG deposited in the libraries of House of Commons and the House of Lords a 'Policy Statement' entitled 'Extension of the nationally significant infrastructure planning regime to business and commercial projects'. This is, currently, the only DCLG guidance on the operation of the new business and commercial regime.

The new PA 2008, ss 35, 35ZA

PA 2008, s 35 gives the Secretary of State power to give a direction for development to be treated as development for which development consent is required, inter alia, if the development is or forms part of 'a business or commercial project (or proposed project) of a prescribed description', will be in England or English waters, and the Secretary of State thinks that the project is of 'national significance' either by itself or when considered with one or more other business or commercial projects (or proposed projects) (see PA 2008, s 35(2)).

PA 2008, s 35ZA sets out various procedural matters in relation to directions given by PA 2008, s 35. Most importantly, for business and commercial projects, PA 2008, s 35ZA(2) make it clear that a PA 2008, s 35 direction in respect of such development may only be made in response to a 'qualifying request' made by:

- a person who proposes to carry out the development to which the request relates;
- a person who has applied, or proposes to apply, for planning permission (or various other consents in PA 2008, s 33(1) or (2); or
- a person who, is a PA 2008, s 35 direction is made, proposed to apply for development consent in respect of the proposed development.

This is important as it is clear that a 'qualifying request' may be made not only by someone who has already applied for planning permission for development, but also by someone proposing to apply for such permission. In practice, the need to draft a development consent order, and provide certain other documents that would normally accompany an application for development consent, will mean that there will be considerable time and procedural advantages in making a 'qualifying request' before making a planning application and, if a PA 2008, s 35 direction is made, proceeding under the PA 2008 regime from the outset.

If a PA 2008, s 35 direction is made, then PA 2008, s 35ZA(3) makes it clear that the Secretary of State may:

- if an application for planning permission (or other PA 2008, s 33(1), (2) consent) has been made, direct that that application be treated as an application for development consent;
- if a person proposes to make an application for planning permission (or other PA 2008, s 33(1), (2) consent), direct that the proposed application be treated as a proposed application for development consent.

Geographical scope of the provisions

As stated above, the new business and commercial provisions in section 35 only apply to development in England and English waters; not to development in Wales. This reflects the devolution settlement in Wales.

It is also worth noting that if all or part of the business or commercial development is in London, the Secretary of State will only make a section 35 direction with the consent of the Mayor of London (see PA 2008, s 35(4)). It is also clear that that consent should be obtained before making any 'qualifying request' to the Secretary of State (see the DCGL 'Policy Statement').

Types of business and commercial development

As stated above, PA 2008, s 35(2) provides that a 'qualifying request' may only be made in respect of 'a business or commercial project (or proposed project) of a prescribed description' (PA 2008, s 35(2)(a)(ii)). It is the BCP Regs that 'prescribe' the descriptions of development in respect of which a direction may be made.

Regulation 2 provides that the descriptions of business and commercial project (or proposed project) in regulation 2(2) are 'prescribed' for the purposes of PA 2008, s 35(2)(a)(ii).

Regulation 2(2)(a) states that a project must be of a description that 'consists wholly or mainly' (emphasis added) of development within SI 2013/3221, reg 2(2)(a)(i) or (ii). Thus it is clear that development forming part of a project falling within the prescribed description can be authorised, if it meets the other requirements in sections 35 and 35ZA.

Regulation 2(2)(a)(i) identifies development comprising the 'construction of buildings or facilities' for the purposes of one or more of the matters in the Schedule to SI 2013/3221. The Schedule identifies the following matters:

- Office use
- Research and development of products and processes
- An industrial process or processes
  - [see the definition of 'industrial process' in reg 1(2)]
- Storage or distribution of goods
- Conferences
- Exhibitions
- Sport
- Leisure
- Tourism

Regulation 2(2)(a)(ii) identifies a further form of development, being the winning and working of minerals in, on or under land. The term 'minerals' for these purposes is defined in SI 2013/3221, reg 1(2), but there is a specific exception for the winning or working of 'peat, coal, oil or gas' (see SI 2013/3221, reg 2(2)(b)(i)). So, for example, 'fracking' would not currently fall within SI 2013/3221, reg 2(2)(a)(ii) and would not, therefore, be development of a prescribed description for the purposes of a PA 2008, s 35 direction.

Establishing national significance

The DCLG consultation on business and commercial development included numerical 'thresholds' for the scale of such development if it was to a regarded as nationally significant. Such thresholds reflected the approach adopted for nationally significant infrastructure projects within PA 2008, ss 15–31.

In the event, the BCP Regs do not have numerical thresholds to indicate national significance, but leave this as a matter of judgement for the Secretary of State on a case-by-case basis.

The DCLG 'Policy Statement', however, does set out the Secretary of State's intended approach to the issue of national significance, as follows:

> 'In considering whether a project is of national significance, the Secretary of State will consider all relevant matters, including:
>
> - whether a project is likely to have a significant economic impact, or is important for driving growth in the economy;
> - whether a project has an impact across an area wider than a single local authority area;
> - whether a project is of a substantial physical size – further details are set out below; or
> - whether a project is important to the delivery of a nationally significant infrastructure project or other significant development.
>
> The Secretary of State will reach a decision on any request on the basis of the information provided by developer. The Secretary of State will also consider any matter which the Secretary of State considers relevant to whether a direction should be made. This will include:
>
> - whether a project is likely to require multiple consents or authorisations, and which, in consequence, would benefit from the single authorisation process offered by the nationally significant infrastructure regime;
> - whether the project is related to a nationally significant infrastructure project being brought forward at the same time and therefore would benefit from the scheme being considered as a single application through the PA 2008 regime.
>
> Each request will be considered on its own merits, but the Secretary of State would expect those developers who are thinking of asking for a direction to bear in mind the following.
>
> Although size in itself will not be the determining factor in whether a project is nationally significant or not, the Secretary of State would not normally expect to receive requests for directions in relation to projects that are not of a substantial size. For example, the Secretary of State would not normally expect to receive requests for construction projects where the gross internal floorspace to be created by the project is less than 40,000m^2; for leisure, tourism and sports facilities where the area to be developed is less than 100 hectares; or for sports stadia where the seating capacity is less than 40,000 seats.
>
> For minerals projects, the Secretary of State would not normally expect to receive requests for projects unless they involve the extraction of a strategically important industrial mineral, or extraction of a mineral on a significant scale, for example where the surface or underground area was over 150 hectares.'

As stated above, this is currently the only guidance on the operation of the regime in relation to business and commercial projects.

Exclusions from the new provisions

As identified above, the winning or working of 'peat, coal, oil or gas' is expressly excluded from the descriptions of business or commercial projects prescribed for the purposes of PA 2008, s 35(2)(a)(ii) (see the BCP Regs, reg 2(2)(b)(i)).

A rather more significant exclusion, however, for many business or commercial projects is the exclusion of 'the construction of one or more dwellings' (see the BCP Regs, reg 2(2)(b)(ii)). This follows the provisions of PA 2008, 35(5) which makes it clear that regulations made under PA 2008, s 35(2)(a)(ii) may not prescribe a description of project which includes the construction of one or more dwellings. It also reflects the approach taken in the PA 2008 generally towards 'associated development', which may not include the construction of one or more dwellings (see PA 2008, s 115(2)(b)).

Thus a mixed-use business, commercial and residential development could not be the subject-matter of a PA 2008, s 35 direction and brought under the PA 2008 regime. In such circumstances any direction could only be made in respect of the business and commercial element.

National Policy Statements

It seems reasonable clear that DCLG does not intend, certainly for the foreseeable future, to publish a National Policy Statement (NPS) for business and commercial development. In reality such development is likely to be far too varied in character to be easily susceptible to a single NPS establishing need and identifying potential impacts.

A consequence of this, however, is that business and commercial projects promoted through the PA 2008 regime will not benefits from presumption in PA 2008, s 104(3) of the Act, but will have to be considered under PA 2008, s 105.

In deciding an application where there is no NPS, PA 2008, s 105(2) requires the Secretary of State to have regard to:

> '(a) any local impact report (within the meaning given by section 60(3)) submitted to the [Secretary of State] before the deadline specified in a notice under section 60(2),
>
> (b) any matters prescribed in relation to development of the description to which the application relates, [none have been prescribed] and
>
> (c) any other matters which the Secretary of State thinks are both important and relevant to the Secretary of State's decision.'

Opting-in to the PA 2008 regime

It is important to recognise that the effect of the substituted PA 2008, s 35 and new s 35ZA is not to require the prescribed forms of business and commercial development to be dealt with under the PA 2008 regime, but simply to give the promoters of such development the opportunity to make a 'qualifying request' to be brought within the regime by a PA 2008, s 35 direction.

Before making such a 'qualifying request' promoters will have to consider a number of tactical issues including;

- the effects on their prospect of success;
- whether they would have needed to apply to more than one local planning authority;
- the likely timescales for achieving development consent;
- the potential effect on relations with the local planning authority and other stakeholders;
- the need for land assembly; and
- the need for other consents.

Making a 'qualifying request' – procedure

A 'qualifying request' must both specify the development to which it relates and explain why the requirements of PA 2008, s 35(2) are met (see PA 2008, s 35ZA(11)).

The decision-maker for business and commercial development applications is the Secretary of State for Communities and Local Government and it is, therefore, to that Secretary of State that any 'qualifying request' should be made. Further information should be available via the National Planning Casework Unit at npcu@communities.gsi.gov.uk (enquiry line – 0303 444 8050).

To enable the Secretary of State to make a decision within the statutory deadline of 28 days (PA 2008, s 35A), developers should provide the following with each request:

- details about the nature of the project including its size;
- the relevant local planning authority or authorities; confirmation that the project falls within the prescribed description;
- and reasons why the Secretary of State should consider the project of national significance.

Applicants should also have regard to the BCP Regs and ensure that their project meets the requirements set out within them.

Preparing an application for development consent following a PA 2008, s 35 direction

Whilst PA 2008, s 35ZA(5) provides that a PA 2008, s 35 direction may provide that specified provisions of the PA 2008, or any other Act, shall have effect in relation to an application with any specified modifications or, indeed, be treated as having been complied with, the Secretary of State is likely to use this power sparingly for fear of creating some procedural unfairness and, therefore, potential target for challenge.

Developers considering making a 'qualifying request' would be well advised, therefore, to anticipate having to comply with the pre-application and application requirements of the PA 2008 regime. These are covered in other articles and in the materials within this work.

Part 5

Pre-application Procedures

Legal Requirements for the Statement of Community Consultation

Written by: Rebecca Clutten, ftb
Edited by: Michael Humphries QC, ftb

The requirement for a Statement of Community Consultation

The PA 2008 places prospective applicants for development consent under an obligation to consult the local community about their proposals. Before any such consultation takes place, however, applicants are required to prepare a statement 'setting out how the applicant proposes to consult, about the proposed application, people living in the vicinity of the land' (PA 2008, s 47(1)). This document is known as the 'Statement of Community Consultation' ('SOCC').

Once a SOCC is prepared, the applicant is under a statutory duty to both publicise the document in the manner specified in the PA 2008, and carry out its consultation in accordance with the proposals identified in it (PA 2008, s 47(7)).

This article provides information on:

- preparing the SOCC;
- consulting in accordance with the SOCC; and
- revisions to the SOCC.

Preparing the SOCC

The content of the SOCC

Save insofar as relates to environmental information (considered further below), there are no specific requirements as to the information the SOCC is to contain. Typically, however, SOCCs that have been submitted with accepted applications include details of:

- the project, including its scale and the positive and negative benefits which might arise;
- how consultation will be carried out, in terms of the methods of consultation to be employed, any phasing of consultation, and provisional periods allowed for responses;
- the information that will be provided to consultees (at each stage for phased consultations);
- who will be consulted; and
- how feedback will be captured and recorded.

The Planning Inspectorate has also suggested (see pages 4 and 5 of the PINS Advice Note 16: The developer's pre-application duties (April 2012)):

- including details of its role as examining authority;
- drawing attention to any relevant National Policy Statements ('NPS') and their status, and
- giving details of any other consultations taking place in the area (to demonstrate that the applicant has had regard to the need to avoid 'consultation fatigue' when programming its own consultation process).

In relation to environmental information, Regulation 10 of the Infrastructure Planning (Environmental Impact Assessment) Regulations 2009 requires that the SOCC contain:

- a statement as to whether the development for which the applicant proposes to make an application is EIA development; and
- if the development is EIA development, how the applicant intends to publicise and consult on the preliminary environmental information ('PEI').

Although a previous version of Advice Note 15 contained a statement suggesting that the PEI must be available at the time the preparation of the SOCC is consulted on (in respect of which, see further below), that advice has now been withdrawn and the Inspectorate has confirmed, in its Register of Advice, that the level of environmental information to be made available is a matter for the applicant. The level of information provided must, however, be enough to enable meaningful consultation. In practice, this means that a local authority must have sufficient information about the environmental impacts of the project to be able properly to advise who should be consulted: see the Register of Advice, Response to Marcus Bate of Pinsent Masons dated 12 December 2011 and Response to Ben Wallace of ESBI Investments dated 26 January 2012.

Consultation on the draft SOCC

The proposed content of the SOCC must itself be consulted upon (PA 2008, s 47(2)). Applicants are required to contact all those local authorities in whose area the land subject of the proposed application falls (ie the PA 2008, s 43(1) authorities) to ascertain their views as to what the statement should contain.

Some NSIPs may have impacts that extend beyond the boundaries of the local authority in which the proposed development is situated. In such cases, applicants are well advised to consult with people living in the wider area who could be affected by the project, and DCLG Guidance suggests that such an intention should be reflected in the SOCC: see paragraph 25 of the DCLG Guidance on the pre-application process (January 2013). If such extended consultation is to be undertaken, it is also advisable that an applicant includes any local authorities for such wider areas in its consultation on the content of the SOCC, notwithstanding the absence of a statutory obligation to do so.

In order to canvass the relevant local authorities' views on the SOCC, the applicant must send to them 'the consultation documents'. There is no statutory requirement or guidance as to the contents of 'the consultation documents' and they are simply defined in PA 2008, s 47(4) as 'the documents supplied to the local authority by the applicant for the purpose of consulting the local authority under subsection (2)'. In practice, however, applicants usually send to the relevant local authorities a draft SOCC and sample consultation materials.

Guidance does identify various aspects of the content upon which applicants should seek local authority input: see paragraph 28 of the DCLG Guidance on the pre-application process (January 2013). These include:

- the size and coverage of the proposed consultation exercise;
- the appropriateness of the techniques proposed, including electronic techniques;
- the design and format of consultation materials;
- the issues to be covered in the consultation materials;
- suggested times and locations for public consultation events;
- local bodies and representative groups who should be consulted; and
- timescales for consultation.

Once it has received 'the consultation materials', a local authority has 28 days within which to respond. Applicants should remind local authorities of the deadline when providing the consultation materials. An applicant has a statutory obligation to 'have regard' to any consultation responses received by the applicant before the expiry of the 28 day deadline – that is, up to and including the 28th day – but consideration of any received after that time will be at the applicant's discretion.

The Planning Inspectorate has noted that 28 days is a short timescale and DCLG Guidance suggests that applicants undertake informal 'pre-consultation consultation' to iron out any issues that might arise in advance of formal consultation: see the DCLG Guidance on the pre-application process at paragraph 26.

The obligation to 'have regard' to local authority responses does not mean that an applicant is under an obligation to give effect to any suggestions made. Where an applicant is unable or unwilling to do so, however, the reason for adopting that course of action should be clearly explained in the application documentation. This will usually be done in the relevant section of the formal Consultation Report.

The Planning Inspectorate may also be able to offer guidance in cases where applicants and local authorities are unable to agree on the consultation process: see the DCLG Guidance on the pre-application process at paragraphs 29–30.

Although local authorities are usually willing to engage with applicants in relation to the SOCC, it is not unheard of for some authorities to fail to respond. In such cases, the applicant must satisfy itself that, and be able to explain in the application document how, its consultation proposals will ensure that all affected and interested parties (including 'hard to reach' and minority groups) will have an opportunity to engage with and comment upon the proposals.

Publicising the SOCC

Pursuant to PA 2008, s 47(6), an applicant is obliged to publicise its final SOCC in two ways:

- by making it available for inspection by the public 'in a way that is reasonably convenient for people living in the vicinity of the land'; and
- by publishing it in a newspaper circulating in the vicinity of the land a notice stating where and when the SOCC can be inspected.

There is also an obligation on applicants to publish in any manner as may be prescribed, although, as yet, no publication requirements have been so prescribed.

In respect of the first requirement above, there is no existing law or guidance on how an applicant should determine whether a location for inspection is 'reasonably convenient for people living in the vicinity of the land'. What would be 'reasonably convenient' location or locations is perhaps best explored with local authorities during the consultation SOCC. It is considered that, if an applicant makes its SOCC available in a manner suggested by the relevant local authority or authorities, the Examining Authority is unlikely to find non-compliance with the requirement.

Consulting in accordance with the SOCC

Once finalised and published, consultation must be carried out in accordance with the contents of the SOCC: see PA 2008, s 47(7)).

There is also a duty, under PA 2008, s 49, for applicants to take into account responses received to consultation carried out in accordance with the SOCC.

Before an application is accepted for examination, the Examining Authority will contact the relevant local authorities (ie those who were or should have been consulted on the SOCC) to ask for their views on the adequacy of the consultation carried out in accordance with the SOCC. Local authorities are therefore able to explain whether or not they agreed with the contents of the SOCC – highlighting *inter alia* any feedback given which was not addressed by the applicant, as the case may be – and whether they consider consultation to have been adequate and carried out in accordance with the SOCC.

Although the ultimate decision as to whether or not an application is to be accepted rests with the Examining Authority, there is clearly considerable merit in trying to resolve any consultation issues with relevant local authorities prior to submission of the application.

Revisions to the SOCC

There is no formal mechanism for revising a SOCC once it has been published. Experience has, however, shown that revisions are sometimes necessary; for example, because changes to the project means that what was originally intended as a single phase consultation instead becomes a multi-phase consultation. In such cases, applicants are, in effect, producing a new SOCC and so would be well-advised to repeat the same procedural steps as were carried out in relation to the original SOCC.

General Principles relating to Consultation

Written by: Richard Honey, ftb
Edited by: Michael Humphries QC, ftb

Introduction

This article focuses on the general common law principles relating to 'consultation' as established through case law. Separate articles will examine the specific legal duties and guidance relating to consultation under the PA 2008.

The duty to consult

There is no general duty to consult. In particular circumstances, however, a duty to consult might arise. In *R (Harrow Community Support Ltd) v Secretary of State for Defence* [2012] EWHC 1921 (Admin) Haddon-Cave J said that 'when decisions will have a specific impact on a definable group, fairness and natural justice may entail a duty to consult with those affected by the decision depending on the context of the decision' (para 28). He went on to say (para 29):

> 'A duty to consult does not arise in all circumstances. If this were so, the business of government would grind to a halt. There are four main circumstances where consultation will be, or may be, required. First, where there is a statutory duty to consult. Second, where there has been a promise to consult. Third, where there has been an established practice of consultation. Fourth, where, in exceptional cases, a failure to consult would lead to conspicuous unfairness. Absent these factors there will no obligation to consult.'

Fundamental rules of proper consultation

Where a duty to consult arises, or where a consultation is voluntarily undertaken, the consultation must be undertaken properly. Lord Woolf MR said in *R v North & East Devon Health Authority, ex parte Coughlan* [2001] QB 213 at paragraph 108 that 'whether or not consultation of interested parties and the public is a legal requirement, if it is embarked upon it must be carried out properly'.

Fair consultation involves giving the persons consulted a fair and proper opportunity to understand fully the matters about which they are being consulted and to express their views, with the person undertaking the consultation thereafter considering those views properly and genuinely (*R v Secretary of State for Trade and Industry, ex p Unison* [1996] ICR 1003).

Four fundamental principles of consultation have been set out by the courts in a number of places and were helpfully summarised by Lord Woolf MR in *Coughlan* at para 108 where he stated that:

> 'To be proper, consultation must be undertaken at a time when proposals are still at a formative stage; it must include sufficient reasons for particular

proposals to allow those consulted to give intelligent consideration and an intelligent response; adequate time must be given for this purpose; and the product of consultation must be conscientiously taken into account when the ultimate decision in taken.'

These four fundamental principles will now be examined in a little more detail.

Consultation must be carried out at a time when proposals are still at a formative stage

In relation to the first principle, it has been said that 'the requirement that consultation must be at a time when proposals are at a formative stage can be expressed as a requirement that the decision maker has not pre-determined the issue upon which he goes out to consultation, i.e. that he has an open mind. That said… to have an open mind does not mean an empty mind': see *Royal Brompton and Harefield NHS Foundation Trust v Joint Committee of Primary Care Trusts* [2011] EWHC 2986 (Admin) at para 16.

Consultation requires that there must be a real opportunity for those consulted to make representations to the decision-maker. The decision-maker should keep a 'responsive and open mind' (*R v Warwickshire City Council, ex p Boyden* [1991] COD 31 at p32) and a 'receptive mind' (*R (Partingdale Lane Residents' Association) v Barnet LBC* [2003] EWHC 947 (Admin) at para 45).

It is well-established that there can be consultation on a 'preferred option'. The fact that a provisional view has been taken, or a preferred option identified, does not prevent a consultation exercise being conducted in good faith at a stage when the position is still formative in the sense that no final decision has yet been made. There is no conflict between a person keeping an open mind and consulting on the preferred route; it is permissible to consult on proposals rather than options which are not being proposed: see *R (Bailey) v Brent LBC* [2011] EWHC 2572 (Admin) at para 90.

The consultation must give sufficient reasons for any proposal to allow intelligent consideration and response

In relation to the second rule, Lord Woolf MR said in *Coughlan* at paragraph 112 that the 'obligation is to let those who have a potential interest in the subject matter know in clear terms what the proposal is and exactly why it is under positive consideration, telling them enough (which may be a good deal) to enable them to make an intelligent response'.

A consultation document must present the issues in a way that facilitates an effective response. It must be clear to the general body of respondents. It must present the available information and the options fairly. It has been said that 'the object of requiring fairness is to ensure high standards in decision-making by public bodies, and to enable responses to be made which will best facilitate a sound decision as a result': see *R (Royal Brompton and Harefield NHS Foundation Trust) v Joint Committee of Primary Care Trusts* [2012] EWCA Civ 472 at para 11.

If during a consultation process, prior to the final decision-making, a new factor or new material emerges which is of potential significance to the decision to be made, fairness may demand that the consultees should be given an opportunity to deal with it: see *R (Edwards) v Environment Agency* [2006] EWCA Civ 877 at para 94.

Similarly, if circumstances change, or what is preferred changes, there may be a duty to re-consult. This will not be the case if the change is trivial, but if there is a fundamental difference between the proposals consulted upon and what is to be adopted then there would be a requirement for a fresh consultation: see *R (M) v Croydon LBC* [2013] EWCA Civ 116 at paras 22-23.

In *R (Devon CC) v SSCLG [2010] EWHC* 1456 (Admin) it was held that a change in approach during a consultation was unfair and deprived the affected councils of the opportunity to make their case in the consultation process (para 98). In that case there had been a last minute change of stance with which the consultees had no chance to anticipate and deal (para 81).

Adequate time must be given for consultation and response

In relation to the third rule, case law sets no prescribed time period for consultation although it is clear that 'adequate' time must be given. Consultation periods can be shorter than usual if there are good reasons for the urgency. Conversely, it has been held that a consultation period of one month including Christmas was too short in the circumstances of a particular case (*R (Green) v Gloucestershire CC* [2011] EWHC 2687 (Admin)).

The courts have rejected the argument that 'a decision-maker can routinely pick and choose whom he will consult', holding that 'a fair consultation requires fairness in deciding whom to consult as well as fairness in deciding the subject matter of the consultation and its timing': see *R (Milton Keynes Council) v SSCLG* [2011] EWCA Civ 1575 at para 32.

The product of consultation must be conscientiously taken into account in finalising the proposals

In relation to the fourth rule, the representations should form 'part of the matrix of the decision-making process': see *R v Warwickshire City Council, ex p Boyden* (1991) COD 31 at p32. The burden created by this rule should not be under-estimated. An example is the HS2 judicial review, where it was held that the consultation on blight and compensation was so unfair as to be unlawful because a particular important consultation response was not conscientiously considered (*Buckinghamshire County Council & Ors v Secretary of State for Transport* [2013] EWHC 481 (Admin)).

Unlawful consultations

Fairness is an intrinsic part of consultation: see *R (Edwards) v Environment Agency* [2006] EWCA Civ 877 at paras 90-94 and 102-106. The substantive test of lawfulness is whether a consultation process was so unfair as to be unlawful. The Court will judge on an objective basis whether the process has been so unfair as to be unlawful in all the circumstances: see *R (JL Baird) v Environment Agency* [2011] EWHC 939 (Admin) at para 51.

It has been held that, provided the fundamental requirements of consultation are observed, a decision-making authority has a comparatively wide discretion as to how the process is carried out, bounded only by irrationality (*Wainwright* at para 11). The threshold to be applied was considered by Sullivan J in *R (Greenpeace) v Secretary of State for Trade and Industry* [2007] EWHC 311 (Admin) where he said at paragraph 62:

> 'A consultation exercise which is flawed in one, or even in a number of respects, is not necessarily so procedurally unfair as to be unlawful. With the benefit of hindsight it will almost invariably be possible to suggest ways in which a consultation exercise might have been improved upon. That is most emphatically not the test. It must also be recognised that a decision-maker will usually have a broad discretion as to how a consultation exercise should be carried out.'

If it is alleged that a consultation process is unfair, clear unfairness must be shown (*Royal Brompton* at para 13). 'In reality, a conclusion that a consultation exercise was unlawful on the ground of unfairness will be based upon a finding by the court, not merely that something went wrong, but that something went 'clearly and radically' wrong' (*Greenpeace* at para 63).

It is not necessary to show that the consultation was in general unfair, merely that it was unfair in relation to a group of persons affected (*Royal Brompton* at para 14).

The aspects of alleged unfairness should be reviewed both individually and in aggregate, as an individual aspect of unfairness may seem trivial on its own but when seen with other aspects of unfairness it may acquire greater significance (*Royal Brompton* at para 12).

PA 2008, s 48 Publicity

Written by: Hereward Phillpot QC, ftb
Edited by: Michael Humphries QC, ftb

Publicity requirements

PA 2008, s 48(1) imposes a duty on the applicant to 'publicise the proposed application in the prescribed manner'. The detailed requirements for publicising the application are to be found in the Infrastructure Planning (Applications: Prescribed Forms and Procedure) Regulations 2009 ('the 2009 Regulations').

In addition to the requirements imposed by the 2009 Regulations, PA 2008, s 50(3) imposes a duty on the applicant to have regard to any guidance issued by the Secretary of State about how to comply with those requirements.

Infrastructure Planning (Applications: Prescribed Forms and Procedure) Regulations 2009

Regulation 4 of the 2009 Regulations prescribes the manner in which an applicant must publicise a proposed application.

The notice must be published for at least two successive weeks in one or more local newspapers, once in a national newspaper and once in the London Gazette (if land in Scotland is affected, it must also be published in the Edinburgh Gazette). It must also be published other specialist publications (Lloyd's List and an appropriate fishing trade journal) where the proposal relates to offshore development.

Although the meaning of 'successive weeks' is not defined, it does not appear to mean every day for two weeks. Rather, the notice must be published once a week for two successive weeks. That is reflected in the CLG's guidance at paragraph 41, which refers to 'the two required local newspaper advertisements'.

Regulation 4 also identifies what the notice must include, namely:

- the name and address of the applicant;
- a statement that the applicant intends to make an application for development consent to the Secretary of State;
- a statement as to whether the application is EIA development;
- a summary of the main proposals, specifying the location or route of the proposed development;
- a statement that the documents, plans and maps showing the nature and location of the proposed development are available for inspection free of charge at the places (including at least one address in the vicinity of the proposed development) and times set out in the notice;
- the latest date on which those documents, plans and maps will be available for inspection (being a date not earlier than the deadline in sub-paragraph (i));

- whether a charge will be made for copies of any of the documents, plans or maps and the amount of any charge;
- details of how to respond to the publicity; and
- a deadline for receipt of those responses by the applicant, being not less than 28 days following the date when the notice is last published.

Applicants would be well advised to pay close attention to the precise terms of each of these requirements, and to ensure that the notices that they publish satisfy them in all particulars. Inevitably, however, there will be occasions when notices are published which fall short of meeting the precise terms of the requirements. In those circumstances the Secretary of State will need to make a judgment as to whether any departure from the requirements is so significant that the applicant has failed to comply with the requirements of Chapter 2 of Part 5 of the PA 2008. If it is, then the application will not be accepted (s 55(3)(e)).

The degree of force with which an objector could argue that a departure should lead to the application being rejected would be likely to depend in large part on whether an individual or individuals could demonstrate a plausible case that they were substantially prejudiced as a result.

The Thames Tideway Tunnel project provides an example of a project where the section 48 notice involved two inadvertent departures from the requirements, but where this was not judged to be so significant as to justify a decision not to accept the application. In that case the Planning Inspectorate noted in its section 55 checklist that the notice did not explicitly state that the documents, plans and maps showing the nature and location of the proposed development were available free of charge, and did not state whether a charge would be made for copies of those documents. Thames Water had itself drawn attention to these departures in the checklist submitted with the application, and set out its reasons for arguing that they were not material. Whilst some objectors sought to persuade the Planning Inspectorate that this was a significant omission, they did not succeed. The Planning Inspectorate concluded that the omissions did not render the notice a nullity, and that it would be unreasonable to conclude as a result of the omission that the applicant had failed to comply with Chapter 2 of Part 5.

Infrastructure Planning (Environmental Impact Assessment) Regulations 2009

Regulation 11 of the Infrastructure Planning (Environmental Impact Assessment) Regulations 2009 requires that where the proposed application is an application for EIA development, the applicant must, at the same time as publishing the PA 2008, s 48 notice, send a copy of that notice to the consultation bodies and to any person notified to the applicant in accordance with regulation 9(1)(c).

Timing of pre-application publicity

CLG Guidance

Paragraph 41 of the CLG's guidance on the pre-application process describes the section 48 publicity as *'an integral part of the local community consultation process'*. It advises that, where possible, the first of the two required local newspaper advertisements should coincide approximately with the beginning of the consultation with communities. However, the guidance also acknowledges that because of the detailed information required for publicity under regulation 4 of the 2009 Regulations (see above) 'aligning publicity with consultation may not always be possible, especially where a multi-stage consultation is intended'.

PINS Guidance

The Planning Inspectorate's Advice Note 16 is similarly limited in the advice it offers in relation to the section 48 stage, but it also suggests it would be 'helpful' if the deadline for responses to section 48 publicity are 'as close as possible to deadlines given to landowners and local authorities etc in the s.42 consultation'.

Relationship to pre-application consultation

The CLG and PINS guidance documents thereby raise, but do not fully resolve, the issue of how the section 48 publicity stage relates to the overall process of pre-application consultation. For smaller and less complex proposals, there may be no difficulty in undertaking pre-application consultation and section 48 publicity at the same time. In larger and more complex cases with multi-stage consultation, however, it may simply be impractical to do that whilst complying with the detailed information requirements set down by regulation 4 of the 2009 Regulations. In such circumstances there does not appear to be any objection in principle to PA 2008, s 48 publicity being undertaken following section 42 and 47 consultation and this was certainly the approach adopted in respect of the Thames Tideway Tunnel project.

Feedback on section 48 publicity

The applicant must have regard to any relevant responses received to section 48 publicity when deciding whether the application that it is actually to make should be in the same terms as the proposed application (s 49(2)).

PA 2008, s 37(3) requires the applicant to submit with his application a consultation report. That report must give details of what has been done in compliance with ss 42, 47 and 48, any relevant responses and the account taken of any relevant responses. This is a useful discipline, because it forces the applicant to engage with the responses it receives at each stage, including what is said in response to s 48 publicity. In writing up the responses, it is important to provide sufficient information so that the reader can understand why changes were or were not made (as the case may be) in response to representations. The Planning Inspectorate can be expected to scrutinise the consultation report with some care to ensure that this has been done carefully and conscientiously.

Taking Consultation into account

Written by: Hereward Phillpot QC, ftb
Edited by: Michael Humphries QC, ftb

The requirements of PA 2008, s 49

Where an applicant has complied with the duties to consult upon and to publicise the proposed application pursuant to PA 2008, ss 42, 47 and 48, and proposes to go ahead with making an application, PA 2008, s 49(2) imposes a duty to first take account of responses to consultation and publicity.

The terms of the duty are expressed as follows:

> 'The applicant must, when deciding whether the application that the applicant is actually to make should be in the same terms as the proposed application, have regard to any relevant responses.'

'Relevant responses' are defined in PA 2008, s 49(3) as those responses received to consultation and to publicity before the deadlines imposed in each case.

In complying with its duty under PA 2008, s 49, the applicant must have regard to any guidance issued by the Secretary of State about how to comply with the requirements of PA 2008, Pt 5, Ch 2 (PA 2008, s 50(1) and (3)).

Compliance with this duty must be demonstrated to the satisfaction of the Secretary of State at the stage of acceptance: see PA 2008, s 55(3)(e), which provides that the Secretary of State may accept the application only if he concludes that the applicant has complied with the pre-application procedures in PA 2008, Pt 5, Ch 2. The key documents to which the Secretary of State is likely to refer in forming a view about the applicant's compliance or otherwise with the duty under PA 2008, s 49 are those to which he is obliged to have regard pursuant to PA 2008, s 55(4): namely, the Consultation Report received under PA 2008, s 37(3)(c), and any adequacy of consultation representation received from a local authority consultee. PA 2008, s 55(4)(c) also obliges the Secretary of State to have regard to the extent to which the applicant has had regard to any guidance issued under PA 2008, s 50.

Published Guidance

DCLG has published guidance under PA 2008, s 50, entitled 'Planning Act 2008: Guidance on the pre-application process' (January 2013) ('the Guidance').

Paragraph 11 of the Guidance lists a series of potentially significant benefits for all parties that can be brought about by the early involvement of local communities, local authorities and statutory consultees. These include allowing members of the public to influence the way projects are developed and how they are integrated into the community, resolving misunderstandings, allowing applicants to obtain important information about the likely impacts of the scheme, enabling potential mitigation measures to be considered and in some cases built into the project, and so on. In order to realise these benefits, however, it is essential that applicants comply with their duty under PA 2008, s 49 and approach the responses received to consultation and publicity with a genuinely open mind. Applicants must be willing to learn from the feedback from consultation and, where it is justified, to adapt their proposals in response.

The Guidance also rightly emphasises the limited scope to make changes to an application once it has been accepted for examination and explains that this is why it is important that issues are made known and explored during pre-application consultation and prior to finalising the application. See also on this issue the DCLG guidance 'Planning Act 2008: Guidance for the examination of applications for development consent' (April 2013) at paragraphs 105 to 107.

Applicants are advised to ensure that their Consultation Report sets out specifically what the applicant has done in compliance with the requirements of the PA 2008, secondary legislation, the Guidance and any relevant policies, guidance or advice published by Government or the Planning Inspectorate. The report should also set out how the application has been influenced by relevant responses to consultation, outlining any changes made as a result, and explain why responses advising on major changes to a project were not followed (paragraph 61).

Applicants need not agree to all suggestions made in response to consultation, but they are required to take them into account. In practice, demonstrating that they have done so requires a clear and coherent explanation as to why a particular suggestion has not been adopted. Formulaic or 'standard' responses to points raised by consultees are not sufficient – the response must engage with the issue raised and enable the reader to understand why it is that a particular suggestion was or was not accepted.

Other relevant aspects of the Guidance are considered below.

General case law on taking consultation into account

There is a well-developed body of case law that addresses what is necessary to ensure that consultation is adequate, including the requirement for a conscientious and open-minded consideration of relevant matters.

The requirements were neatly summarised in *R v North and East Devon Health Authority, ex parte Coughlan* [2001] 2 QB 213 at para 108:

> 'To be proper, consultation must be undertaken at a time when proposals are still at a formative stage; it must include sufficient reasons for particular proposals to allow those consulted to give intelligent consideration and an intelligent response; adequate time must be given for this purpose; and the product of consultation must be conscientiously taken into account when the ultimate decision is taken'.

The courts have elaborated upon that final requirement, explaining that an applicant must embark upon the consultation process prepared to change course, if persuaded by it to do so (*R v London Borough of Barnet, ex parte B* [1994] ELR 357 at 375C).

The duty to take responses conscientiously into account does not equate to a duty not to make a decision without the prior agreement or consensus of the consultees (*R (Smith) v East Kent Hospital NHS Trust* [2002] EWHC 2640 (Admin)). In other words, there is no obligation to agree with the points made by consultees, but it is necessary to show that they have been properly considered and that the reasons for disagreeing with them are rational and properly articulated.

A practical consideration to keep in mind is that in order to demonstrate that responses have conscientiously been taken into account, sufficient time for that to happen must be allowed between the receipt of the response and the final decision. If a consultation response raises complex technical matters, requiring expert consideration, the applicant will need to have allowed itself time – and obtained any necessary expert input – to be in a position properly to have regard to those matters.

The authorities also serve to underline the importance of adequately capturing the reasons why a particular suggestion made in response to consultation has not been accepted, at the time that the decision is made (in the PA 2008 context this would be in the consultation report). Late reasons proffered for taking a particular decision, particularly if provided in response to a subsequent legal challenge to the adequacy of consultation, will be approached with an appropriate degree of scepticism by the courts and are unlikely to be accepted (see eg *R (Medway Council and others) v Secretary of State for Transport* [2002] EWHC 2516 (Admin); *R (Nash) v Chelsea College of Art and Design* [2001] EWHC 538 (Admin)).

Changing a proposed project in response to consultation

The Guidance acknowledges the tension between consulting early but also having project proposals that are firm enough to enable consultees to comment. It encourages applicants to consider undertaking an early stage (or stages) of consultation when options are being considered, which can assist in identifying a preferred option on which to undertake formal statutory public consultation (paragraph 52). One of the obvious advantages of this approach is that it enables applicants to obtain useful input from consultees at an early formative stage where the procedural consequences of making significant changes to the proposals are relatively limited; for example, in respect of the obligation imposed by PA 2008, s 44 at the formal consultation stage to consult all those with an interest in the relevant land.

The courts have accepted that it is lawful to define the parameters of public consultation so as to exclude an option or options (*R (Medway Council and others) v Secretary of State for Transport* [2002] EWHC 2516 (Admin)).

A number of applicants have successfully adopted this staged approach, whereby the options are consulted upon and then narrowed down through an initial round (or rounds) of informal non-statutory consultation, and then statutory consultation is undertaken on a more firm proposal. National Grid, for example, has developed such an approach informed by its early experiences of the PA 2008 process, which it now adopts for all of its grid connection projects.

The Guidance offers advice in relation to the procedural implications of making changes to a proposed project in response to the formal statutory public consultation (paragraphs 55 to 57).

Applicants need not repeat consultation rounds identified in the Statement of Community Consultation 'unless the project proposals have changed very substantially' (paragraph 55). In forming a judgment on that matter, applicants are asked to consider whether what is being taken forward is 'fundamentally different' from what was consulted on, whether the proposed application has changed 'to such a large degree that the proposals could be considered a new application' (paragraph 56), and to use the degree of change, the effect on the local community and the level of public interest as guiding factors (paragraph 55). If the application only changes to 'a small degree' or if the change only affects part of the development, and does not materially change its impacts, it is not necessary to undertake a full re-consultation (paragraph 57). In these respects the Guidance reflects the approach that has been adopted by the courts in considering the need for re-consultation where proposals change (see eg (*R (Smith) v East Kent Hospital NHS Trust* [2002] EWHC 2640 (Admin)).

Ultimately the applicant and its advisors are left to form a judgment as to whether their proposed changes fall on one side of the line or the other. In view of the emphasis placed upon the importance of the pre-application consultation process, and the 'sudden death' nature of the rigorous PA 2008, s 55 acceptance process, applicants tend in practice to be fairly cautious.

Where the judgment is reached that the changes are so significant as to warrant re-consultation, the Guidance suggests that consultees should be supplied with sufficient information to enable them to fully understand the nature of the change and any likely significant impacts – but not necessarily the full suite of consultation documents – and allow at least 28 days for consultees to respond (paragraph 56). This approach of a 'targeted' re-consultation can help to reduce the burden on the applicant, and was successfully adopted by Thames Water Utilities Limited in the pre-application consultation process for the Thames Tideway Tunnel proposals.

Where proposed changes made in response to consultation are judged to be more limited and not to require re-consultation, the Guidance suggests that instead the applicant should ensure that all affected statutory consultees and local communities are informed of the changes (paragraph 57).

Part 6

Information and Surveys

Obtaining Information about Interests in Land

Written by: Douglas Edwards QC, ftb
Edited by: Michael Humphries QC, ftb

Introduction

PA 2008, s 52 comprises a detailed procedure for the obtaining of information concerning the interests held in land affected by a DCO as well as the identity of those who may be entitled to compensation.

In practice, the detailed requirements for pre-application consultation and the requirement in particular to notify the Secretary of State of those affected by proposed compulsory acquisition within a DCO is likely lead to this provision becoming well used.

However, the power to seek such information is limited and is exercisable only following compliance with particular and strict procedural requirements, no doubt at least in part being a recognition of the fact that compelling an individual to disclose information may be considered an infringement of privacy.

PA 2008, s 52 is the subject of PINS Advice Note 4.

The purpose of PA 2008, s 52 and the time at which it may be used

PA 2008, s 52 is available both where a person 'is applying' and where a person 'proposes to apply' for an order granting development consent (s 52(1)). This reflects the purposes of the exercise of the power (s 52(1)), being, to enable to person proposing or promoting a DCO to comply with:

- Chapter 2 of Part 5 of PA 2008 (ie pre-application procedure and in particular the duty under s 44 to consult owners, lessees, tenants and occupiers of land affected by the DCO) or
- Chapter 1 of Part 6 of PA 2008 (eg notification of an accepted application and to those whose interests are to be acquired).

It is likely in practice that it is at the pre-application stage that the power is likely to be of its most use. Since an applicant will generally be expected to have fully identified relevant interests in land to be compulsory acquired it is only exceptionally that the power is likely to fall to be exercised after the DCO application has been made and accepted, possibly where it is known that an interest in land has changed since the original request for information.

The requirement for the Secretary of State's consent

In broad terms, a PA 2008, s 52 notice may require:

- information about landowners or those with an interest in land (s 52(2)), and/or
- information about those who may be able to make a 'relevant claim' (s 52(2A)).

These types of notice are discussed later in this article. In both cases, however, a notice requesting information may not be served without the consent of the Secretary of State.

PINS Advice Note 4 sets out the procedure to be followed and the information required by the Secretary of State where his consent is sought under s 52. The information that should be provided is as follows:

- the contact details of the organisation making the request,
- a demonstration that the request for authorisation is linked to a project requiring development consent,
- a description of the project,
- a table summarising the details of the proposed land for which authorisation for service of a land interests notice is to be sought – a suggested format for the table is annexed to Advice Note 4, and
- a plan (known as Plan A) that shows the land required for or affected by the NSIP – detailed guidance as to the form, scale and colouration of Plan A is given in Advice Note 4.

With regard to the need to demonstrate that the request for authorisation is linked to a project requiring development consent, PINS advice is that:

> 'An explanation should be provided by the developer as to why service of a land interest notice will enable compliance with the pre-application consultation duties or the requirement to notify persons of an accepted application and to give notice to persons interests in land to which a compulsory acquisition request relates. It will be for the developer to seek their own legal advice as to how to best address these matters.'

This advice reflects a recognition that the service of a notice under PA 2008, s 52 on an individual is potentially intrusive and onerous, particularly given the criminal sanctions that apply to non-compliance with such a notice (about which see below). The Secretary of State will need to be satisfied that the service of the notice is therefore genuinely required.

A fee is payable when seeking the consent of the Secretary of State under s 52. The fee is currently set at £1,000 – see regulation 3(1) of the Infrastructure Planning (Fees) Regulations 2010.

PA 2008, s 52 a 'last resort'

There is no statutory requirement to seek any required information voluntarily before making a request under PA 2008, s 52. Advice Note 4 clearly indicates, however, that developers should seek to obtain any required information directly before recourse is had to s 52.

Reference is made in Advice Note 4 to the DCLG Guidance on the Infrastructure Planning (Fees) Regulations 2010, which comments in relation to PA 2008, s 52 (at para 3 of the annex) that 'Applicants are expected to act reasonably, first seeking to obtain relevant information or permission to access land directly before seeking authorisation under these provisions. Specifically, applicants should only submit requests for those aspects of information … where they consider they have been reasonably refused that information.' The same Guidance at paragraph 6 provides that requests under s 52 should only be made as a *'last resort'*.

Advice Note 4 continues as follows:

> 'It is expected that a developer will demonstrate that all reasonable efforts have been made to obtain information about interests in the land identified in green on Plan A, prior to making the request(s), to satisfy the Secretary of State that the authorisation request(s) are a last resort. It is expected that there will have been an exchange of correspondence and dialogue, wherever possible, between the developer and the proposed recipient(s) in an attempt to obtain information about the interests in land, prior to making the s 52 request(s).'

Advice Note 4 provides detailed guidance as to the form of the correspondence and dialogue that is expected to have taken place. Evidence of such correspondence and dialogue (or efforts to stimulate such a dialogue) should be submitted to the Secretary of State with any request under PA 2008, s 52.

As a matter of policy, therefore, the Secretary of State will wish to see other opportunities to obtain the requisite information exhausted before recourse is had to PA 2008, s 52. Thus a developer should have a detailed strategy in place to obtain the required information before the s 52 procedure is engaged. Moreover, an evidence base should be assembled to demonstrate the implementation of this strategy. It is this evidence base that will need to be provided to the Secretary of State in the event that it ultimately becomes necessary to seek a notice under s 52.

Consultation

There is no statutory duty on an applicant, or on the Secretary of State, to consult with 'affected persons' when making or considering a request under PA 2008, s 52.

However, Advice Note 4 makes it clear that an applicant is required to serve a copy of the PA 2008, s 52 notice request, and all accompanying documents, on all proposed recipients of the notice if it were to be served. The letter accompanying service of the request and information should notify the recipient that he/she may make representations to the Secretary of State within 21 days starting the day after the date of the letter. The applicant will be given an opportunity to respond to any comments received before the Secretary of State makes a decision on the request.

Types of PA 2008, s 52 notice

As stated above, in substance PA 2008, s 52 provides for two types of notice to be served with the Secretary of State's consent.

First, a notice may be served under s 52(2) requiring 'the recipient' to give the name and address of any person the recipient believes is one or more of the following, namely:

- an owner, lessee, tenant (whatever the tenancy period) or occupier of the land;
- a person interested in the land;
- a person having power
  - to sell and convey the land, or
  - to release the land.

It is worth noting that 'the recipient' of the notice does not have to be one of the persons identified in s 52(2). The 'person' on whom a notice may be served under s 52(2) (ie 'the recipient') may be any one of those identified in s 52(3), namely:

- an occupier of the land,
- a person who has an interest in the land as freeholder, mortgagee or lessee,
- a person who directly or indirectly receives rent for the land, and
- a person who, in pursuance of an agreement between that person and a person interested in the land, is authorised to manage or arrange for the letting of it.

Thus a managing agent could be 'the recipient' of a notice in respect of the landowner's interest in the land.

It is also worth noting that the notice may require 'the recipient' to give the applicant in writing 'the name and address' of any of the types of person identified in PA 2008, s 52(2). Thus a notice must be carefully drafted so as to specify the full range of interests in respect of which 'the recipient' may be able to supply 'names' and 'addresses'.

The reference above to a 'person interested in the land' would certainly include those with an 'interest in land' as defined in s1 of the Law of Property Act 1925, in order words, easements and 'profit a prendre' etc, and would appear also to include persons with an equitable interest, such as the interest of a tenant for life under a settlement. The name and address of any mortgagee would also fall within s 52(2).

Secondly, a notice may be served under PA 2008, s 52(2A) requiring 'the recipient' to give the name and address of any person who, 'if the order sought by the application or proposed application were to be made and fully implemented, would or might be entitled':

- as a result of implementing the order,
- as a result of the order having been implemented, or
- as a result of the use of the land once the order has been implemented,

to make a 'relevant claim'.

Again, 'the recipient' of any such notice must be a person identified in s 52(3).

A 'relevant claim' is defined in PA 2008, s 52(14) and comprises a claim under s 10 of the Compulsory Purchase Act 1965 or Part 1 of the Land Compensation Act 1973 or s 152(3) of the 2008 Act. In substance, this provision covers an entitlement to statutory compensation for injurious affection or other harm arising from the carrying out of the proposed development and its operation, where no land is acquired.

A notice served under s 52(2A) must explain the circumstances in which a person would be entitled to compensation as mentioned in that subsection: see s 52(5A).

Clearly any determination as to persons who 'would or might' be entitled to make a relevant claim will involve careful judgments as to potential environmental impacts that will have to be clearly justified in making any application for a s 52 notice under s 52(2A).

The form of notice and period for response

There is no statutory form of a notice to be served under PA 2008, s 52. Section 52(4) does, however, identify certain formal requirements; including drawing the recipient's attention to the fact a criminal sanction arises in cases of non-compliance. These are mandatory requirements for a notice.

The notice must be in writing and must specify the deadline by which a response must be given. That deadline must be not earlier than the end of 14 days beginning with the day on which the notice is served on the recipient (s 52(5)). Provisions for service of noticed under the 2008 Act are set out in PA 2008, ss 229 and 230.

Failure to comply with a notice

A failure to comply with a notice served under PA 2008, s 52, without reasonable excuse, amounts to a criminal offence (s 52(6)), as does the giving of information which is false in a material respect and which, when it was given, the person knew or ought reasonably to have known to be false (ss 152(6) and (7)).

Other statutory powers for obtaining information about interests in land

There are several other statutory provisions by which persons may be compelled to disclose the existence of interests in land. Section 16 of the Local Government (Miscellaneous Provisions) Act 1976 is a well-used example and is available to local authorities in respect of 'a function conferred' on that local authority by any enactment. A similar power is available under s 330 of the Town and Country Planning Act 1990 in the context of functions arising under that Act. Furthermore, for the purposes of compulsory acquisition, s 5A of the Acquisition of Land Act 1981 entitles an 'acquiring authority' to serve a notice to secure 'information about land in relation to which an acquiring authority is entitled to exercise a power of compulsory purchase'.

These powers are, however, related to 'functions' of public authorities under other legislation and it seems questionable that they could be used, even by such authorities, for the purpose of promoting an application for a development consent order.

Rights of Entry under the PA 2008 and other Statutory Powers Granting Rights of Entry

Written by: Douglas Edwards QC, ftb
Edited by: Michael Humphries QC, ftb

Introduction

PA 2008, s 53 introduced, with safeguards, a wide ranging power for those proposing or promoting a DCO to enter private land for the purpose of the carrying out of surveys etc.

As is to be expected, however, that power:

- is limited to surveys required for specified purposes;
- requires ministerial consent; and
- is subject to the payment of compensation.

PINS have published guidance, in the form of Advice Note 5, in respect of section 53.

The power

PA 2008, s 53(1) provides that any person duly authorised in writing by the Secretary of State may, at any reasonable time, enter land

- for the purpose of surveying and taking levels of it, or
- in order to facilitate compliance with the Environmental Impact Assessment Directive (85/337/EEC), the EU Habitats Directive (92/43/EC) or any EU instrument replacing those Directives (s 53(1A)),

in connection with:

- an application for a DCO which has been accepted by the Secretary of State, whether in relation to that land or other land (s 53(1)(a));
- a proposed application for a DCO (S 53(1)(b)), where it appears to the Secretary of State that the proposed applicant is considering 'a distinct project of real substance' (s 52(2)); or
- an order granting development consent that includes provision authorising the compulsory acquisition of that land or of an interest in or a right over it (s 53(1)(c)).

It is clear, therefore, that the power to enter land is exercisable pursuant to PA 2008, s 53 (i) before a DCO application has been made, (ii) when that application has been accepted, and (iii) after the DCO has been granted, albeit only in respect of those aspects of the order which concern compulsory acquisition. It is likely to be in the first of those situations that the power will be of most ultility and, in particular, in the context of the design of the scheme or for the purposes of the preparation of the environmental statement or habitats regulations assessment.

The power to enter land for the purpose of surveying that land under PA 2008, s 53(1) includes a power to search and bore for the purposes of ascertaining the nature of the subsoil or the presence of minerals or other matter in it (s 53(3)). This power may be particularly relevant for projects such as underground gas storage facilities within s 17 of the Planning Act 2008. This power is, however, subject to a requirement to give notice of an intention to search and bore etc (s 53(9)) and the authority of the 'appropriate Minister' (see s 53(11)) is the land in question is held by a statutory undertaker and that undertaker objects on the ground that the works would be 'seriously detrimental' to the carrying on of their undertaking.

The power to enter land to facilitate compliance with the two identified EU Directives (above) includes a power to take, and process, samples of

- air,
- water,
- soil or rock,
- flora,
- bodily excretions, or dead bodies, of non-human creatures, or
- any non-living thing present as a result of human activity.

Thus, and by way of example, samples of contamination on the land could be taken to facilitate compliance with a Directive. Living fauna could not however be taken from the land.

It will be apparent from the above that the power is limited to certain specific purposes. As will be made clear below, in considering whether to grant the power to enter private land under PA 2008, s 53, the Secretary of State requires clear and specific detail of the nature of the surveys etc to be carried out.

The requirement for the Secretary of State's consent

A right to enter private land pursuant to PA 2008, s 53 is subject to the consent of the Secretary of State.

The procedure for applying for consent and the information which the Secretary of State requires for the purposes of such an application is set out in PINS Advice Note 5.

There is no prescribed form of application and an application should, therefore, be made by letter. Advice Note 5 provides that '[PINS] has to be satisfied that the developer has a genuine need to enter on to the land in relation to a distinct project which requires, or has already been granted, development consent. Therefore, as much information as possible should be provided to the IPC'.

Advice Note 5 indicates that the following information should be provided when making an application under s 53:

- contact details;
- information linking the request to a project requiring development consent;

- information to demonstrate that the requirements of s 53(2) are met;
- a description of the project requiring development consent;
- a table summarising the details of the land in respect of which the rights of entry are sought - a suggested format of the table is annexed to Advice note 5;
- evidence that the owner / occupier of the land has been consulted (this is not a legal requirement, but is expected);
- a plan of the land, marked as plan A;
- details of the proposed survey and works;
- any conditions which the developer considers should be attached to the authorisation; and
- evidence to demonstrate reasonable efforts have been made to agree access.

PINS Advice Note 5 gives more detailed guidance in relation to each of these items. A fee is payable by a developer for making an application under s 53 and this should also accompany the application.

What runs though the guidance in Advice Note 5 is a requirement for a detailed and full justification as why entry is genuinely necessary, no doubt in recognition of the conflict with privacy and the right to quiet enjoyment of land which the exercise of the powers of entry may generate.

This is particularly the case in respect of a proposed application for a DCO, where, as stated above, the Secretary of State must be satisfied that 'the developer is considering a distinct project of real substance which genuinely requires entry onto the land'.

Moreover, Advice Note 5 offers clear instruction as to the level of detail required of the proposed surveys etc:

> 'The developer should clearly specify what surveys they intend to carry out, outlining their methodology and providing an explanation as to why the surveys are connected with the proposed / accepted / consented DCO. The developer should demonstrate to [PINS] that these surveys comply with the purpose of the s 53 authorisation request in relation to the project. This may include information about the need to investigate and assess environmental impacts … This and the following information should be provided in relation to each land parcel:
>
> - the scope of the environmental surveys that has been agreed with the relevant regulatory/environmental bodies;
> - survey area, timescale and period, together with an indication of whether or not repetitive visits would be required, and
> - any other survey requirements including access into buildings, and night-time surveys.'

As with applications under PA 2008, s 52, there is no express requirement for a developer to exhaust all opportunities by informal means to secure entry onto land for surveys etc, before making an application under s 53. However, Advice Note 5 makes clear that it is the Secretary of State's policy that such applications should be made 'as a last resort' and that he will require clear evidence that 'all reasonable efforts' have been made to obtain entry by negotiation and discussion before resort is had to the powers of compulsion set out in s 53. As such, a developer would be well advised to maintain a documentary record of all correspondence, requests for entry and dialogue that he or she may have had with each landowner before making an application to the Secretary of State under s 53.

The exercise of a power of entry under PA 2008, s 53

A person authorised by the Secretary of State to enter land must serve not less than 14 days' notice of intended entry onto land, where that land is occupied (s 53(4)(b)). Where invasive surveys are to be undertaken under s 53(3) to establish the nature of subsoil and the presence of minerals, then as stated above, the intention to do so must be specified in the notice (s 53(9)). The person entering the land must also produce evidence of the authority to enter and the purpose of entry if requested to do so (s 53(4)(a)), and must comply with any conditions subject to which authorisation of the Secretary of State was given (s 53(4)(c)).

A person who wilfully obstructs a person authorised to enter land under s 53(1) is guilty of an offence (s 53(5)).

Compensation

Where the exercise of a right of entry or the carrying out a survey causes 'damage to land or chattels' compensation may be recovered by the person suffering the damage from the person exercising the right of entry (s 53(7)) and any question of disputed compensation must be referred to and determined by the Upper Tribunal (s 53(8)). It is of note that this right to compensation appears to be limited to physical damage to land or to chattels, and not to any consequential economic loss.

Crown land

By PA 2008, s 54, the right of entry provided for by s 53(1)–(3A) apply to Crown land subject to certain exceptions. Two, in particular, are worthy of note.

First, a person must not enter Crown land unless that person has the permission of (i) a person appearing to be entitled to give such permission, or (ii) the appropriate Crown authority (s 54(2)).

Secondly, the requirements within s 53(4) including the requirement to give 14 days' notice of intended entry onto occupied land, as well as the criminal sanction for obstruction, is disapplied in respect of Crown land.

Other powers to entry for the carrying out of surveys etc

There are other legislative provisions that may be available to applicants, and in particular statutory undertakers, that authorise entry into land to carry out surveys. By way of example, paragraph 10 of Schedule 4 to the Electricity Act 1989 provides the following power to enter land for electricity 'licence holders', that is generating companies, transmission companies and distribution companies holding a licence under s 6 of the 1989 Act:

> '(1) Subject to the following provisions of this paragraph and without prejudice to any other right of entry, a person authorised in writing by a licence holder may, at any reasonable time, enter upon and survey any land for the purpose of ascertaining whether the land would be suitable for use for any purpose connected with the carrying on of the activities which the licence holder is authorised by his licence to carry on.
>
> (2) A person authorised to enter upon any land under this section shall not demand to do so as of right unless—
>
> (a) 14 days' notice of the intended entry has been given to the occupier; and
>
> (b) if required to do so, he has produced evidence of his authority.
>
> (3) The powers conferred by this paragraph shall not be exercisable in relation to land which is covered by a building or will be so covered on the assumption that any planning permission which is in force is acted on.
>
> (4) The power to survey land conferred by this paragraph includes power to search and bore for the purpose of ascertaining the nature of the subsoil; but works may not be carried out on the land for this purpose unless—
>
> (a) notice of the proposed works is included in the notice given under sub-paragraph (2) above; and
>
> (b) where land is held by statutory undertakers who object to the works on the ground that the carrying out of the works would be seriously detrimental to the carrying on of their undertaking, the Secretary of State gives his consent.
>
> (5) Where any person exercises any powers conferred by this paragraph, the licence holder by whom he was authorised shall make good any damage done to the land.
>
> (6) In this paragraph "building" includes any garden, yard, outhouses and appurtenances belonging to or usually enjoyed with a building.'

The Schedule 4 paragraph 10 power is subject to a compensation provision in the following terms (Sch 4 para 11(2)):

> 'Where in the exercise of any power conferred by or under paragraph … 10 above any damage is caused to land or to moveables, any person interested in the land or moveables may recover compensation in respect of that damage from the licence holder on whose behalf the power is exercised; and where in consequence of the exercise of such a power a person is disturbed in his enjoyment of any land or moveables he may recover from that licence holder compensation in respect of that disturbance.'

Whilst the Schedule 4 provisions have some similarities with those under s 53 there are clear differences, including:

- the Schedule 4 paragraph 10 power does not require the authorisation of the Secretary of State, but may be exercised on the authority of the 'licence holder';
- the Schedule 4 paragraph 10 power may not be exercised over land covered by a building, as defined; and
- compensation under Schedule 4 paragraph 11 may be recovered in respect of 'damage' to land and moveables and, furthermore, in respect of disturbance to a person's enjoyment of his land.

Electricity 'licence holders' clearly have an alternative procedure to that availably under PA 2008, s 53 for obtaining entry onto land for the purpose of surveys etc. Similar provisions granting rights of entry are available to other statutory undertakers. Promoters will need to consider carefully whether alternative rights may be available and, where they are available, the relative advantages and disadvantages of each.

PA 2008, s 53 Applications – Seeking Rights of Entry on to Third Party Land for Nationally Significant Infrastructure Projects

Written by: Sarah Merritt and Emma Cottam, Pinsent Masons LLP
Edited by: Michael Humphries QC, ftb

Introduction

PA 2008, s 53 allows the Secretary of State to authorise entry on to third party land, at any reasonable time, for specific purposes in the context of a nationally significant infrastructure project. This power does not, however, extend to Crown land, save with the permission of the appropriate Crown authority.

Whilst various statutory undertakers may already have access to similar rights under their enabling legislation – see, for example, the powers of various license holders under the Electricity Act 1989 – not all applicants under the PA 2008 have such pre-existing rights to access third party land without obtaining the consent of the relevant landowners, which in this article shall be taken to include owners, lessees, tenants or occupiers of the land.

PA 2008, s 53 authorisation, therefore, provides certain applicants with an important new power where a landowner objects to a project and would otherwise be able to prejudice the delivery of such a project – either by virtue of refusing entry to those seeking access to survey the land or by seeking a 'ransom' fee for allowing such access.

Since the PA 2008 came into force, only a handful of projects have applied for and/or been granted a s 53 authorisation; these include the Yorkshire and Humber CCS Cross Country Pipeline, the Wrexham Energy Centre, and the Dogger Bank Teeside A&B wind energy development, amongst others. This article therefore explores the legal parameters of, the procedures for and the timing of these rare (but commercially vital) applications.

PA 2008, s 53 – the legal parameters

PA 2008, s 53 allows an applicant to request authorisation from the Secretary of State for a right of entry to gain access onto land for the purposes of:

- **surveying** – including the power to 'search and bore for the purpose of ascertaining the nature of the subsoil or the presence of minerals or other matter in it' (Planning Act 2008, s 53(3);
- **taking levels or samples** from water, air, soil or rock, flora, bodily excretions, or dead bodies, of non-human creatures, or any non-living thing present as a result of human action; or
- **facilitating compliance with relevant environmental directives** – such as the Environmental Impact Assessment Directive or Habitats Directive.

An applicant can only be granted authorisation for a right of entry if it is in connection with:

- a proposed application for a DCO;
- an application for a DCO which has been **accepted** for examination by the Secretary of State, or
- a DCO (which includes a provision authorising the compulsory acquisition of that land or of an interest or right over it) which has been **granted**.

The key point about a PA 2008, s 53 authorisation is that it is a criminal offence for a person to wilfully obstruct a person exercising a power granted by a s 53 authorisation (see s 53(5)).

The application process for PA 2008, s 53 authorisation

The process for applying for access to land under PA 2008, s 53 is (deliberately) relatively onerous. Any application under s 53 is considered by the Planning Inspectorate ('PINS') to be very much a last resort, although an applicant does not need to wait until a landowner is no longer prepared to negotiate in good faith before initiating the s 53 procedure as such negotiations could go on almost indefinitely. It is clear, however, that a history of negotiations with the relevant landowner(s) needs to have taken place prior to submission of the application and an applicant will need to have had regard to the legislation and the detailed guidance provided in PINS Advice Note 5 (October 2013) and the Department for Communities and Local Government's Guidance: *Planning Act 2008: The Infrastructure Planning (Fees) Regulations 2010* (the 'DCLG Guidance').

There is no set format for a PA 2008, s 53 application; however applicants will need to complete the table and checklist that accompany Advice Note 5 and provide certain plans – including a plan showing: the proposed development; any land controlled by the applicant; and the land over which rights of entry are sought. In addition, applicants are encouraged to notify PINS of an intention to submit an application at least four weeks in advance of submission. It is suggested that applicants will need to consider submitting a suite of documents to make up a PA 2008, s 53 application, all under cover of a letter that demonstrates compliance with the legislation and relevant guidance.

Importantly, there is no prescribed timeframe for the Secretary of State to make a decision on an application under PA 2008, s 53; however experience suggests that section 53 applications are likely to be determined within three months of submission.

For a PA 2008, s 53 application to be successful in the case of a project where a DCO application has not been accepted by PINS or a DCO granted, the applicant must demonstrate that they are 'considering a distinct project of real substance genuinely requiring entry onto the land' (s 53(2)(a)). Evidence of this might include non-statutory or statutory consultation, submission of a Scoping Report to PINS or notification of a project on the PINS website.

Through its suite of PA 2008, s 53 application documents, an applicant will need to provide detailed information about:

- the proposed project/the reference number of the accepted application/a copy of the DCO granted (as appropriate);
- the land over which access rights are being sought and details of those interested in that land;
- what surveys and works the applicant proposes will be required on the relevant land;
- a history of the negotiations that have taken place with the relevant landowner(s) and confirmation as to why an application under Planning Act 2008, s 53 is being made (effectively, why it is an application of last resort and that access has been unreasonably refused);
- confirmation that the relevant landowner(s) have been notified of the application;
- confirmation of payment of the relevant fee(s) (PINS normally requires a fee for each land parcel – as such a single project may require a suite of Planning Act 2008, s 53 applications all bundled together depending on the number of land parcels requiring access); and
- detailed information on matters including the proposed conditions to attach to any authorisation and confirmation as whether there are any issues involved under particular habitats and species legislation.

PA 2008, s 53: the timing

Considering the timing of any PA 2008, s 53 application at a very early stage in the life of a nationally significant infrastructure project is key. Environmental surveys may have very specific windows of time within which the consultant team can carry them out. As such, an applicant will need to factor in negotiation time and time to prepare, submit and for the Secretary of State to determine a s 53 application in order to know what its 'cut-off' date for agreeing access voluntarily may be.

It is worth noting that appropriate Ministerial authority is required if any statutory undertaker is a relevant landowner and objects to the proposed works on the grounds that the proposed works would be 'seriously detrimental' to its undertaking.

PA 2008, s 53 – a balancing Act?

Essentially, any application under PA 2008, s 53 is a justification for the Secretary of State to authorise an interference with a landowner's enjoyment of their land. As such, an applicant needs to make clear that the balance has tipped in favour of an interference being justified (ie that it is lawful, proportionate and in the public interest). This will involve several elements including:

- Detailing the consultation that has taken place with the landowner(s). The DCLG Guidance states that that 'applicant[s] are expected to act reasonably, first seeking to obtain relevant information or permission to access land directly before seeking authorisation under these provisions. Specifically, applicants should only submit requests … where they consider they have been unreasonably refused that information or access'. A rough 'rule of thumb' is that several months' worth of negotiations should have taken place – with this being evidenced in a supporting

Schedule of Correspondence that will form part of the Planning Act 2008, s 53 application.

- Negotiating/discussing the conditions that may be attached to any Planning Act 2008, s 53 authorisation. The conditions (pursuant to s 53(4)(c)) act to limit the applicant's interference with the land. Conditions may include: restricting the time period in which the applicant is authorised to enter the land; limiting the right to of the applicant to gain entry on to the land to working days only; restricting the hours in which the applicant is authorised to enter on to the land, and also prohibiting the applicant from restricting landowner/ occupier access.
- It is worth noting that recent caselaw makes clear that a Planning Act 2008, s 53 authorisation is not a taking of the land, but an application for an authorisation to carry out surveys on the land under a set of conditions which ensures that any damage caused is remedied.

PA 2008, s 53 – considerations once authorisation has been granted

Once a PA 2008, s 53 authorisation has been granted, an applicant will need to be mindful of the potential for affected landowners to judicially review the Secretary of State's decision (at least one of the granted s 53 authorisations has been so challenged, albeit unsuccessfully). This too should be factored into an applicant's overall project programme.

The PA 2008 makes clear (see s 53(4)) that an applicant must when seeking to exercise its powers:

- If required, produce evidence of the person's authority and their purpose of entry;
- Provide 14 days' notice of intended entry where land is occupied; and
- Comply with the conditions of the s 53 authorisation.

In the event that an applicant seeks to use the power to conduct intrusive surveys, this must also be specified in the notice. Indeed, it is worth noting that a landowner can claim (see s 53(7)) for any damage to land or chattels caused in the exercise of the authorisation to enter/survey granted by PA 2008, s 53.

Conclusion

PA 2008, s 53 provides a crucial, commercial lifeline to nationally significant infrastructure projects being promoted by applicants who do not possess statutory powers of entry on to third party land. Any application for an authorisation needs to be thought about early on in the pre-submission programme for a project. An application will be a detailed suite of documents, evidencing a history of unsuccessful negotiations with landowners. Whilst it is a time-consuming process to go through, there are several projects currently before PINS that would arguably not have progressed to the submission stage without this rarely used but vital provision of the PA 2008.

Part 7

Making an Application

Application Documentation

Written by: Isabella Tafur, ftb
Edited by: Michael Humphries QC, ftb

Introduction

An application for development consent must satisfy the requirements of PA 2008, s 37 and reg 5 of the Infrastructure Planning (Applications: Prescribed Forms and Procedure) Regulations 2009 ('the 2009 Regulations'). Regulation 6 deals with the particular requirements for specific types of project, and is explored further in Article 10.2.3. In addition, national policy statements (NPSs) for particular types of infrastructure may also require applicants to supply other specified information as part of the application.

DCLG has produced Guidance on DCO application documents ('Nationally significant infrastructure projects – Application form guidance') and the Planning Inspectorate (PINS) Advice Note 6 ('Preparation and Submission of application documents') also deals with such documents.

The application form

The application must specify the development to which it relates (PA 2008, s 37(3)(a)) and be made in the prescribed form (PA 2008, s 37(3)(b)), which is currently set out at Sch 2 to the 2009 Regulations. Section 2 of the DCLG Guidance (paragraphs 10–48) set out detailed guidance on completing the numbered boxes in the prescribed application form.

The application form requires the applicant to provide a brief explanation of why the application falls within the development consent regime, and a brief non-technical summary of the development proposal and of the location or route of the development (with reference to appropriate plans).

The form also requires the applicant to indicate (with appropriate references) whether any associated development is included in the application and to give references for certain documents, including the consultation report, copies of newspaper notices, the draft order and explanatory memorandum, and the land and works plan.

Where relevant, references must also be given to a number of other documents, such as the environmental statement and, if the application seeks authorisation for compulsory acquisition the statement of reasons, funding statement and book of reference (which comply with reg 7 of the 2009 Regulations).

The DCLG Guidance (paragraph 7) encourages applicants to avoid using complex or technical terminology in the application form. PINS requires three paper copies of the full application to be submitted along with six electronic copies (on DVDs or memory sticks) (PINS Advice Note 6). Electronic documents should not exceed 50MB and each paper copy should be provided to PINS as an individual package.

The consultation report

The application must be accompanied by the consultation report (PA 2008, s 37(3)(c)), which explains what has been done in compliance with PA 2008, ss 42 (duty to consult), 47 (duty to consult local community) and 48 (duty to publicise) in relation to the application, gives details of any relevant responses (defined in s 49(3)) and of the account taken of the relevant responses. Later articles consider the pre-application consultation requirements of the PA 2008.

Prescribed documents and information

Pursuant to PA 2008, s 37(3)(d) the application must also be accompanied by documents and information of a prescribed description. Regulation 5(2) of the 2009 Regulations sets out what constitutes the prescribed documentation and information. It requires an application to be accompanied by the following:

(a) An environmental statement and any scoping or screening or scoping opinions and directions (where applicable);

(b) The draft proposed order;

(c) An explanatory memorandum explaining the purpose and effect of the provisions in the draft order;

(d) A book of reference (where applicable) which complies with the requirements in reg 7 of the 2009 Regulations;

(e) A copy of any flood risk assessment;

(f) A statement dealing with whether the proposal engages one or more of the matters set out in s 79(1) of the Environmental Protection Act 1990 (statutory nuisances), and if so, how the applicant proposes to mitigate or limit them;

(g) A report identifying any European site to which reg 48 of the Conservation (Natural Habitats &c) Regulations 1994 applies or any Ramsar site, which may be affected by the proposed development, together with sufficient information that will enable the Secretary of State to made an appropriate assessment of the implications for the site, if required by regulation 48(1);

It should be noted that this provision appears to contain a drafting error (or a failure to amend), in that it refers to the 1994 Conservation Regulations, which were repealed (in England and Wales) by the Conservation of Habitats and Special Regulations 2010, SI 2010/490. The result is that there does not appear to be a specific requirement, in England or Wales, to identify sites to which the Conservation of Habitats Regulations 2010 apply, or to provide information enabling the Secretary of State to carry out an appropriate assessment (under reg 61 of the 2010 Regulations). However, the intention of the provision is clearly to require the identification and provision of relevant information in relation to European sites and applications should (where relevant) provide this information regardless of the apparent error in reg 5(2)(g);

(h) A statement of reasons and a statement indicating how an order containing the authorisation of compulsory acquisition is proposed to be funded (where the proposed order would authorise the compulsory acquisition of land or an interest in or right over land);

The DCLG Guidance explains that the statement of reasons must set out why the compulsory acquisition is necessary to enable to proposed development to proceed, and that the funding statement must contain sufficient information to enable the Secretary of State to be satisfied that, if such powers are granted, the proposed development is likely to be undertaken and not prevented due to difficulties in obtaining the requisite funding;

(i) A land plan identifying:

  (i) the land required for, or proposed by the development;

  (ii) any land over which it is proposed to exercise powers of compulsory acquisition or any right to use land (where applicable);

  (iii) any land over which it is proposed to extinguish easements, servitude and other private rights; and

  (iv) where the land includes special category land and replacement land, that land;

(j) A works plan showing, in relation to existing features:

  (i) the proposed location or (for a linear scheme) the proposed route and alignment of the development and works; and

  (ii) the limits within which the development and works may be carried out and any limits of deviation provided for in the draft order;

(k) A plan identifying any new or altered means of access, stopping up of streets or roads or any diversions, extinguishments or creation of rights of way or public rights of navigation (where applicable);

(l) A plan with accompanying information identifying (where applicable) –

  (i) any statutory or non-statutory sites or features of nature conservation such as sites of geological or landscape importance;

  (ii) habitats of protected species, important habitats or other diversity features; and

  (iii) water bodies in a river basin management plan,

  together with an assessment of any effects on such sites, features, habitats or bodies likely to be caused by the proposed development;

(m) A plan (where applicable) with accompanying information identifying any statutory or non-statutory sites or features in the historic environment, including scheduled monuments, World Heritage sites, listed buildings and other historic structures, archaeological sites and registered battlefields, together with an assessment of any effects on such sites, features or structures likely to be caused by the proposed development;

(n) A plan with accompanying information identifying any Crown land (where applicable);

(o) Any other plans, drawings and sections necessary to describe the proposals for which development consent is sought, showing details of design, external appearance, and the preferred layout of buildings or structures, drainage, surface water management, means of vehicular and pedestrian access, any car parking to be provided, and means of landscaping;

(p) Any of the documents prescribed by reg 6 (Matters prescribed in relation to applications for specific types of projects) which are relevant to the particular project;

(q) Any other documents considered necessary to support the application; and

(r) If requested by the Secretary of State, three paper copies of the application form and supporting documents and plans.

Regulation 5(3) provides that any plans, drawings or sections required to be provided must be no larger than A0 in size, must be drawn to an identified scale (not smaller than 1:2500) and, in the case of plans, must show north. Where a plan comprises three or more separate sheets, a key plan must also be provided, showing the relationship between the different sheets (reg 5(4)).

Order and format of application documents

PINS Advice Note 6 deals with the order and format of documents submitted with the application. It explains that prior to the submission of an application, applicants will be provided, on request, with a structured electronic application index for arranging the application documents. The application index should identify all documents submitted with the application.

The order in which the documents should be organised is set out in Appendix 1 to Advice Note 6. For more detailed guidance, regard should be had to that Appendix, but in summary, the order of the documents should be as follows:

- Application form;
- Plans/drawings/sections;
- Draft development consent order;
- Compulsory acquisition information;
- Reports/statements;
- Environmental impact assessment and habitat regulations information;
- Photographs;
- Other media;
- Additional information for specific types of infrastructure;
- Other documents.

Summaries

Each document submitted to PINS should include a summary of the key issues contained within the document, which should be no longer than 1,500 words, or 10% of the original document size. Summaries should clearly and accurately highlight the main points and direct the reader to the evidence on which they are based.

References

Each document and plan submitted with the application should be referenced with the following:

- The scheme name;
- A document or plan title;
- A document or plan reference number;
- The appropriate reg 5(2) paragraph number to which the document relates;
- The date of production of the document or plan;
- The author;
- A chronological note of any revisions made to the document or plan, including the revised document or plan.

Pagination, paragraph numbers and font

PINS also sets out the following guidance in Advice Note 6:

- Each application document must be paginated and paragraphs must be numbered.
- The paragraphs within appendices should also be numbered.
- Written document should, as far as is possible, be printed on both sides of the page in order to reduce the overall bulk of the application.
- Unless it is no more than two pages of A4 paper, each document should also contain a table of contents setting out chapter and topic headings.
- The main body of text in reports should have a minimum font size of 12 pt, using a clear and recognisable font such as Arial or Verdana.

Video and audio information

Video and audio information should not be submitted, except in exceptional cases. The PINS advice encourages applicants to consult with PINS before submitting such information.

Photographs

Any photographs should be correctly labelled, annotated and dated, and the location at which the photographs were taken should be identified on a map. The type of lens used to take the photograph must also be specified (eg wide angle).

Glossary, bibliography and links to other documents

A glossary should be included for each written document in order to provide clarification of meaning for all readers, including the general public.

Larger documents, such as the environmental statement, should include a clearly references bibliography. Any links to relevant documents (such as an NPS or development plan) should be made to the specific passage or policy rather than just to the document.

Plans

Each plan must be clearly labelled in the bottom right hand corner with 'title page' information. A list of revisions should be produced to make it easy to identify the latest version of the plan.

The scale used for each plan, drawing or section should ensure that each clearly and accurately portrays the proposals and a scale bar should be included on each plan to prevent any ambiguity when dimensions or distances are measure. Key dimensions and measurements should be notated on each plan, drawing or section. Where sequenced drawings are provided (eg for a linear scheme) a key plan and sequence notation should also be provided.

Appendices

The PINS Advice recognises that appendices are useful for setting out factual, technical and other material upon which the main body of information is based in an ordered and readily identifiable form.

Appendices must be referenced and indexed and divided by section dividers. The relevance of the appendices must be clearly explained in the document to which they relate.

Fees

At the time the application is made, the applicant must pay the correct fee to PINS. The fee is currently £4,500 (reg 5 of the Infrastructure Planning (Fees) Regulations 2010).

Checklist

Appendix 2 to Advice Note 6 contains a checklist to assist decision-makers in determining whether or not to accept an application for examination.

It may be useful for applicants to refer to the checklist in preparing their applications for submission, to ensure that all requirements have been satisfied. Indeed, many applicants submit a copy of the completed checklist with their application.

This checklist is also a useful tool for applicants, as it forces them to review whether procedural requirements that will be considered in determining whether to accept an application have been correctly completed.

Assistance from the Planning Inspectorate

PINS Advice Note 6 encourages an applicant to submit its draft application, DCO and supporting documents to PINS whilst it carries out its consultation and works up detailed proposals, so that any quality control issues can be identified before the application is submitted. This approach will enable PINS to provide (non-binding) feedback as to whether the documents are likely to be of the requisite standard and cover sufficient material, and give the applicant an opportunity to remedy any shortcomings before formal submission of the application.

Applications for a DCO: Formalities

Written by: James Pereira QC, ftb
Edited by: Michael Humphries QC, ftb

Introduction

In order to help applicants to ensure that they comply with the formal requirements of an application, the Planning Inspectorate has published Advice Note Six, 'Preparation and submission of application documents'. The Advice Note is accompanied by an Application Checklist that applicants are encouraged to use to assist with ensuring that the formal contents of the application meet the statutory requirements for acceptance of an application. It is this advice that forms the subject-matter of this article.

Other parts of this work consider the substantive requirements of section 37 (applications for orders granting development consent).

Statutory requirements

PA 2008, s 55 is concerned with the acceptance of applications for DCOs. PA 2008, s 55(3)(f) provides that one of the matters about which the Secretary of State must satisfy himself before accepting an application for a DCO is that:

> '... the application (including accompaniments) is of a standard that the Secretary of State considers satisfactory.'

Section 55(5A) of the PA 2008 provides as follows:

> 'The Secretary of State when deciding whether the Secretary of State may reach the conclusion in subsection (3)(f) must have regard to the extent to which –
>
> a) the application complies with the requirements in section 37(3) (form and contents of application) and any standards set under section 37(5), and
>
> b) any applicable guidance given under section 37(4) has been followed in relation to the application.'

Therefore, quite apart from the other matters set out in PA 2008, s 55, the Secretary of State has a general discretion not to accept an application if the form and content (as opposed to the merits) of the application is not satisfactory in some way. Given the scale and complex nature of NSIPs, together with the focus on written examination under the PA 2008, the power to 'not accept' an application for being of an inadequate standard is necessary and understandable.

Statutory guidance

Paragraph 11 of the DCLG Application form guidance (June 2013) advises as follows:

> 'Applicants are required to submit full application in both electronic and hard copy formats. The applicant should discuss with the Inspectorate the appropriate format for the submission of application documents, for example electronic index, number of electronic and paper copies required, etc.'

Applicants are therefore advised to seek advice from the Planning Inspectorate as to the form and content of applications.

The Planning Inspectorate's guidance

The Planning Inspectorate's guidance on the form and content of applications is found in Advice Note Six: Preparation and submission of application documents. The Advice Note has no statutory status, but compliance with it will increase the likelihood that the application for a DCO achieves the requisite standard for acceptance. Readers are referred to the full text of the advice. An overview is given here, emphasising some key points. Note that applicants are encouraged to submit their application documents in draft while carrying out their consultation and working up detailed proposals, in order to obtain informal advice from the Inspectorate on the content of the application in advance of its formal submission.

Standard application form

The development consent application form is a prescribed form and it must be used to make the application. Statutory guidance on the application form is found in the DCLG Application form guidance (June 2013).

Copies of the application

Applicants are required to submit their full application in both electronic (six copies) and hard copy (three copies) format. Further copies may be sought of the application or of particular documents. Copies of the full application must be made available to all persons notified of the accepted application. The Advice Note gives details of the address and times for submission of an application.

Ordering the application documents

Appendix 1 of Advice Note Six sets out an index and file structure for documents, which can be applied to both electronic and hard copies. This provides a suggested order of information submitted with the application. The advice note states that if any prescribed document type is included within another document, the applicant should make clear in which document it is located and provide a precise reference to it.

Applicants are encouraged to request from the Planning Inspectorate an electronic copy of its application index to ensure that the application is presented in a manner compatible with the Inspectorate's electronic system. File sizes should be kept to a maximum of 50MB each to allow for uploading onto the National Infrastructure Portal.

Appendix 2 of Advice Note Six provides further guidance on the use of the structured electronic application index.

Documents and summaries

Each submitted document should include a summary not exceeding 1,500 words or 10% of the original document size. Summaries should clearly and accurately highlight the main points and direct the reader to the evidence on which they are based. They should not introduce any new material not covered in the main document.

Applicants are encouraged to use appendices to set out in an ordered and readily identifiable form the factual, technical and other material upon which the main body of information is based.

Referencing and heading of plans, documents and photographs

Advice Note Six gives guidance on the referencing of such documents, including (for photos) the need for a photo location plan and details of the type of lens used.

Format of documents

Advice Note Six gives detailed guidance on the format and presentation of documents, including, for example, the use of headings, font size and type, the use of contents and glossaries, double sided printing and so on.

Scale of plans and drawings

Advice Note Six contains general guidance on the scale of plans, drawings and sections. The guidance recognises that the most appropriate scale will depend upon the particular application, and applicants are encouraged to discuss this with the Planning Inspectorate.

Data protection and privacy

Applicants are asked to be mindful of the inclusion of personal data relating to individuals in the documents they submit, in particular the Consultation Report. Advice Note Six advises that the Planning Inspectorate will follow the protocols set down by the Information Commissioner's Office, and that it will redact personal details prior to publication.

Applications in Wales

Particular guidance is given in relation to compliance with the Welsh Language Act 1993.

GIS shapefile

Applicants are requested to provide a GIS shapefile of the land over which authorisation is sought within the application. The Advice Note sets out guidance on what is expected. The shapefile is requested to be submitted at least 2 weeks before the formal submission of the application.

Application fees

The application fee must be paid at the same time the application is made. Further fees are charged at different stages in an application's consideration. Advice Note Six refers to The Infrastructure Planning (Fees) Regulations 2010 (as amended) where details of the fees payable are set out.

Application acceptance checklist

Appendix 3 of Advice Note Six contains an application acceptance checklist. This comprises a checklist based upon the criteria in PA 2008, s 55, which the Planning Inspectorate will use to check compliance with s 55. Applicants are therefore encouraged to refer to the checklist when preparing their application. Note, however, that the Advice Note expressly provides that compliance with the checklist will not be a guarantee that the application will be accepted.

Part 8

Contents of a Development Consent Order

Defining the Nationally Significant Infrastructure Project

Written by: Alex Booth, ftb
Edited by: Michael Humphries QC, ftb

Introduction

There is no single, over-arching definition of a 'nationally significant infrastructure project' ('NSIP') contained in the PA 2008. The closest that the legislation comes to providing such definition is at PA 2008, s 14, of which subsection 14(1) provides a list of 16 'types of project' that may potentially comprise an NSIP.

The spectrum of development identified in subsection 14(1) is diverse. It ranges from highways and harbours to reservoirs and railway infrastructure. However, when seeking to understand the scope of development that may currently be classified as an NSIP, one can at least note that the various forms of development all fall within one of five 'fields'; namely energy, transport, water, waste water and waste. Thus each of the 16 'types of project' falls within one of the five 'fields'.

The purpose of this article is to look firstly at what types of project are capable of amounting to an NSIP, before turning to consider the precise extent of development that is capable of being so regarded.

Types of project

PA 2008, s 14 (as amended) identifies the following 'types of project' as being nationally significant infrastructure projects, subject to the 'thresholds' identified in PA 2008, ss 15–30:

- Energy
    - Generating stations (s 15)
    - Electric lines (s 16)
    - Underground gas storage facilities (s 17)
    - LNG facilities (s 18)
    - Gas reception facilities (s 19)
    - Gas transported pipe-lines (s 20)
    - Other pipe-lines (s 21)
- Transport
    - Highways (s 22)
    - Airports (s 23)
    - Harbour facilities (s 24)

  - Railways (s 25)
  - Rail freight interchanges (s 26)
- Water
  - Dams and reservoirs (s 27)
  - Transfer of water resources (s 28)
- Waste Water
  - Waste water treatment plants (s 29)
  - Infrastructure for the transfer or storage of waste water (s 29)
- Waste
  - Hazardous waste facilities (s 30)

These thresholds determine the scale of development that is deemed to be nationally significant and, therefore, within the ambit of the PA 2008. Thus the pre-existing consenting regimes still apply to projects below the relevant thresholds.

It is important to note that the PA 2008 has not been 'switched on' for all the types of project listed in s 14. The provisions relating to energy and transport types of project came into force on 1 March 2010. The provision relating to water types of project have still not been brought into force. The provisions relating to waste water treatment plants came into force on 6 April 2011. The provisions relating to infrastructure for the transfer or storage of waste water were introduced by the Infrastructure Planning (Waste Water Transfer and Storage) Order 2012 and came into force on 23 June 2013. The provisions relating to waste were brought into force on 1 October 2011.

Statutory power to include/exclude development

It is important to note that whilst the list provided at PA 2008, s 14(1) is expressed in exhaustive terms, the PA 2008 confers on the Secretary of State an express power both to add new types of development to that list and to remove existing ones from it (see s 14(3)). However, the power of the Secretary of State to amend the types of project that may be an NSIP is not without restriction. Only development connected with the five 'fields' of infrastructure project already identified (ie energy, transport, water, waste water and waste) may be added (s 14(5)(a) and (6)); furthermore the development must be one to be carried out entirely in England, its territorial waters, or a Renewable Energy Zone (except one where the Scottish Ministers have functions) (s 14(5)(b) and (7)). There is no corresponding power to add a new type of NSIP in Wales.

So far the PA 2008, s 14(3) power has only been exercised once; that being is relation to waste water infrastructure. The Infrastructure Planning (Waste Water Transfer and Storage) Order 2012 amended s 14 to create a new type of NSIP consisting of 'infrastructure for the transfer or storage of waste water' (amendment to s 14(1)(o)). The Order also created a 'threshold' for this new type of project by amending s 29 and made a 'supplementary provision' relating to compliance with pre-application requirements under the Act and certain regulations.

Thresholds

When a particular development is of a type identified in PA 2008, s 14, the issue as to whether such development comprises an NSIP for the purposes of the PA 2008 turns on the application of the 'threshold criteria' set out in sections 15-30. These criteria are, therefore, of critical importance in determining whether development requires development consent pursuant to the PA 2008 or is to be authorised under some other consenting regime.

The individual thresholds for particular types of project are considered in other articles. What follows are some general points on the approach to thresholds.

Development forming part of an NSIP

The PA 2008 is designed to prevent a developer from artificially defining a project so as to fall below a relevant threshold; thereby avoiding the need to obtain development consent. PA 2008, s 31 states that 'Consent under this Act ('development consent') is required for development to the extent that the development is *or forms part of* a nationally significant infrastructure project' (emphasis added). As discussed above, whether a project is a nationally significant infrastructure project will depend both on the type of project and its relevant threshold. Clearly the words 'or forms part of' are intended to deal with the situation where a developer proposes to bring a project forward in phases with each phase falling below the relevant threshold, but the whole project falling above the relevant threshold. In such circumstances development consent would be required for each phase, as each would form 'part of' an NSIP.

This does raise the issue of what is meant by a 'project' in PA 2008, s 14. Whilst the term is familiar from European environmental law, it is not defined as such within the PA 2008. Much, however, hangs on the proper definition of the term. Clearly it might be possible to bring a development within the PA 2008 regime by claiming that it was an early phase of a much larger project or, alternatively, remove it from the regime by claiming that each phase was an entirely independent project.

The pragmatic solution to this issue may simply be that in most cases the thresholds are so low that nearly all developments within a particular type will be classed as nationally significant and there will be little opportunity for a coherent development below the threshold to be brought forward.

Identity of the applicant

For most types of project the relevant threshold is defined by reference to the scale or capacity of the proposed development. For some, however, it is the identity of the infrastructure provider that it critical. For example, PA 2008, s 20 makes the construction of a pipe-line an NSIP, subject to certain thresholds, where is it is to be constructed by a 'gas transporter'. That term is defined by s 235 as having the same meaning as in Part 1 of the Gas Act 1986. A pipe-line to be constructed other than by a gas transporter, however, is a different type of project and subject to different thresholds under PA 2008, s 21. This distinction would have implications for other provisions within the Act, such as s 156(3).

It is also worth noting that whilst PA 2008, s 22(2)(a) relates to a highway for which the Secretary of State will be highway authority, the applicant for such a highway project may be someone other than the Secretary of State. Clearly, however, such a project could only be promoted with the consent of the Secretary of State. Where the applicant is a highway authority PINS is likely to want to see an agreement under s 6 of the Highways Act 1980 (delegation of functions in relation to trunk roads).

The activity constituting the development

Each of the thresholds also has a term or terms describing the 'activity' that constitutes the development requiring development consent. In many cases this is simply 'construction or extension' – as in 'construction or extension of a generating station' (PA 2008, s 15) – but in other cases alternative terms are used, such as 'improvement', alteration' or 'installation'. These terms often reflect the language of the predecessor consenting regime, which will still apply to development below the relevant threshold. Thus PA 2008, s 16 relates to the 'installation' of an electric line above ground; reflecting the language of section 37 of the Electricity Act 1989.

As underground gas storage may take place in a depleted natural gas field, which is not constructed but is naturally occurring, PA 2008, s 17 makes it clear that the development would be 'starting to use' such a facility (s 17(2)(b)).

In each case it will be important to understand the relevant language and, where there is a choice of 'activity' – for example, the 'construction', 'improvement' or 'alteration' of a highway under PA 2008, s 22 – it will be important for the DCO and its supporting documents to be clear on what 'activity' and, therefore, what threshold applies.

Construction or alteration

In most instances it will be clear whether development is the 'construction' or 'alteration' of a project. However, there may be circumstances where the distinction is not so clear. At what point does the 'alteration' of (say) a gas reception facility under section 19 become so extensive that it is really the 'construction' of a new gas reception facility. Such questions will usually be a matter of fact and degree, but the issue may be an important one.

Taking the above example of a gas reception facility – 'construction' has a threshold of a maximum flow rate of 4.5 million standard cubic metres per day, whereas 'alteration' has a threshold of an 'increase' of 4.5 million standard cubic metres per day. Thus if a gas reception facility with an existing capacity of 3 mscm per day is completely rebuilt in phases with an ultimate capacity of 6 mscm per day, is such development an NSIP or not? The answer may be that if the gas reception facility continued to operate at full capacity throughout the rebuilding that is an alteration, but if it closed down and was rebuilt that is the construction of a new facility.

Extent of an NSIP

Whilst it may often prove straightforward to determine that certain parts of a development comprise an NSIP, or part of an NSIP, this will not always be the case.

Specifically, it may be less than obvious whether development comprises part of the NSIP, or is simply 'associated development' within the meaning of PA 2008, s 115.

The PA 2008 draws a clear distinction between an NSIP for which development consent is required, and 'associated development' that may be included in a development consent order but doesn't have to be. PA 2008, s 115 recognises that these are two elements of development are distinct, one from the another, whilst at the same time making clear that a development consent order may be granted in respect of both.

Other articles deal with 'associated development' and 'associated development in Wales', but the issue of what in the NSIP and what is associated development is particularly pressing in Wales where, subject to a limited exception in relation to underground gas storage projects (see PA 2008, s 115(4)), associated development may not be included in a development consent order.

In England a number of confirmed DCOs do not draw a distinction between those parts of the project that are NSIP and those parts that are not, but others do. There does not appear to be any legal requirement to specify what part of a proposed development is NSIP and what part is not, so long as it is clear that at least some part of the proposed development is an NSIP or part of an NSIP; in other words, as long as it is clear that the proposed development does properly fall within the PA 2008 regime. There may be perfectly valid reasons for not wanting to specify what is NSIP and what is associated development, although as a matter of policy PINS does encourage applicants to make the distinction clear in Schedule 1 to any draft DCO.

Associated Development in England

Written by: Alex Booth, ftb
Edited by: Michael Humphries QC, ftb

Introduction

A development consent order may be granted not only in respect of development for which development consent is required (PA 2008, s 115(1)(a)) – that is, development which is or forms part of a nationally significant infrastructure project ('NSIP') as defined in PA 2008, ss 14-30 – but also in respect of certain other development known as 'associated development' ('AD') (PA 2008, s 115(1)(b)).

As to what comprises AD, PA 2008 itself provides only limited guidance. The term is defined as referring to development which is 'associated' with an NSIP (s 115(2)(a)), but which does not comprise construction/extension of one or more dwellings (s 115(2)(b). In *R (on the application of Innovia Cellophane Ltd) v Infrastructure Planning Commission* [2011] EWHC 2883 the High Court made clear that this exclusion on dwellings did not extend to temporary accommodation for workers.

Associated development can include development in England and in waters adjacent to England (s 115(3)). It can also include development in the field of energy in a Renewable Energy Zone, but not part of any Renewable Energy Zone in relation to which the Scottish Ministers have functions (s 115(3)). Associated development may not include development in Scotland or waters adjacent to Scotland. In Wales, an application for development consent may not include AD, save in respect of surface works, boreholes and pipes associated with underground gas storage by a gas transporter in natural porous strata (s 115(4)).

The remainder of this article is concerned with associated in England and waters adjacent to England; the position in Wales is the subject of a separate article in the Service.

DCLG Guidance on associated development

In the DCLG Guidance on associated development (2013) the Secretary of State will decide on a case by case basis whether development is 'associated development'. The Secretary of State does, however, set out (paragraph 5) certain 'core principles' that will be applied in making any such decision:

- The definition of associated development (in PA 2008, s 115) *requires a direct relationship* between associated development and the principal development. Associated development should therefore either support the construction or operation of the principal development, or help address its impacts.
- Associated development *should not be an aim in itself* but should be subordinate to the principal development.
- Development *should not be treated as associated development* if it is *only necessary as a source of additional revenue* for the applicant, in order to cross-subsidise the cost of

the principal development. This does not mean that the applicant cannot cross-subsidise, but if part of a proposal is only necessary as a means of cross-subsidising the principal development then that part should not be treated as associated development.

- Associated development *should be proportionate to the nature and scale of the principal development.* However, this core principle should not be read as excluding associated infrastructure development (such as a network connection) that is on a larger scale than is necessary to serve the principal development if that associated infrastructure provides capacity that is likely to be required for another proposed major infrastructure project. When deciding whether it is appropriate for infrastructure which is on a larger scale than is necessary to serve a project to be treated as associated development, each application will have to be assessed on its own merits. For example, the Secretary of State will have regard to all relevant matters including whether a future application is proposed to be made by the same or related developer as the current application, the degree of physical proximity of the proposed application to the current application, and the time period in which a future application is proposed to be submitted. [*emphasis added*]

This last point about development being associated with a future application is interesting and is further elaborated in footnote 3 in the DCLG Guidance as follows:

> '... in the case of an application for an offshore generating station, the Secretary of State may consider it appropriate for a degree of overcapacity to be provided in respect of the associated transmission infrastructure, so that the impacts of one or more other planned future projects which could make use of that infrastructure would be reduced by taking advantage of it. Applications that include elements designed for the basis of overcapacity would be expected to demonstrate the need for the overcapacity as well as fully assessing the environmental effects.'

Thus the four core principles in paragraph 5 of the DCLG Guidance are:

- there must be a 'direct' relationship between the NSIP and the AD;
- the AD should not be an aim in itself;
- the AD should not be included only to cross-subsidise the NSIP; and
- the AD should be 'proportionate' to the 'nature and scale' of the NSIP.

Some issues

What is beginning to emerge, however, is that there may not always be clear line between that development which properly forms part of the NSIP itself and that which is AD. For example, are the internal roads within a proposed generating station site part of the NSIP or simply AD? This might not matter in England, where any AD can be included in an application for development consent, but it matters greatly in Wales where such AD would have to be applied for by planning application. Indeed, even in England the distinction may matters as the Planning Inspectorate has started to request applicants to make clear in their DCO schedules what parts of the 'authorised development' are NSIP and what parts AD. In this regard it is interesting to note that whilst some approved DCOs have made this distinction, others have not. Whilst there does not appear to be any legal authority for the Planning Inspectorate's position on this point, it does appear to be developing as a policy position.

It is apparent, therefore, that some tension may exist between what is part of the NSIP and what is AD. Indeed, that tension may pull in different directions in England and in Wales. In England, there may be a tendency to restrict the scope of the NSIP and enlarge that of AD. That would allow a developer to amend or supplement the AD by subsequent applications for planning permission; an avenue not available to development that is or forms part of an NSIP: see PA 2008, s 31. In Wales, by contrast, where AD is only available in the very limited circumstances of certain underground gas storage projects, there may be a tendency to widen the definition of the NSIP to include as much development as possible. Such a result is undoubtedly an unintended consequence of the Welsh devolution settlement, but is unwelcome nevertheless.

The DCLG Guidance on associated development (2013) does encourage applicants to include AD in a single application for development consent under the PA 2008, rather than applying for it via other routes (paragraph 8). That has clear merit in allowing the Examining Authority and Secretary of State to determine an application for the entire project and all its environmental effects; although such a solution is not, for the most part, available in Wales.

Examples of associated development

The DCLG Guidance on associated development (2013) sets out various examples of associated development, being (a) examples of general types of associated development (Annex A) and examples of associated development specific to individual types of major infrastructure projects (Annex B).

However, the guidance identifies three important caveats to the examples provided, being:

- the annexes are not intended to be exhaustive;
- the annexes should not be read as a statement that the development in them should be treated as associated development as a matter of course; 'these lists should be read together with the core principles'; and
- the annexes should not be treated as an indication that the development in them is not an NSIP or an integral part of an NSIP for which development consent is required.

The annexes are, however, a useful starting point from which the core principles can be applied on a case by case basis as suggested by the Secretary of State.

Associated Development in Wales

Written by: Alex Booth, ftb
Edited by: Michael Humphries QC, ftb

Introduction

As compared to the situation in England, which was described in an earlier article, the position regarding what may lawfully comprise 'associated development' ('AD') in Wales is significantly more restricted.

As is the case with England, statutory definition of development in Wales for which a development consent order may be granted is set out in PA 2008, s 115. However, the detail as to what can be considered AD in the two jurisdictions is governed by two different sub-sections; the relevant provisions for England being a combination of sub-ss 115(2) and (3), with those for Wales being sub-ss 115(2) and (4).

This article should be read together with the more general article on 'associated development' in England.

The Limits on 'associated development' in Wales

The criteria for including 'associated development' in an application for development consent in Wales are threefold:

- the first element of the restriction is locational, in that any such development must be *'carried out wholly in Wales'* (PA 2008, s 115(4)(a));
- the second element describes the nature of the development, which is confined to *'the carrying out or construction of surface work, boreholes or pipes'* (PA 2008, s 115(4)(b)); and
- the third element is that the NSIP with which the AD is associated must be development within s 17(3), that is, *'facilities for the storage of gas underground in natural porous strata'* (PA 2008, s 115(4)(c)) – thus an application for development consent for an NSIP comprising the storage of gas underground in cavities (see PA 2008, s 17(6)) would not be able to include AD in Wales. Furthermore the gas storage facility would still have to have to comply with the threshold in s 17(4).

DCLG Guidance on associated development

In the DCLG Guidance on associated development (2013) the Secretary of State will decide on a case by case basis whether development is 'associated development'. The Secretary of State does, however, set out (paragraph 5) certain 'core principles' that will be applied in making any such decision.

Those core principles are discussed in some detail in the article on associated development in England, but in broad terms they can be summarised as follows:

- There must be a 'direct' relationship between the NSIP and the AD;
- The AD should not be an aim in itself;

- The AD should not be included only to cross-subsidise the NSIP; and
- The AD should be 'proportionate' to the 'nature and scale' of the NSIP.

The DCLG Guidance on associated development (2013) also sets out various examples of associated development, being: (a) examples of general types of associated development (Annex A); and (b) examples of associated development specific to individual types of major infrastructure projects (Annex B).

Some issues

As discussed in the context of the article on associated development in England, the distinction between the NSIP itself and AD does create some tensions in the definition of these terms, particularly in Wales.

These tensions came to the fore in the examination of the Brechfa Forest West wind farm application in Wales, where Carmarthenshire County Council ('CCC') argued that certain elements of the proposed wind farm (for example, an access roads) were not within the definition of a generating station and therefore not part of the NSIP. This would have meant, in Wales, that they could not be included in an application for development consent.

The Examining Authority considered this jurisdictional issue in the context of the 2009 version of the DCLG Guidance on associated development, which was current at the time. The key passage in that guidance stated (paragraph 10) that 'Development should not be treated as associated development if it is actually an integral part of the NSIP'.

The Examining Authority reported its consideration on this issue as follows:

> '**Scope of proposed works**
>
> 4.139 The proposed authorized project is described in Schedule1 Part 1 of the draft DCO. It includes provision for an access track, a borrow pit and an electricity sub-station.
>
> 4.140 CCC noted in its relevant representation that in Wales consent cannot be given within the DCO for works which are associated development (RREP2 LA). While the legislation is a little more complex than this, CCC's interpretation in respect of this project, an onshore electricity generating station, appears sound. CCC referred to guidance issued by the Department for Communities and Local Government (DCLG) (Guidance on Associated Development, Applications to the Infrastructure Planning Commission, DCLG, September, 2009). This included as examples of associated development some work items included within the applicant's schedule of works for which development consent is sought. CCC requested that I consider whether the application included elements of work that should be considered to be associated development, and thus not be included within the DCO.
>
> 4.141 I asked CCC whether they wished to offer any comments to inform this consideration. CCC raised the issue of the proposed site access, but offered no assessment as to whether this, or other elements of

the proposed development, might be more properly identified as associated development, rather than seen as integral to the project (REP2 LA).

4.142 Examples included in Annex A of DCLG's guidance, which are of potential relevance to this application, include vehicular access arrangements and sub-stations. In assessing this I have also given consideration to the borrow pit which might, in appropriate circumstances, be properly identified as associated.

4.143 I note a number of points on this issue before addressing the substance:

- The DCLG guidance is not directly applicable to this project; a DCO consenting an electricity generating station in Wales cannot include associated development.
- Nevertheless, some of the analysis in the guidance is relevant.
- The list of examples in the guidance is clearly identified as types of development which 'may qualify as associated development', with the list acknowledged to be neither exhaustive nor prescriptive.
- The guidance advises that development should not be treated as associated development if it is an integral part of the NSIP.

4.144 Given that this is an electricity generating station in Wales the key consideration is whether the individual elements of work can properly be seen as integral to the development of this project.

4.145 The applicant addressed this issue directly in the explanatory memorandum to the draft DCO, submitted as part of the initial application (APP4, paras 2.12 et seq). This argued that all works items for which consent is sought are integral to the development. I find the arguments convincing. In particular, I note the consideration of the definition of a generating station in the explanatory memorandum, and that none of the works identified have a purpose other than the construction and/or operation of the wind farm. The sub-station sits within the site boundary and is required for the production of electricity. The borrow pit is also within the site boundary, and has no wider function than providing material for the construction of the wind farm. The access track is required to connect the main site to the highway network for construction, maintenance and in due course removal.

4.146 I conclude that each of the elements identified in the draft DCO forms an integral part of the proposed development.'

The Secretary of State endorsed that conclusion and all elements of the generating station (including the access road etc) were granted development consent. Interestingly, the key passage from the 2009 DCLG Guidance that the Examining Authority relied on – 'Development should not be treated as associated development if it is actually an integral part of the NSIP' – was omitted from the latest 2013 version on the DCLG Guidance on associated development. It is not absolutely clear, therefore, to what extend Brechfa represents the correct approach under the latest guidance.

Associated Development: Providing Over-capacity for Future Projects

Written by: Hereward Phillpot QC, ftb
Edited by: Michael Humphries QC, ftb

The issue

Can a development consent order (DCO) authorise works whose purpose is *prima facie* to cater for the requirements of future nationally significant infrastructure projects (NSIPs)?

The law

Under the PA 2008, s 115(1) where development consent is granted for an NSIP, consent may also be granted for 'associated development'. The PA 2008, s 115(2) defines 'associated development' as meaning development which:

- is associated with the development within PA 2008, s 115(1)(a) (ie development for which development consent is required) or any part of it;
- is not the construction or extension of one or more dwellings, and
- is within PA 2008, s 115(3) or (4).

Beyond the (slightly circular) definition in PA 2008, s 115(2), associated development is not further defined in the 2008 Act.

So far, there has only been one case that has come before the courts considering the PA 2008: *R (Innovia Cellophane Ltd) v Infrastructure Planning Commission* [2011] EWHC 2883 (Admin), but the issue in dispute there was whether proposed temporary campus accommodation for construction workers constituted the construction of 'dwellings'. *Innovia* offers no wider assistance in interpreting PA 2008, s 115, save for emphasising the purpose of the legislation in avoiding a piecemeal consent system (judgement paragraph 29).

Government guidance

The DCLG *'Guidance on associated development applications for major infrastructure projects'* (April 2013) (the DCLG Guidance) explains (paragraph 5) that it is for the Secretary of State to decide on a case by case basis whether or not development should be treated as associated development, and identifies a series of 'core principles' that will be taken into account for these purposes.

The first and fourth of those core principles are of direct relevance here:

> '(i) The definition of associated development, as set out in paragraph 3 above, requires a direct relationship between associated development and the principal development. Associated development should therefore either support the construction or operation of the principal development, or help address its impacts.

...

(iv) Associated development should be proportionate to the nature and scale of the principal development. However, this core principle should not be read as excluding associated infrastructure development (such as a network connection) that is on a larger scale than is necessary to serve the principal development if that associated infrastructure provides capacity that is likely to be required for another proposed major infrastructure project. When deciding whether it is appropriate for infrastructure which is on a larger scale than is necessary to serve a project to be treated as associated development, each application will have to be assessed on its own merits. For example, the Secretary of State will have regard to all relevant matters including whether a future application is proposed to be made by the same or related developer as the current application, the degree of physical proximity of the proposed application to the current application, and the time period in which a future application is proposed to be submitted.' (emphasis added).

The term 'principal development' in the first core principle above is defined in paragraph 2 of the DCLG Guidance as 'the development for which development consent is required under Part 3 of the Act' (ie the NSIP).

A footnote in the DCLG Guidance to the fourth core principle (above) states that:

> 'For example, in the case of an application for an offshore generating station, the Secretary of State may consider it appropriate for a degree of overcapacity to be provided in respect of the associated transmission infrastructure, so that impacts of one or more other planned future projects which could make use of that infrastructure would be reduced by taking advantage of it. Applications that include elements designed for the basis of overcapacity would be expected to demonstrate the need for overcapacity as well as fully assessing the environmental effects.'

The DCLG Guidance is helpful, and plainly proceeds on the basis that there will be circumstances where overcapacity to cater for future NSIPs can be 'associated development'. However, it is only guidance and not law, and does not clearly articulate how such development can be said to be 'associated with' the NSIP for which development consent is sought, as opposed to the future NSIP(s).

Consideration by the Secretary of State

This issue came to a head during the examination of the application for the proposed East Anglia One Offshore Windfarm (EA One) in 2013. The EA One proposals included the provision of onshore ducting and cables for the NSIP, together with the provision of ducting which would be designed to accommodate (in due course) cabling for two future offshore NSIPs which were then in the pre-application stage.

The effect of including the additional ducting was that a wider strip of land was needed along the cable route, and construction would take slightly longer in order to carry out the additional works. However, the approach adopted would result in less disruption and associated adverse environmental effects, and a reduced area affected by compulsory acquisition, by comparison to the position that would arise if the works were authorised and undertaken sequentially as each NSIP came forward. In simple terms, the suggested approach avoided the need for repeated entry onto the land to undertake excavation and ducting works over a number of years (as the cables for the future NSIPs could simply be pulled through the then existing cable ducts). The promoter, local authorities and (ultimately) the landowners were agreed that it was a sensible and pragmatic approach, but the Examining Authority had to grapple with whether it was lawful and to this end they asked a number of questions of the promoter, both in written questions and at the compulsory acquisition hearing.

EA One relied on the following key points:

a The PA 2008, s 115(2) definition is broad – the development need only be 'associated with' the development for which development consent is required. The Planning Act 2008 imposes no additional constraint.

b In ordinary usage, 'associated with' means 'connected with'.

c The issue in each case is, therefore, a matter of fact and degree for the Secretary of State to determine the degree of connection between the NSIP and the proposed associated development.

d That approach is reflected in the DCLG Guidance, and it can fairly be said that the EA One application is the paradigm case of the type of overcapacity provision that would properly qualify as associated development.

e There is no difference in principle between the provision of, say, a slightly larger cable which will have capacity for more than one NSIP, and multiple ducts, some of which will carry cables for the present NSIP, others of which will carry cables for future NSIPs. In both cases what is being provided is more ducting and/or cabling capacity than is required purely to cater for the needs of the present NSIP.

f The impacts of the present NSIP must include its cumulative impacts with other future projects, which are sufficiently likely to require to be assessed for the purposes of environmental impact assessment. If the proposed overcapacity is intended to help to address the cumulative impacts of the present NSIP, it is 'associated with' that NSIP and thus falls within the scope of PA 2008, s 115(2).

The Examining Authority and the Secretary of State accepted those arguments, and authorised both the associated development and the powers of compulsory acquisition needed to enable it to be implemented.

The status of the additional ducting was addressed at paragraphs 4.5 to 4.17 of the Examining Authority's report, and further consideration was given to this issue in paragraphs 5.111 to 5.117 (in the context of the powers of compulsory acquisition that had been sought). Having set out the statutory context and the relevant passages from the DCLG Guidance, and with reference to the two future projects EA Three and EA Four, the Examining Authority concluded as follows:

> '4.13 The development consent applications for East Anglia Three and Four would either be submitted by the same or by a related developer. A high degree of physical proximity would exist between the schemes. The onshore cable ducts to accommodate East Anglia Three and Four would be laid along the same route as the onshore cables for East Anglia One to connect to their respective convertor stations adjacent

to the East Anglia One convertor station at Bramford. It is anticipated that the applications for development consent for East Anglia Three and East Anglia Four would be made within a reasonable timescale. In particular at the ISH [HE-31] it was made clear that studies were well advanced for the future wind farms.

4.14 The applicant's representation [REP-196] submitted as part of its responses to the ExA's questions also demonstrated that the applicant had considered a number of alternatives and having taken into account the environmental effects, considered that construction of ducts for future wind farms along with laying of cables for East Anglia One to be the most appropriate.

4.15 The AD Guidance, at paragraph 5 (i), states: 'Associated development should either support the construction or operation of the principal development, or help address its impacts.' At the CAH, the applicant emphasised that the East Anglia Three and Four related aspects of the scheme had been included following engagement and consultation with other parties, including the local authorities and at their express suggestion. Suffolk County Council (SCC) confirmed that the preferable option would be to install the ducts for East Anglia Three and Four along with the cables for East Anglia One. This would have the benefit of avoiding a repeat cable-laying operation along the route in the future thereby reducing the overall disturbance caused to individuals and local communities. The LIR [REP-231] and representations from the local authorities [REP-276] made clear the reduced impacts that would arise from simultaneous construction of the ducts for future wind farms with the cabling for East Anglia One.

4.16 There is obviously a key relationship between the laying of the ducts for East Anglia Three and Four and the East Anglia One project. The inclusion of the ducts as associated development for the project would assist in addressing the cumulative impacts of the scheme. Having regard to the recently revised AD Guidance and, in particular footnote 3 to paragraph 5(iv), there can be no doubt that what is proposed represents the type of overcapacity provision that is envisaged in the guidance.

4.17 The Panel concludes, as a matter of fact and degree, that the connection between the East Anglia One project and the laying of the ducts for East Anglia Three and Four is such that the latter can be appropriately regarded as development which is associated with the former' (emphasis added).

The Examining Authority also accepted that as the additional ducting constituted associated development for these purposes, it formed part of the development comprised in the DCO for which development consent was sought (see PA 2008, s 122(2)(a)), it was therefore lawful to grant powers of compulsory acquisition to enable it to take place (report paragraph 5.116).

In his decision letter dated 17 June 2014, the Secretary of State endorsed the examining authority's conclusions on this issue, and its analysis (decision letter paragraphs 4.4 and 4.74).

Whilst the issue has yet to be tested in the courts, the Secretary of State's decision in the EA One case provides an important precedent for those seeking to include provision for over-capacity within their applications.

Discussion

For those considering seeking approval for overcapacity, it is important not only to seek to meet the terms of the DCLG Guidance, but also to give careful consideration to the wider implications of such an approach when preparing the application.

a If the justification for the provision of the overcapacity includes the minimisation of adverse environmental effects through undertaking the works at the same time, that will need to be reflected in a suitable requirement ensuring that is in fact what happens.

b If the DCO includes powers of compulsory acquisition that are needed to enable the overcapacity to be provided, the applicant will need to show a compelling case in the public interest for the overcapacity. That consideration will also tend to militate in favour of some suitable requirement ensuring that the development is undertaken as envisaged; rather than the provision of the overcapacity being an option to be exercised at the promoter's election. Clearly, if the provision may or may not happen, it could be difficult to say there is a compelling case for acquiring land simply to keep the option open.

c In the EA One DCO, requirement 29 requires simultaneous installation of the ducts, subject to the ability of the Secretary of State to waive that requirement if on application by the promoter he is satisfied that the relevant future NSIPs 'have been abandoned or will not come forward within a reasonable time frame' (report paragraphs 4.529 – 4.531).

d That caveat is important, because in those circumstances it would not necessarily be in the public interest for there to continue to be an obligation on the promoter to execute the additional works. In particular, it avoids:

  i unnecessarily wide temporary and permanent interference with landowners' enjoyment of their land;

  ii unnecessary additional construction impacts; and

  iii wastage of equipment, energy and expenditure.

e Depending on the circumstances of the particular case, the caveat need not give rise to difficulties in terms of EIA. It is likely to be the case that the actual impacts would be reduced from those assessed, and any potential cumulative impacts associated with the future NSIP(s) would no longer be 'likely' for the purposes of EIA. All of that would need to be considered through the EIA process, not least in the consideration of alternatives.

f Similarly, it need not give rise to difficulties in terms of compulsory acquisition. Provided that the requirement is drafted in suitable terms, the decision that the caveat applied would necessarily have arisen before the relevant works for the current NSIP had occurred. Thus no temporary land take would be likely at that stage, and nor would there have been any permanent acquisition of the relevant land. The DCO would need to make provision to address this, and to ensure that any temporary and permanent land take in circumstances where the caveat applies would be confined to those areas needed for the present NSIP only. In order to do this, it would be necessary to establish through evidence what land would be needed in those circumstances, and for this to be marked on the plans.

As will be apparent, however, the issues arising are not straightforward, and introduce additional complexity to the process of EIA, the drafting of the DCO and the Statement of Reasons, and generally in the presentation of the case in the application documents and at examination. In the right circumstances, however, the ability to provide overcapacity makes practical sense, and can be to the mutual benefit of the promoter and those most directly affected by the proposed works.

DCO Model Provisions

Written by: Michael Humphries QC, ftb

Introduction

Regulation 5(2)(b) of the Infrastructure Planning (Applications: Prescribed Forms and Procedure) Regulations 2009, SI 2009/2264 ('the Applications Regulations') requires that an application for an order granting development consent must be accompanied by 'the draft proposed order'.

It needs to be stressed that the drafting of a 'draft proposed order' is a very technical legal exercise and, as PINS Advice Note 13 makes clear, 'Developers are strongly urged to take appropriate legal advice at all stages in the preparation and examination of a draft DCO'.'

This article will examine the role of 'model provisions' in the drafting of a 'draft proposed order'.

The status of model provisions

PA 2008, s 38(1) (as originally enacted) allowed the Secretary of State by order to prescribe 'model provisions' for incorporation in a draft order accompanying an application for an order granting development consent. Furthermore, s 38(2) required the then IPC to 'have regard' to any such prescribed model provisions, although it was made clear (s 38(3)) that it was not mandatory for provisions included in a draft order to be in the prescribed form.

The Secretary of State exercised the power under Planning Act 2008, s 38 in prescribing the Infrastructure Planning (Model Provisions) (England and Wales) Order 2009, SI 2009/2265. ('the Model Provisions Order').

The Explanatory Memorandum to the Model Provisions Order states (paragraph 7.8) that the order was 'intended to assist the applicant in preparing the draft proposed order, and to enable common issues across all or most applications to be addressed in a consistent manner'. The Government had consulted on a draft version of the order in 2009 and in the Explanatory Memorandum reported (paragraph 8.11) that 'The predominant view of respondents was that the model provisions were helpful, and would assist applicants when they come to formulate an application to the IPC'.

Despite this seeming endorsement of the role of model provisions, the Localism Act 2011 repealed PA 2008, s 38 with effect from 1 April 2012. Paragraph 1.2.9 of 'Statutory Instrument Practice' (November 2006) published by the Office of Public Sector Information observes that 'If an enabling Act, or the enabling section of it, is repealed, instruments made under it will lapse unless they are saved, ie continued in effect.' The Model Provisions Order does not appear to have been 'saved' and so should formally be regarded as having lapsed.

Despite this, it remains clear that PINS still wishes to be informed of any departures from the model provisions. Current guidance in PINS Advice Note 13 is as follows:

> 'Model provisions were intended as a guide for developers in drafting orders, rather than a rigid structure, but aided consistency, and assisted developers to draft a comprehensive set of lawful provisions.
>
> In the absence of relevant guidance published by DCLG, it would be helpful for the Planning Inspectorate to receive a track-change draft of the DCO showing any departures from the model provisions. The Planning Inspectorate would wish to receive such a track-change draft of the DCO both at the pre-application stage and with the formal submission of the application for development consent.' (emphasis added)

Interestingly, Examining Authorities will also often ask parties to a DCO Issue Specific hearing why a model provision should be followed. It is clear, therefore, that for the moment at least the Model Provisions Order will continue to play a role in the Planning Act 2008 regime.

For this reason, this article will continue to describe, in broad terms, the structure of the Model Provisions Order

The structure of the Model Provisions Order

The Model Provisions Order contains four schedules comprising:

- General model provisions;
- Model provisions for railways;
- Model provisions for harbours; and
- Model provisions in respect of requirements.

The Explanatory Memorandum to the Model Provisions Order states (paragraph 7.9) that 'The model provisions Order is constructed in such a way that promoters of nationally significant infrastructure projects only need look to the Schedule which is relevant to the infrastructure type.'

As will be seen in the text below, for most DCOs this statement goes too far and those drafting a DCO are likely to have to look beyond the schedule relevant to any particular infrastructure type.

In that context, however, it is worth noting that the DCLG 'Application Form Guidance' (September 2008) states (paragraph 20) that the Explanatory Memorandum for a DCO 'should also clearly explain if and why any provisions in the draft order diverge from the model provisions in the Infrastructure Planning (Model Provisions) Order 2009'.

General model provisions

During consultation on the draft Model Provisions Order, some respondents requested that DCLG produce bespoke model provisions for each infrastructure type within sections 15-30 of the 2008 Act. Whilst the Explanatory Memorandum to the Model Provisions Order make it clear that DCLG considered doing this, it goes on to make clear (paragraph 8.12) that 'we found it impossible to fulfil all such requests, as many infrastructure types would only require 'general' model provisions, or would need provisions that are so specific to the project in question that model provisions would not assist.'

Having referred to the model provisions for railways and harbours, the Explanatory Memorandum to the Model Provisions Order states (paragraph 7.10), therefore, that:

> 'We have not set out a complete set of model provisions for other NSIP types, since promoters of such projects are likely to need provisions which are bespoke to that project. However, Schedule 1 sets out a series of model provisions which may be relevant to a large number of infrastructure projects, which cover a number of issues common to large construction projects, such as the compulsory acquisition of land and stopping up of streets. In all cases, individual applicants will need to decide if they need to modify the model provisions for the purposes of their own draft development consent orders.'

Schedule 1 is not, therefore, put forward as a complete list of provisions likely to be relevant to all projects, but is clearly a menu of model provisions that may be relevant to any particular project and from which a promoter can select and, as appropriate, adapt and supplement DCO provisions.

Model provisions for railways

The Explanatory Memorandum to the Model Provisions Order states (paragraph 7.9) that:

> 'Schedule 2 sets out a complete set of model provisions to be used in nationally significant infrastructure projects (NSIP) relating to railways, and is based largely on the contents of the existing Transport and Works (Model Clauses for Railways and Tramways) Order 2006 (SI 2006/1954).'

Again, early experience seems to suggest that, far from regarding the Schedule 2 model provisions as a 'complete set', promoters are adapting and supplementing them.

The Doncaster and Ipswich Chord DCOs provide a helpful precedent for drafting detailed provisions in a rail DCO.

Model provisions for harbours

The Explanatory Memorandum to the Model Provisions Order further states (paragraph 7.9) that:

Schedule 3 sets out a complete set of model provisions to be used in NSIP harbour projects, and is based on provisions stemming either from the Transport and Works (Model Clauses for Railways and Tramways) Order 2006, SI 2006/1954 or from one or more Harbour Revision Orders or Harbour Empowerment Orders.'

Again, as with Schedule, 2 above, early experience seems to suggest that, promoters are adapting and supplementing the Schedule 3 model provisions. Indeed, Part 2 of the Hinkley Point C (Nuclear Generating Station) Order 2013 is an example of a highly adapted use of some of the Schedule 3 model provisions.

Model provisions in respect of requirements

The Explanatory Memorandum to the Model Provisions Order further states (paragraph 7.11) that:

> 'The model provisions Order also includes (at Schedule 4) a series of model 'requirements' (akin to planning conditions under existing regimes). We expect that applicants will include what they consider to be suitable requirements, in the draft proposed order they submit along with their application.'

Whilst the 'model provisions in respect of requirements' cover a broad range of issues, they will almost certainly need to be amended and supplemented to meet the needs of any particular project.

Guidance has not yet been published on the drafting of DCO requirements. In essence, however, the requirements in a DCO will be similar to the conditions attached to a grant of planning permission and so the advice in circular 11/95 may be of some assistance.

The predecessor regimes as a basis for precedent

The Explanatory Memorandum to the Model Provisions Order appears to acknowledge, not surprisingly, that even the Model Provisions Order itself has borrowed from previous model clauses and, indeed, from actual clauses in orders made by the Secretary of State. This is helpful as in early DCO examinations the then Commissioners were often reluctant to recognise the value of draft DCO provisions adapted from other regimes. More recently, however, PINS appears to have accepted the assistance that may be derived from other regimes. PINS Advice Note 13 states that:

> 'Provisions used in 'predecessor' regimes such as for Transport and Works Act Orders or Harbour Empowerment Orders may be helpful in the drafting of a DCO. Developers should satisfy themselves that the inclusion of particular wording is appropriate and relevant in all the circumstances of a given project. The relevant precedent and the rationale for including the particular wording of a provision will need to be set out and justified in the explanatory memorandum.'

There seems little doubt that provisions from previous orders, whether made under the Planning Act 2008 or otherwise, will continue to be a useful source of precedent in drafting DCO provisions. What is clear, however, is that PINS will expect the Explanatory Memorandum for any such draft DCO to set out and justify the proposed wording. Indeed, recent experience in examinations tends to indicate that Inspectors will not only seek an explanation for any departure from a model provision, but also, on occasion, an explanation for compliance with a model provision.

Drafting conventions for statutory instruments

If the 'draft proposed order' makes provision for: (a) the making of byelaws; (b) the creation of offences; (c) the application, modification or exclusion of a statutory provision; or (d) the making of amendments, repeals or revocations of statutory provisions of local application, then that 'draft proposed order' must be contained in a statutory instrument: see PA 2008, s 117(4). Experience so far with applications for development consent has shown that most DCOs will indeed need to 'apply, modify or exclude' statutory provisions and will, therefore, have to be made in the form of a statutory instrument.

An 'SI template' is available on the Office of Public Sector Information (OPSI) website, together with an 'SI template user manual'.

The Office of Parliamentary Counsel (OPC) has published 'Drafting Guidance' (December 2011) for the drafting of legislation that sets out a number of general drafting principles as well has detailed drafting guidance. Although this guidance is designed for members of OPC in the drafting of Bills, it is also clearly helpful for those drafting statutory instruments.

Conclusions

Although the Model Provisions Order has formally lapsed, it is clear that PINS continues to regard the model provisions as a helpful template and applicants need to be prepared, therefore, to justify departures from those provisions. As more DCOs are made, however, an expanding data base of acceptable provisions, for each NSIP type, will become available and, in these circumstances, it may be that the current standing of the model provisions will begin to fade.

Defence to Proceedings in Respect of Nuisance

Written by: James Pereira QC, ftb
Edited by: Michael Humphries QC, ftb

Introduction

This chapter considers PA 2008, s 158. This section provides statutory authority for certain activities authorised by an order granting development consent, for the purpose of conferring a defence in civil or criminal proceedings in nuisance. Note that s 158 confers statutory authority rather than blanket immunity from actions in nuisance. It must therefore be read alongside relevant case law on the scope of the defence of statutory authority. It should also be read alongside PA 2008, s 152, which provides an entitlement to claim compensation where land has been injuriously affected by the carrying out of works. These and other matters are discussed in more detail below.

Statutory basis

PA 2008, s 158 provides as follows:

> "**Nuisance: statutory authority**
>
> (1) This subsection confers statutory authority for—
>
> > (a) carrying out development for which consent is granted by an order granting development consent;
> >
> > (b) doing anything else authorised by an order granting development consent.
>
> (2) Statutory authority under subsection (1) is conferred only for the purpose of providing a defence in civil or criminal proceedings for nuisance.
>
> (3) Subsections (1) and (2) are subject to any contrary provision made in any particular case by an order granting development consent."

The scope of PA 2008, s 158

The proceedings that fall within PA 2008, s 158(2)

The statutory authority is only conferred for the purpose of providing a defence in civil or criminal proceedings for nuisance: see PA 2008, s 158(2). Such proceedings would include private nuisance and public nuisance at common law.

The position in relation to statutory nuisance proceedings under the Environmental Protection Act 1990 is less clear. The Divisional Court in *Camden LBC v LUL* [2000] Env LR 369 (DC) at [25] has expressed the preliminary, non-binding, view on a similarly worded provision in the Railways Act 1993, s 122(3) that it would apply to proceedings by way of an appeal against a statutory nuisance abatement notice served under the Environmental Protection Act 1990, s 80 where that notice alleged a statutory nuisance amounting to a common law nuisance, but it would not apply where the notice alleged a statutory nuisance amounting to prejudice to health.

In the same case, the Divisional Court expressed the view that criminal proceedings for a nuisance order under the Environmental Protection Act 1990, s 82 would be criminal proceedings for nuisance. Proceedings under section 82 are started by laying an information in the magistrates' court and are therefore criminal in nature: see *Botross v London Borough of Hammersmith and Fulham* [1995] Env LR 217. Consistent with this view, General Model Provision 7 ('GMP7') in the Infrastructure Planning (Model Provisions) (England and Wales) Order 2009 makes express provision for a defence to proceedings under the Environmental Protection Act 1990, s 82 to be conferred upon a defendant in certain circumstances. This is addressed further below.

Activities that fall within PA 2008, s 158

The statutory authority extends to the carrying out of development for which consent is granted under the DCO (PA 2008, s 158(1)(a)), and to other activities (which need not amount to development) which are authorised by an order granting development consent (PA 2008, s 158(1)(b)). The defence therefore covers not only the construction of an NSIP, but also its operation. It could also extend to other activities that may be authorised by the NSIP, such as those associated with the lopping of trees or the carrying out of survey work.

The scope of a defence of statutory authority

It is important to note that the scope of the defence of statutory authority generally has been the subject of a number of court decisions which are therefore relevant to the scope of PA 2008, s 158.

A defence of statutory authority is only available where the nuisance created could not have been prevented by reasonable measures or due diligence by the perpetrator: see *Allen v Gulf Oil* [1981] AC 1001. It must be the inevitable result of carrying out the development or undertaking the activities in question: see *Managers of the Metropolitan Asylum District v Frederick Hill and Others* (1881) 6 App Cas 193 at 213. Hence where the nuisance has come about because of the negligence of the operator, the defence will not succeed.

Model provisions

As stated above, GMP7 makes express provision for a defence to proceedings for a nuisance order brought by an individual under the Environmental Protection Act 1990, s 82 in certain circumstances. The relevant circumstances are as follows.

For proceedings in relation to a nuisance caused by the carrying out of development, the defendant must show that the nuisance:

- relates to premises used by the undertaker for the purposes of or in connection with the construction or maintenance of the authorised project and that the nuisance is attributable to the carrying out of the authorised project in accordance with a notice served under the Control of Pollution Act 1974 s 60 (control of noise on construction site), or a consent given under s 61 (prior consent for work on construction site) or 65 (noise exceeding registered level); or

- is a consequence of the construction or maintenance of the authorised project and that it cannot reasonably be avoided.

For proceedings relating to nuisance caused by the operation of the project the defendant must show that the nuisance:

- relates to premises used by the undertaker for the purposes of or in connection with the use of the authorised project and that the nuisance is attributable to the use of the authorised project which is being used in accordance with a scheme of monitoring and attenuation of noise agreed with the Commission as described in requirement 25; or
- is a consequence of the use of the authorised project and that it cannot reasonably be avoided.

As a consequence of the above, GMP7 also disapplies certain statutory provisions where the consent relates to the use of premises by the undertaker for the purposes of or in connection with the construction or maintenance of the authorised project. These provisions are the Control of Pollution Act 1974, s 61(9) (consent for work on construction site to include statement that it does not of itself constitute a defence to proceedings under section 82 of the Environmental Protection Act 1990, s 82) and s 65(8) of that Act (corresponding provision in relation to consent for registered noise level to be exceeded).

Guidance

Paragraph 38 of the DCLG Application Form Guidance (2013), referring to Box 19 of the application form, advises that the applicant should refer to the Environmental Protection Act 1990, s 79(1) in order to consider whether the development proposal would engage one or more of that section's issues relating to nuisance. If it does, the applicant's statement should set out its proposals for mitigating or limiting them.

Compensation

It is not the purpose of this work to give a detailed account of the law of compensation. Users of this Service who have a specific issue in relation to compensation should refer to a specialist text on this subject. This article does, however, give an overview of the entitlement to compensation arising under PA 2008, s 152.

Landowners whose ability to bring an action in nuisance has been curtailed by PA 2008, s 158 are provided with a right to claim compensation under PA 2008, s 152 subject to meeting the requirements of that provision. In simple terms, PA 2008, s 152 provides a right to compensation to any person whose land is injuriously affected by the carrying out of authorised works (see s 152(3)) or depreciated in value by physical factors caused by the use of the NSIP (see s 152(7)). Importantly, the right to compensation does not depend upon any land having been acquired by the use of compulsory purchase powers.

Section 152(3) provides that if, by virtue of section 158 or an order granting development consent, there is a defence of statutory authority in civil or criminal proceedings for nuisance in respect of any authorised works than

> '(3) A person by whom or on whose behalf any authorised works are carried out must pay compensation to any person whose land is injuriously affected by the carrying out of the works.'

It is made clear that the Compulsory Purchase Act 1965, s 10(2) (limitation on compensation) applies to sub-s (3) of this section as it applies to that section: see PA 2008, s 152(5). It is also made clear that the Land Compensation Act 1973, Part 1 (compensation for depreciation of land value by physical factors caused by use of public works) applies in relation to authorised works as if: (a) references in that Part to any public works were to any authorised works; (b) references in that Part to the responsible authority were to the person for whose benefit the order granting development consent has effect for the time being; and (c) ss 1(6) and 17 were omitted: see PA 2008, s 152(7).

An order granting development consent may not include provision the effect of which is to remove or modify the application of any of s 152(1)–(7).

Compensation for injurious affection caused by the carrying out of authorised works

It seems likely from the wording of PA 2008, s 152(3) and (4) that the provision is to be applied in a similar manner to section 10 of the Compulsory Purchase Act 1965. However, by analogy with section 10, compensation would be payable where the following criteria are met:

- the loss has resulted from an act made lawful by the order granting development consent;
- the loss is such that in the absence of PA 2008, s 158 it would have given the landowner an entitlement to recover damages;
- the loss must arise from the physical interference with the land or with a right enjoyed with it, and must result in a depreciation of the value of the claimant's land; and
- the loss must arise from the execution of the authorised works and not from their use.

Note that under PA 2008, s 152(4) a dispute as to the principle or the amount of compensation may be referred to the Upper Tribunal (Lands Chamber).

Compensation for depreciation of land value caused by the use of public works

PA 2008, s 152(7) applies the Land Compensation Act 1973, Part 1 with the modifications set out under s 152(7)(a)–(c) (above). The result is that a right to compensation exists where the following conditions are met:

- the value of the claimant's interest in land has been depreciated (Land Compensation Act 1973, s 1(1));
- the depreciation is caused by 'physical factors'. These are defined as noise, vibration, smell, fumes, smoke, artificial lighting and the discharge on to the land in respect of which the claim is made of any solid or liquid substance (Land Compensation Act 1973, s.1(1) and (2));
- the physical factors are caused directly by the use of the authorised works;
- the claimant has a qualifying interest (Land Compensation Act 1973, s 1(1)). [Reference should be made to the Land Compensation Act 1973, s 2 for the specific statutory wording and requirements in relation to qualifying interests. Only an overview is given here.] This means that the claimant must have purchased his interest before the date on which the authorised works were first used, that in the case of a dwelling the claimant has a freehold interest or a tenancy with not less than three years unexpired term remaining at the date of the claim (and where the claimant is entitled to occupy the land he must do so as his residence), and that in the case of property that is not a dwelling, the claimant must be an owner occupier and the land must either be an agricultural unit or have an annual value which is less than the prescribed amount (Land Compensation Act 1973, s 2(1)–(6));
- the claimant has made his claim at the correct time and in the correct manner (see Land Compensation Act 1973, ss 3, 8, 10 and 19 in relation to the manner and timing of making a claim); and
- the compensation claimed exceeds £50 (Land Compensation Act 1973, s 7).

By PA 2008, s 152(7)(b) the compensation is payable by the person for whose benefit the order granting development consent has effect for the time being. Section 152(7)(b), therefore, modifies the effect of the Land Compensation Act 1973, s 1(1) and (4).

Removal of other Consent Requirements

Written by: Michael Humphries QC, ftb

Introduction

In the 2007 White Paper 'Planning for a Sustainable Future', the Government identified one of the problems of the Town and Country Planning Act 1990 regime as being that:[1]

> 'There are too many different and overlapping development consent regimes. A single project can require multiple permissions under several different regimes, particularly projects involving linked developments – for instance, there a port expansion needs road and rail links. Most of these different statutory consent processes have their own procedural rules and, while there are similarities, there are also some important differences. This can significantly increase the costs of applications and can act as a real barrier to bringing forward proposals and to participating in the debate about them.'

In response to this problem, the Government proposed to:[2]

> 'Streamline the procedures for infrastructure projects of national significance by rationalising the different development consent regimes and improving the inquiry procedures for all of them. This will harmonise requirements on developers *and, as far as possible, create a single application process for all of the development authorisations needed for nationally significant infrastructure projects.*' (emphasis added)

The PA 2008 regime clearly aims to meet that objective by removing the requirement to obtain various permissions, consents and authorisations for development where development consent is required. PA 2008, s 33 sets out the effect of the requirement for development consent on various other consent regimes.

As the 2007 White Paper made clear, however, a single application process was only to be created 'as far as possible' and the reality is that the new regime is some way from being a complete 'one stop shop'. PA 2008, s 150, however, does provide a mechanism for including certain additional consents and authorisations within a DCO.

PA 2008, s 150

PA 2008, s 150 provides as follows:

> '(1) An order granting development consent may include provision the effect of which is to remove a requirement for a prescribed consent or authorisation granted, only if the relevant body had consented to the inclusion of the provision.
>
> (2) 'The relevant body' is the person of body which would otherwise be required to grant the prescribed consent or authorisation.'

1 Planning for a Sustainable Future (2007) para 2.8(c)
2 Planning for a Sustainable Future (2007) para 2.13(d)

The 'prescribed consents or authorisations' for the purposes of PA 2008, s 150 are set out at reg 2 of, and the Schedule to, the Infrastructure Planning (Miscellaneous Prescribed Provisions) Regulations 2010 ('the 2010 Regulations'). The Schedule to the 2010 Regulations identified some 78 'other' consents and authorisations that may be brought within the 2008 Act regime. This Schedule was, however, amended by the Infrastructure Planning (Miscellaneous Prescribed Provisions) (Amendment) Regulations 2013, SI 2013/520 ('the 2013 Regulations') with effect from 6 April 2013.

It is important to note, however, that the effect of the provisions is to enable a DCO to contain provisions for removal of a prescribed consent or authorisation, only where the 'relevant body' that would otherwise be required to grant the prescribed consent or authorisation has consented to the inclusion of the provision.

The 'relevant bodies' under the Schedule

The Schedule (as amended) lists the consents and authorisations by reference to the sections of the relevant legislation. The Schedule does not list the current relevant consenting bodies. Part 1 of the Schedule lists those consents that are relevant to both England and Wales. Part 2 of the Schedule lists those consents that only relate to Wales.

The intention in drafting the list for Wales was to ensure that no devolved consent should be included in a draft DCO without the agreement of the relevant consulting body in Wales.

The following table lists all the consents and authorisations listed in the 2010 Regulations, as amended by the 2013 Regulations. The effect of those amendments was that 16 consents and authorisations that originally appeared in Part 1 of the Schedule (England and Wales) were moved to Part 2 (Wales only). In the table below those consents and authorisations appear in italics. The relevant bodies are also shows for each consent or authorisation:

Act	Section/ Regulation	Consent/ Authorisation	Relevant Consenting Body
PART 1 of SCHEDULE 1 (England and Wales)			
Electricity Act 1989	6	Licences authorising supply	Gas and Electricity Markets Authority
Gas Act 1986	7, 7ZA, 7A	Licensing of public gas transporters, gas interconnectors, gas suppliers and gas shippers	Gas and Electricity Markets Authority
Petroleum Act 1998	3	Licence to search, bore for and get petroleum	Secretary of State
Petroleum Act 1998	14	Authorisation for construction and use of a pipeline in controlled waters	Secretary of State

Act	Section/ Regulation	Consent/ Authorisation	Relevant Consenting Body
Energy Act 2008	4	Licences in relation to combustible gas importation and storage	Secretary of State; Welsh Ministers; Scottish Ministers; Department of Enterprise, Trade and Investment in Northern Ireland
Energy Act 2008	18	Licences in relation to the storage of carbon dioxide	Secretary of State; Welsh Ministers; Scottish Ministers; Department of Enterprise, Trade and Investment in Northern Ireland
Nuclear Industries Security Regulations 2003	5, 6, 8	Approval of security plans	Secretary of State
Justification of Practices Involving Ionising Radiation Regulations 2004	9, 10	Justifying determinations in relation to new and existing practices relating to ionising radiation	Secretary of State; Scottish Ministers; a Northern Ireland department; the National Assembly for Wales
Energy Act 2008	46	Approval of a funded decommissioning programme	Secretary of State
Conservation (Natural Habitat, &c) Regulations 1994	44	Revoked in England and Wales[3]. In Scotland, licence for taking, possession or control of certain specimens	Marine Management Organisation, Countryside Council for Wales, Welsh Ministers
Offshore Marine Conservation (Natural Habitats. &c) Regulations 2007	49	Licence in relation to the use, capture or keeping of wild birds	Marine Management Organisation

3 Currently, Part 1 of Schedule 1 (England and Wales) does not refer to regulations 53, 54, and 55 of the Conservation of Habitats and Species Regulations 2010, which contains the updated provisions.

Act	Section/ Regulation	Consent/ Authorisation	Relevant Consenting Body
Protection of Badgers Act 1992	10	Licences to kill, take or interfere with badgers	Natural England, Countryside Council for Wales, Welsh Ministers
Wildlife and Countryside Act 1981	16	Licences in relation to wild birds	Natural England, Countryside Council for Wales, Welsh Ministers
Environmental Permitting (England and Wales) Regulations 2010	Permit	Environmental Permit or exemption from the requirement for a Permit	Environment Agency
Water Resources Act 1991	24, 25	Abstraction and impounding licences	Environment Agency
Water Resources Act 1991	32, 109, 164 and byelaws under 5, 6, 6A of Sch 25	Consent for abstraction; consent for structures in over or under a main river; consent for discharges; byelaws for flood defences; byelaws for fisheries purposes and fisheries byelaws for marine or aquatic environmental purposes	Environment Agency
Water Resources Act 1991	73	Ordinary and emergency drought orders	Environment Agency
Water Resources Act 1991	79A	Drought permits	Environment Agency
Water Industry Act 1991	166	Consent for certain discharges under s165	Environment Agency
Land Drainage Act 1991	17, 23	S17 repealed. S23 consent for erecting an obstruction in a watercourse	Environment Agency
Greenhouse Gas Emissions Trading Scheme Regulations 2005	Permit	Repealed[4]. Listed as a permit in the 2010 Regulations	Environment Agency

4 Part 1 of Schedule 1 has not yet been updated to take account of the Greenhouse Gas Emissions Trading Scheme Regulations 2012.

Act	Section/ Regulation	Consent/ Authorisation	Relevant Consenting Body
Persistent Organic Pollutants Regulations 2007	8	Authorisation to be dealt with under Part 2 of Annex V of Regulation (EC) No. 850/2004	Environment Agency
Water Industry Act 1991	Part 4, Ch 3	A notice of determination of a reference in relation to discharge of trade effluent into a public sewer	Sewerage undertaker
PART 2 of SCHEDULE 1 (Wales only)			
Planning (Listed Buildings and Conservation Areas) Act 1990	8	Authorisation of works, Listed building consent	Local Planning Authority/Secretary of State
Planning (Listed Buildings and Conservation Areas) Act 1990	74	Conservation area consent for demolition	Local Planning Authority/Secretary of State
Ancient Monuments and Archaeological Areas Act 1979	2, 3	Scheduled monument consent	Secretary of State
Protection of Wrecks Act 1973	1	Restricted area licence	Secretary of State
Town and Country Planning Act 1990	198	Consent under a tree preservation order	National Assembly for Wales
Town and Country Planning Act 1990	211	Consent in relation to trees in a conservation area	Local Planning Authority
Planning (Hazardous Substances) Act 1990	13, 17, 18	Hazardous substance consent	Hazardous Substance Authority, usually the district council
Salmon and Freshwater Fisheries Act 1975	26	Confirmation or variation of an order in relation to limitation of fishing licences	Water authority, confirmed by Welsh Ministers. The Environment Agency may also make orders

Act	Section/ Regulation	Consent/ Authorisation	Relevant Consenting Body
Hedgerows Regulations 1997	5	Removal of hedgerows consent	Local Planning Authority
Public Health Act 1936	263	Approval to culvert or cover a watercourse in an urban district	Local Authority
Coast Protection Act 1949	16	Coastal protection work consent	Coast Protection Authority (district council)
Coast Protection Act 1949	18	Excavation of materials on or under the seashore licence	Coast Protection Authority (district council)
Food and Environment Protection Act 1985	8	Licence in relation to deposits into the sea (Scotland only)	Licensing Authority
Water Industry Act 1991	110A	Order of the Authority in relation to new connections to public sewers	Water Services Regulation Authority
Water Industry Act 1991	118	Consent for discharge of trade effluent into a public sewer	Sewerage undertaker
Clean Air Act 1993	4	Approval of installation notice in relation to a new furnace	Local Authority
Clean Air Act 1993	6, 8, 15	Approval of plant for arresting grit and dust; approval for height of chimney	Local Authority
Clean Air Act 1993	7	Exemption from s6(1) of the Act	Local Authority
Clean Air Act 1993	14	Exemption from height of chimney regulations	Local Authority of Secretary of State
Clean Air Act 1993	16(2)	Height of other chimneys prevention of the smoke, grit, dust or gases from becoming prejudicial to health or a nuisance	Local Authority
Clean Air Act 1993	20	Exemption of fireplaces in relation to smoke in a smoke control area	Local Authority

Act	Section/ Regulation	Consent/ Authorisation	Relevant Consenting Body
Environmental Permitting (England and Wales) Regulations	Permit	Environmental Permit where the local authority is the regulator	Local Authority
Pipe-lines Act 1962	15	Consent to place a pipeline in a street	Street Authority
Road Traffic Regulation Act 1984	1, 9, 14, 15, 22B	Traffic regulation order; experimental traffic order; temporary restriction or prohibition on roads; 22B repealed	Local Traffic Authority
Town and Country Planning Act 1990	247	Stopping up or diversion of a highway order	Secretary of State
Town and Country Planning Act 1990	257	Stopping up or diversion of a footpath, bridleway or restricted byway	Local Authority
Inclosure Act 1845	147	Repealed by Commons Act 2006	
Inclosure Act 1847	4	Repealed by Commons Act 2006	
Inclosure Act 1852	14	Order distinguishing allotments, town and village greens by metes and bounds (but not fenced)	Commissioners
Inclosure Act 1854	5, 9, 11	Order of exchange, partition or division; fencing and making roads dispensed with; order apportioning rent and fixed payments and determining extent, identify and boundaries of land charged	Commissioners
Inclosure Act 1857	1, 5	Disposal of fences; Repealed by Commons Act 2006	Commissioners

Act	**Section/ Regulation**	**Consent/ Authorisation**	**Relevant Consenting Body**
Commons Act 1876	15	Consent or authorisation required under byelaws made by owners in relation to pasture land	Lord of the Manor
Commons Act 1899	1, 10	Consent or authorisations required under byelaws or made under a scheme for regulation and management of a common	District Council
Law of Property Act 1925	193	Impositions of limitations on rights of access	Welsh Ministers
Coity Wallia Commons Act 1976	6, 10	Private Act. Consents in relation to Coity Wallia Common	Conservators
Health and Safety at Work Act 1974	16	Approval of codes of practice	Health and Safety Executive
Ionising Radiations Regulations 1999	5	Authorisation of specified practices in relation to x-ray and accelerator equipment	Health and Safety Executive
Radiation (Emergency Preparedness and Public Information) Regulations 2001	4, 5	Any assessment required in relation to hazard identification and risk evaluation	Health and Safety Executive
Conservation of Seals Act 1970	10	Licence to kill or take seals	Marine Management Organisation
National Parks and Access to the Countryside Act 1949	20	Authorisation pursuant to byelaws for the protection of nature reserves	Natural England
Deer Act 1991	8	Licences in relation to moving deer or taking deer alive	Natural England, Countryside Council for Wales, Welsh Ministers
Wildlife and Countryside Act 1981	28E	Consent for operations within a SSSI	Natural England

Act	Section/ Regulation	Consent/ Authorisation	Relevant Consenting Body
Wildlife and Countryside Act 1981	53	An order in relation to the duty to keep the definitive map and statement under continuous review	Natural England
Countryside and Rights of Way Act 2000	17	A consent or authorisation required under byelaws in relation to rights of access	Natural England
Countryside and Rights of Way Act 2000	24, 25, 26	Direction in relation to the exclusion or restriction of access in relation to land management, fire risks, salt flats and nature conservation	Coastal Margin – Natural England; Land in a National Park – National Parks Authority; any other land – appropriate countryside body
Salmon and Freshwater Fisheries Act 1975	30	Consent for introduction of fish into inland waters	Environment Agency
Import of Live Fish (England and Wales) Act 1980	1	Consent in relation to import, keeping or release of non-native live fish	Environment Agency, Secretary of State and Natural England/ Countryside Council for Wales
Water Resources (Environmental Impact Assessment) Regulations 2003	9	Consent in relation to abstracting or impounding water	Environment Agency
Environmental Protection (Disposal of Polychlorinated Biphenyls and other Dangerous Substances) (England and Wales) Regulations 2000	9	A registration with regards to inventories of contaminated equipment	Environment Agency

Act	Section/ Regulation	Consent/ Authorisation	Relevant Consenting Body
Control of Pesticides Regulations 1986	Consent	Consent in relation to advertising, control, storage, supply and sale of pesticides	Ministers
Hazardous Waste (England and Wales) Regulations 2005	21	A registration in relation to notification of premises	Environment Agency

Obtaining the consent of the relevant body

Experience is tending to demonstrate that the 'relevant bodies' are often reluctant to give up their consenting or authorising powers and that it is, in fact, proving difficult to promoters to include Schedule 1 consents and authorisations in a DCO.

Indeed, the Planning Inspectorate's own guidance in relation to the Countryside Council for Wales as a consenting authority notes that in relation to the consents listed in Part 2 of Schedule 1 to the Regulations:

> 'These are consents that would normally be granted by CCW. CCW would generally not agree to these consents being included within a development consent order but will consider this on a case by case basis.'

PINS Advice Note 11: 'Working with public bodies in the infrastructure planning process' provides the following guidance to promoters:

> 'Certain prescribed consents etc can be consented separately or included in a DCO. s150 of the 2008 Act provides that these consents can only be included in a DCO if the relevant consenting body agrees to their inclusion. *Developers will need to engage early in the pre-application stage with consultees that have such consenting powers, so that it is clear by the time an application is submitted whether such consents are to be included in a draft DCO.*' (emphasis added)

Paragraph 19 of DCLG's 'Guidance on the pre-application process' (January 2013) provides the following advice to relevant consenting bodies and promoters:

> 'Where an applicant proposes to include non-planning consents within their Development Consent Order, the bodies that would normally be responsible for granting those consents should make every effort to facilitate this. They should only object to the inclusion of such non-planning consents with good reason, and after careful consideration of reasonable alternatives. It is therefore important that such bodies are consulted at an early stage.'

Expanding and improving the 'one stop shop' approach to consents

On 22 November 2012 DCLG published a consultation seeking views on proposals to expand and improve the 'one stop shop' approach for consents under the 2008 Act.

In its response, published in March 2013, the Government announced its proposals to establish a 'Consents Service Unit' (CSU) within PINS and to make changes to streamline the Infrastructure Planning (Miscellaneous Prescribed Provisions) Regulations 2010 and the Infrastructure Planning (Applications: Prescribed Forms and Procedure) Regulations 2009.

In April 2013 the Government established a new 'Consents Service Unit' within PINS and, in its response to consultation document (Major infrastructure planning: expanding and improving the 'one stop shop' approach for consents – summary of responses and government response') is stated (paragraph 14) that:

> 'The Consents Service Unit, to be based in the Planning Inspectorate, will be operational from April 2013 and will offer a bespoke service to those developers that want to use it. It will provide a lead contact to work with the developer and relevant consenting bodies (with a strong emphasis on the pre-application stage), to coordinate a logical and systematic approach to the handling of 12 different consents which may be required in addition to development consent under the 2008 Act. These consents could be required during the construction phase and/or the operational phase. The aim is to ensure that, where possible, these are dealt with in parallel. The Unit's key role will be to facilitate effective and efficient decision-making, including identifying any process blockages and resource needs, and escalate such issues where necessary.'

In May 2013 PINS published the 'Consents Service Unit for Nationally Significant Infrastructure Projects – Prospectus for Developers' and a 'Frequently Asked Questions' document that both explain the workings of the CSU.

The Discharge of DCO Requirements

Written by: Michael Humphries QC, ftb

Introduction

PA 2008, s 120(1) provides that an order granting development consent may impose 'requirements' in connection with the development for which development consent is granted.

PA 2008, s 120 further provides that:

'(2) The requirements may in particular include –

(a) requirements corresponding to conditions which could have been imposed on the grant of any permission, consent or authorisation, or the giving of any notice, which (but for section 33(1)) would have been required for the development;

(b) requirements to obtain the approval of the Secretary of State or any other person, so far as not within paragraph (a).'

This article considers the following matters in relation to the discharge of DCO requirements:

- Drafting requirements to be discharged;
- The appropriate discharge body;
- Appealing the discharging authority's decision; and
- Fees.

Drafting requirements to be discharged

Requirements are frequently drafted so as to require the submission of written details of an aspect of the development to a 'discharging authority' that then has the power to 'approve' or otherwise such details prior to development, or a stage of the development, commencing. Such pre-commencement requirements are commonplace as planning conditions and considerable judicial authority exists on their interpretation.

The DCO procedure does give the opportunity, however, to create bespoke requirements and definitions to suite the particular circumstances of a project. Three concepts will be considered:

- The definition of the term 'commence';
- The expression 'unless otherwise approved'; and
- Non-material changes.

The definition of the term 'commence'

Model requirement 2 in Schedule 4 to the Infrastructure Planning (Model Provisions) (England and Wales) Order 2010 ('the Model Provisions Order') states that 'The authorised development must be *begun* within [insert number] years of the date of this order.' (emphasis added). PA 2008, s 155 defines when development is taken to have 'begun' for the purposes of s 154 and such a definition is also relevant to a requirement (such as model requirement 2) in a DCO.

The Model Provisions Order, however, also make extensive use of the term 'commence', such as in model requirement 3 ('No authorised development shall commence until …'). However this term is not defined in the Model Provisions Order, either in the General Model Provisions (Schedule 1) definitions or in the 'model requirements' (Schedule 4) definitions. Nor is the term defined in the 2008 Act itself. Thus if the term 'commence' is not to be given its 'ordinary meaning', it may be appropriate to define it in the DCO itself.

> In the Hinkley Point C nuclear generating station DCO (Schedule 2 paragraph 1 – interpretation) the term 'commencement' (and the words 'commence' and 'commenced') as being *'the carrying out of a material operation, as defined in section 155 of the Planning Act 2008 (which explains when development begins), comprised in or carried out for the purposes of the authorised project'*.

In the North London Reinforcement Project draft DCO (Schedule 2 paragraph 1 – definitions) the term 'commence' was defined negatively so as to exclude certain activities that might otherwise have been captured by the ordinary meaning of the word. In that draft DCO the term 'commence' was defined as follows:

> ''commence' in relation to any part of the authorised development, does not include any demolition, site clearance, devegetation, remediation, environmental (including archaeological) investigations, site or soil survey, erection of contractors' work compound, erection of site office, erection of fencing to site boundaries or marking out of site boundaries.'

Such a definition would allow the promoter to undertake the identified preparatory works before discharging the terms of any pre-commencement requirement.

The expression 'unless otherwise approved'

Expressions such as 'unless otherwise approved' or 'save to the extent that revised plans [etc] have been submitted to and approved' have been relatively common in planning conditions and are similarly being proposed in DCO requirements.

In the Hinkley Point C nuclear power station DCO requirement PW4 provides that:

> '(1) Buildings and structures comprising Works Nos … shall be carried out in accordance with the plans as set out in … of this Order, *save to the extent that revised plans* relating to the siting, scale or appearance *have been submitted to and approved by the local planning authority*.' (emphasis added)

In relation to planning conditions, the Courts have generally been reluctant to endorse expressions such as 'unless otherwise approved', as they may have the effect of allowing a form of development that was not assessed or permitted: see, for example, *Henry Boot Home Limited v Bassetlaw DC* [2002] EWCA Civ 983 at paras 51-54. Having said that, the Courts have accepted there may be some scope for non-material amendments to a permitted development.

> In *R (Midcounties Co-operative Limited) v Wyre Forest DC* [2009] EWHC 964 the Court considered a planning condition (condition 6) that set a retail floorspace limit but then stated *'unless otherwise agreed in writing with the Local Planning Authority'* and a further condition (condition 4) that required 'strict compliance' with various plans and drawings *'unless other minor variations are agreed in writing after the date of this permission and before implementation with the Local Planning Authority.'*

In relation to the condition 6 'tailpiece' the court held (para 70) that:

> 'As I shall come to in connection with another condition, I accept the existence of a very limited power to make immaterial variations informally. But while the tailpiece in the condition in question could be applied in that way, it contains no words purporting to limits its application.'

In relation to condition 4, however, the Court held (para 79) that:

> 'I do not regard this tailpiece as unlawful. Its clear scope is to enable 'minor variations' to an obligation otherwise to develop 'in strict accordance' with plans and drawings. Both parts of the condition operate to limit the flexibility which the tailpiece provides.'

The court added (para 81) that:

> 'In my judgement this scope covers at least those circumstances in which the change is immaterial in the sense that no reasonable local planning authority could refuse it, or take enforcement proceedings lawfully in respect of its implementation. I do not exclude other jurisprudential bases.'

There does appear to be, therefore, some limited flexibility for a planning condition to vary a permitted development. See also the approach of the Court in *R (Halebank PC) v Halton BC* 2012 EWHC 1889 (Admin) applying the approach in Mid-Counties and rejecting the approach taken by the deputy judge in *R (Warley) v Wealden DC* [2011] EWHC 2083 (Admin) (see paras 100/101).

In the Hinkley Point C nuclear generating station DCO, the applicant included a provision in the following terms (see Schedule 11 para 1(5) (interpretation)):

> 'Where any requirement specifies 'unless otherwise approved' by the discharging authority or requires the applicant to demonstrate the existence of exceptional circumstances such approval shall not be given or exceptional circumstances agreed except in relation to minor or immaterial changes where it has been demonstrated to the satisfaction of the discharging authority that the subject-matter of the approval sought or the undertaker's proposed response to exceptional circumstances is unlikely to give rise to any materially new or materially different environmental effects from those assessed in the Environmental Statement.' (emphasis added)

This form of wording appears to be acceptable to the Secretary of State and may form a precedent for other DCOs.

Non-material changes

PA 2008, s 153, Sch 6, para 2 enables the Secretary of State to make certain changes to a DCO if the Secretary of State is satisfied that the change is not material. In deciding whether a change is material, the Secretary of State must have regard to the effect of the change, together with any previous changes made under paragraph 2, on the DCO as originally made. The power allows the Secretary of State to impose new requirements in connection with the development, as well as removing or altering existing requirements. The power in paragraph 2 may only be exercised on an application made to the Secretary of State made by, or on behalf of, the applicant or a successor in title of the applicant; a person with an interest in land; or, any other person for whose benefit the DCO has effect.

This approach broadly reflects that set out at section 96A of the Town and Country Planning Act 1990. That section allows a local planning authority to make 'non-material changes' to a planning permission. In principle, it would appear that this provision could be applied and adapted to permit a local planning authority to make non-material changes to the requirements under a DCO. PA 2008, s 120(5) allows a DCO to apply, modify or exclude a statutory provision which relates to a matter for which provision may be made in the order, although it would be a matter for the Secretary of State whether such a provision was necessary or appropriate.

The appropriate discharge authority

In the 'model requirements' at Schedule 4 to the Model Provisions Order it is clearly contemplated that DCO requirements will be discharged by the (then) Infrastructure Planning Commission ('the IPC'), now the Planning Inspectorate ('PINS'). Model requirement 3, for example, states that: 'No [stage of the] authorised development shall commence until [for that stage] written details of the following have, after consultation with the relevant planning authority, been *submitted to and approved by the Commission.'* (emphasis added).

Since the 'model requirements' were published in 2009, however, the IPC has made it clear that it is not resourced to act as the 'discharge authority' for DCO requirements and PINS appears to be adopting the same position. In its 'Guidance for local authorities' (March 2010), DCLG stated that:

> 'as is the case under the previous regime, scheme promoters should normally be able to appeal local authority decisions on a subsequent approval – though not by appealing under the TCPA. Instead t*he IPC can include provision in each Development Consent Order that allows it to determine any subsequent approval in default of agreement or approval by the LPA*. We will be amending the Infrastructure Planning (Model Provisions) Order 2009 to reflect this is due course.' (emphasis added). Although no such amendment was made to the Model Provisions Order, the change of emphasis from the Commission as the primary discharge authority to the commission as default or appeal discharge authority is clear.

In 18 January 2012 the IPC stated in a response in its website 'Register of Advice' that 'Generally discharges of requirements are dealt with by the relevant local authority or statutory undertaker rather than the IPC.' In its April 2012 Advice Note 13 PINS stated (page 4) that 'The developer should seek to agree wording for proposed requirements with the body to whom details are to be submitted for subsequent approval, and in any event seek the local planning authority's views on proposed requirements as they will enforce any breach of terms of any order granted.' This last advice appears to contemplate that the 'discharge authority' could be a body other than the local planning authority, although the local planning authority's role as consultee 'in any event' is emphasised as is its role in enforcing any requirements.

This last point seems important. The PA 2008 makes a breach of the terms of a DCO a criminal offence (see s 161), but makes the relevant local planning authority responsible for the service of a notice of unauthorised development under s 169. It is likely, therefore, that in most cases the most appropriate discharge authority for a DCO requirement will be the relevant local planning authority. That is not to suggest that other bodies may not be the discharge authority in particular circumstances, but PINS is likely to need some convincing that a requirement should be discharge by one body, but enforced by another. Certainly the Secretary of State has shown no enthusiasm for take on the role of discharge authority, although the Secretary of State could be asked to take on that role if particular circumstances indicated that it was appropriate.

Certainly the experience so far is that it is the relevant local planning authority which has been given responsibility for the discharge of DCO requirements.

Appealing the discharging authority's decision

Where conditional planning permission is granted under s 72 of the Town and Country Planning Act 1990 an applicant may appeal to the Secretary of State against a local planning authority's decision to 'refuse an application for any consent, agreement or approval of that authority required by a condition imposed on the grant of planning permission or grant it subject to conditions': see s 78(1)(b) of the 1990 Act. Similarly, an applicant may appeal to the Secretary of State where the local planning authority has failed to determine such an application: see s 78(2) of the 1990 Act. Section 79 deals with the determination of appeals under s 78. Regulations and guidance set out the procedures to be followed in relation to such appeals.

No such equivalent procedure is prescribed under the Planning Act 2008 and neither is there a model provision in the Infrastructure Planning (Model Provisions)(England and Wales) Order 2009, SI 2009/2265 ('the Model Provisions Order') that sets out a preferred appeal mechanism following refusal or conditional grant of an application under a DCO requirement.

In broad terms, emerging practice has identified two solutions to this issue, being:

- The application and adaptation of Part III of the Town and Country Planning Act 1990; and
- The creation of a bespoke system for the discharge of requirements.

The application and adaptation of Part III of the Town and Country Planning Act 1990.

This solution simply seeks to incorporate, with any necessary modifications, the system for appealing planning conditions contained within Part III of the Town and Country Planning Act 1990. Typically, a DCO provision will simply allow an appeal against refusal, grant subject to conditions or non-determination of an application to discharge a DCO requirement to be made under Part III of the 1990 Act as if the requirement were a condition under s 78 of that Act. An example of this approach may be found in the Preesall underground gas storage project DCO. In principle, this approach could allow some adaptation of the 1990 Act system by, for example, modifying timescales or other procedural steps. Any wholesale amendment of the 1990 system, however, is likely (in effect) to fall within the second of the above approaches.

The creation of a bespoke system for the discharge of requirements

An alternative approach seeks to create a bespoke system for the discharge of DCO requirements. This approach may be less straight forward, but does give the opportunity to tailor a system for the discharge of DCO requirements to the particular circumstances of the project. For example, it may be possible to create a 'fast track' written representations system with tight timescales for the exchange of representations and other procedural steps.

Such an approach was adopted in the Hinkley Point C nuclear generating station DCO: see Schedule 14 to that Order.

Fees

As stated above, PA 2008 does not create a mechanism for the discharge of DCO requirements and so does not, therefore, specify any fee structure for local planning authorities acting as the discharge authority under any such requirements.

Three potential mechanism exist under which a fee structure may be identified, being:

- Planning Performance Agreements;
- PA 2008, s 106 obligations; and
- DCO provisions/schedules.

Planning Performance Agreements

Planning Performance Agreements (PPAs) between local planning authorities (LPAs) and applicants for major development projects have been around since 2007, following a Planning Advisory Service and ATLAS pilot project in 2006. The Communities and local Government (CLG) and ATLAS Guidance Note, 'Implementing Planning Performance Agreements', advises that 'Planning Performance Agreements are essentially a collaborative project management process primarily aimed at complex development proposals.'. PPAs can be drafted to set *inter alia* target timetables for the performance of identified steps in the consideration of applications for major development projects.

The CLG/ATLAS Guidance Note observes, at paragraph 2.3, that 'The PPA process could be used at any stage in a development project, from Area Action Plan formation through to reserved matters.' It seems clear, therefore, that there is no objection in principle to PPAs being used in the context of the discharge of planning conditions, and, by extension therefore, DCO requirements. A number of bodies have produced 'good practice' guidance on PPAs.

In a circular letter to local authorities from the Department for Communities and Local Government and the Department of Energy and Climate Change dated 16

July 2009, it was made clear that PPAs are a mechanism available to LPAs within the context of PA 2008.

If performance under a PPA would involve an LPA in additional costs beyond those reflected in any application fee, then this can be recovered through the PPA. This may be particularly attractive to local planning authorities discharging 'requirements' under a DCO where there is no formal application fee mechanism. It does need to be stressed, however, that PPAs are collaborative agreements and cannot be imposed on a hostile local planning authority or, for that matter, an unwilling developer.

PA 2008, s 106 obligations

An appropriately drafted planning obligation may present a further or alternative opportunity to set out a mechanism for the payment of fees to local planning authorities discharging DCO requirements. Indeed, the opportunity to submit a unilateral planning obligation may be particularly attractive where a local planning authority is unable or unwilling to enter into a PPA. Such a mechanism may also be drafted so as to incentivise early decision making by the discharge authority.

A unilateral PA 2008, s 106 obligation cannot, however, impose any positive obligation on a non-party. In other words, a unilateral section 106 obligation cannot require a local planning authority to meet particular positive performance targets, although it may provide for payments based on a local planning authority meeting particular timescales for the determination of discharge applications.

In relation to the Preesall underground gas storage project, the applicant recognised that the relevant local planning authority could have resourcing issues in discharging DCO requirements and set up a 'Discharge Contribution' mechanism in Pt 4 of Sch 1 to its s 106 obligation. The Preesall s 106 obligation set up a mechanism for the discharge of DCO requirements that included 'discharge contributions' to cover the local planning authority's costs; 'timescales' for the determination of discharge applications; and 'penalties' in the event of timescales being exceeded.

DCO provisions/schedules

PA 2008, s 120(5)(d) provides that a DCO may include 'This power would appear to be wide enough to allow the DCO to make provision for payments to be made to local planning authorities discharging DCO requirements. Such a provision would appear to be 'incidental' or 'consequential' upon any DCO provision or requirement making a local planning authority the 'discharge authority' for a DCO requirement.

The Relationship between Development Consent and Marine Licensing

Written by: Michael Humphries QC, ftb

Introduction

A number of Nationally Significant Infrastructure Projects (NSIPs) and associated development are proposed partly on land and partly within the UK marine licensing area, where development would normally require a marine licence granted by the Marine Management Organisation (MMO) or the Welsh Government Marine Consents Unit under Part 4 of the Marine and Coastal Access Act 2009. PA 2008 allows a DCO to include a *deemed* marine licence, thereby removing the requirement to seek separate consent under the 2009 Act. This micro-article examines the relationship between development consent and marine licensing.

A general discussion of the role of the MMO within the Planning Act 2008 regime is set out at Annex B of PINS Advice Note 11: working with public bodies in the infrastructure planning process.

Development within the UK marine licencing area

Part 4 of the Marine and Coastal Access Act 2009 sets up a regime for the licensing of 'licensable marine activities' within 'the UK marine licensing area': see ss 65 and 66 of the 2009 Act. There is a long list of 'licensable marine activities' within s 66 of the 2009 Act which would encompass most forms of 'development' likely to be the subject-matter of an application for development consent. 'Section 66(4) of the 2009 Act defines 'the UK marine licensing area' as consisting of 'the UK marine area' other than the Scottish inshore region. The term 'UK marine area' is itself defined in s 42 of the 2009 Act to include the area of sea within the seaward limits of the territorial sea adjacent to the United Kingdom, any area of sea within the limits of the 'exclusive economic zone', and the area of sea within the limits of the UK sector of the continental shelf. The term 'sea' is defined in s 42 to include any area submerged at mean high water spring tide.

PA 2008, s 31 makes it clear that development consent is required for development to the extent that the development is, or forms part of, an NSIP. The classes of NSIP for which development consent is required are defined by ss 14–30 and, in many cases, include: (a) development in waters adjacent to England and Wales up to the limits of the territorial sea; and (b) development in a Renewable Energy Zone (except where the Scottish Ministers have functions). Furthermore, by PA 2008, s 115(1), development consent may also be granted for 'associated development' if it is to be carried out in England, waters adjacent to England up to the limits of the territorial sea, or in a Renewable Energy Zone (except where the Scottish Ministers have functions). Note that a DCO may not include 'associated development' in waters adjacent to Wales.

It is clear from the above, however, that development consent may be required for development that would also be a 'licensable marine activity' under the 2009 Act.

Development consent

By PA 2008, s 103, it is the Secretary of State that has the function of deciding an application for an order granting development consent and, as stated above, development consent may be granted for both the development for which development consent if required (ie the NSIP) and for 'associated development'.

PA 2008, s 149A provides that:

> "(1) An order granting development consent may include provision deeming a marine licence to have been issued under Part 4 of the Marine and Coastal Access Act 2009 (marine licensing) for any activity only if the activity is to be carried out wholly in one or more of the areas specified in subsection (2).
>
> (2) The areas are –
>
> (a) England,
>
> (b) waters adjacent to England up to the seaward limits of the territorial sea,
>
> (c) an exclusive economic zone, except any part of an exclusive economic zone in relation to which the Scottish Ministers have functions,
>
> (d) a Renewable Energy Zone, except any part of a Renewable Energy Zone in relation to which the Scottish Ministers have functions,
>
> (e) an area designated under section 1(7) of the Continental Shelf Act 1964, except any part of that area which is within a part of an exclusive economic zone or Renewable Energy Zone in relation to which the Scottish Ministers have functions."

A deemed marine licence under s 149A is, therefore, part of the DCO granted by the Secretary of State and is not actually a marine licence granted by the MMO under the 2009 Act. Furthermore, to the extent that a DCO includes a deemed marine licence, then it is axiomatic that the 'activities' covered by that deemed licence will not require a separate marine licence granted by the MMO under the 2009 Act.

The role of the MMO in relation to applications for development consent

The MMO has an important role in relation to applications for development consent. This role is set out in s 23 of the 2009 Act, which makes various amendments to PA 2008.

PA 2008, s 42 is amended to inset a new subsection (1)(aa) so that there is a duty to consult the MMO 'in any case where the proposed development would affect, or would be likely to affect, any of the areas specified in subsection (2)'. A new subsection (2) is then inserted, as follows:

'(2) The areas are –

(a) waters adjacent to England up to the seaward limits of the territorial sea,

(b) an exclusive economic zone, except any part of an exclusive economic zone in relation to which the Scottish Ministers have functions,

(c) a Renewable Energy Zone, except any part of a Renewable Energy Zone in relation to which the Scottish Ministers have functions,

(d) an area designated under section 1(7) of the Continental Shelf Act 1964, except any part of that area which is within a part of an exclusive economic zone or Renewable Energy Zone in relation to which the Scottish Ministers have functions.'

For shorthand, these are simply referred to below as 'the s 43(2) areas'.

Thus the MMO's role as consultee extends beyond the circumstances where development is actually proposed within any of the s 42(2) areas and includes circumstances where the proposed development would affect, *or would be likely to affect*, any such area.

Interestingly, section 23(7) of the 2009 Act provides that the Secretary of State must give guidance to the MMO as to 'the kind of representations which may be made by the MMO' under (a) Chapter 2 of Part 5 of PA 2008 (pre-application procedure), or (b) Part 6 of that Act (deciding applications for orders granting development consent). This guidance was issued by Defra as 'Government guidance to the Marine Management Organisation (MMO) on its role in relation to applications, and proposed applications, to the Infrastructure Planning Commission (IPC) for development consent under the Planning Act 2008' (September 2008).

Paragraph 29 of the Defra guidance states that;

> "The MMO is the UK Government's expert body on marine management and it is in this capacity that the MMO should contribute to proposed applications. Therefore, when the MMO is consulted it should limit its representations and comments on the proposed application to those matters that directly relate to its marine management role. A matter is directly related to the MMO's functions only insofar as the proposed development involves an activity or operation which the developer intends to carry out in an area, or likely to affect an area, mentioned above [that is, one of the section 42(2) areas]. It would, for example, be appropriate for the MMO to comment on any piers or jetties associated with an onshore power station development, as these may affect the areas specified in the MCA Act."

Section 23 of the 2009 Act also amends s 56 (duty to notify persons of accepted applications) and s 102 (definition of 'interested party') to include reference to the MMO "where the development for which the application seeks development consent would involve the carrying on of any activity" in one or more of the s 42(2) areas. Thus for the purposes of ss 56 and 102, the MMO's role is confined to circumstances where the 'activity' would actually be carried on within any of the s 42(2) areas.

By making the MMO an 'interested party' it is clearly contemplated that the MMO will be given the opportunity to play a role during the examination of any application for development consent. Paragraph 42 of the Defra guidance states that: 'The MMO will be invited to any specific issue hearings (see section 91 of the Planning Act) or open floor hearings (see section 93 of the Planning Act) where it can submit representations orally.'

Paragraph 43, however, puts this in context by making clear that: 'When the MMO attends a preliminary meeting or subsequent hearings or makes written representations to the IPC, the MMO should limit its representations on the application to those that directly relate to its marine management role, for example, as a licensing authority or marine planning authority.'

DCO 'requirements' and deemed marine licence 'conditions'

PA 2008, s 120 states that:

'(1) An order granting development consent may impose requirements in connection with the development for which consent is granted.

(2) The requirements may in particular include –

(a) requirements corresponding to conditions which could have been imposed on the grant of any permission, consent or authorisation, or giving of any notice, which (but for section 33(1)) would have been required for the development;

(b) requirements to obtain the approval of the Secretary of State or any other person, so far as not within paragraph (a).

(3) An order granting development consent may make provision relating to, or matters ancillary to, the development for which consent is granted.

(4) The provision that may be made under subsection (3) includes in particular provision for or relating to any of the matters listed in Part 1 of Schedule 5.'

The list of matters in Part 1 of Schedule 5 includes the following:

'30A Deeming a marine licence under Part 4 of the Marine and Coastal Access Act 2009 to have been given by the Secretary of State for activities specified in the order and subject to such conditions as may be specified in the order.

30B Deeming any such conditions to have been attached to the marine licence by the Secretary of State under that Part.'

It is important to note, however, that both the 'requirements' under the DCO and the 'conditions' under the deemed marine licence are all part of the DCO granted by the Secretary of State. In other words, the conditions attached to the deemed marine licence are simply DCO provisions that happen to be in a schedule to the DCO entitled 'Deemed Marine Licence'. A deemed marine licence will typically be included in a schedule to the DCO in a form that mimics an actual marine licence, but that should not obscure its status as part of the development consent granted by the Secretary of State.

This may be relevant in circumstances where a single DCO 'work' is partly on land and partly within the UK marine licensing area. It may be inappropriate, in relation to a single 'work', to have one body (possibly the local planning authority) responsible to the discharge and enforcement of 'requirements' for that part of the work on land and another body (the MMO) responsible for the discharge and enforcement of 'conditions' for that part of the work within the UK marine licensing area.

Exactly this situation occurred in relation to the Preesall Underground Gas Storage DCO, where part of an underground gas storage cavern was several hundred metres below land and part of it was several hundred metres below an estuary that was within the UK marine licencing area. Clearly it made no sense to have the local planning authority responsible for the discharge and enforcement of requirements relating to part of a cavern and the MMO responsible for the discharge and enforcement of identical conditions relating to the other part of a cavern. In that case the promoter and the two discharging /enforcing authorities agreed that the caverns should be granted a deemed marine licence in respect of such parts that fell within the UK marine licencing area, but that they should be exempted from the conditions imposed under the deemed marine licence and, instead, made the subject of requirements under the DCO.

This reallocation of functions between the local planning authority and the MMO does not cause any jurisdictional conflict, however, in circumstances where the deemed marine licence is simply part of the DCO granted by the Secretary of State.

Enforcement of conditions in a deemed marine licence

DCO requirements are enforced under Part 8 of PA 2008. Deemed marine licence conditions, by contrast, are enforced under Part 4 of the 2009 Act.

PA 2008, s 160 makes it an offence to carry out, or cause to be carried out, development for which development consent is required at a time when no development consent is in force in respect of the development. PA 2008, s 161 creates a further offence where, without reasonable excuse, a person: (a) carries out, or causes to be carried out, development in breach of the terms of an order granting development consent; or (b) otherwise fails to comply with the terms of an order granting development consent.

PA 2008, s 161, therefore, makes it an offence not to comply with a DCO 'requirement' and, it might be thought, a deemed marine licence 'condition'. The 2009 Act, however, inserted a new s 149A(4) into PA 2008, which provides as follows in relation to deemed marine licence conditions:

> '(4) A person who fails to comply with such a condition does not commit an offence under section 161 of this Act.'

This provision does not prevent s 161 being used to enforce any DCO requirement, as opposed to deemed marine licence condition, that happens to apply to the UK marine licensing area.

The enforcement provisions for marine licences are set out at Part 4, Chapter 3 of the 2009 Act. Sections 85-89 set out provisions relating to offences where there has been failure to comply with a condition of a marine licence and ss 90–92 set out provisions relating to enforcement notices where there has been failure to comply with a marine licence condition.

Paragraph 45 of the Defra Guidance (above) states that:

> 'The MMO should prosecute any alleged offences in the marine area under the MCA Act, though it is open to bring legal proceedings for offences in the marine area under sections 160 or 161 of the Planning Act 2008 should this be deemed appropriate (for instance, where particular terms of a DCO do not flow into a deemed marine consent).'

PA 2008, s 120(9)

Written by: Hereward Phillpot QC, ftb
Edited by: Michael Humphries QC, ftb

PA 2008, s 120(9)

PA 2008, s 120 identifies what may be included in an order granting development consent. PA 2008, s 120(9) provides as follows:

> 'To the extent that provision for or relating to a matter may be included in an order granting development consent, none of the following may include any such provision –
>
> (a) an order under section 14 or 16 of the Harbours Act 1964 (c 40) (orders in relation to harbours, docks and wharves);
>
> (b) an order under section 4(1) of the Gas Act 1965 (c 36) (order authorising storage of gas in underground strata);
>
> (c) an order under section 1 or 3 of the Transport and Works Act 1992 (c 42) (orders as to railways, tramways, inland waterways etc.)'.

The effect of this provision

PA 2008, s 120(9) is not particularly clearly drafted, and (at least initially) this led to different suggested interpretations being advanced as to its meaning and effect.

In approaching its interpretation, it is important to bear in mind that PA 2008, s 120 is not itself concerned with the consenting of development, rather it is concerned only with the nature of the matters ancillary to development (see s 120(3)) which may or may not be authorised via orders under three separate statutory regimes that confer order-making powers.

Restrictions on the consenting of development are to be found elsewhere in the PA 2008. It is clear that once development consent has been granted under the PA 2008 authorising a particular associated development, that development cannot subsequently be authorised under any of these separate order-making powers. This is because PA 2008, s 115(5) applies s 33(2) to 'associated development' for which development consent exists. The effect is to remove jurisdiction for that development under those other statutory regimes.

This statutory restriction operates in one direction only. It prevents the granting of, say, a Harbour Empowerment Order (HEO) for an associated development *after* the grant of a Development Consent Order (DCO) authorising that development, but not before.

Although the matter has not been tested in the courts, it is suggested that the effect of PA 2008, s 120(9) is twofold:

1 Once a DCO has been granted, it operates to prevent the granting of an order under the other statutory regimes which varies the ancillary matters authorised

in that DCO. Any such variations would therefore need to be obtained via the procedure in the Infrastructure Planning (Changes to, and Revocation of, Development Consent Orders) Regulations 2011, SI 2011/2055.

2 It prevents promoters from obtaining consent for associated development in a DCO, but at the same time seeking authorisation for the necessary ancillary powers under a separate statutory regime. This supplementing of DCO powers via other statutory regimes is only permissible under PA 2008, s 120(9) where the provisions in question could not have been included in the DCO itself. Now that the former restriction on the creation of offences in a DCO has been revoked, there are likely to be few such provisions in practice.

Parallel applications

Subject to the important issue of relative timing, there is therefore nothing in PA 2008, s 120(9) which would prevent a promoter seeking an order under one of the other statutory regimes whilst at the same time seeking a DCO containing the same or similar provisions.

Neither PA 2008, s 115(5) nor s 120(9) prevents the relevant decision-maker from granting such an order in advance of the same development and ancillary matters being approved in a DCO. This remains the case even where an application has been made for the DCO in question.

This approach was used by EDF Energy in relation to the development of the Hinkley Point C new nuclear power station. EDF's proposal included the construction and operation of a large aggregates jetty (as associated development), to allow the import by sea of the majority of the aggregates needed to construct the power station. The early construction and availability of this jetty facility was considered likely to accelerate the construction of the power station itself, and to reduce its adverse effects, if and when that was authorised under the Planning Act 2008. EDF therefore sought and obtained powers to construct and operate the jetty through an application for a HEO under the Harbours Act 1964 and a Transport and Works Act Order (TWAO) under the Transport and Works Act 1992. Essentially identical powers were sought and subsequently obtained in the DCO.

In advance of the public inquiry into the application for a HEO and TWAO, the Department for Energy and Climate Change wrote to EDF asking for its views on whether PA 2008, s 120(9) caused any difficulties in reconciling the making of a HEO/TWAO with the existence of an application for a DCO which contains the same provisions. EDF responded to say that no such difficulties arose, for reasons which reflect the analysis set out above, and in due course the HEO and TWAO were both made and not challenged.

It should also be noted that shortly after that public exchange of correspondence, the IPC published Annex B to its then Advice Note 11 (Working with Public Bodies), which confirmed that such an approach was legitimate. The same advice is now to be found in Annex B to PINS Advice Note 11.

Part 9

Compulsory Purchase

Compulsory Purchase Powers in a DCO

Written by: Richard Honey, ftb
Edited by: Michael Humphries QC, ftb

Introduction

A development consent order (DCO) under the PA 2008 can authorise the compulsory acquisition of land or of an interest in or right over land. DCOs are unusual in that they are a means by which even purely private developers may secure compulsory purchase powers. Before the PA 2008 this was not possible; save in the case of the privatised utility companies and under the Pipelines Act 1962.

Even so, the Government's policy position appears still to be that promoters should seek to acquire land by negotiation wherever practicable and that powers of compulsory acquisition should only be sought where attempts to acquire land or rights by agreement have failed.

In this article, as in DCOs themselves, references to acquiring a right over land include acquiring it by the creation of a new right as well as by the acquisition of an existing one (PA 2008, s 159(3)). Particular provision is made for the acquisition of rights in relation to underground gas storage facilities, which is dealt with in PA 2008, s 133. That section covers rights to store gas in underground gas storage facilities, to stop up a well, borehole or shaft, or prevent its use by another person, and rights of way over land.

Conditions for the exercise of compulsory purchase powers

There are important conditions attaching to the use of compulsory purchase powers through DCOs. First, a DCO can include provision authorising the compulsory acquisition of land only if the Secretary of State is satisfied that the land (PA 2008, s 122):

- is required for the development to which the development consent relates (s 122(2)(a));
- is required to facilitate that development (s 122(2)(b);
- is incidental to that development (s 122(2)(b)); or
- is replacement land which is to be given in exchange for the order land (s 122(2)(c)).

The Inspectorate has said that the 'facilitate' and 'incidental' provisions in PA 2008, s 122(2)(b) could encompass the acquisition of land for the construction of development (eg a gas pipeline) which was not authorised by the DCO but which would be authorised by a later consent (register of advice, 17 November 2011, North Killinghome Power Project). In this regard, see also footnote 3 at paragraph 5 of the DCLG Guidance on associated development.

These are wide powers of compulsory purchase that are likely to be sufficient for promoters in most, if not all, cases. The further removed the land is from actually being required for the development, however, the more difficult it is likely to be in practice to justify the acquisition of the land in question.

Secondly, a further important condition must be satisfied under PA 2008, s 122(3), namely that there is a 'compelling case in the public interest' for the land to be acquired compulsorily. Whilst this wording reflects a long-standing policy test and had appeared in various court decisions (see, for example, *De Rothschild v Secretary of State For Transport* (1989) 57 P&CR 330), it was not previously a statutory requirement; indeed, s 122 remains the only place where it does appear as a statutory requirement.

Thirdly, a DCO can only authorise compulsory acquisition of land if one of three further conditions is met (PA 2008, s 123). They are that:

- the application for the order included a request for compulsory acquisition of the land to be authorised (s 123(2));
- all persons with an interest in the land consent to the inclusion of the provision (s 123(3)); or
- the prescribed procedure has been followed in relation to the land (s 123(4)).

The third condition above is based on an equivalent provision in the Acquisition of Land Act 1981. It deals with 'additional land', that is land which it is proposed shall be subject to compulsory acquisition and which was not identified in the book of reference submitted with the application. The procedure for the purposes of PA 2008, s (4) is prescribed in the Infrastructure Planning (Compulsory Acquisition) Regulations 2010, SI 2010/104.

Justification for the exercise of compulsory purchase powers

As well as satisfying the fundamental conditions set out above, it is necessary to show that the compulsory purchase proposed is properly justified.

The DCLG 'Guidance related to procedures for the compulsory acquisition of land' (September 2013) explains what justification will be sought for a DCO authorising the compulsory acquisition of land, including factors to which the decision-maker must have regard (paragraphs 8–19). This includes that:

- all reasonable alternatives to compulsory acquisition (including modifications to the scheme) have been explored (paragraph 8);
- the proposed interference with the rights of those with an interest in the land is for a legitimate purpose and is necessary and proportionate (paragraph 8);
- the applicant must have a clear idea of how it intends to use the land to be acquired (paragraph 9);
- there is a reasonable prospect of the requisite funds becoming available (paragraph 9);
- the purposes for which an order authorises the compulsory acquisition of land are legitimate and sufficiently justify interfering with the human rights of those with an interest in the land affected (paragraph 10);
- the land to be acquired is no more than is reasonably required for the purposes of the development (paragraph 11(i));

- there is compelling evidence that the public benefits that would be derived from the compulsory acquisition will outweigh the private loss that would be suffered by those whose land is to be acquired (paragraph 12).

In determining where the balance of public interest lies, the DCLG Guidance makes it clear (paragraph 14) that 'the Secretary of State will weigh up the public benefits that a scheme will bring against any private loss to those affected by compulsory acquisition.'

An applicant will also be required to provide a funding statement providing as much information as possible about the resource implications of both: (a) acquiring the land; and (b) implementing the project for which the land is required (paragraph 17).

Interestingly, the guidance does not say that the compulsory purchase of land is intended as a last resort in the event that attempts to acquire by agreement fail, as was stated in ODPM circular 06/2004 ('Compulsory Purchase and the Crichel Down Rules').

Nonetheless, applicants should not underestimate how hard it can be to demonstrate that these policy tests are satisfied in practice. In some cases, such as the expansion of an airport or a harbour, it may not be too difficult to show that the particular land is required. Similarly, in the case of linear schemes such as road and rail routes, it may be easier to show that there are no alternatives but to acquire compulsorily the interests in land which have not been acquired by agreement in advance. In other cases, however, such as offsite ecological compensation works or landscape planting, it may be very hard to show that the particular land is required. The DCLG Guidance states (paragraph 11(ii)) that the Secretary of State needs 'to be satisfied that the development could only be landscaped to a satisfactory standard if *the land in question* were to be compulsorily acquired' (emphasis added). This could be very hard to demonstrate in practice.

Types of land

There are various protective provisions in the Act for certain types of land, which are explained in turn below. It should be noted that the Growth and Infrastructure Act 2013 reduced the circumstances in which the special parliamentary procedure was to be engaged.

Statutory undertakers

PA 2008, s 127 provides protective provisions for the land of statutory undertakers which apply where land has been acquired, and is used, by a statutory undertaker for the purpose of its undertaking, and the undertaker makes a representation on the application. In those circumstances s 127(2) provides that the DCO can only include provision authorising the compulsory acquisition of the undertaker's land where the Secretary of State is satisfied that the nature and situation of the land are such that either:

- it can be purchased and not replaced without serious detriment to the carrying on of the undertaking, or

- if purchased it can be replaced by other land belonging to, or available for acquisition by, the undertakers without serious detriment to the carrying on of the undertaking.

PA 2008, s 127(5) makes a similar provision in relation to the acquisition of a right over the undertaker's land.

PA 2008, s 138 relates to DCOs which authorise the acquisition of land in which there subsists a right vested in a statutory undertaker for carrying on their operations or where there is on, under or over the land apparatus of the undertaker. This encompasses statutory undertakers as defined in Part 11 of the Town and Country Planning Act 1990 and electronic communications code network operators. The DCO can include provision for the extinguishment of the relevant right, or the removal of the relevant apparatus, only if the Secretary of State is satisfied that this would be necessary for the purpose of carrying out the development to which the DCO relates.

The Growth and Infrastructure Act 2013 had the effect of removing the special parliamentary procedure in cases where a statutory undertaker or local authority holds land.

National Trust

PA 2008, s 130 applies to land belonging to the National Trust which is held by the Trust inalienably. It provides that to the extent that the DCO authorises the compulsory acquisition of such land it must be subject to special parliamentary procedure if a representation has been made by the Trust about the application objecting to the compulsory acquisition of land.

Commons, open spaces etc

Commons and open spaces are covered in PA 2008, ss 131–132, along with land forming part of a fuel or field garden allotment. Section 131 relates to the acquisition of land and s 132 relates to the acquisition of rights over land. Under s 131 a DCO would be subject to special parliamentary procedure save in particular circumstances. Those circumstances are:

- replacement land has been or will be given in exchange for the order land and the replacement land has been or will be vested in the prospective seller and subject to the same rights, trusts and incidents as attach to the order land (s 131(4));
- for open space only, either there is no suitable land available to be given in exchange for the order land or any suitable land available to be given in exchange is available only at prohibitive cost, and it is strongly in the public interest for the development for which the order grants consent to be capable of being begun sooner than is likely to be possible if the order were to be subject (to any extent) to special parliamentary procedure (s 131(4A));
- for open space only, where the order land is being acquired for a temporary (although possibly long-lived) purpose (s 131(4B));
- where the order land does not exceed 200 sq m or is required for the widening or drainage of an existing highway, and the giving in exchange of other land is

unnecessary, whether in the interests of the persons, if any, entitled to rights of common or other rights or in the interests of the public (s 131(5)).

PA 2008, s 132 sets out similar provisions in relation to the compulsory purchase of rights over land, although there are differences between the two provisions.

Green Belt

PA 2008, s 147 applies where the DCO includes the compulsory acquisition (or exchange or appropriation) of Green Belt land. It requires that the Secretary of State must notify the relevant local authorities of the proposed acquisition.

Notification requirements

For pre-application consultation, PA 2008, ss 42 and 44 apply to people who are owners, tenants or occupiers of affected land and people the promoter thinks would or might be entitled to make a claim for compensation under s 10 of the Compulsory Purchase Act 1965 or Part I of the Land Compensation Act 1973. The same categories of persons must also be notified under s 56 and s 59.

Where a DCO is made which includes provision authorising the compulsory acquisition of land, PA 2008, s 134 requires that the promoter (known as a prospective purchaser) serve a 'compulsory acquisition notice' on owners, lessees and occupiers of the land that is to be acquired or to subject to rights being acquired. The persons who have to be served are those who would be qualifying persons for the purposes of s 12(1) of the Acquisition of Land Act 1981. The promoter also has to erect a compulsory acquisition notice on a conspicuous object or objects on or near the order land and, so far as practicable, keep it in place for six weeks, and publish a notice in one or more local newspapers.

PA 2008, s 134(7) explains that a compulsory acquisition notice is a notice in the prescribed form describing the order land (or the right if appropriate), stating that the DCO includes provision authorising the compulsory acquisition of land or a right over the land, where and when a copy of the order is available for inspection, and that a person aggrieved by the DCO may challenge it only in accordance with s 118. The form of notice is found in Schedule 1 to the Infrastructure Planning (Compulsory Acquisition) Regulations 2010.

Procedural requirements

There are various procedural provisions which apply to applications for a DCO where compulsory acquisition powers are sought. For example, the Infrastructure Planning (Applications: Prescribed Forms and Procedure) Regulations 2009, SI 2009/2264 require the provision with such applications of:

- a statement of reasons;
- a statement to indicate how the DCO is proposed to be funded;
- a land plan identifying land over which it is proposed to exercise powers of compulsory acquisition or any right to use land; and

- a book of reference.

There are also particular certification requirements in relation to s 56 (notification of an accepted application).

The DCLG Guidance related to procedures for compulsory acquisition provides advice on what is required for the land plans, funding statement and the statement of reasons. The Inspectorate has said that it would be prepared to provide advice on the content of draft funding statements (register of advice, 25 October 2012, Thames Tideway Tunnel). Funding is likely to be more of an issue with DCOs than traditional compulsory purchase orders because the compulsory acquisition powers in a DCO are often given to purely private bodies and carry with them the liability to pay proper compensation for land and rights acquired.

The guidance also encourages the use of alternative dispute resolution techniques to resolve concerns about the compulsory acquisition of land, including both mediation and early neutral evaluation.

The September 2013 version of the DCLG Guidance omitted what was said in the February 2010 version to the effect that a promoter should be negotiating in parallel with the compulsory purchase process to acquire land by agreement. It is unlikely, however, that this omission was intended to signal a significant change of position on the part of the Government. It remains advisable for promoters to seek to acquire land by agreement where possible and where appropriate within the financial constraints of the project.

PA 2008, s 106 provides that in deciding an application for an order granting development consent, representations may be disregarded if they relate to compensation for compulsory acquisition of land or of an interest in or right over land.

The duration of a DCO authorising the compulsory acquisition of land is covered in s 154, which provides that steps in relation to the acquisition must be taken within a particular time limit. That time limit is to be set out in the DCO and is commonly five years.

PA 2008, s 175 extends the blight regime in the Town and Country Planning Act 1990 to include land identified in a DCO to be subject to compulsory acquisition.

Illustrations from practice

An example of a DCO that included compulsory acquisition powers is the Hinkley Point C (Nuclear Generating Station) Order 2013, SI 2013/648, which grants powers for both the compulsory acquisition of land (art 24) and rights over land (art 27). It also includes powers for the temporary possession of land (art 33). It is notable that during the examination of that application the promoter offered a parent company guarantee of £10 million for the funding of compulsory acquisition compensation in order to satisfy the panel that adequate funding was in place. There was also a debate during the application about the permanent acquisition of land in circumstances where it was in fact only required temporarily, albeit for a period of years. The panel considered that if an owner offered to lease the land there would be no justification for compulsory acquisition but, in the absence of such an offer, a compelling case for the acquisition of the freehold would have been made out. The time limit for the exercise of compulsory acquisition powers was set as five years (art 26).

Incorporation of the Compulsory Purchase Code

Written by: Richard Honey, ftb
Edited by: Michael Humphries QC, ftb

Introduction

Where compulsory acquisition powers are incorporated into a development consent order, it is necessary for them to rely on the mechanisms and processes set out in other legislation for their efficacy. The 'compulsory purchase code' is the name that is commonly given to the disparate group statutory provisions that relate to compulsory purchase, supplemented by case law.

Parts of the compulsory purchase code

In essence, there are four parts to the compulsory purchase code being:

- the statutory power authorising compulsory purchase;
- the procedure for seeking an 'order' by which a statutory power authorising compulsory purchase is applied to a particular parcel of land;
- the implementation of the 'order' (particularly in relation to entry on the land and the transfer of title); and
- compulsory purchase compensation.

The statutory power authorising compulsory purchase

In relation to the PA 2008, s 122 grants the statutory power to include provision authorising the compulsory acquisition of land in a DCO. Subject to the requirements of s 122, that power is, therefore, available to any person who may properly apply for a development consent order.

This makes the powers of compulsory purchase potentially available to a whole range of developers who would not otherwise have had direct access to such powers. This can be contrasted to the compulsory purchase powers available under other regimes where the power is normally only available to a clearly defined class of person; for example, the relevant local authority under s 226 of the Town and County Planning Act 1990 or the relevant highway authority under s 239 of the Highways Act 1980. No such limitations exist under the Planning Act 2008.

The procedure for seeking an 'order' by which a statutory power authorising compulsory purchase is applied to a particular parcel of land

The procedure for seeking a development consent order is dealt with elsewhere in this work.

It is worth reminding the reader, however, that the Infrastructure Planning (Compulsory Acquisition) Regulations 2010, SI 2010/104 set out various procedural requirements that relate particularly to the compulsory acquisition of 'additional land' that was not included in the Book of Reference.

The implementation of the 'order' (particularly in relation to entry on the land and the transfer of title)

PA 2008, s 125 relates to the application of certain other parts of the compulsory purchase code in a development consent order and, in particular, relating to the implementation of the compulsory purchase powers within a DCO. The section applies if a DCO includes provision authorising the compulsory acquisition of land. It provides that Part 1 of the Compulsory Purchase Act 1965 ('CPA 1965') (procedure for compulsory purchase) applies to the compulsory acquisition of land under the DCO as it applies to a compulsory purchase to which Part 2 of the Acquisition of Land Act 1981 applies, as if the DCO were a compulsory purchase order under the 1981 Act. The provisions of the CPA 1965 govern the procedures to be followed once the compulsory acquisition of land has been authorised in the DCO.

PA 2008, s 125 provides however that, subject to any contrary provisions made by the DCO, Part 1 of the CPA 1965 will have effect with the omission of s 4 (time limit for exercise of compulsory purchase powers), s 10 (compensation for injurious affection) and paragraph 3(3) of Schedule 3 (provision as to giving of bonds).

The Planning Inspectorate has made clear that 'broadly, the same legislation applies in respect of procedural matters and how compensation is assessed and paid under the 2008 Act regime as for compulsory purchase under other regimes' (register of advice, 16 December 2010, Rampion Offshore Wind Farm).

The effect of PA 2008, s 125 would also apply Part 1 of the CPA 1965 to any acquisition of land following the service of a blight notice on the grounds that the land is blighted because its compulsory purchase is proposed in an application for a DCO. Section 175 amends the Town and Country Planning Act 1990 to apply the blight provisions to land in an application for a DCO or a DCO which is for compulsory acquisition and also land identified in national policy statements as suitable or potentially suitable for a development.

The procedures for implementing compulsory acquisition powers under a DCO are, therefore, the same as those for a compulsory purchase order, namely through Part 1 of the CPA 1965 and notices to treat and of entry. In addition, however, as is explained below, many DCOs also apply the Compulsory Purchase (Vesting Declarations) Act 1981. This creates an alternative means of implementing the compulsory purchase powers contained in a DCO and would allow the use of general vesting declarations.

Compulsory purchase compensation

Section 1 of the Land Compensation Act 1961 provides as follows:

> 'Where by or under any statute (whether passed before or after the passing of this Act) land is authorised to be acquired compulsorily, any question of disputed compensation and, where any part of the land to be acquired is

subject to a lease which comprises land not acquired, any question as to the apportionment of the rent payable under the lease, shall be referred to the [Upper Tribunal] 2 and shall be determined by the Tribunal in accordance with the following provisions of this Act.'

Thus, where there is a dispute as to compensation, the compulsory purchase compensation provisions in the LCA 1961 are automatically applied to any compulsory purchase of land by the terms of s 1, unless specifically disapplied. The 'following provisions' of the 1961 Act referred to in s 1 include the six rules for assessing compensation set out in s 5, as follows:

'Compensation in respect of any compulsory acquisition shall be assessed in accordance with the following rules:

(1) No allowance shall be made on account of the acquisition being compulsory:

(2) The value of land shall, subject as hereinafter provided, be taken to be the amount which the land if sold in the open market by a willing seller might be expected to realise:

(3) The special suitability or adaptability of the land for any purpose shall not be taken into account if that purpose is a purpose to which it could be applied only in pursuance of statutory powers, or for which there is no market apart from [...] 1 the requirements of any authority possessing compulsory purchase powers:

(4) Where the value of the land is increased by reason of the use thereof or of any premises thereon in a manner which could be restrained by any court, or is contrary to law, or is detrimental to the health of the occupants of the premises or to the public health, the amount of that increase shall not be taken into account:

(5) Where land is, and but for the compulsory acquisition would continue to be, devoted to a purpose of such a nature that there is no general demand or market for land for that purpose, the compensation may, if the [Upper Tribunal] 2 is satisfied that reinstatement in some other place is bona fide intended, be assessed on the basis of the reasonable cost of equivalent reinstatement:

(6) The provisions of rule (2) shall not affect the assessment of compensation for disturbance or any other matter not directly based on the value of land:

and the following provisions of this Part of this Act shall have effect with respect to the assessment.'

These rules form the starting point in most assessments of compulsory purchase compensation, although it needs to be recognised that the 1961 Act contains a number of other important provisions relating to the assessment of compulsory purchase compensation.

Part 1 of the Land Compensation Act 1973 (compensation for depreciation of land value by physical factors caused by use of public works) applies in relation to works authorised under a DCO, by means of s 152(7) of the 2008 Act, as if references in the LCA 1973 to 'public works' were references to 'authorised works' in the DCO. Part 1 of the LCA 1973 is however applied with the omission of s 1(6) and s 17, which relate to statutory immunity from nuisance.

Compensation is payable pursuant to s 165(4), for damage caused to land or chattels in the exercise of a relevant right of entry, by the local authority that authorised the entry to any person suffering damage. In circumstances where a dispute about such compensation is referred to the Upper Tribunal (Lands Chamber) for determination, s 165(6) provides that the provisions of s.4 of the LCA 1961 apply (with any necessary modifications). Section 4 of the LCA 1961 deals with the costs of Tribunal proceedings.

One important aspect of the compulsory purchase code that is amended by the PA 2008 is the disapplication of s 10 of the CPA 1965 (compensation for injurious affection) and its replacement by a bespoke provision. PA 2008, s 152 applies where a person affected by a DCO has no right to claim in nuisance (eg because of the provision in s 158 which gives a defence of statutory authority in civil or criminal proceedings for nuisance). PA 2008, s 152 gives a right to compensation for injurious affection in cases where a person would not be able to succeed in a claim for nuisance in respect of works authorised by the DCO.

By PA 2008, s 152(1), the section applies if by virtue of s 158 of the DCO there is a defence of statutory authority in civil or criminal proceedings for nuisance in respect of any authorised works. It defines 'authorised works' as including both development for which consent is granted by the DCO and anything else authorised by the DCO. The substantive obligation is in s 152(3), which provides that the person by or on whose behalf any authorised works are carried out must pay compensation to any person whose land is injuriously affected by the carrying out of the works. Section 152(8) provides that a DCO may not include provision the effect of which is to remove or modify the application of any of s 152(1)–(7), so that the provision is 'locked-in' to the DCO system.

The provision for compensation in PA 2008, s 152 effectively applies in lieu of s 10 of the CPA 1965. PA 2008, s 152(5) goes as far as to apply the limitation on compensation in s 10(2) of the CPA 1965 to compensation under s 152(3). Furthermore, s 152(6) applies to the construction of s 152(3) 'any rule or principle applied to the construction of section 10'. Section 152(3) provides compensation where 'land is injuriously affected by the carrying out of the works'. Section 10 of the CPA 1965, by contrast, provides compensation where a person's interest in land is injuriously affected by the execution of the works. It appears, therefore, that there is little difference between the ambit of the two provisions and that the intention is that the approach under s 10 of the CPA 1965 would apply to compensation for injurious affection under PA 2008, s 152.

Ability to modify or exclude a 'compensation provision'

It is important to note that the ability to 'modify' the application of a 'compensation provision', that is a provision in or made under an Act which relates to compulsory purchase compensation, is very limited by the terms of PA 2008, s 126 and can only be included to the extent necessary to apply the provision to the compulsory acquisition of land authorised by the order. Furthermore, a DCO may not include a provision the effect of which is to 'exclude' the application of a 'compensation provision'.

That said, there does appear to be some scope to introduce new provisions into a DCO relating to compulsory purchase compensation where the effect does not modify or exclude the application of an existing 'compensation provision'.

Compulsory purchase provisions in DCOs

As the number of projects passing through the Planning Act 2008 regime increases examples are beginning to emerge of additional or alternative compulsory purchase provisions in DCOs made by the Secretary of State. Some of these derive from the (now lapsed) Infrastructure Planning (Model Provisions)(England and Wales) Order 2009 and others are new.

Taking as an example the Hinkley Point C (Nuclear Generating Station) Order 2013, SI 2013/648, the DCO makes various additional provision for the application of the compulsory purchase code. SI 2013/648, art 27(3), Sch 11 provides for the modification of compensation and compulsory purchase statutes to deal with the creation of new rights.

Article 29 provides for the application of the Compulsory Purchase (Vesting Declarations) Act 1981 to the DCO as if it were a compulsory purchase order, with certain modifications. This enables the use of a general vesting declaration with DCOs, as opposed to notices to treat and of entry as would otherwise be the case.

Article 30 empowers the promoter to acquire only so much of, or such rights in, the subsoil of land as may be required, instead of acquiring the whole of the land. In such cases, Art 31 (considered below), applies where the promoter acquires a cellar, vault, arch or other construction forming part of a house, building or manufactory. The word 'manufactory' has been interpreted to mean a building whose main use is for manufacturing purposes, including ancillary or associated structures (see Roots, Humphries et al *The Law of Compulsory Purchase* (2nd edn, Bloomsbury Professional) at para D385).

By contrast, in the Network Rail (North Doncaster Chord) Order 2012, SI 2012/2635, art 27 applies not only to subsoil but also to 'the airspace over the land' (see also eg the Lancashire County Council (Torrisholme to the M6 Link (A683 Completion of Heysham to M6 Link Road)) Order 2013, SI 2013/675, art 25).

Article 31 of the Hinkley Point C (Nuclear Generating Station) Order 2013 deals with the acquisition of part of certain properties. It applies in place of s 8(1) of the CPA 1965 (which would otherwise apply by virtue of PA 2008, s 125) where a notice to treat is served on the owner of land forming only part of a house, building or manufactory or of land consisting of a house with a park or garden, to enable the owner to serve a counter-notice within 21 days objecting to the acquisition but stating that the owner is willing and able to sell the whole of the land. Unless the promoter agrees to acquire the whole then the issue of whether the owner should be required to sell only the land subject to the notice to treat must be referred to the Lands Chamber of the Upper Tribunal for determination. On such a reference the test is whether the land subject to the notice to treat can be acquired without material detriment to the remainder of the land subject to the counter-notice, or, where the land subject to the notice to treat consists of a house with a park or garden, without material detriment to the remainder of the land subject to the counter-notice and without seriously affecting the amenity and convenience of the house. If so, then the owner is required to sell the land subject to the notice to treat. Where under this process a notice to treat is deemed to cover less land or more land than originally specified in the notice, the promoter has 6 weeks in which it can withdraw the notice. If it does, then it must pay the owner compensation for any loss or expense caused by the giving and withdrawing of the notice to treat. Art 31(10) provides that where the owner is required to sell only part of the land or property, compensation is payable by the promoter for severance.

In arts 33 and 34 relating to the temporary use of land for carrying out and maintaining the project, it is provided that s 13 of the CPA 1965 relating to refusal to give possession to the authority applies to the temporary use as it would to the compulsory acquisition of land under the DCO.

There are various provisions in the Hinkley Point C (Nuclear Generating Station) Order 2013 which confer on persons affected by the exercise of powers under the DCO an entitlement to compensation, to be determined under Part 1 of the LCA 1961 where it is disputed. These provisions cover for example:

- any person who suffers loss by the suspension or extinguishment of any private right of way under art 15 (permanent stopping up of streets);
- any person who suffers loss by the suspension of any private right of way under art 17 (temporary stopping up of streets);
- owners and occupiers of any building or land in relation to which rights under art 22 (protective work to buildings) have been exercised for any loss or damage arising to them by reason of the exercise of those rights;
- owners and occupiers of the relevant land for any loss or damage arising by reason of the exercise of the authority conferred by art 23 to survey and investigate land;
- any person who suffers loss by the extinguishment or suspension of any private right of way under art 28 (private rights of way);
- any person who is an owner or occupier of land appropriated under art 32(1) (rights under or over streets), without the promoter acquiring any part of that person's interest in the land, and who suffers loss as a result;
- owners and occupiers of land of which temporary possession is taken under art 33 (temporary use of land for carrying out authorised project) for any loss or damage arising from the exercise in relation to the land of any power conferred by art 33;
- owners and occupiers of land of which temporary possession is taken under art 34 (temporary use of land for maintaining authorised project) for any loss or damage arising from the exercise in relation to the land of the provisions of art 34;
- any person who suffers any loss or damage arising from unnecessary damage to any tree or shrub when carrying out felling or lopping trees under art 41;
- any person who suffers any loss or damage arising from unnecessary damage to any tree or shrub subject to a tree preservation order under art 42.

Moreover, the Lancashire County Council (Torrisholme to the M6 Link (A683 Completion of Heysham to M6 Link Road)) Order 2013, SI 2013/675 contains in art

18 powers temporarily to close, interfere with and undertake works in the Lancaster Canal. art 18(7) provides that any person who suffers loss or damage as the result of either the suspension of any private right of navigation or any effect of the exercise of the art 18 powers on the functioning of any intake or discharge along the canal is entitled to compensation for such loss or damage.

Returning to the Network Rail (North Doncaster Chord) Order 2012, SI 2012/2635, art 41 of that DCO deals with the application of the Land Compensation Act 1973. It provides that regulations on the sound proofing of buildings affected by public works (eg the Noise Insulation (Railways and Other Guided Transport Systems) Regulations 1996, SI 1996/428 and the Noise Insulation Regulations 1975, SI 1975/1763) apply to the railway comprised in the authorised development under the DCO as if that railway was provided or used in the exercise of statutory powers.

Extinguishment of Public Rights of Way

Written by: Alex Booth, ftb
Edited by: Michael Humphries QC, ftb

Introduction

This article is concerned with the extinguishment of public rights of way and, in particular, PA 2008, ss 136 and 137.

Section 136 provides that a DCO may extinguish public rights of way, subject to one of two criteria contained in s 136(1) being met to the satisfaction of the Secretary of State. Section 136 is otherwise concerned with the procedure of extinguishment in circumstances where the land over which the right exists is authorised for acquisition by the DCO.

Section 137 is a discrete provision, relating to the extinguishment of rights over land that accommodates either apparatus belonging to statutory undertakers, or apparatus operated in connection with an electronic communications code network.

To date, the extent to which the relevant provisions have been considered during the examination process is limited. Furthermore, no guidance has yet been issued which might indicate how the provisions are intended to operate.

General provision as to extinguishment

PA 2008, s 136(1) stipulates that a DCO may only extinguish a public right of way if the Secretary of States is satisfied either:

> '(a) an alternative right of way has been or will be provided, or
>
> (b) the provision of an alternative right of way is not required.'

The inclusion of a discretion for the Secretary of State to authorise the extinguishment of a public right of way without replacement, in the event of his/her concluding that such replacement is not required, would appear to provide potential for dispute. The exercise of such discretion would presumably be subject to regulation by the courts by means of judicial review, the period for challenge being limited to six weeks from the date of publication of the order granting development consent by virtue of the Highways Act 1980, s 118(7).

In terms of the tests likely to be applied by the Secretary of State in this context, some limited assistance may be gained from decisions of the Courts in connection with the Highways Act 1980, s 118. Sections 118(1) and (2) require respectively:

(i) that a highways authority, when considering whether to extinguish a public right of way, should determine whether 'it is expedient that the … way should be stopped upon on the ground that it is not needed for public use'; and

(ii) that the Secretary of State, when considering whether to confirm an order for extinguishment, should only do so having determined that 'it is expedient so to do having regard to the extent … that the path or way would … be likely to be used by the public, and having regard to the effect which the extinguishment or the right of way would have ...'

The decisions of Phillips J in *R v Secretary of State ex parte Stewart* (1980) 39 P&CR 534 and Auld J in *R v Secretary of State ex parte Cheshire County Council* [1991] JPL 537 both offer some insight in this regard, though necessarily they are concerned with the statutory wording of s 118 as opposed to PA 2008, s 136. In the former, and as regards the second of the two tests, Phillips J effectively concluded in *ex p Stewart* (p 541) that where there was material demand for the route in question, it would not be 'expedient' to extinguish it.

However, the test in PA 2008, s 136(1)(b) is more broadly worded so as to suggest that a wide range of matters might be taken into consideration by the Secretary of State in the exercise of his discretion; such discretion to be exercised 'in the round'. At present, the extent to which the benefits of delivering the NSIP giving rise to the need for the extinguishment might fall to be considered in this context is unclear. However, it should be noted that, as regards development consented pursuant to the Town and Country Planning Act 1990, s 247 of that Act confers on the Secretary of State a broad discretion to stop up/extinguish any right of way if it is considered 'necessary' to enable development to be carried out. Paragraph 7.15 of the Rights of Way Circular 1/09 speaks in terms of the decision-maker weighing up 'the advantages' of making an order to extinguish a right of way; such 'advantage' must necessarily include the benefit that the consented development would deliver.

As regards provision of alternative routes pursuant to s 136(1)(a), potentially problematic is the absence of any temporal requirement as to when a replacement right of way must take be provided. The reference to an alternative right that 'has been ... provided' must of course relate to a right which has come into existence prior to the date of the Secretary of State's decision in respect of the application. However the reference to the Secretary of State being 'satisfied' that an alternative right 'will be provided', without any requirement as to the date by which such replacement provision must available, might be thought to leave some scope for dispute regarding the sufficiency of the replacement right of way.

The provision in practice

The Rookery South development consent order application provides a useful illustration of how the provision may be expected to work in practice.

In that instance the DCO sought (and ultimately published) provided for the extinguishment of two short sections of footpath: see article 11 of and Schedule 3 to the DCO. By way of mitigation, the promoters were also proposing to upgrade various existing routes, as well as to provide limited new stretches of footpath/cycleway; the improvements to be provided by, s 106 obligation. Notwithstanding that the proposed new provision did not in any sense 'replicate' the routes lost (which routes the Examining Panel observed were 'effectively short stubs and [did] not lead anywhere'), the Panel felt able to conclude (para 5.144) that: 'We are satisfied therefore that alternatives would be provided to enable these public rights of way to be extinguished'.

Accordingly, at least in this instance, the decision-maker did not consider that an 'alternative right of way' being provided pursuant to PA 2008, s 136(1)(a) need reflect or even approximate the route which it replaced. Rather, it was enough that an additional route was being provided. This is significant, in that in the ordinary course of events one might have expected a 'replacement' route to serve the same function as the route to be extinguished, on a 'like for like' basis.

Procedural requirements

Extinguishment where land acquired

PA 2008, s 136(2) and (3) are concerned with circumstances where the order granting development consent makes provision for the acquisition of land, compulsorily or by agreement, and the order extinguishes a right of way that is not a right enjoyed be vehicular traffic. Section 136(3) proves in these circumstances that the order granting development consent may not provide for the right of way to be extinguished from a date which is earlier than that on which the order is 'published'.

It is worth pausing to consider the use of the word 'published' in this context. The term is used in a number of provisions within the PA 2008, but is not defined in s 235 or elsewhere. Its precise meaning in the context of PA 2008 is significant, if only because the six week period within which judicial review proceedings must be brought in respect of legal challenge to the grant of a DCO pursuant to the Highways Act 1980, s 118(1), runs from the date on which the DCO or the statement of reasons in respect of it are 'published' (s 118(1)(b)).

As yet there is no judicial interpretation as to the statutory meaning of the term, either in the context of, PA 2008, s 136(3) or anywhere else in the PA 2008. However, read so as to give practical meaning to the provision, it appears that the intention of the draftsman was to preclude the extinguishment of a public right of way by a DCO until such time as the DCO has been formally 'published' by the HMSO (as the Queen's Printer of Acts of Parliament).

Revival of right of way where acquisition of land abandoned

The remaining provisions of PA 2008, s 136 (s 136(4), (5) and (7)) relate to the circumstances where a public right of way has been extinguished by a DCO, but the anticipated acquisition of land over which the right formerly existed has not been completed. In these circumstances, where 'it appears to the Secretary of State that the proposal to acquire the land has been abandoned' (s 136(4)(b)), then the Secretary of State must make an order 'reviving' the extinguished right.

The provision is clearly intended to avoid the permanent loss to the public, of rights of way the extinguishment of which was not ultimately necessary – either because the NSIP was not constructed, or because it was constructed in such a way as did not require acquisition of the land over which the public rights historically ran.

It should be noted that PA 2008, s 136(7) expressly provides that the 'revival' of a right of way pursuant to s 136(5) is no bar to 'the making of a further order extinguishing the right of way'. The use of the term 'further order' suggests that this provision is not intended for some further extinguishment under the existing DCO, but rather either a fresh DCO or else another, wholly separate, order such as one sought pursuant to the Highways Act 1980, s 118ZA.

The 'apparatus' exception

PA 2008, s 137 is engaged where an order granting development consent makes provision for the acquisition of land, compulsorily or by agreement, and a public right of way (not being a right enjoyed by vehicular traffic) exists over the land in circumstances where either '*on, over or under*' that land there is:

(a) apparatus belonging to a statutory undertaker (the term statutory undertaker as defined in Part 11 of the 1990 Act); or

(b) electronic communications apparatus kept installed in connection with an electronic communications code network.

In such circumstances, s 137(3) provides that the right of way in question may only be extinguished with the consent of the undertaker or operator of the network in question.

Unsurprisingly, the legislation provides that consent must not be unreasonably withheld: see PA 2008, s 137(4)(b). In this context it should be noted s 137(5) provides that any dispute as to whether or not any party is acting unreasonably in withholding consent, falls to be determined not by the courts, but by the Secretary of State. This jurisdiction on the part of the Secretary of State would however be subject to regulation by the courts by means of judicial review (s 118(7)).

As to when the requirement to secure 'consent' pursuant to PA 2008, s 137 is engaged, it appears at first that that a distinction of sorts is being drawn between statutory undertakers and the operators of an electronic communications code network.

For statutory undertakers generally the protection in PA 2008, s 137 is afforded where there island on, over or under which there is '*apparatus belonging to statutory undertakers*'. The test, therefore, is simply one ownership. For electronic communications apparatus, however, that apparatus must be '*kept installed for the purpose of an electronic communications code network*' (emphasis added). This appears to imply something other than ownership, but in reality simply reflects the terms of the electronic communications code that provides that apparatus may be installed or 'kept installed' in land.

As regards what comprises 'apparatus' in this context, for the purposes of PA 2008, s 137(2(b) the terminology relating to electronic communications is defined as per the Communications Act 2003, Sch 17, para 1(1). In contrast, there is no definition of the term 'apparatus' as applicable to a statutory undertaker for the purposes of s 137(2)(a). However in, s 138 (a related provision concerned with private, as opposed to public rights), the term 'relevant apparatus' is defined with reference to statutory undertakers as: 'apparatus vested in or belonging to statutory undertakers for the purpose of carrying out their undertaking'.

Notwithstanding the slight difference in terminology in the two provisions (ie 'apparatus' as opposed to 'relevant apparatus'), it would be surprising indeed if the term 'apparatus' were not accorded the same or very similar meaning in both PA 2008, ss 137 and 138. This is perhaps particularly the case given that, for the purposes of an electronic communications code network, s 138 defines 'relevant apparatus' in precisely the same terms as for s 137. As such, whatever else may be in dispute, there seems little doubt that in order for s 137 to engage the apparatus belonging to a the statutory undertaker must be held by that undertaker for 'for the purpose of carrying out [its] undertaking'.

Temporary Possession

Written by: Richard Honey, ftb
Edited by: Michael Humphries QC, ftb

Introduction

It is possible in practice for DCOs to provide for the temporary possession of land for the purposes of the carrying out of the project or maintaining the project once completed. This is the case even though the PA 2008 contains no express power to take temporary possession. Where temporary possession is taken, it would allow the undertaker to occupy and control the land to the exclusion of everyone else, including the landowner and any lessee. It would authorise what would otherwise be a trespass. If the land were subject to a tenancy, taking temporary possession would have no direct legal effect on the operation of the tenancy, which would continue to apply to the land including obligations to pay rent; although such a tenant might seek to argue as against its landlord that the tenancy had become frustrated as the landlord was not providing vacant possession and, in any event, would have a claim in compensation for loss or damage against the person taking temporary possession.

Temporary possession can be both controversial as far as affected landowners and occupiers are concerned, and problematic to operate in practice as far as the compensation provisions are concerned. Periods of temporary possession can last for many years and can also be of uncertain duration as at the date that possession is taken. This can give rise to problems for the assessment of compensation and for the operation of the six year limitation period for compensation claims. Moreover, during this period landowners cannot deal with the land in the way that they normally could and occupiers must remove themselves from the land and seek other land to carry on their operations. Furthermore, the promoter cannot be forced to acquire the land permanently even where the landowner or occupier would prefer that.

Temporary possession powers were included in Model Provisions 28 and 29 of the general model provisions in the Infrastructure Planning (Model Provisions) (England and Wales) Order 2009, SI 2009/2265. Such powers have been included in many DCOs, for example in Articles 31 and 32 of the National Grid (North London Reinforcement Project) Order 2014, SI 2014/1052 and in Articles 28 to 30 of the Network Rail (Norton Bridge Area Improvements) Order 2014, SI 2014/909.

It is important to note that a power of temporary possession is *not* a power of compulsory acquisition, but simply a power to enter on and take temporary possession of land for a specified purpose; the undertaker acquires no interest or right in the land itself.

Temporary use of land for carrying out the authorised project

Model Provision 28 and a number of DCOs grant an undertaker power, in connection with the 'carrying out' of the authorised project, to enter on and take possession of land specified in a schedule to the order for purposes also specified in the schedule related to a specific part of the project. In practice, land subject to temporary possession for the carrying out of the project is included in the definition of 'Order Land' along with the land to be acquired or used within the limits of deviation.

The Planning Inspectorate has advised that where temporary possession of land is required, The Infrastructure Planning (Applications: Prescribed Forms and Procedure) Regulations 2009, SI 2009/2264, reg 7 applies, so that the land plan must identify the plot with a number and state the area in square metres (Register of Advice, 28 February 2011, Willington Gas Pipeline).

It is also possible for a DCO to include a provision to the effect that temporary possession may be taken of not only that land listed in the schedule to the order for temporary possession but also any land subject to compulsory purchase under the order where the compulsory acquisition process has not been commenced. This is intended to allow temporary possession, rather than permanent acquisition, where the promoter decides to switch to temporary possession. The rationale is that if, during the design development process, it appears that permanent acquisition is not necessary for the purposes of the project, and that temporary possession would suffice, the change can be made. This obviously assists the promoter and may in some cases assist the landowner or occupier; sometimes however the landowner or occupier may want the land taken permanently rather than subject to temporary occupation for a period of in some cases many years.

Otherwise, Model Provision 28 provides that the undertaker may not compulsorily acquire land scheduled for only temporary possession (save in relation to acquiring compulsorily rights or subsoil only) and that where the undertaker takes temporary possession of land, it should not be required to acquire the land or any interest in it.

Model Provision 28 also confers powers to remove any buildings and vegetation from the land and to construct temporary works (including the provision of means of access) and buildings on the land. These powers have been widened in some DCOs as made. For example, Article 31 of the North London Reinforcement DCO (SI 2014/1052) also includes powers to construct other works and mitigation works. It is not unusual now for DCO applications to include powers for temporary possession which go beyond the Model Provisions, in allowing works for mitigation, ground strengthening and the like to be constructed and left on land where only temporary possession has been taken so that the works are left there permanently. An example of where the DCO allows the construction of permanent works on land of which only temporary possession is taken is Article 28 of the Norton Bridge Area Improvements Order 2014, SI 2014/909.

The Model Provisions include a requirement on the undertaker, before giving up the temporary possession, to remove all temporary works and restore the land to the reasonable satisfaction of the landowner, subject to a proviso that the undertaker shall not be required to replace a building removed under the temporary possession power. This provision is extended in practice sometimes so that, where permanent works are to be constructed on land temporary possession of which has been taken, the DCO also provides that the undertaker is not required to remove permanent works constructed on the land, eg mitigation or ground strengthening works. This was done, for example, in Article 28 of the Norton Bridge Area Improvements Order 2014, SI 2014/909; see also the Redditch Branch Enhancement Order 2013, SI 2013/2809, the North Doncaster Chord Order 2012, SI 2012/2635 and the Ipswich Chord Order 2012, SI 2012/2284.

The need for clarity over what works are temporary and what works are permanent is important for a variety of reasons, not least the assessment of compensation. The report of the Examining Authority dated 12 June 2012 into the Ipswich Chord Order 2012, SI 2012/2284 records that the draft DCO in that case was altered to clarify which of the proposed works were permanent and which were temporary so that the land had to be restored.

The reinstatement provision can be important in certain cases. In paragraph 97 of the Examining Authority's report on the North Doncaster Chord Order 2012, SI 2012/2635 dated 31 July 2012, the ExA records that the draft DCO contained a provision that the undertaker should not be required to reinstate any ground used during construction and that it questioned whether this was reasonable as the affected land could include farmland. As a result, the undertaker deleted the provision from the draft DCO.

Model Provision 28 provides that the authority for the temporary possession of land for the purposes of carrying out the project ceases five years after the date on which the relevant DCO is made. This is subject to a proviso that the time limit does not prevent the undertaker from remaining in possession of land, if the land was entered and possession was taken before the end of that period. In Network Rail's Norton Bridge DCO (SI 2014/909), the Secretary of State for Transport inserted a provision to make clear that the authority for temporary possession of land granted under that DCO to National Grid (separate from that granted to Network Rail) also expired five years after the DCO comes into force (decision letter dated 31 March 2014, para 38).

Model Provision 28 provides that not less than 14 days' notice has to be given to owners and occupiers before the undertaker enters on and takes temporary possession of land. Some DCOs as made – for example the Redditch Branch Enhancement Order 2012, SI 2013/2189 and the Norton Bridge Area Improvements Order 2014, SI 2014/909 – have voluntarily included 28 days instead of 14 days' notice.

The Crossrail and HS2 Hybrid Bills both included 28 days' notice provisions. The 'Post Legislative Assessment of the Crossrail Act 2008' published by the Department for Transport (Cmd 8676, July 2013) stated that 'the provision for 28 days' notice to be given for temporary possessions has proven to be sufficient'.

The question of 14 or 28 days' notice was the subject of debate in the case of the National Grid (North London Reinforcement Project) Order 2014, SI 2014/1052. The Examining Authority's report dated 23 January 2014 at paragraph 6.137 contained the conclusion that a period of 14 days was 'so short as to be unreasonable' and recommended a change to 28 days. But the Secretary of State disagreed in his decision letter dated 16 April 2014, stating:

> '4.16 The Secretary of State notes the ExA's view [ER 6.137] that a notice period of 14 days for entering on and taking possession of land was unreasonably short. However, taking into account the strong need for the timely delivery of the project to avoid works in the winter months to mitigate harm to European Sites and species, and the need to avoid any delays in the planned outage timetables which have been calculated to be carried out when forecast network demand can accommodate them, the Secretary of State does not agree that the period is unreasonable. A 14 day notice period is consistent with precedents, including the Infrastructure Planning (Model Provisions) (England and Wales) Order 2009 (now repealed), and section 11

of the Compulsory Purchase Act 1965. The Secretary of State also considers that any unnecessary delays in the ability for NGET to enter on and take temporary possession of land could constrain the delivery of the Project. The Secretary of State considers that a notice period of 14 days is sufficient.'

A time limit is also set on the duration of the occupation. The Model Provisions provide that the undertaker may not, without the agreement of the landowner, remain in possession of any land for longer than one year after the completion of the part of the project specified in the schedule for the relevant land. In the Secretary of State for Transport's decision letter dated 19 March 2013 on the Heysham to M6 Link Road DCO (SI 2013/675) the Secretary of State included references to work numbers in the schedule to the DCO 'so as to provide greater precision about the deadline for LCC to give up possession of land used temporarily for the purposes of the scheme'.

In the Model Provisions, Article 22(3) provides that all private rights of way over land of which temporary possession is taken shall be suspended and unenforceable for as long as the undertaker remains in lawful possession of the land. This has been extended in some DCOs made. For example, in the North London Reinforcement DCO (SI 2014/1052), Article 26(4) covers all private rights and restrictive covenants, rather than just private rights of way.

All temporary possession provisions include an obligation to pay compensation to the owners and occupiers of land for any loss or damage arising from the exercise of any power contained in the relevant article of the DCO. Disputes as to compensation are dealt with by the Upper Tribunal (Lands Chamber) under Part I of the Land Compensation Act 1961. The provisions also contain a saving that the liability to pay compensation does not affect a person's entitlement to compensation under the Planning Act 2008, s 152 (or the Compulsory Purchase Act 1965, s 10, if applicable).

If the land is being used as a business, the compensatable loss will be the genuine net profit which the business would have earned from its legitimate activities on the affected land, over the relevant period of time (see by analogy eg *Pennine Raceway Ltd v Kirklees MBC* [1984] RVR 85 and *Hobbs (Quarries) Ltd v Somerset CC* (1975) 30 P&CR 286). Where land is occupied by someone other than the owner, the relevant period will run from when temporary possession was taken until the earliest possible date on which the owner could have obtained possession of the land. Any entitlement to compensation is subject to the usual requirements of causation, remoteness and mitigation. The burden of proof to establish the loss or damage, and its quantum, will lie on the claimant.

As noted above, the compensation regime is problematic in relation to limitation periods and uncertain durations of possession. The regime also lacks many of the features of compensation for acquisition, such as entitlements to advance payment, loss payments and statutory interest. This adds to the complexity of dealing with compensation for temporary possession and potentially operates to the detriment of landowners and occupiers in certain cases.

Temporary use of land for maintaining authorised project

Model Provision 29 and many DCOs also contain powers for temporary use of land for the purposes of 'maintaining' the authorised project after its completion. The power shares many of the same features with the construction temporary possession power described above. The main features of the maintenance power are:

- the power applies at any time within a specified maintenance period, usually defined as five years from the date on which the relevant part of the project was first opened for use;
- the power does not apply to any house, or garden belonging to a house, or any other building which is occupied at the time;
- the power is to enter on and take temporary possession of any land within the Order limits, provided it is reasonably required for the purpose of maintaining the project
- buildings on the land, provided they are reasonably necessary for the purpose of maintaining the project
- the power is subject to giving 28 days' notice to the owner and occupier of the land;
- the power is limited to allow temporary possession only for so long as may be reasonably necessary to carry out the maintenance of the part of the project for which possession of the land was taken
- before giving up possession, the undertaker must remove all temporary works and restore the land to the reasonable satisfaction of the owners of the land;
- the power is subject to an obligation to pay compensation to the owners and occupiers of the land for any loss or damage arising from the exercise of the power in relation to the land.

Compulsory Purchase Compensation

Written by: Richard Honey, ftb
Edited by: Michael Humphries QC, ftb

Introduction

The Inspectorate has stated in terms that 'the assessment of compensation is complex and governed by other legislation and extensive case law' (register of advice, 21 February 2012, Dyfnant Forest Wind Farm). That is a fair summary of the position. The Inspectorate has also made it clear repeatedly in its register of advice that it will have nothing to do with claims for compensation (see also eg PA 2008, s 102(4)(e)(i)).

That said, the examining authority may, in some cases, need to give some consideration to the overall amount of compensation payable in connection with consideration of whether there are sufficient funds available to pay compensation. In the Hinkley Point case, the promoter had taken expert advice on the likely cost of implementing the proposed development, including the cost of the necessary land acquisition (panel report, 19 December 2012, para 7.35).

A similar position existed in relation to the Rookery South application (panel decision, 13 October 2011, paras 7.25, 7.100). Although the Examining Authority was hesitant to go too far into considering the quantum of compensation (paras 7.81, 7.83), it did accept that 'a misunderstanding of the likely quantum of compensation could lead the Applicant to underestimate the likely compensation payable, which in turn could impact on viability and thus affect the argument for a compelling case' (para 7.98). Ultimately a provision was included in the DCO (Art 8) to the effect that the development could not be commenced unless either a guarantee in respect of the promoter's liabilities to pay compensation or an alternative form of security for that purpose was in place.

Similarly, the Examining Authority may need to consider the availability of compensation in particular circumstances as part of its consideration of the proportionality of the proposed compulsory acquisition of land. In the case of the Ipswich Rail Chord, the authority had to consider the entitlement to compensation of tenants with an interest of less than six months. The Examining Authority concluded that the resultant interference with the tenants' human rights was proportionate and in the public interest (panel report, 12 June 2012, para 5.91; see also the Rookery South decision at paras 7.102–7.103).

An overview of compulsory purchase compensation under the PA 2008

Save in the case of s 10 of the CPA 1965, which is considered further below, the compensation provisions arising from a DCO are substantially the same as other similar orders. The text below gives a very brief overview of the compensation entitlements that arise and the main rules which apply to them.

Value of the land acquired

The principle underlying compensation for compulsory acquisition of land is that fair compensation should be given to the owner whose land has been taken. The aim is to provide a fair financial equivalent for the land taken. The owner is entitled to be compensated fairly and fully for his loss, but he is not entitled to receive more than fair compensation: see *Transport for London v Spirerose* [2009] 1 WLR 1797 at 1822C–D and *Waters v Welsh Development Agency* [2004] 1 WLR 1304 at 1306E, 1309B–D. Compensation cannot, and must not, exceed the owner's total loss, for, if it did, it would put an unfair burden on the public purse and it would transgress the principle of 'equivalence', which is at the root of statutory compensation, namely that the owner shall be paid neither less nor more than his loss (*Horn v Sunderland Corporation* [1941] 2 KB 26 at 49). A claimant is not entitled to receive more than fair compensation: a person is entitled to compensation for losses fairly attributable to the taking of his land, but not to any greater amount (*Director of Buildings and Lands v Shun Fung* [1995] 2 AC 111 at 125D).

The primary statutory rules for assessing compensation are found in s 5 of the LCA 1961. Under s 5(2) of the LCA 1961 the value of land is taken to be the amount which the land if sold in the open market by a willing seller might be expected to realise. As to what the land might be expected to realise, this refers to the expectations of properly qualified persons who have taken pains to inform themselves of all the particulars ascertainable about the property, and its capabilities, and the demand for it (*Inland Revenue Commissioners v Clay* [1914] 3 KB 466 at 475). It must be assumed that the hypothetical vendor and purchaser did whatever reasonable people buying and selling such property would be likely to have done in real life; the hypothetical buyer is assumed to have behaved reasonably and made proper enquiries about the property and not to have appeared too eager to buy (*Ryde v London Regional Transport* [2004] RVR 60 at paras 18–19). So far as possible the assessment of compensation should reflect what would be likely to happen if the property were actually sold at the valuation date (*Waters* at p 1313C).

The principles applying to an open market valuation of land were summarised by Hoffmann LJ in *IRC v Gray* [1994] RVR 129 at 136:

> 'one assumes that the hypothetical vendor and purchaser did whatever reasonable people buying and selling such property would be likely to have done in real life. The hypothetical vendor is an anonymous but reasonable vendor, who goes about the sale as a prudent man of business, negotiating seriously without giving the impression of being either over-anxious or unduly reluctant. The hypothetical buyer is slightly less anonymous. He too is assumed to have behaved reasonably, making proper inquiries about the property and not appearing too eager to buy. But he also reflects reality in that he embodies whatever was actually the demand for that property at the relevant time. It cannot be too strongly emphasised that although the sale is hypothetical, there is nothing hypothetical about the open market in which it is supposed to have taken place. The concept of the open market involves assuming that the whole world was free to bid, and then forming a view about what in those circumstances would in real life have been the best price reasonably obtainable.'

The willing seller is a hypothetical character and the personal characteristics of the actual seller are not to be taken into account.

The starting point is that a search for the value of land at a particular date must take account of the attributes of the land at that date (*Spirerose* at p 1801G). As a generality, land is to be valued in the state in which it was in and in the circumstances prevailing at the valuation date. Where property is to be valued on an open market basis as at a certain date, no counter-factual assumptions should be made other than those which are inherent in the valuation exercise or those which are directed by statute (*Spirerose* at p 1814C). An interest in land is assumed to be sold in the state in which it existed as at the valuation date, taking into account any tenancies or restrictions to which it was subject. There are particular statutory rules and provisions arising from case-law (including *Pointe Gourde v Sub-Intendant of Crown Lands* [1947] AC 565) which require the effect on value of the scheme underlying the compulsory acquisition to be ignored in certain circumstances.

Where a DCO grants the power to create new rights in land it may need to apply parts of the statutory compensation code with necessary modifications: see, for example, Schedule 10 to the Lancashire County Council (Torrisholme to the M6 Link (A683 Completion of Heysham to M6 Link Road)) Order 2013.

Where temporary possession of land is taken, the promoter must pay compensation to the owners and occupiers of the land for any loss or damage arising from the exercise of the power. If the land is being used for the purposes of a business then the compensatable loss may properly reflect net profit which the business would have earned from its legitimate activities on the affected land, over the relevant period of temporary possession: see by analogy *Pennine Raceway Ltd v Kirklees MBC* [1984] RVR 85 and *Hobbs (Quarries) Ltd v Somerset CC* (1975) 30 P&CR 286. Where land is occupied by someone other than the owner, the relevant period would be from when temporary possession was taken until the earliest possible date on which the owner could have obtained possession of the land. The entitlement to compensation would be subject to the usual requirements of causation, remoteness and mitigation. The burden of proof to establish the loss or damage, and its quantum, would lie on the claimant.

Section 37 of the LCA 1973 provides an avenue for compensation where a claimant has no compensatable interest in the land acquired. This would apply to persons in occupation under a licence, a tenancy at will, or holding over after a lease. Section 37 applies where a person is displaced from land in consequence of the acquisition of the land by an authority possessing compulsory purchase powers and he had no compensatable interest in the land but was in lawful possession of it. The displaced person is entitled to a disturbance payment.

Disturbance

Section 5(6) of the LCA 1961 provides compensation for disturbance, known as Rule 6 compensation. This covers both the cost of being disturbed, or 'displaced', from the land, under the first limb, but also, under the second limb, any other matter not directly based on the value of the land. The second limb of Rule 6 was described as being potentially wide in *Ryde* (para 24). Consequential or economic losses other than those directly related to the value of the land itself are in principle recoverable as compensation under the second limb of Rule 6, including on the part of investment owners. A claim under Rule 6 may be made for consequential loss even it does not stem from a loss of occupation.

Any loss recoverable under Rule 6 must be a loss properly and actually incurred by a claimant. Moreover, such claims are subject in law to three particular tests. To be recoverable:

- there must be a causal connection between the compulsory acquisition and the loss (see *Shun Fung* a p 126A);
- the loss must be reasonably foreseeable and not too remote (see *Shun Fung* at p 126D-F); and,
- the claimant must behave reasonably in taking steps to eliminate or reduce any loss (see *Shun Fung* at pp 126F-G, 127C-E, 138A, 138F).

It is the first of these, causation, which seems to give rise to most problems in practice. In *Wrexham Maelor BC v MacDougall* [1993] 2 EGLR 23 at 32J what was recoverable was described by the Court of Appeal as 'significant damage consequent upon the taking of his interest, other than costs and expenses, which is the natural and reasonable consequence of the taking of his interest and not too remote'. In *Shun Fung* it was said that 'there must be a causal connection between the resumption or acquisition and the loss in question' (at 126A).

Pre-possession losses may be claimed if they are due to the compulsory acquisition. They are only recoverable, however, where they are incurred in anticipation of the compulsory acquisition and because of the threat of compulsory acquisition (*Shun Fung* at 137H–138A). Save for the need to avoid double counting in relation to overlap with the value of the land, judged as at the valuation date, there is no difference in principle as to the recoverability of pre and post-possession losses.

A range of losses may be claimed under Rule 6. Lost profits arising from temporary or permanent loss of business as a result of a compulsory acquisition are generally recoverable. The expenses of removal to new premises are generally recoverable, including the costs of searching for and finding alternative premises, removal costs and the costs of setting-up the new premises. Consequential or economic losses, including taxation liabilities, are generally recoverable, subject to compliance with the three fundamental requirements for Rule 6 claims. The Court of Appeal in *Wrexham Maelor BC* recognised that claims for compensation for losses such as lost earnings or lost profits are not excluded in principle. Rule 6 also encompasses compensation for reasonable surveyor's, legal and other professional fees incurred as a direct consequence of the compulsory acquisition, and compensation for the personal time actually and reasonably spent by a claimant dealing with matters caused by the acquisition, and charged at a fair and reasonable hourly rate.

Severance and injurious affection

Where land is taken, a landowner may suffer loss by the detrimental effect of such acquisition on other land that he retains. Section 7 of the CPA 1965 provides compensation for severance and injurious affection. Section 7 provides that in assessing compensation for land taken, regard must be had to the damage to be sustained by the landowner through any injurious effect on that landowner's other land by reason of the exercise of the relevant statutory powers. This has been described as loss caused to the retained land by the works or use of the land acquired for the statutory purpose. Section 7 requires, in effect, that where a person's land is compulsorily acquired, if certain retained land suffers a diminution in value because of the project, then that diminution in value should be included in the compensation paid for the acquisition. Any loss of amenity which affects the value of the retained land could also give rise to a claim for compensation.

The main requirements in a claim for s 7 compensation for injurious affection are:

- land must have been acquired compulsorily from the claimant;
- the harm must be caused by the exercise of the statutory powers;
- injurious affection can arise from both the execution and the use of the works or the land taken, and would include temporary loss during the execution of the works;
- there is no need for there to be an underlying right to claim in tort;
- injurious affection extends beyond matters that would normally be compensatable in tort, such as loss of privacy and general amenity;
- the injurious effect may arise from the works as a whole and not just from that part of the works on the land taken from the owner;
- compensation may (and ought to) be prospective, to include what is reasonably anticipated to happen as it must be claimed once and for all; and
- damage to purely personal rights unconnected with the land is not compensatable.

The 'other land' (the retained land) must be held with the land taken, but it need not be contiguous with or indeed part of the same title, or used in the same way or occupied by the same person, as the land taken. The two parcels of land must merely be owned by the same person and 'so near to each other, and so situated that the possession and control of each gives an enhanced value to all of them' (*Cowper Essex v Acton Local Board* (1889) 14 App Cas 153 at 167).

For there to be a claim for injurious affection under s 7 of the CPA 1965, the value of the owner's retained land must have been depreciated by injurious affection as a result of the construction or use of the scheme or the acquisition of land. Section 7 provides that compensation is payable for injury done 'by the exercise of the powers conferred by... the special Act'. The injury must be caused by the exercise of the relevant statutory powers. The measure of compensation is the diminution in value of the owner's retained land, and compensation is not to be measured by the costs the owner incurs to overcome the consequences of the construction or use of the scheme (*Cowper Essex* at pp 166, 178).

The provisions of PA 2008, s 152 are explained elsewhere in this work. The effect of s 152(3) is that the promoter must pay compensation to any person whose land is injuriously affected by the carrying out of the authorised works. The provision in s 10(2) of the CPA 1965 is to be applied and, furthermore, any rule or principle applied to the construction of s 10 must also be applied to the construction of s 152(3). It appears that the effect of s 152 is intended to be equivalent to that of s 10 of the CPA 1965.

For PA 2008, s 152 to apply it is not necessary for a person to have had any land taken for the scheme. However, the land must be affected in a way that reduces its value and the injury can only arise from the carrying out of the works, not from the subsequent use of the works. Entitlement to compensation would be limited to cases where a person would have had a claim in tort but for the statutory authority conferred by the DCO. Entitlement only arises where a remedy would have been available in damages but for the defence of statutory authority.

The operation of s 10 of the CPA 1965 has become subject to a series of rules or conditions, known as the McCarthy rules after *Metropolitan Board of Works v McCarthy* (1874) LR 7 HL 243. The same rules would apply to a claim under s 152, pursuant to s 152(6). They are:

- the injurious affection must be the consequence of the lawful exercise of statutory powers;
- the injurious affection must be such that, if not done under statutory authority, would have given rise to a cause of action;
- compensation is payable only for damage to the claimant's land or interest in land; and
- compensation is payable in respect of only the execution of works and not their use.

These rules were summarised in *Clift v Welsh Office* [1999] 1 WLR 796 at 801B-C, with another point added: the compensation must be ascertainable in accordance with the general rules applicable to damages in tort. This includes the tortious requirements of foreseeability and directness of harm. The measure of damages is usually the diminution in the value of the interest in land affected, assessed at the date of the injury, for all the anticipated injury. The value of a claimant's interest in land must be affected by physical interference with some legal right, public or private, of which the claimant is entitled to make use in connection with his property (*McCarthy* at 253 and 256), irrespective of whether the damage was caused by permanent or temporary interference.

Damage arising from business lost by reason of an obstruction or interference making land less accessible or attractive to customers is recoverable, where such loss of business reduces the value of land (see *Wildtree Hotels v Harrow LBC* [2001] 2 AC 1). However, compensation is not available for personal losses, including lost business profits.

Another form of injurious affection compensation is provided under Part 1 of the LCA 1973, which is applied to works authorised under a DCO by s 152(7). Part 1 compensation is in essence compensation for depreciation of land value by physical factors caused by use of public works. Section 1 of the LCA 1973 provides that where the value of an interest in land is depreciated by 'physical factors' caused by the use of public works then, subject to certain conditions, compensation is payable for that depreciation. In addition to compensation, reasonable valuation and legal expenses are also payable (s 3(5)). The 'physical factors' are defined in s 1(2) as noise, vibration, smell, fumes, smoke, artificial lighting and the discharge of any solid or liquid substance (eg dust). Noise is the most common physical factor in relation to which claims are made. The source of the physical factors must be situated on or in the public works the use of which is alleged to be their cause.

Part 1 claims may be made one year after the opening of the relevant public work. Compensation is assessed by reference to prices one year after opening, applying s 5(2)–(4) of the LCA 1961, less deduction for betterment. Reasonably expected intensification of the use of the works is taken into account. Section 9 of the LCA

1973 makes similar provision to s 1 but in circumstances where there are alterations to pre-existing public works (eg road widening).

Some additional points

In terms of procedure, the DCLG 'Guidance related to procedures for compulsory acquisition' (February 2010) says that promoters should seek to acquire land by negotiation wherever practicable (para 39). The guidance urges promoters to use alternative dispute resolution including in relation to agreeing the compensation payable for property acquired (para 42). Mediation and early neutral evaluation are mentioned.

It is also notable that the guidance suggests that in order 'to alleviate concerns about future compensation entitlement' a promoter could enter into agreements with those whose land is to be acquired which guarantee a minimum compensation payment, if the project proceeds (para 44). This would be without prejudice to a claimant's ability to seek a higher level of compensation in the future. Such an approach may assist both in allowing those whose land is being acquired to plan for relocating or dealing with the acquisition, as well as reducing the objections which are made to DCOs on a protective basis.

Disputes about compensation which cannot be resolved must be referred to the Lands Chamber of the Upper Tribunal under the Tribunal Procedure (Upper Tribunal) (Lands Chamber) Rules 2010, SI 2010/2600.

The DCLG guidance also refers readers to ODPM circular 06/2004 entitled 'Compulsory Purchase and the Crichel Down Rules'. DCLG also published in October 2004 a series of guidance documents on the compulsory purchase system. These cover compensation to agricultural owners and occupiers, compensation to business owners and occupiers, and compensation to residential owners and occupiers.

More information on compensation for compulsory purchase can be found in Roots et al *The Law of Compulsory Purchase* (2nd edn, Bloomsbury Professional).

Part 10

Environmental Impact Assessment and Habitats Regulations Assessment

Requirement for Environmental Impact Assessment

Written by: Gregory Jones QC, ftb
Edited by: Michael Humphries QC, ftb

What is EIA?

Environmental Impact Assessment (EIA) is a means of drawing together, in a systematic way, an assessment of the likely significant environmental effects arising from a proposed development.

What type of NSIP Projects are Covered by EIA?

The EIA Directive (Directive 85/337/EEC as amended by Directives 97/11/EC and 2003/35/EC now consolidated as European Directive 2011/92/EU) requires that projects of a description contained within Annexes I and II of the Directive likely to have significant effects on the environment by virtue *inter alia* of their nature, size or location are made subject to an assessment of their environmental effects (Article 2(1)).

These projects are defined in Article 4 and listed in Annex I and Annex II of the EIA Directive. An EIA is always required for projects included in Annex I. Projects of the categories listed in Annex II shall be made subject to an assessment when Member States determine that they are likely to have significant effects on the environment.

Those categories of development within Annex I are all assumed to have likely significant environmental effects and thus an EIA is always mandatory for a development of the type included within Annex 1. Those in Annex II will require an EIA, if in the view of the Examining Authority they are likely to have significant effects on the environment. It is important to note that the requirement is triggered by *any* likely significant environmental effects not merely any *adverse* significant environmental effects (*British Telecommunications plc v Gloucester City Council* [2001] EWHC 1001 (Admin); (2002) 2 P&CR 33; *R (Stephen Prophet) v York City Council* [2002] EWHC 588 (Admin). Hence, promoters of NSIPs should assume that it is most likely that all NSIP applications will be subject to EIA. This is because whilst it may be theoretically possible to devise a nationally infrastructure project that does not require an EIA, in practice it is difficult to imagine a nationally significant infrastructure project will not have a likely significant environmental effect, even if its overall effect is beneficial. Indeed, the 'primary position' of the Institute of Environment Management Assessment is that EIA should be made a mandatory requirement for all NSIPs. Its 'secondary position' is that all non-Annex I developments should undergo formal, case by case, screening opinion produced by the EA, developed through consultation with environmental stakeholders.

The Infrastructure Planning (Environmental Impact Assessment) Regulations 2009

The Infrastructure Planning (Environmental Impact Assessment) Regulations 2009, SI 2009/2263 (as amended) ('the IP EIA Regulations') came into force on 1 October

2009 and are intended to set out the procedures that must be followed so that the consideration of applications for NSIPs fully reflect the requirements of the EIA Directive.

The EIA screening and scoping process for NSIPs under the IP EIA Regulations and the PA 2008 is summarised below.

Summary of EIA Process for NSIP

Screening

- Screening Opinion within 21 days of request

Scoping

- Desk top baseline review and Gap Assessment
- Preliminary stakeholder engagement
- Scoping Report
- Scoping Opinion within 42 days of receiving request

Preliminary Environmental Information

- 28 days consultation as part of PA 2008, ss 42 and 47 consultation

Environmental Impact Assessment

- Baseline
- Project Definition (iterative process)
- Assessing Effects
- Reporting – Environmental Statement (ES)

How to Approach EIA

In seeking to ensure that the NSIP application is made and assessed in accordance with the EIA Directive and Regulations, it is critical to have a basic understanding of the way in which EU law obligations are to be interpreted, particularly those directed towards environmental protection. Such obligations – as Lord Hoffmann made clear in *R v North Yorkshire , ex parte Brown* [2000] 1 AC 397 at 401D – must be interpreted in accordance with the principles of European law. This means, for example, not only examining the English language version of the EIA Directive – and where appropriate a comparison with other language versions – but also possessing an understanding of the purpose of the EIA Directive.

The EIA Directive will also be interpreted in the light of the EU Treaty obligations imposed upon the United Kingdom. In *Berkeley v Secretary of State for the Environment* [2001] 2 AC 603, Lord Hoffmann expressly relied upon what is now article 4(3) of the Treaty on the European Union ('the TEU') in support of his view that national authorities including the courts must ensure the full effectiveness of the EIA Directive by interpreting very narrowly their discretion not to quash a decision taken in breach of the EIA Directive. Article 4(3) of the TEU states that:

> 'The Member States shall take any appropriate measure, general or particular, to ensure fulfilment of the obligations arising out of the Treaties or resulting from the acts of the institutions of the Union (this includes the EIA Directive). The Member States shall facilitate the achievement of the Union's task.'

The European Court of Justice (ECJ) has also relied upon the obligation contained in this Treaty article in order to create the principles of direct and indirect effect (see further below).

Article 191 of the Treaty on the Functioning of the European Union ('the TFEU') is another important Treaty obligation for the purposes of the EIA Directive. It provides amongst other things that:

> 'Union policy on the environment shall aim at a high level of protection taking into account the diversity of situations in the various regions of the Union. It shall be based on the precautionary principle and on the principles that preventive action should be taken, that environmental damage should as a priority be rectified at source and that the polluter should pay.'

See also the Communication from the Commission on the precautionary principle – Brussels, 02.02.2000 COM (2000). The 'precautionary principle' is, for example, relevant to many practical issues in respect of the EIA of an NSIP, such as the quality of scientific evidence required in EIA.

Relationship between the EIA Directive and the NSIP EIA Regulations

If the IP EIA regulations implement the EIA Directive, why can't we forget about the EIA Directive? It is generally accepted that the EIA Directive is capable of 'direct effect' (*Kraaijveld v Gedeputeerde Staten Van Zuid-Holland* (Case C-72/95)). This means if the IP EIA Regulations have not correctly implemented the EIA Directive into the English domestic law, an individual may nonetheless rely directly upon rights conferred by the EIA Directive to enforce those rights against emanations of the state such as the Secretary of State. This is so, even if it means quashing development consent granted to a private company or individual (see eg *R v Durham County Council and Sherburn Stone Company Ltd, ex p Huddleston* [2000] 1 WLR 1484).

Where direct effect cannot be relied upon, the IP EIA Regulations must nonetheless be interpreted to give full effect to the requirements of the EIA Directive, even if that means stretching their ordinary meaning in the English language (see, eg Case C-106 *Marleasing SA v La Comercial International de Alimnetacion SA* [1990] ECR I-4135). This practice is sometimes inaccurately referred to as 'indirect effect' or more precisely, as the 'duty of loyalty' or 'cooperation': see also *R v Durham County Council and Sherburn Stone Company Ltd, ex p Huddleston* [2000] 1 WLR 1484.

The Purpose of the EIA Directive

Given that the ECJ takes a so-called purposive approach to the interpretation of EU law, it is important therefore for those applying for development consent to understand two key aspects about the purpose of the EIA Directive. The first is, as Advocate General Elmer stated in *Commission of the European Communities v Federal Republic of Germany* (Case C-431/92) [1995] ECR I-2189, 2208-2209 that:

> 'the provisions of the Directive are essentially of a procedural nature. By the inclusion of information on the environment in the consent procedure it is ensured that the environmental impact of the project shall be included in the public debate and that the decision as to whether consent is to be given shall be adopted on an appropriate basis.' (approved in *Berkeley*).

Accordingly, since its substance is procedure, flaws in procedures adopted in an EIA may be regarded as substantive flaws and are thus less likely to be excused by the courts or the Examining Authority.

The second point is that the purpose of the EIA Directive is not only that the Secretary of State has all the environmental information before him when he makes a decision on whether to make a development consent order, though that is, of course, a key requirement. Lord Bingham in *Berkeley* held that the directly enforceable right of the citizen which is accorded by the EIA Directive is not merely a right to a fully informed decision on the substantive issue. It must have been adopted on an appropriate basis and that requires the inclusive and democratic procedure prescribed by the Directive in which:

> 'the public, however misguided or wrongheaded its views may be, is given an opportunity to express its opinion on the environmental issues.'

As Advocate General Elmer also made clear in *Aannemersbedrijf P K Kraaijeveld BV v Gedeputeerde Staten van Zuid-Holland* (Case C-72/95) [1996] ECR I-5403, 5427, para 70):

> 'Where a member state's implementation of the Directive is such that projects which are likely to have significant effects on the environment are not made the subject of an environmental impact assessment, the citizen is prevented from exercising his right to be heard.'

The importance attached to the right of public participation the EIA decision making process in respect an NSIP has been further emphasised by the Aarhus Convention on Access to Environmental Justice.

Front-loaded EIA

The courts have also stressed the need to ensure that the environmental effects of a development including cumulative effects are assessed at the earliest possible opportunity in the development consent process (see eg *R (Brown) v Carlisle City Council* [2010] EWCA Civ 523 [2011] Env LR 5 and *R (on the application of Barker) v Bromley LBC* [2006] UKHL 52; [2007] Env LR 20 per Lord Hope at [22]). This requirement fits in with the general front loaded philosophy of the NSIP regime.

What is EIA Development?

The NSIP EIA Regulations impose procedural requirements for carrying out EIA for NSIPs which fall to be considered as 'EIA development' under the EIA Regulations.

The schedules to the EIA Regulations contain the following two broad categories of projects:

- Schedule 1 projects replicate those contained in Annex I to the EIA Directive – these are always EIA development and include, for example, nuclear power stations. By definition it is presumed that such projects are always likely to have significant effects upon the environment.
- Schedule 2 projects replicate those contained in Annex I to the EIA Directive and are only EIA development if the individual project is likely to have significant effects on the environment. Schedule 2 includes, for example, wind farms and overhead cables. Schedule 2 to the EIA Regulations applying to NSIPS does not include applicable thresholds and criteria (unlike the Town and Country Planning (Environmental Impact Assessment) Regulations 2011). But it must be recalled that the European Court of Justice has held that the projects identified in Schedule 2 should be given a *'wide scope and broad purpose'* (*Dutch Dykes – Kraaijveld v. Gedeputeerde Staten van Zuid-Holland* (Case C-72/95) [1997]. Env LR 3, 265).

EIA Scoping

Written by: Hereward Phillpot QC, ftb
Edited by: Michael Humphries QC, ftb

The Infrastructure Planning (Environmental Impact Assessment) Regulations 2009, SI 2009/2263

The Infrastructure Planning (Environmental Impact Assessment) Regulations 2009, SI 2009/2263 (the 'EIA Regulations'), reg 8 sets out the procedure for obtaining a written opinion as to the information to be provided in an environmental statement (ie a 'scoping opinion'). The procedure is only available to a person who proposes to make an application for a development consent order ('DCO') (reg 8(1)), or an application to discharge a requirement (reg 8(2)).

The procedure is not compulsory. Whilst it is, therefore, a matter of choice for applicants whether or not they apply for a scoping opinion, in practice almost all do. It is an important part of the Environmental Impact Assessment ('EIA') process and is regarded as good practice. The advantages are obvious, in that obtaining a scoping opinion helps to focus the process of environmental impact assessment and ensure that the concerns of key stakeholders are identified and addressed at an early stage. It also allows issues to be 'scoped out' of the EIA process at an early stage, which can save time and money.

An effective scoping process makes it less likely that the environmental statement ('ES') submitted with the application will be rejected as inadequate, or that requests will need to be made for additional information. There is no obligation to follow the advice given in the scoping opinion, but again, for obvious enough reasons, most applicants will choose to do so to reduce the prospect of their application being rejected.

Procedural steps

The main procedural steps are the same whether the applicant is seeking a scoping opinion from the Secretary of State pursuant to reg 8(1), or from the authority responsible for the discharge of the requirement (the 'relevant authority') pursuant to reg 8(2).

Once a request has been made, the Secretary of State/relevant authority must consult the person who made the request and the 'consultation bodies' (reg 8(6)). Regulation 2(1) defines 'the consultation bodies' as meaning:

> '(a) a body prescribed under section 42(a) (duty to consult) and listed in column 1 of the table set out at Schedule 1 to the Infrastructure Planning (Applications: Prescribed Forms and Procedure) Regulations 2009 where the circumstances set out in column 2 are satisfied in respect of that body;
>
> - each authority that is within section 43 (local authorities for the purposes of section 42(b)); and

- if the land to which the application, or proposed application, relates or any part of that land is in Greater London, the Greater London Authority.'

If a consultation body fails to reply within 28 days of being consulted, the Secretary of State/relevant authority is entitled to assume it has no comments to make.

Before adopting a scoping opinion, the Secretary of State/relevant authority must take into account: (a) the specific characteristics of the particular development; (b) the specific characteristics of development of the type concerned; (c) the environmental features likely to be affected by the development; and (d) in the case of an application to discharge a requirement, the ES submitted with the original application (reg 8(9)).

The Secretary of State/relevant authority must provide a scoping opinion within 42 days from receipt of the request. There are only two exceptions to this timescale. First, where additional information has been requested, the 42-day period runs from receipt of that additional information (reg 8(6)). Secondly, where the request for a scoping opinion has been accompanied by a request for a screening opinion, the 42-day period runs from the date that the screening opinion was adopted (reg 8(7) and (8)).

In practice, most applicants will undertake at least some form of informal consultation with the main consultation bodies before submitting a request to the Secretary of State. This allows their views to be considered and, where appropriate, reflected in the information accompanying the request and reduces the likelihood of significant dispute as to the appropriate scope of the EIA. As explained below, it is also important in enabling the applicant to satisfy the Secretary of State's expectations as to the information that ought to accompany a request for a scoping opinion, and to comply with the guidance issued by the Planning Inspectorate on his behalf.

Documents accompanying request

The formal requirements for making a valid request for a scoping opinion are very limited.

Where the request is to the Secretary of State in relation to a proposed application for a development consent order, the only obligatory requirements are:

- a plan sufficient to identify the land;
- a brief description of the nature and purpose of the development and its possible effects on the environment; and
- such other information or representations as the person making the request may wish to provide or make (reg 8(3)).

Where the request is to a relevant authority in relation to the discharge of a requirement, in addition to the reference number of the DCO, the applicant must provide:

- an explanation of the likely effects on the environment which were not identified at the time the DCO was made; and
- such other information or representations as the person making the request may wish to provide or make (reg 8(4)).

In practice there is generally a need to provide a fairly substantial amount of information with the request in order to make it possible for the decision-maker to give an informed (and thus useful) scoping opinion. The precise level of information that ought to be provided will be a matter of judgment in each individual case, depending on the nature of the development and the area(s) where its effects might occur.

A common approach (and one recommended by the Planning Inspectorate – see below) is to submit a scoping report, which is structured in a similar way to an ES, explaining the nature and purpose of the proposed development, describing the receiving environment, setting out the proposed approach to the process of environmental impact assessment, and then identifying the scope of the proposed assessment on a topic-by-topic basis.

Form of scoping opinion

A number of scoping opinions provided by the IPC and subsequently the Planning Inspectorate (on behalf of the Secretary of State) in relation to on-going projects are available to download from the Planning Inspectorate's website, and provide a useful guide as to what to expect.

The structure adopted by the Planning Inspectorate for its scoping opinions is to provide:

- an executive summary;
- an introductory section which identifies what the Secretary of State has done in order to satisfy the requirements of reg 8 and to inform his opinion;
- a description of the proposed development and the site and surroundings based on the information provided by the applicant, together with the Secretary of State's comments on that information to inform the process of environmental impact assessment;
- specific comments on the applicant's approach to EIA and the relevant topic areas set out in the applicant's scoping report; and
- a final section which does not formally comprise part of the scoping opinion, but responds to other issues the Secretary of State has identified which may help to inform the preparation of the application for the DCO. This might include information on additional procedural steps made necessary (or desirable) by the presence of protected habitats or species in the receiving environment, the need for information on other regulatory regimes etc.

Appended to the scoping opinion should be a list of consultees, copies of the responses received to consultation and general advice on the presentation of information in the ES.

Secretary of State not precluded from asking for further information

Obtaining a scoping opinion, and then undertaking the process of EIA in a way that reflects that opinion, does not guarantee that the resulting ES will be judged to be adequate. Regulation 8(10) makes explicit that neither the Secretary of State nor a relevant authority shall be precluded from asking for further information, notwithstanding what may have been said in the scoping opinion.

Guidance

The Planning Inspectorate's advice on the scoping process is set out in Advice Note 7: Screening and Scoping under the EIA Regulations. No further advice has been provided by the Department for Communities and Local Government, although applicants may also wish to have regard to the guidance issued by the European Commission on Scoping in 2001: see 'Guidance on EIA: Scoping' (June 2001).

Information requirements

In addition to summarising the relevant requirements under the EIA Regulations, Advice Note 7 explains that the Planning Inspectorate would find it helpful to be provided with the following additional information identified in s 3 (screening).

- The plan to identify the land required under reg 8(3) should include the following:
  - the proposed DCO site boundary;
  - the location of the NSIP and any associated development;
  - any permanent land take required for the NSIP;
  - any temporary land take required for construction, including off-site construction compounds;
  - any retained infrastructure which would be retained or upgraded for use as part of the NSIP and any existing infrastructure which would be removed; and
  - features including planning constrains and designated areas on and around the site, such as national parks or historic landscapes.
- Where practical the information should be included on a single plan. Where more than one plan is used, the plans should be at the same scale and a key plan should be provided.
- Photographs of the site and sensitive receptors, and photomontages as appropriate.
- OS Grid references (for linear schemes).
- In describing the development and its possible effects, the information should be set out using the headings in Sch 3 to the EIA Regulations and applicants should ensure that all aspects of the environment likely to be significantly affected by the development are addressed.

Developers are advised to consider the timing of any request carefully so as to obtain the most benefit from the process, waiting until there is sufficient certainty about the description of the scheme likely to have a significant environmental effect.

The Advice Note recommends that the applicant should submit the request in the form of a scoping report, and provides the following advice as to what such a report should contain.

- An outline of the main alternatives considered and the reason for selecting a preferred option.
- Results of desktop and baseline studies where available.
- Guidance and best practice to be relied upon, and whether this has been agreed with the relevant bodies, together with copies of correspondence to support these agreements.
- Methods used or proposed to be used to predict impacts and the significance criteria framework used.
- Any mitigation proposed and predicted residual impacts.
- Where cumulative development has been identified, how the developer intends to assess these impacts in the environmental statement.
- An indication of any European designated nature conservation sites that are likely to be significantly affected, and the nature of those effects.
- Where a developer seeks to scope out matters, a full justification for doing so, preferable supported by evidence of agreement with the relevant bodies (preferably presented in a tabular format).
- Key topics covered as part of the scoping exercise.
- An outline of the structure of the proposed ES.

It is also suggested that the scoping report should identify the details of the proposed NSIP likely to have significant environmental effects. Where there is uncertainty, as much detail as possible should be provided in the form of parameters, or a worst case should be assumed.

A completed trans-boundary screening matrix should also be provided to facilitate the Secretary of State's consideration under reg 24 of the EIA Regulations.

Procedural advice

Developers are advised to undertake their own informal consultation with the prescribed consultation bodies prior to submitting their request to the Secretary of State, so as to inform the request that they make.

They are also advised to give the Planning Inspectorate a minimum of ten working days' notice in advance of seeking a scoping opinion, accompanied by a GIS shapefile to identify the land in question. This will enable the Planning Inspectorate to allocate resources and identify the prescribed consultation bodies.

Advice Note 7 also contains more detailed advice on referencing and administrative matters, which applicants should follow when preparing their requests.

Preparation of an Environmental Statement

Written by: Hereward Phillpot QC, ftb
Edited by: Michael Humphries QC, ftb

Infrastructure Planning (Environmental Impact Assessment) Regulations 2009, SI 1009/2263

The Infrastructure Planning (Environmental Impact Assessment) Regulations 2009, SI 2009/2263 (the 'EIA Regulations'), reg 9 sets out a procedure intended to facilitate the preparation of an environmental statement (ES).

Pursuant to reg 9(1) and (2), the procedure may be triggered by one of four possible events:

- the applicant notifying the Secretary of State under regulation 6(1)(b) of the EIA Regulations that it intends to provide an ES in respect of a proposed application for a development consent order (DCO);
- the applicant notifying the authority responsible for the discharge of a requirement on an existing DCO (the relevant authority) under regulation 6(2)(b) of the EIA Regulations that it intends to provide an updated ES in respect of a proposed application to discharge the requirement;
- the Secretary of State giving a screening opinion in respect of a proposed application for a DCO to the effect that the proposed development is EIA development; or
- the relevant authority giving a subsequent screening opinion to the effect that supplementary information is needed to enable it to determine an application to discharge a requirement.

The procedure itself is prescribed by reg 9(1), and involves a number of steps that the Secretary of State or the relevant authority, as the case may be, must follow.

The consultation bodies (defined in reg 2(1) of the EIA Regulations) must be notified in writing of the name and address of the applicant, and of the duty imposed on those bodies by reg 9(3) to make information available to that person. The duty is subject to the exceptions from the duty to disclose environmental information under the Environmental Information Regulations 2004 or the equivalent Scottish legislation (see reg 9(4)).

The applicant must be notified in writing of the names and addresses of the bodies so notified.

The applicant must also be notified in writing of any person whom it considers: (a) to be, or to be likely to be, affected by or to have an interest in the proposed development; and (b) to be unlikely to become aware of the proposed development by means of the pre-application and application procedure in Part 5 of the Planning Act 2008 (ie pre-application consultation etc).

Preparation of ES

The law, guidance and good practice on the preparation of ES is extensive, and it would be unrealistic to seek to provide a comprehensive guide to those matters in this article. Instead, the article to provide a brief overview of the key points, including those which have now been set down in the guidance issued by the Planning Inspectorate on behalf of the Secretary of State.

General case law

As the courts have become increasingly familiar with the process of EIA, so the potential pitfalls have become better mapped and understood, and the degree of risk associated with the process has reduced and become more readily manageable. A realistic and pragmatic approach to the process of EIA and the contents of ES has developed, recognising that there will often be room for legitimate disagreement as to the appropriate scope and content of an ES, without any issue of law arising.

The following key principles can be discerned:

- The ES does not have to contain every scrap of environmental information, and need only cover the main effects or likely significant effects. Excessive information can be a hindrance to good decision-making (see eg *R v Rochdale Metropolitan Borough Council, ex parte Milne* (2000) 81 P&CR 27; *R (Bedford) v London Borough of Islington* [2002] EWHC 2044 (Admin); *Derbyshire Waste Ltd v Blewett and Secretary of State for the Environment* [2004] EWCA Civ 1508).
- Where a project is to be approved in stages, with details of some matters reserved for approval at a later stage, the ES accompanying the application for the 'in principle' approval must allow the decision-maker to understand the likely significant effects of the project as a whole (see eg *R v London Borough of Bromley, ex parte Barker* [2006] UKHL 52).
- To enable this to be done, clear parameters will need to be established for the purpose of EIA, and secured in the approval so that the effects of the development as approved do not exceed those assessed (see *R v. Rochdale Metropolitan Borough Council, ex parte Milne* (above)). This will often be an important issue with NSIPs, where much of the detail is likely to remain at large at the DCO stage. In this regard, further guidance has been issued by the Planning Inspectorate on how to deal with the resulting uncertainties (see below).
- Where a development is linked to a larger project, the ES for that development must consider the cumulative effects that are likely to arise as a result (see eg *R (Brown) v Carlisle City Council* [2010] EWCA Civ 523).
- It is important that members of the public do not have to engage in a 'paper chase' to piece together the ES, which must therefore be a properly integrated and accessible document accompanied by a non-technical summary (see *Berkeley v Secretary of State for the Environment* [2001] 2 AC 603).
- An ES will not be adequate if it lacks a key piece of information necessary to ascertain whether significant effects are likely. It is not acceptable to leave the gathering of that additional information until after consent has been granted

(*R v Cornwall County Council, ex parte Hardy* [2001] Env LR 25). That is to be distinguished from situations where it is possible to reach a conclusion on likely significant effects without certain information, but provision is made for that information to be gathered after permission is granted so as to inform mitigation measures etc (see eg *R (PPG 11 Ltd) v Dorset County Council* [2003] All ER (D) 68 (Jun)).

- Mitigation measures can be taken into account in determining likely significant effects, although these must be secured in any consent that is granted, and their likely effectiveness must be taken into account (see eg *R (PPG 11 Ltd) v Dorset County Council* (above)).

Guidance

The Planning Inspectorate's guidance on the preparation of an ES is contained in a series of Advice Notes. Those of most direct relevance here are Advice Note 3: EIA Consultation and Notification, and Advice Note 9: Using the 'Rochdale Envelope'.

Advice Note 3: EIA Consultation and Notification

Advice Note 3 sets out the approach to be taken by the Secretary of State when identifying consultation bodies to be notified under reg 9 of the EIA Regulations and, where relevant, consulted on the scope of the ES under reg 8.

It explains that in addition to providing the applicant with the list of the notified consultation bodies, the Secretary of State will also provide details of any 'non-prescribed consultation bodies', where appropriate. These 'non-prescribed' bodies are those with relevant functions and responsibilities but which are not prescribed under s 42(a) of the PA 2008. The applicant is therefore not obliged to consult with them in order to satisfy the pre-application consultation obligations.

The Secretary of State's list of notified consultation bodies will be used in due course as part of the process of determining whether the applicant has complied with the pre-application procedure. If the applicant identifies and consults fewer bodies than appear on the list, a clear explanation will be needed.

The Advice Note sets out in detail the approach that the Secretary of State will adopt when consulting and notifying in relation to the following activities:

- identifying local authorities;
- applying the 'relevance test' of the APFP Regulations;
- applying the 'circumstances test' of the APFP Regulations;
- identifying statutory undertakers as prescribed in the APFP Regulations;
- identifying parish/community councils;
- notifying and consulting in Wales;
- notifying and consulting the devolved administrations and the British Crown dependencies;

- notifying and consulting where a proposed NSIP includes an offshore element; and
- notifying other European Economic Area states.

Advice Note 9: Using the 'Rochdale Envelope'

The principles behind the use of the 'Rochdale Envelope' and the guidance on its use in Advice Note 9 are both considered in more detail in Article 11.2.5 ('Flexibility and alternatives'), but the points summarised below are of particular relevance to the preparation of the ES.

- The developer should seek to identify those aspects of the development that are likely to give rise to significant adverse impacts, such that the maximum potential adverse impacts have been properly assessed and can be taken into account.
- The ES must consider the inter-relationship between aspects of the proposed development, and explain how these have been assessed to address the environmental impacts as a whole.
- Where certain details remain unresolved, the ES will need to clearly identify those elements; provide reasons why these cannot be finalised at this stage; and assess variations of the proposals so as to capture the likely worst case within the parameters set (this should be done as simply as possible, and in a manner that aids the making of recommendations and decision-making).
- In identifying potential cumulative impacts with other major developments, applicants should seek to identify relevant developments through consultation with local planning authorities and other relevant authorities on the basis of those that are:
    - under construction;
    - permitted application(s) not yet determined;
    - projects on the Planning Inspectorate's Programme of Projects;
    - identified in the relevant Development Plan (and emerging Development Plans – with appropriate weight being given as they move closer to adoption); and
    - identified in other plans and programmes which set the framework for future development consents/approvals, where such development is likely to come forward.
- The applicant will need to judge whether the undecided parameters are such as to preclude a robust assessment in the ES, and should ensure that the parameters are not so wide ranging as to represent effectively different schemes. The parameters need to be clearly defined in the draft DCO and in the ES.

Environmental Impact Assessment: Trans-Boundary Consultation

Written by: Hereward Phillpot QC, ftb
Edited by: Michael Humphries QC, ftb

The issue

When should the Secretary of State initiate the process of trans-boundary consultation on the environmental effects of a proposed nationally significant infrastructure project (NSIP), how is the decision made, and what steps should be taken by promoters to address this question?

The law

The relevant law is to be found in the Infrastructure Planning (Environmental Impact Assessment) Regulations 2009, SI 2009/2263 (the '2009 Regulations'), reg 24 which transpose the requirements of Article 7 of EU Directive 2011/92/EU (the EIA Directive) into domestic law. Article 7 and Regulation 24 apply to European Economic Area ('EEA') States by virtue of section 2(2) of the European Communities Act 1972 as modified by section 2(5) of the European Economic Area Act 1993.

Regulation 24 provides:

> '(1) This regulation applies where–
>
> (a) one of the events mentioned in regulation 4(2) occurs; or
>
> (b) it otherwise comes to the attention of the Secretary of State that development proposed to be carried out in England, Wales or Scotland is the subject of an EIA application, and the Secretary of State is of the view that the development is likely to have significant effects on the environment in another EEA State; or
>
> (c) another EEA State likely to be significantly affected by such development so requests.
>
> (2) Where this regulation applies, the Secretary of State must–
>
> (a) send to the EEA State as soon as possible and no later than their date of publication in The London Gazette referred to in sub-paragraph (b), the particulars required by paragraph (3) and, if it thinks fit, the information referred to in paragraph (4);
>
> (b) publish the information in sub-paragraph (a) in a notice placed in–
>
> (i) the London Gazette, in relation to all proposed development; and
>
> (ii) the Edinburgh Gazette, in relation to development proposed to be carried out in Scotland,

indicating the address where additional information is available; and

(c) give the EEA State a reasonable time in which to indicate whether it wishes to participate in the procedure for which these Regulations provide.

(3) The particulars mentioned in paragraph (2)(a) are–

(a) a description of the development, together with any available information on its possible significant effect on the environment in another EEA State; and

(b) information on the nature of the decision which may be taken.

(4) Where an EEA State indicates, in accordance with paragraph (2)(c), that it wishes to participate in the procedure for which these Regulations provide, the Secretary of State must as soon as possible send to that EEA State the following information–

(a) a copy of the application concerned;

(b) a copy of any environmental statement in respect of the development to which that application relates; and

(c) relevant information regarding the procedure under these Regulations,

but only to the extent that such information has not been provided to the EEA State earlier in accordance with paragraph 2(a).

(5) The Commission must also ensure that the EEA State concerned is given an opportunity, before development consent for the development is granted, to forward to the Secretary of State, within a reasonable time, the opinions of its public and the authorities referred to in Article 6(1) of the Directive on the information supplied.

(6) The Commission must in accordance with Article 7(4) of the Directive–

(a) enter into consultations with the EEA State concerned regarding, inter alia, the potential significant effects of the development on the environment of that EEA State and the measures envisaged to reduce or eliminate such effects; and

(b) determine in agreement with the other EEA State a reasonable period of time for the duration of the consultation period.

(7) Where an EEA State has been consulted in accordance with paragraph (6), on the determination of the application concerned the Secretary of State must inform the EEA State of the decision and must forward to it a statement of–

(a) the content of the decision and any requirements attached to it;

(b) the main reasons and considerations on which the decision is based including relevant information about the participation of the public; and

(c) a description, where necessary, of the main measures to avoid, reduce and, if possible, offset the major adverse effects of the development.'

Thus the trans-boundary consultation process can be triggered either by the Secretary of State reaching the view that the proposed development is likely to have significant effects on the environment in another EEA State, or as a result of a request from another EEA State. An example of the latter scenario occurred during the process of determining the application for the proposed new nuclear power station at Hinkley Point in Somerset, where the Austrian Government made a request following the close of the examination. The Austrian Government consulted its own people on the proposed application, and the views expressed in response were taken into account by the Secretary of State in reaching his decision.

All NSIPs that are EIA development will be screened by the Planning Inspectorate on the Secretary of State's behalf on a case by case basis for likely significant effects on another EEA State.

In reaching a view on whether to initiate the process, the Secretary of State must decide whether significant environmental effects on other EEA States are 'likely'.

The Court of Appeal has held that for these purposes 'likely' should be interpreted in the same way as it has been where it appears elsewhere in the 2009 Regulations and the EIA Directive (*R (on the application of An Taisce) v (1) The Secretary of State for Energy and Climate Change (2) NNB Generation Company Limited* [2014] EWCA Civ 1111). An Taisce (The National Trust for Ireland) had argued that a significant adverse effect should be considered 'likely' if it cannot be excluded on the basis of objective evidence. This approach, mirroring that taken by the ECJ to the Habitats Directive in the *Waddenzee* case, was rejected by the Court of Appeal, which held that:

1 The words 'likely to have significant effects on the environment' must have the same meaning throughout the EIA Directive.

2 'Likely' for these purposes does not mean more probable than not.

3 There is a clear distinction between the Habitats Directive and the EIA Directive for these purposes.

4 The 'real risk' approach to likelihood that the domestic authorities have so far adopted when considering the EIA Directive embodies a precautionary approach.

5 Adopting An Taisce's suggested approach would be contrary to the objectives of the EIA Directive as the public and decision-makers would be likely to 'lose the wood for the trees', thereby causing the EIA process to become less effective as an aid to good environmental decision-making.

In deciding whether a project is 'likely' to have a significant adverse effect on the environment of another EEA State, the Secretary of State should therefore approach the question on the basis of whether this is a 'real risk' or a 'serious possibility'. This involves considering both the magnitude and complexity of the potential impact, and the probability of it occurring. The greater the potential impact, the lower will be the level of probability at which the competent authority will decide that it should be subject to the environmental impact assessment process (see *Miller v North Yorkshire CC* [2009] EWHC 2172 (Admin) per Hickinbottom J at paragraphs 31 and 32). The competent authority must therefore make a judgment, balancing the severity of any potential environmental harm against the probability of it occurring.

Once triggered, the process takes place in two stages. First, the paragraph (2) stage involves notification of the EEA State concerned, and providing it with an opportunity to consider whether it wishes to participate. For these purposes the EEA State need only be given relatively limited information about the project (paragraph (3)), although in practice it is likely that it would be provided with a copy of the environmental statement.

If the EEA State in question decides that it does not wish to participate, that is the end of the process. However, if it decides to participate it is then sent a copy of the application, the environmental statement and procedural information and given an opportunity to consult its public and provide their views to the Secretary of State (paragraphs (4) and (5)).

It is the EEA State concerned that must consult its public, and not the Secretary of State. The Secretary of State's role is confined to facilitating the process of consultation through notification and the provision of information, and then taking the results of that consultation into account in making his decision on the application. If the consultation process undertaken by the relevant EEA State is materially defective, however, there may be grounds on which the Secretary of State's ultimate decision could be challenged in the Courts.

Guidance

The Planning Inspectorate's guidance on the trans-boundary consultation process is contained in Advice Note 12: Development with significant trans-boundary impacts consultation (2012).

In addition to providing an explanation of the legal background and the approach adopted by the Planning Inspectorate and the Government, Advice Note 12 also guides promoters on their role in making sure that the relevant information is available at the appropriate times.

Whilst it is important to read the guidance as a whole, the following key points emerge for those who are promoting NSIPs:

1. It is for promoters, and it is in their best interests, to undertake consultation with specific EEA States where they believe there may be significant trans-boundary effects. They may also wish to consult environmental bodies and relevant interest groups within that State. This should be done as part of the process of pre-application consultation.
2. Care must be taken in seeking to identify the relevant bodies and groups in other States. The Planning Inspectorate's list of contacts in the closest EEA States to the UK is set out in Annexe 3 to Advice Note 12.
3. Promoters are strongly encouraged to grapple with the issue of potential trans-boundary impacts as part of their request for a scoping opinion. This should be done as early as possible.

4 It is recommended that a screening matrix is used for these purposes, and a checklist indicating the level of detail to be provided is set out in Annexe 4 to Advice Note 12.

5 Where relevant, the draft application and environmental statement should be sent to the EEA State concerned as soon as they are sufficiently detailed to enable meaningful comments to be made.

6 Engagement with such EEA States should take place as early as possible, not least to reduce the prospects of it being found that there are likely to be significant adverse trans-boundary effects which the developer has not taken appropriate steps to avoid, reduce and if possible offset. If that situation were to arise, 'there may be no alternative at that stage but to refuse development consent'.

7 Unless developers are able to demonstrate to the Planning Inspectorate's reasonable satisfaction that their development will not have significant trans-boundary effects, they should act with caution and prepare their application documents and undertake consultation on the basis that there may be such effects and the Secretary of State will notify the relevant EEA State.

The guidance explains that the Secretary of State will adopt a precautionary approach to the issue of likelihood, although in itself this does not seem to represent any deviation from what is required in any event as a matter of law (see the *An Taisce* case above). However, it then goes further and states that as 'a rule of thumb ... unless there is compelling evidence to suggest otherwise' it is likely that nuclear power stations and off-shore generating stations in a Renewable Energy Zone will be considered likely to have significant trans-boundary effects.

So far, only one new nuclear power station has been screened by the Planning Inspectorate (using the 2011 version of Advice Note 12 which contained the same guidance), and in that case it was considered that there was compelling evidence that significant trans-boundary effects were not likely. The reason for reaching this view was that reliance could be placed on the strict system of licensing and regulation to ensure that accidental release of radioactive materials was not likely to occur. On the basis that the same system applies to all new nuclear power stations in the United Kingdom, it seems unlikely that any other such proposals would be regarded as likely to give rise to significant trans-boundary effects by reason of accidental release of radioactive materials.

Advice Note 12 also gives guidance on the approach to be taken to the timing of the different stages of the trans-boundary process. A period of six weeks will usually be provided for the initial stage of notification (subject to considering reasonable representations from the EEA State concerned that a longer period should be allowed). Similarly, it is said that a six week period would be reasonable for the second stage, namely consultation with the public of the EEA State concerned. In order to meet the statutory examination deadline the consultation period should in any event close no later than the first month in the examination period.

Discussion

The profile of the issue of trans-boundary consultation has been raised as a result of the *An Taisce* litigation. It is also important to note that the Committee set up to monitor compliance with the obligations created by the original legal source of the trans-boundary consultation requirement – the UNECE Convention on Environmental Impact Assessment in a Trans-boundary Conext (the Espoo Convention) – has become increasingly active and interventionist.

Failure to undertake trans-boundary consultation where it ought to have taken place can therefore present a significant litigation risk.

Whilst the Court of Appeal in the *An Taisce* case rejected the argument that a significant trans-boundary effect was 'likely' for these purposes if it cannot be excluded on the basis of objective evidence, it did not entirely close the door on future litigation to determine what is in fact the correct approach to likelihood for the purposes of EIA. On the facts of that particular case it was successfully argued by the Secretary of State and the promoter that no matter how low the threshold might be set by the Court of Justice of the European Union (CJEU), the Secretary of State's decision would still be lawful. Once the Claimant's 'zero risk' approach had been rejected, it was therefore unnecessary to decide whether the 'real risk' approach might be overturned by the CJEU in order to dispose of the case.

However, at paragraph 33 Sullivan LJ said that if the Court of Appeal were a court of final appeal, and it was therefore necessary to apply the '*CILFIT* test':

> '... I could not say that I was convinced that the other Member States and the CJEU would necessarily conclude that the 'real risk' approach is the correct approach to the likelihood of significant effects on the environment for the purposes of the EIA Directive'.

The '*CILFIT* test' is a reference to the case of *CILFIT (Srl) v Ministry of Health* (Case 283/81) [1982] ECR 3415, concerning the approach to be taken by a court of final appeal to the issue of whether or not a reference should be made to the European Court of Justice (CJEU). In the *CILFIT* case the CJEU said that the national court could only refrain from submitting a question of EU law to the CJEU if it is convinced that the correct application of EU law is so obvious as to leave no scope for any reasonable doubt as to the manner in which the question raised is to be resolved, and convinced that the matter would be equally obvious to the courts of the other Member States and the CJEU.

Sullivan LJ's comment seems to create room for future argument as to what the correct approach should be, albeit in another case with stronger facts. Importantly, it creates room for an argument that a reference ought to be made to the CJEU, an outcome which any promoter should regard with great concern because of the considerable delay and uncertainty that a reference necessarily brings with it.

The cautious approach espoused by the guidance would therefore seem prudent. In most cases promoters ought not to have much to fear from the trans-boundary consultation process. If there is a real risk of significant adverse trans-boundary effects, the process of assessment and pre-application consultation itself may be complicated by the need to deal with another State, but if done properly it is likely to be less risky than the alternative.

Habitats Regulations Assessment

Written by: Gregory Jones QC, ftb
Edited by: Michael Humphries QC, ftb

Introduction

This article considers the circumstances in which an NSIP will require an appropriate assessment under the Conservation of Habitats and Species Regulations 2010, SI 2010/490 (as amended) ('the Habitats Regulations'), the information that should inform such an assessment and the consequences arising out of such an assessment.

This article should be read in conjunction with those considering the EIA process, which will often overlap with assessment under the Habitats Regulations. Although the EIA process is designed to *inform* the final decision, whereas assessment under the Habitats Regulations may, in certain circumstances, actually *determine* the final decision, (see eg Lord Carnwath Foreword to Jones: 'Habitats Directive: A Developer's Obstacle Course?).

The legislative background

The UK is bound by the terms of Council Directive 92/43/EEC of 21 May 1992 on the conservation of natural habitats and of wild fauna and flora ('the Habitats Directive') which has been transposed into domestic law through the Habitats Regulations. Although we are here mainly concerned with Articles 2 and 3 of the Habitats Directive, as the case law has emphasised the need for it to be considered as a whole, the whole of Article 6 is set out below:

1 For special areas of conservation, Member States shall establish the necessary conservation measures involving, if need be, appropriate management plans specifically designed for the sites or integrated into other development plans, and appropriate statutory, administrative or contractual measures which correspond to the ecological requirements of the natural habitat types in Annex I and the species in Annex II present on the sites.

2 Member States shall take appropriate steps to avoid, in the special areas of conservation, the deterioration of natural habitats and the habitats of species as well as disturbance of the species for which the areas have been designated, in so far as such disturbance could be significant in relation to the objectives of this Directive.

3 Any plan or project not directly connected with or necessary to the management of the site but likely to have a significant effect thereon, either individually or in combination with other plans or projects, shall be subject to appropriate assessment of its implications for the site in view of the site's conservation objectives. In the light of the conclusions of the assessment of the implications for the site and subject to the provisions of paragraph 4, the competent national authorities

shall agree to the plan or project only after having ascertained that it will not adversely affect the integrity of the site concerned and, if appropriate, after having obtained the opinion of the general public.

4 If, in spite of a negative assessment of the implications for the site and in the absence of alternative solutions, a plan or project must nevertheless be carried out for imperative reasons of overriding public interest, including those of a social or economic nature, the Member State shall take all compensatory measures necessary to ensure that the overall coherence of Natura 2000 is protected. It shall inform the Commission of the compensatory measures adopted.

5 Where the site concerned hosts a priority natural habitat type and/or a priority species, the only considerations which may be raised are those relating to human health or public safety, to beneficial consequences of primary importance for the environment or, further to an opinion from the Commission, to other imperative reasons of overriding public interest.

The effect of these provisions in the UK is that any plan or project which may affect a Special Area of Conservation ('SAC'), a candidate SAC or a Special Protection Area ('SPA') is subject to Regulations. In addition, the UK Government has a policy of applying their provisions to both Ramsar sites and potential SPAs. In the text that follows, these are referred to simply as 'sites'.

The process of assessment under the Habitats Regulations

PINS Advice Note 10 on *Habitats Regulation Assessment* (January 2013) follows the European Commission's *Methodological Guidance on the Provisions of Articles 6(3) and (4) of the Habitats Directive* in breaking down the process down into four stages (screening, appropriate assessment, alternative solutions and imperative reasons of overriding public interest, or 'IROPI'), and that approach is adopted here for consistency.

In relation to stages 3 and 4, it is noted that the Department for the Environment, Food and Rural Affairs has recently consulted upon draft guidance on *Alternative solutions, imperative reasons of overriding public interest (IROPI) and compensatory measures.* It is to be expected that final guidance on these matters will be forthcoming in due course.

Stage 1: Screening

Article 6(3) of the Directive requires an Appropriate Assessment to be carried out where there is a plan or project, that is not connected to the management of the site, but is 'likely to have a significant effect' upon the site either individually or in combination.

In Case C-258/11 *Sweetman v An Bord Pleanála*, in her opinion, the Advocate-General ('the AG') succinctly summed up in plain language the purpose behind this stage as requiring developers to ask the question 'should we bother to check' whether the plan or project adversely affects the integrity of the site? Stage 1 is therefore a preliminary stage.

When is an effect 'likely'? It does not have the same meaning as the English civil law test of 'more likely than not' (ie more than 50%). Applying the so-called 'precautionary approach' (see micro article 100) the courts have given the word 'likely' a much wider definition that an ordinary reading of the word might suggest. While to most it suggests an event that might well occur, cases such as Case C-127/02 *Landelijke Vereniging tot Behoud van de Waddenzee* [2004] ECR I-7405, *R (Loader) v Secretary of State for Communities and Local Government* [2012] EWCA Civ 869 and *R (Bateman) v South Cambridgeshire DC* [2011] EWCA Civ 157 put it beyond doubt that the correct approach is to look for effects that 'such a risk exists if it cannot be excluded on the basis of objective information that the plan or project will have significant effects on the site concerned' and 'in the case of doubt about the absence of significant effects … an assessment must be carried out' (see *Waddenzee*, para 44). An effect is therefore likely where there is only a risk, or a mere possibility, of it occurring.

What is a 'significant effect'? To all intents and purposes, the definition of significant effects appeared settled after *Waddenzee*, which held that where 'a plan or project has an effect on that site but is not likely to undermine its conservation objectives, it cannot be considered likely to have a significant effect on the site concerned' (see para 47). *Waddenzee* continued at para 48 to say that where those objectives were undermined, it necessarily followed that there were significant effects. The focus therefore was clearly on the 'characteristics and specific environmental conditions of the site concerned by that plan or project' that went to the sites conservation objectives (also at para 48).

However, the recent *Sweetman* case, on one reading, modifies this approach. There, the AG's opinion's was that 'significant' set a 'very low' de minimis threshold excluding only those sites that have 'no appreciable effect on the site'. That threshold 'operates as a trigger, in order to determine whether an appropriate assessment must be undertaken'. However, the AG also considered that the threshold was not so low as to not exclude plans or projects 'having any effect whatsoever on the site' (emphasis added) so as not to prevent all activities on or near the site becoming 'impossible by reason of legislative overkill' (see paras 48 to 49).

Although the AG did not refer to *Waddenzee* in this part of her opinion, the Court did in its decision, albeit only to set out what was said in *Waddenzee*: 'Where a plan or project not directly connected with or necessary to the management of a site is likely to undermine the site's conservation objectives, it must be considered likely to have a significant effect on that site. The assessment of that risk must be made in the light of, in particular, the characteristics and specific environmental conditions of the site concerned by such a plan or project' (see para 30). It therefore seems that the better view is that the focus remains on the site's conservation objectives.

In assessing both significance and likelihood, it is permissible and indeed desirable, to have regard to mitigation measures. If the appropriate authority considers that those measures will be effective, it can base its conclusion that significant effects are unlikely upon then, and dispense with the need for an appropriate assessment. In *Feeney v Secretary of State for Transport* [2013] EWHC 1238 (Admin), Ouseley J held that if the appropriate authority 'lawfully concludes that the [mitigation] would exclude [the risk of a significant effect] on the basis of objective information, it is difficult to see on what basis an appropriate assessment could still be required' (see para 53). However, as the *A5 Alliance* [2013] NIQB 30 case demonstrates, doubts about the efficacy of proposed mitigation measures will prevent a conclusion that significant effects are unlikely, and an appropriate assessment will be required.

Although the recent decision in *Champion v North Norfolk DC* [2013] EWHC 1065 (Admin) appears to cast doubt on this approach when it comes to mitigation in the form of planning conditions, it is respectfully suggested that the approach is not likely to be followed by the ECJ. There it was held that a decision maker could not determine that no appropriate assessment was required (ie that significant effects were not likely) while at the same time requiring a condition to mitigate effects (as that condition would not be necessary if those effects were not likely). This appears to be taking two limbs of what is a sequential in reverse order. The first question ought to be whether the plan or project has a condition attached to it, and the second question is whether, given that condition, the project is likely to have significant effects. If it is not, then an appropriate assessment will not be required.

The evidence base at Stage 1 screening

Regulation 61(2) of the Habitats Regulations places a mandatory requirement on a person applying for development consent to provide the appropriate authority with such information as may be required: (a) for the purposes of the appropriate assessment; or (b) to enable them to determine whether an appropriate assessment is required. If insufficient information is submitted for those purposes, the competent authority may, and most likely will, refuse to accept the application for a DCO.

It is therefore necessary to engage in a robust process of pre-application consultation with the relevant statutory nature conservation bodies to ensure that the potential impacts of the development have been identified and addressed in sufficient detail before submission. It is likely that this process will overlap with the consultation required for EIA purposes. It is also good practice to consult more widely.

It is noted here that practice in the UK in relation to the information to be provided at the screening stage goes beyond what would otherwise be thought to be required in light of the AG in *Sweetman* characterising the first stage as the 'should we bother to check?' stage. Instead, as PINS Guidance Note 10 makes clear, the level of detail expected to accompany application is high, such that it 'should result in information which will show beyond reasonable doubt whether any European sites are likely to be affected... describe the likely impacts on the conservation objectives of the European sites ... and describe whether the impacts are likely to be significantly adverse'. It is therefore the case that a substantial amount of work may have to be undertaken prior to submission in order to clear this hurdle, notwithstanding that the European approach seems to contemplate a less exacting standard at this stage of the process.

PINS Guidance Note 10 lists the following as issues that developers 'may' (read 'should') wish to include in their stage one screening assessment or report:

- a detailed description of the development, processes, timings, and method of work;
- proposed details of the methodology used to determine which European sites to include within the assessment;
- a plan and description of the European site(s) and all of the associated interest features potentially affected;
- an appraisal of the project's likely impacts on the European site(s);

- an outline and interpretation of baseline data;
- an appraisal of any other plans or projects likely to have a significant effect in combination with the proposed development;
- an evaluation of the potential for the scheme to require two or more appropriate assessments by different competent authorities, and;
- a statement which specifies where the site boundaries of the scheme overlap into devolved assemblies or other European member states.

That screening report will have to come to one of two conclusions: (a) there is no potential likely significant effect on a site; or (b) an anticipated potential significant effect on a site exists.

Where screening concludes that there will be no potential likely significant effect on a site, it will be necessary to produce a 'no significant effects screening report'. There is no template for this report, but it must make it clear what the developer's view is and contain sufficient information to enable the competent authority to reach its own (hopefully concurring) view.

Where screening concludes that there is an anticipated potential likely significant effect on a European site, alone of in combination with other projects, the applicant's HRA needs to move to Stage 2 (Appropriate Assessment) of the HRA process.

The report on the outcome of screening assessment should clearly identify which European sites are being taken forward to Stage 2 (Appropriate Assessment) and which have been screened out.

Stage 2: Appropriate Assessment

Having established that a plan or project is likely to have significant effects on the site, the next stage is to subject the plan or project to an 'appropriate assessment of its implications for the site in view of the site's conservation objectives'.

The question the appropriate assessment addresses is whether the plan or project will 'adversely affect the integrity of the site concerned'. It is not immediately clear from the English language version what that phrase means, and its interpretation was precisely the question the court considered in *Sweetman*.

The AG's opinion was that 'integrity' was directed at the 'essential unity' of the site (see paras 53 to 56). Adopting a purposive approach to interpretation, in making the determination as to whether integrity was affected, it was again necessary to focus on why the site was designated and what its conservation objectives were. If attributes of the site going to its designation and conservation objectives were adversely affected by the proposed plan or project, then so would be its integrity. Further, it was necessary to make the assessment on the basis of the precautionary principle – only if the appropriate authority were 'convinced' that the plan or project would not affect the integrity of the site could that finding properly be made (see para 51). On that basis, a temporary loss of part of the site, perhaps during construction works, is less likely to result in an adverse effect on integrity than a permanent loss.

The CJEU expressly adopted the AG's opinion in holding that the integrity of a site will not be adversely affected where the plan or project permits the 'lasting preservation of the constitutive characteristics of the site concerned that are connected to the presence of a natural habitat type whose preservation was the objective justifying the designation of that site…' (see para 39).

The CJEU emphasised (at para 40) that having made that assessment, the precautionary principle required that authorisation could only be granted 'on condition that the competent authorities – once all aspects of the plan or project have been identified which can, by themselves or in combination with other plans or projects, affect the conservation objectives of the site concerned, and in the light of the best scientific knowledge in the field – are certain that the plan or project will not have lasting adverse effects on the integrity of that site. That is so where no reasonable scientific doubt remains as to the absence of such effects.'

The PINS Guidance suggests that as a minimum, the applicant's HRA report should contain:

- evidence about the project's impacts on the integrity of protected sites
- a description of any mitigation measures proposed which avoid or reduce each impact, and any residual effect
- a schedule indicating the timing of mitigation measures in relation to the progress of the development
- cross references to the relevant DCO requirements and development consent obligations that secure these mitigation measures, and identification of any factors that might affect the certainty of their implementation
- a statement as to whether any residual effects constitute an adverse impact on the integrity of European sites
- evidence to demonstrate that the applicant has fully consulted and had regard to comments received by the relevant SNCBs during pre-application consultation.

Stage 3: Assessment of alternative solutions

Where, having carried out an appropriate assessment and come to the view that the integrity of the site will be adversely affected, authorisation can only be granted where a further assessment has been carried out and concluded that there are no alternative *solutions* to the proposed development, not just alternative developments. This is an onerous hurdle to clear and will require a detailed and thorough examination of alternative solutions to deliver the objectives of the project. That assessment will include considering, at a minimum, not going ahead with the project, as well as locating the project in other regions or even countries. It must be objectively demonstrated that there are no other feasible alternatives that will not affect the integrity of the site, and that the proposal is the least damaging of all the solutions as regards the integrity of the site and the habitats and species therein. The assessment of whether there are alternative sites must be based solely on ecological criteria; matters of economics and social policy are only considered at stage 4.

Stage 4: Imperative Reasons of Overriding Public Interest ('IROPI')

If it is concluded that there are no alternative solutions, then development consent can only be granted if there are IROPI for granting consent. In such a case, compensatory measures must be taken.

Where the site hosts a protected species or habitat, IROPI must relate to human health, public safety or beneficial consequences of the development of primary importance to the environment or other reasons of IROPI where the advice of the European Commission has been sought and had regard to. In all other cases, this is unnecessary.

IROPI may be social or economic, but the use of the words 'imperative' and 'overriding' indicate that this too is a high threshold: the development must in essence be indispensable, and the *public* interest in it going ahead must clearly outweigh protecting the conservation objectives of the site.

Compensatory measures

Although not given as a separate stage 5 in the guidance, compensatory measures follow on from a finding that IROPI has been made out. Such measures will need to be agreed with the appropriate statutory nature conservation body and may well be both expensive and a cause of delay. Compensatory measures must protect the overall coherence of the network of European sites and may include extending sites or recreating sites elsewhere. It will usually be necessary, except where this is not possible, for compensatory measures to be delivered before the site is adversely affected. In framing compensatory measures it should be borne in mind that these measures are to 'compensate'; they do not require more than is necessary to replace what is lost.

Part 11

Other Application Documents

Book of Reference

Written by: Richard Honey, ftb
Edited by: Michael Humphries QC, ftb

Introduction

A DCO 'book of reference' is a schedule of parcels of land affected by an order, identifying persons with some connection to the land. A book of reference is not physically part of the DCO (ie it is not a schedule to the order itself), but is a separate document referred to in a DCO and thereby, in effect, incorporated within the terms of the DCO.

The book of reference to a DCO is important because the order will authorise the undertaker to acquire compulsorily the land and rights described in the book of reference and shown on the plans. Similarly, the undertaker may be authorised to remove or reposition apparatus belonging to statutory undertakers, which is described in the book of reference. For the order to work properly in practice, the book of reference needs to be accurate and complete. The book of reference also identifies particular categories of land, such as land forming part of a common, open space, or fuel or field garden allotment.

Requirements

Where relevant, an application for a DCO should be accompanied by a book of reference (the Infrastructure Planning (Applications: Prescribed Forms and Procedure) Regulations 2009, SI 2009/2264, reg 5(2)(d)).

The requirements for a book of reference are specified in reg 7. It has to be in five parts, as follows:

(1) names and addresses for service of each person within Category 1 (owner, lessee, tenant or occupier) and Category 2 (person interested in the land or having power to sell, convey or release the land), as defined in the Planning Act 2008 (PA 2008), s 57, for any land to be subject to:

  (i) powers of compulsory acquisition;

  (ii) rights to use land; or

  (iii) rights to carry out protective works to buildings (eg underpinning or strengthening);

(2) names and addresses for service of each person within Category 3 in s.57 (persons who after diligent enquiry might be entitled to make a relevant claim if the development consent order were to be made and fully implemented);

(3) names of all those entitled to enjoy easements or other private rights over land (including private rights of navigation over water) to be extinguished, suspended or interfered with;

(4) the owner of any Crown interest in the land which is proposed to be used for the purposes of the order;

(5) land:

(i) the acquisition of which is subject to special parliamentary procedure;

(ii) which is special category land; and

(iii) which is replacement land for land being compulsorily acquired.

For each part of the book of reference, the area of the land in m^2 should be stated for each plot of land within which it is intended that all or part of the proposed development and works shall be carried out.

It is important not to omit land that is to be compulsorily acquired from the book of reference, otherwise it may have to be dealt with as 'additional land' under the Infrastructure Planning (Compulsory Acquisition) Regulations 2010, SI 2010/104. Where land is being acquired by agreement it would not need to be included in the book of reference unless for example there are restrictions on the title that need to be overcome. Having said that, undertakers often include land that is to be acquired by agreement to give protection against unknown third party rights or a landowner's failure or inability to complete a sale by agreement.

Guidance

The *Planning Act 2008: Guidance related to procedures for the compulsory acquisition of land* (September 2013) makes some additional practical points, including:

- each part in the book of reference serves a different purpose and persons may need to be identified in one or more parts;
- applicants should not add any further (non-prescribed) parts to a book of reference;
- ambiguous descriptions should be avoided;
- where it is proposed to create and acquire new rights compulsorily they should be clearly identified;
- the book of reference should cross-refer to the relevant articles of the order.

The point that a person can be in more than one PA 2008, s 57 category, and listed in more than one part of the book of reference, is an important one to remember. Persons identified in Part 3 of the book of reference should generally also be recorded in Part 1, as persons within PA 2008, s 57 categories 1 or 2. If there is doubt whether a private right or easement qualifies for Part 1 it should be included in both Parts 1 and 3 so as to err on the side of caution. If a person is not identified in Part 1 of the book of reference then they would not be an affected person under PA 2008, s 92, and would not be notified under PA 2008, s 59, and so would be deprived of the opportunity to seek a compulsory acquisition hearing.

A book of reference may need to be updated during the course of an application, because information changes or new persons are identified. Amended versions could sensibly be provided to the Inspectorate with the PA 2008, s 58 certificate of compliance and also before the end of the examination.

An issue has arisen in practice where applicants have included in books of reference schedules listing 'statutory undertakers and other like bodies having or possibly having a right to keep equipment on, in or over the land within the Order Limits'. The September 2013 DCLG guidance specifically advises that this should not be done (Annex D, para 9). The Inspectorate has advised that this is not something which it expects to see and that, if such a schedule is included, then the reason for it should be explained in the application documentation (register of advice, 19 September 2012, Daventry International Rail Freight Terminal). The Inspectorate has also advised applicants to prepare a justification as to the purpose of such a schedule and the reasons why it has been included in case the inclusion of such a schedule is questioned by the Examining Authority (register of advice, 27 June 2014, Progress Power Station).

Funding Statement

Written by: James Pereira QC, ftb
Edited by: Michael Humphries QC, ftb

The need for a funding statement

Where an applicant for development consent intends to apply for authorisation to compulsorily acquire land, interests in land or a right over land, he is required to provide with the application 'a statement to indicate how an order that contains the authorisation of compulsory acquisition is proposed to be funded': see The Infrastructure Planning (Applications: Prescribed Forms and Procedures) Regulations 2009, SI 2009/2264, reg 5(1)(h) and DCLG Application Form Guidance (2013), paragraph 26. This statement is commonly referred to as a 'funding statement'.

A funding statement must also be produced where it is proposed to include a provision in the DCO to authorise the acquisition of land that was not shown in the book of reference submitted with the application and a person having an interest in the land does not consent to the inclusion of that provision: see the Infrastructure Planning (Compulsory Acquisition) Regulations 2010, SI 2010/104, reg 5. The funding statement in such a case must relate to the funding of the acquisition proposed by the additional provision.

The contents of a funding statement

As to the contends of a funding statement, the DCLG Application Form Guidance (paragraph 26) explains that it should contain

> '... sufficient information to enable the Secretary of State to be satisfied that, if he was to grant the compulsory acquisition request, the proposed development is likely to be undertaken and not be prevented due to difficulties in sourcing and securing the necessary funding.'

A more detailed consideration of what a funding statement should contain is found later in this article.

The purpose of a funding statement

The 2009 version of the DCLG Application Form Guidance (paragraph 24) stated as follows about the need for a funding statement:

> 'This is necessary because it is not appropriate for people's ownership of land, interest in land or rights over land to be compulsorily taken from them, if there is doubt as to whether the development will proceed after those rights, etc, have been taken away.'

This text does not exist in the equivalent paragraph 26 of the 2013 version on the Guidance.

The funding statement in the examination process

More detail on the approach that will be taken is given in the DCLG Guidance on procedures for compulsory acquisition (2010). This advises (paragraph 21) that:

> 'The promoter must have a clear idea of how it intends to use the land which it is proposing to acquire, and should be able to demonstrate that there is a reasonable prospect of the requisite funds becoming available. Otherwise, it will be difficult to show conclusively that the compulsory purchase of land meets the two conditions in section 122 … and is therefore justified in the public interest at that time.'

In summary the two conditions in s 22 referred to above are that the land is required for the development and that there is a compelling case in the public interest for the acquisition.

The resource implications of the proposed scheme are elaborated in the DCGL Guidance on compulsory acquisition procedures (paragraphs 33–34) in the following terms:

> 'As stated above, any application for a consent order authorising compulsory acquisition must be accompanied by a statement explaining how it will be funded. This statement should provide as much information as possible about the resource implications of both acquiring the land and implementing the project for which the land is required. It may be that the project is not intended to be independently financially viable, or that the details cannot be finalised until there is certainty about the assembly of the necessary land. In such instances, the promoter should provide an indication of how any potential shortfalls are intended to be met. This should include the degree to which other bodies (public or private sector) have agreed to make financial contributions or to underwrite the scheme, and on what basis such contributions or underwriting is to be made.
>
> The timing of the availability of the funding is also likely to be a relevant factor. Regulation 3(2) of [the Infrastructure Planning (Miscellaneous Prescribed Provisions) Regulations 2010] allows for five years within which any notice to treat must be served beginning on the date on which the order granting development consent is made, though the decision-maker does have the discretion to make a different provision in an order granting development consent. Promoters should be able to demonstrate that adequate funding is likely to be available to enable the promoter to carry out the compulsory acquisition within the statutory period following the order being made, and that the resource implications of a possible acquisition resulting from a blight notice have been taken account of.'

The guidance on funding in this context is very similar to that given under ODPM circular 06/04 in relation to compulsory acquisition under the Acquisition of Land Act 1981: see ODPM Circular 06/04, paragraphs 20–21.

Practical issues and experience to date

The decisions and advice to date have highlighted a number of matters for consideration in this context. These are considered under the headings below.

Expect a high level of scrutiny, but note that the process is quite flexible

Applicants can expect that their funding statements and s 106 obligations will be scrutinised very closely by the Inspectorate. It is common for funding issues to be subject to extensive written questions and answers during the examination process, and also to be subject to oral examination at any oral hearing dealing with compulsory purchase. They are also fairly soft targets for objectors. So applicants need to be prepared.

Experience shows that the inquisitorial nature of the examination works well in this context. It should therefore be possible to ensure that all the Inspectors' concerns have been addressed whether by providing greater security or by explaining why such security is not appropriate in the particular case.

The inquisitorial nature of the process can sometimes be daunting for applicants who are used to an adversarial system, because of the more interventionist approach of the decision-maker during the examination. In particular, it is tempting to view questions from the Inspectors as indicating disapproval or criticism. This temptation should be resisted. While each matter must be judged on its merits, questions from Inspectors are just as likely to be motivated by their need to understand the applicant's position and to have matters explained and justified to them more clearly, as they are to be motivated by some underlying criticism of the applicant's case. As with all aspects of the examination process, it is therefore necessary to critically evaluate the questions being put and decide whether they require a change in the applicant's position or simply a better explanation of what that position is.

Contrary to the fears held by some before the new system got underway, Inspectors are generally content to receive updated funding statements and to accommodate travelling drafts of any planning obligation that is being offered to provide the legal safeguards necessary. In this way the relevant documents can be drafted to reflect the issues raised during the examination. There should be no need to be in the dark about the issues by the end of the examination process. See, for example, the extent to which the funding position evolved during the Rookery South examination.

Note too that the advice given by the Secretary of State in the Galloper wind farm application, which contemplated that further information, might be requested from the applicant after the close of the examination if funding became a particular issue or concern. That is obviously a proportionate approach to take where the alternative would be to refuse the application.

Matters to be covered in a funding statement

The DCLG Guidance on compulsory purchase procedures (paragraphs 33–34) indicates that the following should be addressed in the funding statement:

- The resource implications of the project, including:
  - acquiring the land;
  - implementing the project;
- The sources of funding;

- How potential shortfalls in funding are expected to be met;
- The basis upon which funding is being provided;
- The timing of available funding, in particular by reference to:
  - the time period for the exercise of powers of compulsory acquisition;
  - the possibility of a blight notice being served;
- Any uncertainties (eg around securing funding, or around the viability of the project), their implications, and how they are to be addressed.

In addition, the following points may be important:

- Contextual points about the standing of the Applicant, its parents, the importance of the project etc.
- Any points thought necessary to address particular funding concerns that have been raised during the application process, particularly where changes have not been made in response to issues raised by the Inspectorate.
- An explanation of how the funding is to be secured. Usually this will be an explanation of how the section 106 obligation which contains the necessary legal requirements for funding security will work.

The relevance of compensation

The extent to which the level of expected compensation is relevant to these issues is a moot point. Traditionally, it is said that matters of compensation are for the Upper Tribunal and not for the authority being asked to approve powers of compulsory acquisition. On the other hand, the level of expected compensation must be relevant to understanding whether the level of any funding is adequate to fund acquisitions.

The Inspectorate has shown itself willing to accept the proposition that a misunderstanding about the likely level of compensation required could undermine an applicant's arguments on whether there is a compelling case: see the Rookery South report at paragraph 7.98. Applicants are naturally – and quite properly – cautious about providing details of the amount of expected compensation. However, one way of dealing with this may for applicants to refer to the fact that expert advice has been taken on quantum, and that the level of funding for compensation that is available is considerably above the level so advised. In this way applicants are able to address this point without being over-exposed to examination of their precise compensation assessment, and while also giving comfort that any potential underestimate of liability is not a cause of concern: see, for example, the Galloper Wind farm Funding Statement at paragraph 4.15.

Single purpose corporate vehicles (SPVs) and parent companies

It is common for the funding statement submitted with the application to be quite light on detail. In particular, where an applicant is an SPV or subsidiary company with limited assets itself, the funding statement can be expected to refer to the financial standing of the parent(s). Usually such statements are superficially very impressive, because the parent company will often be a major corporate body of substance with a huge turnover. Nevertheless, the concern of the Planning Inspectorate is to ensure that the 'particular' applicant has or will have the necessary funds. Accordingly the examination of a funding statement of this sort will inevitably move on from these general statements to the particular issues surrounding the application and applicant in question, and indeed to the detailed mechanisms by which funding security will be secured. Therefore, while there is often good sense in starting out in a fairly high level way, such an approach may not stand up during the course of the examination process.

It is probably the case that publicly funded projects promoted by a public authority will get an easier ride. The notion of compulsory acquisition by a statutory body funded by the public purse is a more comfortable one than such acquisition by a private commercial body. Moreover, there is probably – rightly or wrongly – an implicit acceptance that that standing of a public authority and the public law principles which govern its conduct make it more accountable, and that when a public body says that it will commit funds to a project it will do just that.

Mechanism for securing the funding

The general guidance on the need for funding and the reasons for it has been referred to already. But what of the particular form or mechanism for securing funding in circumstances where there is doubt as to the particular applicants financial standing or the enforceability of any commitments to funding? The short answer is that each case will be judged on its own merits and the Secretary of State does not as yet have any best practice guidance to provide.

Experience of the examination process to date would suggest, however, that a section 106 obligation will usually be required to ensure that the necessary funding will be in place before the project commences.

Applicants that are commercial enterprises, and in particular SPVs, can be expected to have to give consideration to the following being given by way of a planning obligation:

- Security for a particular, or minimum, sum of money for land acquisitions (which applicants usually see as preferable to an open-ended guarantee). It would be appropriate to time limit the duration of any security, provided the time limit is sufficiently lengthy to allow for disputes as to the amount of compensation payable. The type of security that will be provided (bond, bank guarantee, etc) should be specified.
- A power to approve the security, to be held by the local planning authority.
- A covenant not to exercise any powers of compulsory acquisition until the security in question has been approved.
- A covenant that the applicant will not place itself into voluntary liquidation.
- A covenant not to transfer the benefit of the DCO without first procuring equivalent obligations from the transferee. It may also be appropriate for the provisions of the DCO relating to the transfer of powers to third parties to make it clear that the transferee is under the same obligations as the (original) undertaker.

The need to demonstrate funding to meet compensation claims for severance, injurious affection and/or disturbance caused by the construction or operation of the project may well be challenging, as such compensation may be very difficult to quantify before a project has been implemented. Nevertheless, a funding statement should make it clear that such compensation has, at least, been considered where it might be relevant.

Although the DCLG Guidance on compulsory purchase procedures (paragraph 33) also refers to the need to identify the resource implications of 'implementing' the project, it is in the nature of large infrastructure projects that securing the necessary funding for their development in advance of the grant of development consent is often a wholly unrealistic expectation. Nevertheless, the funding statement should address the funding for the implementation of the scheme, even if it is necessary to do so at a relatively high level at the application stage. In some cases more detail will be required.

Part 12

Pre-Examination, Examination and Post-Examination

Timescales for Pre-Examination, Examination and Post-Examination Procedures

Written by: Isabella Tafur, ftb
Edited by: Michael Humphries QC, ftb

Introduction

One of the guiding principles behind the development consent regime was a need to improve the efficiency of the planning process for dealing with major infrastructure projects, which was too slow and complicated: see Planning for a Sustainable Future, White Paper 2007, paragraph 1.20. The Government considered that prolonged procedures increased costs, resulted in years of blight for individuals and communities and put the country's economic and environmental well-being at risk. As a consequence, the PA 2008 regime contains a prescribed timetable to facilitate faster decision-making.

This article examines the individual elements within the overall prescribed timetable and considers how the timetable is performing in practice.

Acceptance of an application

The timing of any application for development consent under the PA 2008 is, obviously, within the control of the applicant. However, it is from the date of application that the prescribed timetable applies.

The Secretary of State must decide whether or not to accept the application (PA 2008, s 55) within 28 days from the day after the receipt of an application purporting to be an application for development consent under PA 2008, s 37.

The Secretary of State must notify the applicant of its decision of whether it has accepted the application (s 55(6) and (7)). Although there is no prescribed time period for such notification, experience suggests that PINS will notify the applicant promptly.

Notification of acceptance

If the application has been accepted, the applicant must then notify certain persons – as set out in PA 2008, s 56(2) and Sch 1 to the Infrastructure Planning (Applications: Prescribed Forms and Procedure) Regulations 2009 ('the 2009 Regulations') – in accordance with reg 8 of the 2009 Regulations. The notice of acceptance under s 56(2) must also notify such persons of the deadline for making representations to the Secretary of State of their interest in, or objection, to the application (s 56(4)).

The deadline for making representations under section 56(4) must not be earlier than the period of 28 days that begins with the day after the day on which the person receives the notice (s 56(5)). The applicant must also publicise the application in the manner prescribed by reg 9 the 2009 Regulations.

Pursuant to PA 2008, 56, the applicant must certify to the Secretary of State that it has complied with the notification and publication requirements in s 56. This certificate must be in the form prescribed by the 2009 Regulations (set out in Sch 3 to those Regulations), and must be sent to the Secretary of State within 10 *working* days from the deadline set for the making of representations (reg 10 of the 2009 Regulations). Note this is the only reference to 'working days'; all other statutory deadlines under the PA 2008 and the 2009 Regulations are calendar days. At the same time, if the application includes a request to authorise compulsory purchase powers, the applicant must send the Secretary of State a notice of the affected persons (PA 2008, s 59 and reg 10 of the 2009 Regulations): see, for example, the North London Reinforcement Project application for an example of PINS's approach of where all persons under s 56(2) had not been correctly notified.

Initial assessment and preliminary meeting

The Examining Authority must make an initial assessment of the principal issues arising on the application within 21 days from the day after the applicant notified the relevant persons of the acceptance of the application under s 56.

Having made the initial assessment, the Examining Authority must hold a preliminary meeting (PA 2008, s 88), to which it must invite the applicant, interested parties (s 102), statutory parties (s 88(3A)) and each local authority (s 88A). It may also invite other persons.

There is no prescribed timeframe during which the preliminary meeting must be held. This is significant and gives PINS the opportunity to set the date of the preliminary meeting with a view to allowing adequate preparation time for the examination of a complex or controversial application.

At the preliminary meeting, or as soon as practicable thereafter, the Examining Authority must set a timetable for the examination of the application (Infrastructure Planning (Examination Procedure) Rules 2010, SI 2010/103, reg 8). The timetable must set out, *inter alia,* the date by which representations must be received by the Examining Authority; the period within which the Examining Authority will ask questions in writing and seek further written information; the period within which the applicant will have the opportunity to comment in writing on the relevant representations and any responses to written questions; the period within which the applicant and any interested party must agree a statement of common ground and the date of any issue specific hearing.

Examination

The day after the preliminary meeting (or the last day of the preliminary meeting, if it runs over more than one day) is the start date for the examination of the application. The Examining Authority must complete the examination of the application within six months of the start date (PA 2008, s 98).

The Examining Authority must report to the Secretary of State within three months of the deadline for completion of the examination (or, if it completed the examination earlier than that, within three months of completing the examination) (PA 2008, s 98(3)).

There is a power for the Secretary of State to extend this time limit in s 98(4), provided he notifies all interested parties of the new deadline, and publicised the new deadline in the manner he considers appropriate. The Secretary of State must also make a statement to the Houses of Parliament, announcing the new deadline: see the Able Marine Energy Park application for an example of the Secretary of State extending the three month period for making a decision.

Decision

The Secretary of State must then decide an application within three months from the date on which he received the Examining Authority's report (PA 2008, s 107).

The Secretary of State has a power to extend that time limit, pursuant to s 107(3), provided he notifies interested parties of his decision, publicises the new deadline and announces the new deadline to the Houses of Parliament.

Experience so far

Set out at Table 1 below is a summary of the times within which the various procedural steps have been taken for the first 25 projects that have reached the section 55 decision stage (whether to accept the application).

A number of themes emerge:

- the range of periods from acceptance of the application to preliminary meeting is quite wide at 98 days (Redditch Branch Enhancement Scheme and Stafford Area Improvements Norton Bridge Railway) to 215 (North London Electricity Line Reinforcement) where there had been a procedural error in the s 56(2) notices – although the typical range is about 100 days to 130 days;
- there appears to be some correlation, although not a particularly strong one, between the length of period from acceptance of the application to preliminary meeting and whether the Examining Authority is a Panel or a single appointed person;
- the range of period from application to decision is relatively constant at between 14 and 18 months (excluding projects that have gone to Special Parliamentary Procedure) and that even for the largest projects, including the Thames Tideway Tunnel (18 months).

Table 1

PROJECT	APPLICATION	SECTION 55 DECISION	PRELIMINARY MEETING [days after s 55 decision]	REPORT [days after s 55 decision]	DECISION	TOTAL (MONTHS) [days after s 55 decision]	COMMENTS
Overhead electricity line to connect Maesgwyn Wind Farm	3.8.10	31.8.10	N/A				Application not accepted
Rookery South Energy from Waste Generating Station	5.8.10	26.8.10	17.1.11 [144 days]	N/A IPC made the decision	13.10.11	14 [413 days]	DCO only published on 26.3.13 following SPP
Brig y Cwm Energy from Waste Generating Station	31.12.10	26.1.11	7.6.11 [132 days]	N/A			Application withdrawn following refusal to allow amendment
North Doncaster Rail Chord	22.6.11	19.7.11	16.11.11 [120 days]	31.7.12 [378 days]	16.10.12	16 [455 days]	
Ipswich Rail Chord	29.6.11	21.7.11	9.11.11 [111 days]	12.6.12 [327 days]	5.9.12	15 [412 days]	
Kentish Flats Extension	14.10.11	10.11.11	22.2.12 [104 days]	29.11.12 [385 days]	19.2.13	16 [467 days]	
Hinkley Power Station	31.10.11	24.11.11	21.3.12 [118 days]	19.12.12 [391 days]	19.3.13	17 [481 days]	

Brechfa Forest West Wind Farm	4.11.11	30.11.11	13.3.12 [104 days]	12.12.12 [378 days]	12.3.13	16 [468 days]	
Galloper Offshore Wind Farm	21.11.11	19.12.11	29.5.12 [162 days]	27.2.13 [436 days]	24.5.2013	18 [522 days]	
Preesall Saltfield Underground Gas Storage	1.12.11	23.12.11	24.4.12 [123 days]	22.1.13 [396 days]	9.4.2013	16 [473 days]	
Heysham to M6 Link Road	6.12.11	23.12.11	3.4.12 [102 days]	19.12.12 [362 days]	19.3.13	15 [452 days]	
Able Marine Energy Park	19.12.11	12.1.12	24.5.12 [133 days]	25.2.13 [410 days]	18.12.13	23 [707 days]	DCO delayed due to SPP
Triton Knoll Offshore Wind Farm	31.1.12	23.2.12	23.7.12 [151 days]	17.4.13 [419 days]	11.7.13	16 [505 days]	
East Northants Resource Management Facility	14.3.12	11.4.12	26.7.12 [106 days]	22.4.13 [376 days]	11.7.13	13 [457 days]	
Port Blyth New Biomass Plant	15.3.12	11.4.12	2.8.12 [113 days]	2.5.13 [386 days]	24.7.13	15 [470 days]	
M1 Junction 10a Grade Separation – Luton	29.6.12	27.7.12	15.11.12 [111 days]	13.8.13 [382 days]	30.10.13	15 [461 days]	
Roosecote Biomass Power Station	3.7.12	31.7.12	N/A				Application withdrawn

PROJECT	APPLICATION	SECTION 55 DECISION	PRELIMINARY MEETING [days after s 55 decision]	REPORT [days after s 55 decision]	DECISION	TOTAL (MONTHS) [days after s 55 decision]	COMMENTS
Kings Lynn B Connection Project	27.7.12	21.8.12	11.1.13 [143 days]	10.10.13 [415 days]	18.12.13	16 [485 days]	
Fieldes Lock – Rail linked power station	14.8.12	7.9.12					Application withdrawn
North London (Electricity Line) Reinforcement	30.8.12	27.9.12	30.4.2013 [215 days]	23.1.14 [483 days]	16.4.14	18 [567 days]	Preliminary meeting postponed after it became apparent that the applicant had not fully complied with its obligation under s 56(2) to notify certain persons of the application.
Redditch Branch Enhancement Scheme	4.9.12	1.10.12	7.1.13 [98 days]	2.8.13 [305 days]	31.10.13	13 [369 days]	
East Anglia ONE Offshore Windfarm	21.11.12	14.12.12	25.6.2013 [193 days]	18.3.14 [459 days]	17.6.14	18 [551 days]	
Stafford Area Improvements Norton Bridge Railway	19.12.12	10.1.13	18.4.13 [98 days]	3.1.14 [358 days]	31.3.14	15 [446 days]	

Daventry International Rail Freight Terminal	22.2.13	20.3.13	8.7.2013 [110 days]	7.4.14 [383 days]	3.10.14	18 [563 days]	Re-submitted application following non-acceptance of application on 29.11.12
Thames Tideway Tunnel	28.2.13	27.3.13	12.9.13 [170 days]	12.6.14 [442 days]	12.9.14	17 [535 days]	

From experience, it is also possible to give some broad indications of the likely timetable for an examination. Table 2 below sets out a typical timetable. This can be helpful in identifying potential peak periods of activity.

Table 2

EVENT	**APPROX PERIOD AFTER PRELIMINARY MEETING**
PRELIMINARY MEETING	0
Notice of procedural decisions following Preliminary Meeting (incl Timetable for examination; ExA's first written questions; Note of Preliminary Meeting)	1–2 weeks
Deadline for receipt of Responses to ExA's first written questions; Written representations; Local Impact Reports	5–6 weeks
Deadline for receipt of Comments on relevant / written reps Comments on LIRs Comments on responses to ExA's first written questions	9–10 weeks
ExA's second written questions	11–12 weeks
Deadline for receipt of Responses to ExA's second written questions	15–16 weeks
Deadline for receipt of Comments on responses to ExA's second written questions	17–18 weeks
Issue specific hearings Compulsory acquisition hearings Open floor hearings	A few days within range (say) 12–20 weeks
CLOSE OF EXAMINATION	24 weeks

PA 2008, s 56 Notice and Relevant Representations

Written by: Hereward Phillpot QC, ftb
Edited by: Michael Humphries QC, ftb

PA 2008, s 56(2) notice

The PA 2008, s 56(2) places a duty on the applicant to give notice of the application to certain individuals and organisations.

The form and content of the notice

The notice must include the information prescribed by the Infrastructure Planning (Applications: Prescribed Forms and Procedure) Regulations 2009, SI 2009/2264, reg 8(2): see PA 2008, s 56(3).

The applicant must make available to each person required to be notified a copy of the application and certain prescribed documents: see PA 2008, ss 56(6)(b), 37(3)(d) and SI 2009/2264, reg 6.

Who must be notified?

Notification must be given to 'such persons as may be prescribed' (PA 2008, s 56(2)(a)), the identity of 'such persons' to be determined by reference to SI 2009/2264, reg 8(1), Sch 1. Column 1 of SI 2009/2264, Sch 1 provides a list of statutory bodies, and Column 3 identifies the circumstances in which each of those bodies must be notified. For example, Natural England must be notified in the case of all applications likely to affect land in England

Notification must also be given to the Marine Management Organisation ('MMO') where the proposed development involves activity within its jurisdiction (PA 2008, s 56(2)(aa), (2A)), each local authority that is within PA 2008, s 56A (PA 2008, s 56(2)(b)), the Greater London Authority ('GLA') where the application site (or part of it) is within Greater London (PA 2008, s 56(2)(c)), and each person who is within one or more of the categories set out in PA 2008, s 57 (PA 2008, s 56(2)(d)).

PA 2008, s 57 identifies three categories of person. Those who the applicant knows, after making diligent inquiry, have a legal interest in, and/or are occupiers of, land forming all or part of the application site, fall within 'Category 1': see PA 2008, s 57(1). Those known to have an interest in, or the power to sell and convey or release, such land, fall within 'Category 2': see PA 2008, s 57(2). Category 3 is less straightforward, and comprises those that the applicant thinks would or might be entitled to 'make a relevant claim' if the order were to be made and fully implemented: see PA 2008, s 57(4)–(6). A 'relevant claim' for these purposes is defined by subsection (6) as one under section 10 of the Compulsory Purchase Act 1965 (compensation where satisfaction not made for the taking, or injurious affection, of land subject to compulsory purchase), Part 1 of the Land Compensation Act 1973 (compensation for depreciation of land value by physical works caused by use of public works), or PA 2008, s 152(3) (a claim by a person whose land is injuriously affected by the carrying out of works authorised by the DCO).

Publicity

In addition to the requirement to notify certain persons, the applicant must also publicise the application in the prescribed manner: see PA 2008, s 56(7). SI 2009/2264, reg 9 stipulates that this is to be done by way of a notice containing specified details, published in the same way as a proposed application and also displayed at or near to the site.

PA 2008, s 56(4) deadline for receipt of relevant representations

The applicant's notice must also identify the deadline for receipt by the Secretary of State of representations giving notice of the person's interest in, or objection to, the application: see section 56(4). The minimum period that must be allowed is 28 days beginning with the day after that on which the person receives the notice: see PA 2008, s 56(5). The same minimum period has been prescribed for the purposes of the publicity notice under PA 2008, s 56(7): see PA 2008, s 56(8) and SI 2009/2264, reg 9(3).

PA 2008, s 102(2), (4) definition of 'representation' and 'relevant representation'

PA 2008, s 102(1) defines who will qualify as an 'interested party' for the purposes of the examination into the application and, in addition to the applicant, comprises those falling into one of the three categories identified in PA 2008, s 57 (above), the MMO (where relevant), the local authorities and the GLA (where relevant), and anyone who has 'made a relevant representation'.

This is important as, once a person has acquired the status of an 'interested party', such a person also acquires certain rights before, during and after the examination process. These include the right to be invited to a preliminary meeting; the right to require, and be heard at, an open-floor hearing; the right to be heard at an issue-specific hearing, if one is held; the right to be notified of when the Examining Authority has completed its examination; and the right to be notified of the decision: see paragraph 27 of the CLG Guidance on the examination of applications (February 2010). More detail on who is, and may apply to become, an interested party, and the status of interested parties during the examination, is provided in [Micro-article 125 below]

A 'representation' for these purposes is defined inclusively, so as to include evidence: see PA 2008, s 102(2). A 'relevant representation' is one that satisfies all of the following requirements (PA 2008, s 102(4)):

- it is about the application;
- it is made in the prescribed form and manner, and within the prescribed time limit;

- it contains material 'of a prescribed description'; and
- it is not concerned with compensation for compulsory acquisition, the merits of policy in the NPS, and is not vexatious or frivolous (for example, where the points raised are considered to be so trivial in the context of the application that they are not worthy of serious consideration).

The CLG Guidance on the examination process cautions that deciding to treat a representation as 'vexatious or frivolous' is not a step to be undertaken lightly, as a person aggrieved by such a decision may challenge it by way of judicial review. In borderline cases, the guidance recommends giving the benefit of the doubt to the person making the representation: see CLG Guidance on the examination of applications, paragraph 35. That would appear to be sensible.

The Infrastructure Planning (Interested Parties) Regulations 2010, SI 2010/102 prescribe the form and manner in which relevant representations must be made. SI 2010/102, reg 4 requires relevant representations to be in the form of a registration form, and to include certain basic information about the person registering (for example, name, address of the person/agent, interest in land affected by the application (if any) etc), as well as 'an outline of the principal submissions which the person registering intends to make in respect of the application' (SI 2010/102, reg 4(e)). It must also state whether the person registering intends to make oral representations at any hearings that may be held (SI 2010/102, reg 4(f)).

Guidance on what is meant by an 'outline of the principal submissions' is to be found in the CLG Guidance on the examination process at paragraphs 32–33. A person's relevant representation does not need to set out in full the arguments which the person intends to make during the examination, but it should contain sufficient information to enable the Examining Authority to understand which aspects of the application the person supports or objects to, and the reasons why. This will help the Examining Authority identify the main issues likely to feature in the examination, guide its structure and programme, and suggest where interested parties with similar cases might consider collaborating to present a joint case.

The guidance also suggests that this process of considering the relevant representations will help the Examining Authority to see whether there are any relevant issues at risk of not being properly covered, and how to remedy this. In practice this is unlikely to arise very often, as the prolonged and detailed pre-application process should ensure that all of the potentially important issues are flushed out in advance of the application being made.

Infrastructure Planning (Examination Procedure) Rules 2010, SI 2010/103

Rule 3 – relevant representations

Further provision in relation to relevant representations is made in the Infrastructure Planning (Examination Procedure) Rules 2010, SI 2010/103, r 3.

Those making relevant representations must ensure that they are received by the Examining Authority by the later of the dates specified in the notices required by PA 2008, s 56(4), (8). Any written comment on relevant representations that are made must be received either by the date on which the preliminary meeting is held, or, if later, the date specified in the timetable set by the Examining Authority pursuant to SI 2010/103, r 8.

The Examining Authority can ask for further information about matters contained in a relevant representation, or a comment made in respect of such a representation, and set a date by which such information must be provided.

All relevant representations and comments must be made available by the Examining Authority as soon as practicable after receipt, in accordance with SI 2010/103, r 21. This involves publishing the material on the PINS website http://infrastructure.planningportal.gov.uk/ and making hard copies available for inspection and copying – see SI 2010/103, r 21(2).

Time periods

Later representations

The examination process involves a series of stages at which further representations will be sought by the Examining Authority from interested parties. At the preliminary meeting, or as soon as practicable thereafter, the Examining Authority will publish a timetable in accordance with SI 2010/103, r 8. That timetable will set a date for the making of written representations, for the Examining Authority to ask questions in writing about any matter contained in the application, in relevant representations, written representations, or anything else it considers relevant, and for the applicant and interested parties to comment in writing on any relevant or written representations or responses provided to written questions.

The timetable will tend to evolve during the course of the examination, with further deadlines being set for additional rounds of questions and comments, hearings and written representations. In order to keep the examination to time, these deadlines are generally fairly tight, and a great deal of effort is required in order adequately to deal with the multiple (and often complex) matters of law and evidence arising in the limited time available.

SI 2010/103, r 23 – allowing extra time

The Examining Authority does have the power to allow extra time for the taking of any step which may or must be taken under the 2010 Rules: see SI 2010/103, r 23.

Whilst this is a power exercised from time to time (see, for example, the extension of time allowed for the making of comments on written representations in the Able marine energy park examination), the Examining Authority is likely to be reluctant to allow more time unless there are very good reasons for doing so and it would not put at risk the prospects of finishing the examination on time. Generalised pleas for more time because of the very significant administrative and cost burdens involved in sticking to the tight timetables needed to complete the examination on time are likely to be refused (see, for example, the Examining Authority's rejection of a request made for an extension of time by the joint local authorities at the examination into the proposals for a new nuclear power station at Hinkley Point C in Somerset).

Interested Parties

Written by: Hereward Phillpot QC, ftb
Edited by: Michael Humphries QC, ftb

PA 2008, ss 102, 102A, 102B

The main participants in an examination held under the PA 2008 are those who have, or acquire, the status of 'interested parties'. Designation as an interested party carries with it important consequences in terms of notification, the right to make and receive representations, and the right to require and to participate in hearings.

PA 2008, s 102

PA 2008, s 102(1) defines who is or may become an 'interested party' for the purposes of the examination of any individual application.

The applicant and the local authority in whose area the land is located are automatically accorded the status of Interested Parties (s 102(1)(a),(c) and (8)). In addition, the Marine Management Organisation and the Greater London Authority are automatically given the status of interested parties where the development proposed falls within their respective areas of jurisdiction (s 102(1)(ba) and (d)).

Other persons can become interested parties in the following ways:

- By reason of being notified of the application in accordance with s 56(2)(a) (s 102(1)(aa)) (see Micro-article 124 above).
- By reason of a decision by the Examining Authority under s 102A that the person is within one of the categories set out in s 102B (s 102(1)(ab) (see below).
- In the case of 'statutory parties' (see s 88(3)(c) and below) and local authorities within s 88A, by notifying the Examining Authority of a desire to become an interested party following the preliminary meeting (s 102(1)(ca)).
- By making a relevant representation (s 102(1)(e)) (see Micro-article 124 above for the definition of a 'relevant representation').

Once a person has become an interested party, he may choose to relinquish that status by notifying the Examining Authority to that effect (s 102(1ZA). For example, various Interested Parties wrote to the Examining Authority to relinquish their status during the examination into the East Northants Research Management Facility.

PA 2008, ss 102A and 102B

The purpose of PA 2008, ss 102A and 102B is to enable the Examining Authority to accord interested party status to those who should have been, but were not, notified of the acceptance of the application under section 56 (and thus acquired interested party status via that route).

PA 2008, s 102A allows for those who consider themselves to be in this position to ask the Examining Authority to become interested parties. On receipt of a request which meets the requirements set out in section 102A(1), the Examining Authority must decide whether the person is within one or more of the categories set out in section 102B. If it is satisfied to that effect, it must then notify that person and the applicant that the person has become an interested party (s 102A(3)).

There are four requirements which PA 2008, s 102A(1) sets before the obligation under subsection (2) arises:

- The person must have made a request to the Examining Authority to become an Interested Person;
- The request must state that the person claims to be within one or more of the categories in section 102B;
- The person must not have been notified of the acceptance of the application in accordance with section 56(2)(d); and
- The applicant must have issued a section 58 certificate in relation to the application (certifying compliance with the section 56 requirement to notify persons of the accepted application).

PA 2008, s 102B identifies three categories of person, corresponding to the categories of person who should have been notified under section 56(2)(d) (see Article 124 above).

The Infrastructure Planning (Interested Parties) Regulations 2010, SI 2010/102

As explained above, PA 2008, s 102(1) provides that a 'statutory party' may become an interested party. Section 88(3A) provides that a 'statutory party' means a person specified in, or of a description specified in, regulations made by the Secretary of State.

The Infrastructure Planning (Interested Parties) Regulations 2010, SI 2010/102 contain the relevant specifications. Regulation 3 provides that the persons specified for these purposes are:

- Those listed in Column 1 of the Schedule to the Regulations in the circumstances specified in Column 2 to that Schedule; and
- Any affected person.

Column 1 lists various persons, and Column 2 lists the circumstances in which those persons are deemed to be statutory parties. So, for example, the Welsh Ministers are a statutory party for all applications likely to affect land in Wales, and the Health and Safety Executive is a statutory party for all applications.

Affected persons are defined in regulation 2(1) as meaning a person whose name has been given to the Examining Authority in a notice under PA 2008, s 59 (notice of persons interested in land to which a compulsory acquisition request relates). All 'affected persons' are therefore also interested parties, and have all the entitlements associated with that status. In addition, they may also request that a compulsory acquisition hearing be held to consider the issues arising in connection with the proposed compulsory acquisition of land.

Status of 'Interested Parties' in the examination process

The Act provides Interested Parties with a particular status in the examination process. In particular:

- Interested Parties must be invited to the preliminary meeting (PA 2008, s 88(3)(b)) and have a right to participate in that meeting (s 88(4)(a)).
- Procedural decisions made by the Examining Authority must be notified to all Interested Parties (s 89(2A) and (4)).
- In determining whether a hearing should be held, the Examining Authority is required to ensure that 'an interested party has a fair chance to put the party's case' (s 91(1)(b)), and hence Interested Parties have a special status when considering the fairness of the examination procedure.
- Interested Parties are entitled to make oral representations at hearings (s 91(3)).
- Interested Parties are entitled to require to be heard at an open floor hearing (s 93(1)) and to make oral representations about the application at that hearing (s 93(3)).
- Notification of, and participation in, site visits is limited to Interested Parties Infrastructure Planning (Examination Procedure) Rules 2010, rule 16 (see eg the invitation to Interested Parties to make submissions on locations for the site visit at the Galloper Offshore Windfarm examination).
- The Secretary of State must notify Interested Parties of the deadline for the decision on the application, and of any changes to that deadline (s 98).

Participation by those who are not Interested Parties

The Examining Authority retains a discretion to allow participation in the examination by those who are not interested Parties. It is a discretion that has already been exercised in a number of examinations, including those into the Triton Knoll Offshore Wind Farm and Preesall Saltfield Underground Gas Storage proposals.

The CLG Guidance has this to say about the exercise of that discretion:

> 'It is for the Examining Authority to decide whether to allow persons other than those categorised as interested parties to participate in the examination of the application, including expert witnesses. But where a request is received from an interested party to allow an expert witness to take part in the examination of the application, the Secretary of State considers that this should be given serious consideration, in the interests of informed decision making' (paragraph 43).

This needs to be read and understood together with paragraph 29 of the CLG Guidance, which states that where an interested party wishes to take part in an oral hearing, they may appoint a representative, including a legal representative, to speak on their behalf at the hearing.

In practice the nature and format of issue specific hearings often makes it necessary for the panel's questions to be answered by more than one person. For example, a question might require both the explanation of a point of law, or DCO drafting, and the giving of expert evidence on the practicalities lying behind that point. Participants at issue specific hearings sometimes therefore adopt an approach whereby questions are dealt with by a rotating cast of individuals from within the team. Lawyers cannot give evidence, and whilst they can relay instructions to the panel in response to questions, it will often be much more sensible and efficient simply to ask the relevant member of the team to deal with a point. That should not require an application for the Examining Authority's consent on each occasion, and a pragmatic approach seems to have been adopted in hearings so far.

Local Impact Reports

Written by: Hereward Phillpot QC, ftb
Edited by: Michael Humphries QC, ftb

PA 2008, s 60

PA 2008, s 60 provides that certain local authorities are to be invited to produce a 'Local Impact Report' (LIR) in order to inform the examination of the likely impact of the proposed development on that authority's area. In some cases the invitation to produce such a report will be made to a number of different authorities who may choose to co-operate to produce a combined LIR (for example, at the examination into the Galloper Offshore Windfarm proposal Suffolk CC and Suffolk Coastal DC provided at joint LIR: see preliminary meeting notes at paragraphs 4.18–4.19). There is no obligation on an authority that receives such an invitation to produce a LIR, but it is strongly encouraged to do so: see PINS Advice Note 1: Local Impact Reports.

The Act defines a LIR as follows: 'a report in writing giving details of the likely impact of the proposed development on the authority's area (or any part of that area)' (PA 2008, s 60(3)).

PA 2008, s 104(2)(b) imposes an obligation upon the Secretary of State to have regard to any LIR submitted to him within the relevant time limit.

Procedural requirements and timescales

The invitation to produce a LIR is triggered by a notice given by the Secretary of State (section 60(2)), which must also specify the deadline for receipt of the LIR (PA 2008, s 60(5)). The Secretary of State must give the requisite notice once the application has been accepted and he has received a PA 2008, s 58 certificate (certifying compliance with the requirements of section 56) and (where it applies) notification under section 59.

PINS Advice Note 1: Local Impact Reports explains that the Examining Authority will take account of the complexity of the application and other relevant matters, and also the overall timescale set by the Act for examining the application. In practice, this last factor means that the deadline set by the notice is likely to be quite short.

The deadline for receipt of the LIR will be one of the items included amongst the procedural decisions made following the preliminary meeting, together with the period within which Interested Parties (including the applicant) will have the opportunity to make written comments on any LIRs that are submitted.

Authorities are advised in PINS Advice Note 1 not to wait until the deadline has been set before commencing the preparation of their LIR, because of the scale of the task and the limited time likely to be available between notification and expiry of the deadline. The consultation and pre-application periods are likely to be the most appropriate time to commence the evaluation of impacts and gathering of material. The LIR can then be compiled once the application has been accepted and the invitation to submit a LIR has been received. The Examining Authority may agree to an extension of time for an authority to complete its LIR, but this is likely to be a discretion exercised only rarely, and then only to allow a limited additional period of time (see, for example, the approach taken in the examination into the Brechfa Forest West Wind Farm application).

Authorities should also take account of the other deadlines that are likely to be looming for them at this stage of the examination, such as those for production of Statements of Common Ground and written representations (see, for example, the notes of the Hinkley Point C preliminary meeting at paragraphs 5.2, 5.11–5.16).

PA 2008, s 56A identifies which adjoining authorities (unitary authorities, lower-tier district councils and upper-tier county councils), in addition to the authority (or authorities) within whose area the development is to be located, are to be invited to submit a LIR. In respect of offshore proposals, it may be the case that there are no local authorities who would be invited to produce a LIR, although in those circumstances the nearest local authority has sometimes voluntarily produced a LIR in any event (see, for example, the discussion reported in the notes of the Triton Knoll Offshore Windfarm preliminary meeting at paragraphs 3.24 to 3.26).

Contents and style of a LIR

Provided that the LIR satisfies the statutory definition, the precise style and content of the document is a matter of choice for each individual authority.

Contents

Section 10 of the CLG's Guidance for local authorities contains some guidance on the contents of LIR, but it is somewhat limited. It explains two important points:

1 There is no need for the LIR to replicate the Environmental Impact Assessment produced by the applicant. This is of great practical significance because of the highly complex and technical nature of such assessments, and the length of the Environmental Statements to which the assessment process leads.

2 The LIR should be distinguished from any representation a local authority may choose to make in respect of the merits of an application. Again, this is a significant point because maintaining that distinction should make the task of producing the LIR more manageable, and help the authority to focus on the proper role of that document.

More detailed guidance is available in PINS Advice Note 1: Local Impact Reports, which contains the following very helpful list of topics that may be of assistance in compiling the LIR:

1 Site description and surroundings/location

2 Details of the proposal

3 Relevant planning history and any issues arising

4 Relevant development plan policies, supplementary planning guidance or documents, development briefs or approved master-plans and an appraisal of their relationship and relevance to the proposals

5 Relevant development proposals under consideration or granted permission but not commenced or completed

6 Local area characteristics such as urban and landscape qualities and nature conservation sites

7 Local transport patterns and issues

8 Site and area constraints

9 Designated sites

10 Socio-economic and community matters

11 Consideration of the impact of the proposed articles and requirements within the draft Order (such as the scheme) in respect of all of the above

12 DCO obligations and their impact on the local authority's area.

Both the CLG Guidance and the PINS Advice Note stress the importance of using the LIR to provide local knowledge and experience, and evidence of local concerns and issues to the Examining Authority. Examples given in the PINS Advice Note include local evidence of flooding, local social or economic issues or local knowledge of travel patterns to community facilities. This should ensure that local issues which might not otherwise come to the attention of the examination are properly taken into account.

PINS Advice Note 1 indicates that LIRs are also expected to contain the local authority's appraisal of the proposed development's compliance with local policy and guidance. This may well be a material consideration, but it must also be remembered that the development plan has no particular status in decision-making under the PA 2008.

PINS Advice Note 1 encourages local authorities to give their views on the relative importance of different social, environmental or economic issues and the impact of the scheme on them, on the basis that they are well placed to appreciate the impacts of proposals, for example in terms of employment, local services, associated development, or DCO obligations under s 174 of the PA 2008.

National Policy Statements (NPSs) may also be helpful to local authorities in preparing their LIRs as a guide to matters of local impact that are likely to be relevant to the determination of an application. However, local authorities are advised by in PINS Advice Note 1 that there is no need for them to undertake an assessment of compliance with an NPS as this would duplicate the Examining Authority's role.

PINS Advice Note 1 also suggests that where an NPS is locationally specific, the local authority should consider those local impacts of a development proposal which would not have been considered at the national policy development stage. In such instances there may be local impacts on sensitive receptors not apparent at the NPS stage, stemming from, for example, the particular layout, design, scale, appearance, or access arrangements of the scheme.

An important task for local authorities in compiling the LIR is to consider in detail the impact of the proposed DCO articles, requirements and DCO obligations, and any changes or additions which the local authority consider to be needed. These matters are likely to be the focus of much of the Examining Authority's attention during the course of the examination, and it is essential that local authorities get to grips with the detail of these matters at the earliest opportunity. By doing so, they will also help to ensure that their LIR and written representations are properly focussed, and maximise the prospects of influencing the Secretary of State's decision.

Style

PINS Advice Note 1 suggests that the LIR should consist of a statement of positive, neutral and negative local impacts, but it does not need to contain a balancing exercise between positives and negatives, as that is a matter for the Examining Authority; nor does it need to take the form of a formal committee report.

Emerging good practice

It is inevitable that the approach taken to the production of the LIR will differ from authority to authority and from project to project. Much may depend on the scale and complexity of the individual proposal, and the extent to which it has been possible to agree statements of common ground with the applicant.

For example, in the Hinkley Point C examination, the two District Councils and the County Council produced a joint LIR. The LIR was a very substantial document, supported by detailed appendices, but its nature and scale were not dictated simply by the complex nature and scale of the development to be assessed and the fact that it involved multiple sites in a number of quite different locations. In that case there had been a failure to agree much in the way of common ground in advance of the production of the LIR, and the impacts were in dispute between the authorities and the applicant.

The overall structure of the LIR in that case was as follows:

1 An Executive Summary, identifying the structure and role of the LIR, its contents and the key impacts identified.

2 A main LIR, divided into three parts:

 a Site related matters.

 b opic-based matters.

 c Community/area based matters.

3 A set of Appendices, comprising:

 a Figures

 b Topic papers (the evidence and supporting data said to justify the impacts articulated in the main LIR).

 c A list of documents used in compiling the LIR.

 d Preliminary comments on draft requirements.

Whilst the contents and focus of the LIR were the subject of lengthy and detailed criticism by the applicant during the examination process, the broad structure adopted may nevertheless offer some assistance for other authorities dealing with large and complicated applications.

By contrast, the LIR submitted in the Preesall Saltfield Underground Gas Storage examination was a relatively simple, single volume document of just under 50 pages in length. That relatively modest document was supplemented by a series of Statements of Common Ground, to which it made cross-reference as appropriate, and might be seen as representing a more manageable approach in less complex cases.

Initial Assessment of Issues

Written by: Isabella Tafur, ftb
Edited by: Michael Humphries QC, ftb

Introduction

While it is for the Examining Authority to decide how to examine an application, in making any decision about how the application will be examined, it must comply with the provisions in the PA 2008, Chapter 6. Pursuant to PA 2008, s 88, the examining authority must make an initial assessment of the principal issues arising on the application prior to the Preliminary Meeting.

Initial assessment of the principal issues

In making its initial assessment of the principal issues, the Examining Authority will have regard to the application documents and is also likely to take into account the relevant representations received from interested parties: see para 37 of the DCLG Guidance 'Planning Act 2008: Guidance for the examination of applications for development consent' and PINS Advice note 8.3 (under the heading 'What is a relevant representation?).

Rule 5 of the Infrastructure Planning (Examination Procedure) Rules 2010, SI 2010/103 requires the Examining Authority to make the initial assessment of issues within 21 days from the day after the deadline for the receipt of representations by the Secretary of State (as specified by the applicant in its PA 2008, s 56 notification letter).

Notification of the initial assessment

Having made the initial assessment of principal issues, the Examining Authority will hold a Preliminary Meeting. Rule 6 of the Infrastructure Planning (Examination Procedure) Rules 2010 requires the Examining Authority to give notice of that Meeting, and to notify all those invited of the matters to be discussed at the Preliminary Meeting. This is done by a 'Rule 6 letter'.

The Examining Authority's initial assessment of principal issues will usually be listed as Appendix C to the Rule 6 letter. The Examining Authority makes it clear that it is not a comprehensive or exclusive list of all relevant matters, as it will have regard to all the important and relevant matters raised during the examination. This last point is important, as the list of principal issues will not preclude parties from raising other issues, nor the Examining Authority from considering them during the examination.

The initial assessment of principal issues will also usually then form an agenda item at the Preliminary Meeting allowing parties the opportunity to comment on the initial assessment list and raise potential additional issues. PINS Advice Note 8.1 states that 'The meeting may include questions and answers about the key issues that will need to be examined, the timetable for the examination and other important organisational details.'

At, or more usually following, the Preliminary Meeting the Examining Authority will set out the timetable for the examination: see Rule 8 of the Infrastructure Planning (Examination Procedure) Rules 2010. This is usually done by issuing a 'Rule 8 letter' a few days after the close of the Preliminary Meeting. The Rule 8 letter will also contain the Examining Authority's list of principal issues or refer back to the initial assessment of principal issues if the list has not changed.

Conclusion

Given the relatively short time-scales for responding to written questions during the examination period, the initial assessment of principal matters can provide applicants and interested parties with a useful steer in identifying areas in which further work could usefully be focused.

Examples of initial assessments

Typically the list of principal issues will include numbered headings, with short explanatory notes below. Below are a number of examples of the lists of principal issues generated by the applications for development consent for three very different types of NSIP.

Rampion offshore wind farm

1 *Biodiversity, biological environment and ecology*

Including effects on marine and terrestrial life, onshore and offshore ornithology and on protected areas and species including in combination effects.

2 *Compulsory powers*

Including whether there is a compelling case in the public interest.

3 *Development Consent Order and Deemed Marine Licence*

Including consideration of the appropriateness of the powers that would be conferred and whether the Order and the Licence would secure the mitigation relied on by the applicant in the Environmental Statement or which is otherwise considered necessary (Note:This topic will necessarily have to be considered on a 'without prejudice' basis.)

4 *Effects during construction and operation*

Including the cable route corridor, substation site and effect of electro-magnetic fields on receptors.

5 *Landscape/seascape, visual and heritage*

Including effects on the South Downs National Park, the Sussex Heritage Coast and on heritage assets including buried archaeological remains onshore and offshore.

6 *Marine and coastal physical processes*

Including waste and debris with dredging and disposal, chemical pollutants, scouring and scour protection, effects on the coast (erosion and flooding), effects on sea defences and physical effects on port approaches (eg deep water channels).

7 *Navigation and risk*

Including safety during construction and operation, effects of maintenance of shipping lanes and anchorages, effects on commercial and recreational vessels, local ports and search and rescue operations.

8 *Socio-economic*

Including effects on tourism and recreation (land and water based), effects on local businesses (land and water based) and effects on nearby ports and commercial fishing.

9 *Transport and traffic*

Including effects that traffic generated by the proposal could have on the highway network during construction and operation, environmental effects, in combination effects with other proposals and effects on other road users.

Daventry International rail freight terminal

1 *Combination with other development proposals*

- The relationship between the proposed development and the adjacent major sustainable urban extension (SUE) of Rugby, both forming part of the former Rugby Radio Station site.
- The policy and development plan context for examining the application.
- The details of the application particularly concerning a new junction with the A5, rail connections, and the main warehouse buildings within the context of the parameters included in the main site and rail framework plans and schedule.

2 *Transport*

- The calculation of additional traffic generated by the proposed development, the impact on the trunk road network, the adequacy of proposals for junction improvements and mitigating transport impacts on local roads and communities adjacent to the development.
- The capacity of the rail network to accommodate the predicted additional rail flows from the development.

3 *Heritage impacts*

- The consequences of the development for the scale of mediaeval and later ridge and furrow cultivation which has survived as a feature of the former Rugby Radio Station site.
- The extent to which the proposed Lilbourne Meadows provide for a satisfactory retention of the existing ridge and furrow.

4 *Landscape and visual impacts*

- The impact of lighting from the proposed development on surrounding areas.
- The extent to which the proposed warehousing buildings will be visible from surrounding areas, including the degree to which these would result in adverse visual impacts and the likely success of proposed mitigation.

- The nature and adequacy of Lilbourne Meadows to provide a visual buffer between Lilbourne and the main development, and the mechanisms for implementation.

5 *Ecology impacts*

- The nature and adequacy of Lilbourne Meadows to provide habitat mitigation for protected species

6 *Drainage and flooding*

- Given the large area of hard standing proposed, the suitability of land drainage proposals, including the diversion of Clifton Brook and its tributary.

7 *Traffic management*

- How the impact of heavy goods vehicles on the local environment can be mitigated, for example restricting/preventing the use of laybys for overnight lorry parking to reduce the consequent general degradation and appearance of the area caused by litter, low standard of maintenance and misuse of land.

8 *Construction impacts*

- The impact from vibration during the construction phase.
- The effects of earthwork operations during construction on dust emissions and reduction in air quality.

9 *Noise*

- The impact of noise generated by the railway proposals (including on the proposed SUE development) and from HGV traffic to and from the site once the development is operational.
- Given that the site is proposed to be operated 24-hours a day, noise impacts generated from the main site on Lilbourne village.

Thames Tideway tunnel

1 *Air quality and emissions*

Matters include but are not limited to:

- The effects on air quality from dust and particulates from construction and transportation.
- Odour, particularly during operation.
- Adequacies of the baseline assessment, the assessments of likely significant effects and any proposed monitoring regime and mitigation. Any measures to avoid, reduce and compensate for adverse impacts.

2 *Biodiversity, biological environment and ecology*

Matters include but are not limited to:

- Implications for European sites and protected species.
- Loss of or change to habitats, both estuarine and terrestrial, including timing of works and activities and resultant seasonal effects.

- Potential impacts of waste disposal transportation and method and location of disposal.
- Adequacies of the baseline assessment, the assessments of likely significant effects and any proposed monitoring regime and mitigation. Any measures to avoid, reduce and compensate for adverse impacts.

3 *Coastal/river change*

Matters include but are not limited to:

- The effects of the application proposals on channel, bank and foreshore erosion and deposition (affecting flood defence structures, transport infrastructure, ecology, recreation and heritage assets).
- Restoration of and works to foreshore.
- Any proposed monitoring and measures to avoid, reduce and compensate for adverse impacts.

4 *Compulsory acquisition and related matters*

Matters include but are not limited to:

- Justification for compulsory acquisition of the land, rights and powers that are sought by the draft development consent order.
- Alternatives both in relation to individual plots and specific sites.
- Statutory undertaker land and apparatus and potential detriment to the carrying on of an undertaking and any need for replacement land in that context.
- Open space land and rights over that land, loss of open space and any need for replacement land in that context.
- Resource implications in particular the availability and certainty of funding for the project, blight and hardship matters and compensation.
- Considerations in relation to mooring rights and displacement both permanent and temporary.
- Protective provisions and indemnities.
- Limitations on rights of way, access and works to property likely to have a direct effect beyond the property interests and Book of Reference defined limits of compulsory acquisition sought.

5 *Design, landscape and visual impact*

Matters include but are not limited to:

- The extent to which the design would be attractive, durable, resilient and adaptable and whether the project would demonstrate good design in terms of siting in relation to existing and proposed townscape, landscape, local context and setting.
- The main alternatives to the designs considered.
- Visual impact and public perceptions of the landscape, riverscape and townscape of the area.

- Loss of and change to existing tree and vegetation cover, the duration of impact and the delivery mechanisms and timescales for mitigation.
- The extent to which the design would meet the functional objectives of the project and operational, safety and security requirements.

6 *Flood risk and climate change*

Matters include but are not limited to:

- Appropriate adaptation and consequential impacts and mitigation.
- Potential impact of settlement on flood defence assets.
- The extent to which design and landscape measures maximise permeability and the potential for preventing rainwater from entering the sewerage system.
- Lifetime and capacity of new infrastructure.
- Any update required against UK Climate Projections.

7 *Historic environment*

Matters include but are not limited to:

- The effects on the significance of buildings and structures identified as heritage assets.
- The effects of settlement on heritage assets.
- The effects on the settings of heritage assets and the wider historic environment.
- The measures to protect heritage assets which are as yet undiscovered.

8 *Land use including regeneration and open space*

Matters include but are not limited to:

- The effects on current and planned regeneration schemes and housing delivery.
- The effects on open space including Metropolitan Open Land.

9 *Noise and disturbance*

Matters include but are not limited to:

- The effects of noise and vibration on residential amenity (including shift workers) and other sensitive receptors such as recording studios and schools.
- Noise and vibration from transportation particularly during construction.
- Use of assessment methodologies and mitigation and thresholds proposed for construction and operational noise levels and the 'Thames Tideway Tunnel noise insulation and temporary re-housing policy' and 'compensation programmes'.

10 *Rationale for the selection of worksites and drive strategies*

Matters include but are not limited to:

- Detail of specific sites, routes, designs, layout, construction programmes and operational processes.

- Sites and alternatives including Carnwath Road Riverside, Chambers Wharf and the matters relating to the drive to versus the drive from these locations, Deptford Church Street, King Edward Memorial Park Foreshore and the considerations raised by the potential for use of land at Heckford Street.

11 *Socio-economic effects*

Matters include but are not limited to:

- Health and wellbeing including any measures to avoid, reduce or compensate for adverse impacts.
- The effects of the proposed development on the community including amenity, use and enjoyment of open space and equalities impacts.
- The effects on river access, occupiers (residential, leisure and business) and users.
- The effects on schools, businesses and tourism.
- Baseline assessment methodologies and mitigation.

12 *Traffic, travel and transportation*

Matters include but are not limited to:

- The effects in relation to waste management and disposal strategy.
- The effects of settlement on transportation bridges and tunnels (road, rail and pedestrian/cycle etc).
- The effects on existing transport networks (highway, waterway, rail and pedestrian/cycle etc) and parking and the capacity for and impacts on existing users.

13 *Water quality and resources*

Matters include but are not limited to:

- The effects of proposed project on water quality – discharges during construction, maintenance periods and operation.
- The effects of the proposed design for reduction of discharges from each combined sewer overflow connection site.
- Relationship with the River Basin Management Plans, estuary management plan and water resources management plans and the requirements of the Water Framework Directive.
- Mitigation and management during construction, operational and decommissioning phases.

Statements of Common Ground

Written by: James Pereira QC, ftb
Edited by: Michael Humphries QC, ftb

Introduction

Paragraph 57 of the DCLG Guidance for the examination of applications for development consent (April 2013) describes a statement of common ground in the following way:

> 'A statement of common ground is a written statement prepared jointly by the applicant and another party or parties, setting out any matters on which they agree. As well as identifying matters which are not in real dispute, it may also be useful for a statement to identify areas where agreement has not been reached. The statement should include references to show where those matters are dealt with in the written representations or other documentary evidence.'

Statements of common ground are given legislative recognition in rule 8 of the Infrastructure Planning (Examination Procedure) Rules 2010, SI 2010/103 (as amended), which provides that among the matters to be included in the timetable which is set at, or shortly after, the Preliminary Meeting on the DCO application, is the period within which the application and any interested party must agree a statement of common ground.

The purpose of a statement of common ground

Statements of common ground are useful documents to assist the parties and the Examining Authority in identifying and understanding what are the issues of dispute and what are the issues that are agreed between the parties to the statement. This is useful to ensure that the evidence and the examination focuses on the material differences between the parties. The effective use of such statements is expected to lead to a more efficient examination process.

The form and content of statements of common ground

A statement of common ground is a written statement prepared jointly by the parties to the statement. It will usually be signed by a representative from each party. It is possible for the parties to an examination to enter into more than one statement of common ground, and for there to be different statements of common ground between different parties.

The content of a statement of common ground will depend upon the subject-matter of the statement, which in turn will depend upon the issues raised by the particular application. Paragraph 59 of the DCLG Guidance for the examination of applications for development consent (April 2013) advises as follows:

> 'The statement should contain the basic information on which the parties have agreed, such as the precise nature of the proposed infrastructure, a description of the site and its planning history. In addition to basic information about the application, agreement can often be reached on technical matters and topics that rely on basic statistical data. For example, traffic evidence can be simplified and the issues refined by agreeing matters such as traffic flows, design standards, and the basis for forecasting the level of traffic the application would generate . . .'

The following points should be noted:

- It would be usual for there to be statements of common ground between the applicant for the DCO and the main statutory parties who are relevant to the application. This might include, for example, bodies such as the local planning authority, the local highway authority, the Environment Agency, Natural England, English Heritage and, where appropriate, the Marine Management Organisation.
- Cross referencing to other documents that are before the Examining Authority, or annexing documents that support propositions in the statement of common ground, can be a useful means of increasing the weight that such documents carry. It also helps the reader of the statement to understand the basis of the agreement (or disagreement), which in turn will help to shape the examination process.
- Statements of common ground are often made on a topic or issue basis. For example, in any one application there may be a statement of common ground setting out a general description of the project, another statement of common ground on pre-application procedures, another on noise impacts, another on nature conservation matters, and so on.
- In cases where the statement of common ground concerns matters of expert evidence and opinion, it is good practice for it to be signed by the parties' relevant experts, and for it to carry an appropriate experts' declaration. This will assist the examining authority in assessing the weight to be given to the statement, and will help it decide who to question about the statement, should questioning be necessary.

The timing of statements of common ground

It is usual for the Examining Authority to set a deadline for the submission of statements of common ground in the formal letter which is sent out after the Preliminary Meeting has been held following acceptance of the DCO application. However, the early submission of statements of common ground is encouraged, and applicants are advised that they need not wait until the examination period to prepare or submit statements of common ground. The DCLG Guidance gives particular encouragement to reaching agreement about any requirements (ie conditions) that should be attached to a development consent order if granted before the examination commences. The Planning Officer's Society has endorsed the DCLG's encouragement of making statements of common ground at the pre-application stage (see paragraph 3.28 of 'Responding to Nationally Significant Infrastructure Projects' Advice Note, August 2010 (Planning Officer's Society)).

Preparing statements of common ground

There is no set way of preparing a statement of common ground. Paragraph 60 of the DCLG Guidance for the examination of applications for development consent (April 2013) advises as follows:

> 'How such agreement is reached will vary depending on the nature and complexity of the application and the matters at issue. Where there are only two or three major parties involved and the issues are fairly straightforward, the Examining Authority may encourage the parties at the preliminary meeting to get together with a view to producing a single statement of common ground containing agreed facts. For more complex applications it may be necessary for the applicant to agree a number of statements of common ground with different parties, each focused on separate aspects of the application.'

It is to be remembered that the parties are expected to co-operate with the examination process, and hence in the preparation of statements of common ground. Where the statements involve matters of expert opinion, any experts involved in preparing the statement of common ground should do so in accordance with their overriding duty to the Examining Authority.

The effect of a statement of common ground

It is important to recognise that the Examining Authority is not bound to accept the contents of a statement of common ground, nor are participants in the examination process who are not parties to the statement. Parties to statements of common ground therefore need to be prepared to answer questions on the contents of the statement and to justify the agreement reached.

As paragraph 61 of the DCLG Guidance for the examination of applications for development consent (April 2013) makes clear:

> 'The duty of the Examining Authority is not simply to accept the statement of common ground or to react to the evidence presented. The role of the Examining Authority is to ensure that all aspects of any given matter are explored thoroughly, especially with regard to the matters fundamental to the decision, rather than simply accepting the statement of common ground without question.
>
> Consequently, the Examining Authority should probe the evidence thoroughly if their judgement or professional expertise indicates that either:
>
> - all of the evidence necessary for a soundly reasoned decision has not been put before them, or
> - that a material part of the evidence in front of them has not been adequately tested.'

However, it is important that any questioning or challenge to the statement of common ground from the Examining Authority is conducted fairly. It is good practice to ensure that fair, advanced, warning is given by the Examining Authority of any questioning or examination of matters that are agreed in the statement of common ground. In extreme cases, where the parties have proceeded on the basis that an issue is agreed but the decision-maker goes back on that agreement in its decision without giving fair warning to the parties, and without allowing them to comment, the courts may be prepared to quash the decision as being procedurally unfair: see *Edward Ware New Homes v Secretary of State* [2003] EWCA Civ 566, where an Inspector's decision letter following a planning appeal was quashed because he had reached a contrary view on an issue which was agreed in the statement of common ground between the parties at the inquiry, and which had not been treated as controversial at the inquiry, without giving the parties the opportunity to comment first.

Compulsory Acquisition Hearings

Written by: Richard Honey, ftb
Edited by: Michael Humphries QC, ftb

Introduction

This article examines the various provisions relating to a compulsory purchase hearing. Unlike an issue specific hearing, a compulsory acquisition hearing may be required as of right in defined circumstances.

Requiring a compulsory acquisition hearing

Where an application for a development consent order (DCO) includes a request for authorisation of compulsory acquisition of land or an interest in or right over land, the Examining Authority must fix, and cause each 'affected person' to be informed of, the deadline by which an affected person must notify the Secretary of State that the person wishes a compulsory acquisition hearing to be held (PA 2008, s 92(2)).

PA 2008, s 92(5) defines an 'affected person' by reference to section 59(4) of the Planning Act 2008 which states that 'A person is an affected person … if the applicant, after making diligent inquiry, knows that the person is interested in the land to which the compulsory acquisition request relates or any part of that land.'

At or as soon as practical after the end of the Preliminary Meeting for an examination held pursuant to PA 2008, s 88, rule 8 of the Infrastructure Planning (Examination Procedure) Rules 2010, SI 2010/103 ('the 2010 Rules') require the Examining Authority to set the timetable for the examination of the application including '(g) the date by which any affected person must notify the Examining authority or their wish to be heard at a compulsory acquisition hearing'. This timetable is set out in what is generally known as the Examining Authority's Rule 8 letter. Rule 13 of the 2010 Rules provides that at least 21 days notice must be given of a deadline for an affected person to give notice requesting a compulsory acquisition hearing.

If any such a request is duly made, then PA 2008, s 92(3) makes clear that a compulsory acquisition hearing must be held. The 2010 Rules also provide that at least 21 days notice must be given to an affected person of the date, time and place of the compulsory acquisition hearing itself (rule 13(3)). In practice considerably more notice is likely to be given.

Arrangements for compulsory acquisition hearings

The Preliminary Meeting held under rule 7 will usually consider, where necessary, how compulsory acquisition hearings are to be arranged and timetabled, prior to the timetable actually being issued. Even before then, it is normal for persons to have indicated in their relevant representations whether they qualify as an affected person and whether they would like a compulsory acquisition hearing to be held.

It is possible for the Examining Authority to consider all compulsory acquisition requests relating to the same application at the same compulsory acquisition hearing, although it can also convene separate compulsory acquisition hearings (rule 15(2)).

The conduct of compulsory acquisition hearings

It is for the Examining Authority to decide how a compulsory acquisition hearing is to be conducted (PA 2008, s 94(3)). Within that context, however, both the applicant and each affected person are 'entitled' to make oral representations about the compulsory acquisition of land at a compulsory acquisition hearing (s 92(4)).

The DCLG 'Guidance for the examination of applications for development consent' (April 2013) states that a compulsory acquisition hearing is intended to consider the issues arising in connection with the authorisation of the compulsory acquisition of land (para 30). It also says that affected persons 'may make oral representations about the compulsory acquisition requests' (para 83) and that 'a key matter to be considered will be whether there is a compelling case in the public interest for the compulsory acquisition of land' (para 87).

The general provisions in relation to hearings at a DCO examination are found in PA 2008, ss 94, 95 and 95A. A hearing must be in public (s 94(2). The Examining Authority has the power to decide how the hearing is to be conducted. PA 2008, s 94(4) states that it is for the authority to decide whether a person making oral representations may be questioned, and the matters on which they may be questioned, as well as the amount of time for making representations and asking questions. PA 2008, s 94(7) goes on to provide that the Examining Authority must apply the principle that any oral questioning should be undertaken by the Examining Authority itself, except where the it thinks that oral questioning by another person is necessary in order to ensure 'adequate testing of any representations' or 'that a person has a fair chance to put the person's case'. The Examining Authority can refuse to allow representations to be made at a hearing for a number of reasons, including that they relate to compensation for compulsory acquisition of land or of an interest in or right over land (s 94(8)).

The 2010 Rules set more detailed rules for the conduct of hearings. Rule 14(2) obliges the Examining Authority to identify at the start of any hearing the matters to be considered at the hearing and any matters on which they require further explanation. Rule 14(3) provides that oral representations must be based on representations submitted in writing earlier in the process, but rule 14(4) allows other issues to be referred to. Rule 14(9) entitles an affected person to be represented by any other person at a hearing.

The DCLG 'Guidance for the examination of applications for development consent' (April 2013) provides that hearings should be 'carried out as efficiently as possible, whilst remaining fair to all parties and thorough in their examination of evidence' (para 86). In relation to compulsory acquisition, it is likely that the Examining Authority will allow more latitude to objectors than in other types of hearings, as they are subject to appropriation of land or rights against their will.

The DCLG guidance provides that the examining authority 'will probe, test and assess the evidence through direct questioning of persons making oral representations' (para 92). The Examining Authority is able to appoint a barrister or solicitor itself to test evidence through oral questioning. The DCLG guidance also says that the Examining authority may allow cross-examination 'where it considers that this is necessary to ensure the adequate testing of any representations, or where it considers that it is necessary to allow an interested party a fair chance to put their case' (para 94) and goes on to say that the authority 'will ensure that parties are not denied the opportunity to ask questions where the answers are required in order to complete their cases' (para 95).

It is possible for the Examining Authority to allow witnesses to be called at compulsory acquisition hearings. The DCLG guidance explains that although there is no automatic right to call witnesses, the authority has the discretion to allow this to be done either by the authority of its own volition or upon the request of a party (para 97).

Whilst PA 2008, s 92 entitles certain parties to make 'oral representations' and s 94 places limits on the questioning of a person making oral representations other, that is, than by the Examining Authority itself, experience so far suggests that Examining Authorities do on occasion conduct compulsory acquisition hearings in a reasonably formal way.

For example, at the first compulsory acquisition hearing in June 2011, which was in relation to an application for an energy recovery facility at Rookery South, the Examining Authority allowed the calling and cross-examination of witnesses by counsel and the making of opening and closing submissions, over four days. The main issues covered at that hearing were the justification for the development proposed (scale and need), alternative sites and the policy context. The Examining Authority's decision dated 13 October 2011 records that at the hearing 'some issues relevant to the consideration of the grant of development consent were examined further in the context of compulsory acquisition' (para 7.87).

In this context it is perhaps interesting to note that, in relation to compulsory purchase orders, the Compulsory Purchase (Inquiries Procedure) Rules 2007, SI 2007/3617 set out an entitlement to cross-examine witnesses (rule 16(3)).

Other compulsory acquisition hearings have been structured more like other hearings, that is, with an agenda of issues to be addressed in turn and very much led by the Inspector(s) (see, for example, the Ipswich Rail Chord agenda for hearing in February 2012 and the King's Lynn B Power Station Connection agenda for hearing in April 2013). In other cases witnesses have prepared statements of evidence in support of the acquisition (see, for example, the Redditch Branch Enhancement hearing in April 2013).

Perhaps the underlying message here is that practice is still emerging, but the procedural rules are sufficiently flexible to allow a range of responses appropriate to the particular circumstances.

Open Floor Hearings

Written by: Hereward Phillpot QC, ftb
Edited by: Michael Humphries QC, ftb

PA 2008, s 93

PA 2008, s 93 establishes a duty on the Examining Authority to cause an open floor hearing (OFH) to be held where one is duly requested by an interested party (IP). The purpose of an OFH is to hear, first hand, from IPs about their thoughts on the proposed development.

The Examining Authority must first fix and inform IPs of a deadline by which they must notify the Secretary of State of their wish to be heard at an OFH (PA 2008, s 93(1)). Where at least one notification has been received in time, the Examining Authority is obliged to cause an OFH to be held (s 93(2)), at which each IP is entitled to make oral representations about the application.

The deadline for the purposes of PA 2008, s 93(1) must be at least 21 days after the date on which notice of the deadline is given (Infrastructure Planning (Examination Procedure) Rules 2010, SI 2010/103 (the 2010 Rules), r 13(1)). The Examining Authority must notify all IPs of the date of any OFH as soon as practicable after the expiry of the deadline (r 13(3)).

Procedural rules

The 2010 Rules do not make very detailed provision for the procedure to be adopted at hearings, leaving the precise procedure to the discretion of the Examining Authority. They do, however, set some important ground ruless, which apply to both OFHs and issue specific hearings (ISH).

The Examining Authority shall determine the procedure at the hearing (r 14(1)), identifying at the start of the hearing the matters to be considered, and any matters where it requires further explanation from IPs (r 14(2)). That does not prevent additional matters being referred to during the hearing, subject to the Examining Authority's discretion as to how the hearing is to be conducted (r 14(4)).

Any oral representations must be based on either the relevant or written representations made by or on behalf of the IP (r 14(3)).

The Examining Authority may proceed with the OFH even if the IP who requested it does not attend (r 14(7)).

DCLG/PINS Guidance

The main guidance on hearings (including OFHs) is provided in the DCLG Guidance document *Planning Act 2008: Guidance for the examination of applications for development consent*. A summary of some of the points made in the CLG Guidance is to be found in PINS *Advice Note 8.5: Participating in the examination*, but the latter document adds nothing of substance.

The DCLG Guidance explains that, subject to the Examining Authority's powers of control over the conduct of the hearing, all IPs will have an opportunity to make oral representations about the application (paragraph 85). However, it also underlines the point that it is for the Examining Authority to determine how the hearing is conducted, including the amount of time to be allowed for the making of a person's representations. The Examining Authority is expected to use this power to ensure that hearings are carried out 'as efficiently as possible, whilst remaining fair to all parties and thorough in their examination of evidence' (paragraph 86). In practice the emphasis has tended to be on efficiency and expedition, not only to keep the examination timetable on track, but also to try to make time for all IPs to have their say. IPs will generally be reminded that the process is primarily a written one, and that there is no need to repeat points that have already been made in writing.

Those with similar interests, who are likely to submit similar evidence, are encouraged to work to agree upon a spokesperson to put forward a joint case. Repetition of points is strongly discouraged (paragraph 91).

Any questioning of IPs will generally be undertaken by the Examining Authority itself, or an advocate appointed to assist it, and should not be aggressively adversarial (paragraph 92). In certain circumstances cross-examination may be allowed (paragraphs 93 and 95), but in practice this would be highly unusual (see below) and there will generally be little if anything to be gained on the part of the applicant from the cross-examination of IPs at an OFH.

There is no automatic right to call witnesses at hearings, but the Examining Authority has a discretion to permit any person other than the IP to make oral representations. Where an IP asks for an expert witness to be allowed to take part in the examination, the request should not be denied unreasonably (paragraph 97). In practice evidence from expert witnesses will tend to be confined to ISHs.

The recording and filming of proceedings is allowed, subject to it not disrupting the hearing (paragraph 98).

Practice at OFHs

The following points can be made about the emerging practice at OFHs:

- PINS makes audio recordings of the hearings, and these recordings (together with written summaries) are made available on the PINS website. Listening to these recordings provides an invaluable insight into how an OFH is likely to be conducted.
- The Examining Authority does not generally allow IPs to use the OFH as an opportunity to question the applicant.
- Responses by the applicant to points made by IPs at OFHs will generally be expected to be provided in writing in due course (sometimes alongside responses made to written representations).
- Therefore, whilst a representative of the applicant will usually be in attendance, this may well not be the applicant's advocate.

- If large numbers of IPs register a wish to speak at an OFH, then the time available for each IP will be correspondingly limited (for example, in some of the OFHs held in relation to EDF's application for its new nuclear power station at Hinkley Point in Somerset, a limit of 3 minutes per person was adopted). Objectors should therefore be aware that mass participation in an OFH may ultimately be counter-productive.
- Although there can be a temptation on the part of applicants to view OFHs as little more than an opportunity for objectors to let off steam (akin to hearing from members of the public in a planning inquiry under the Town and Country Planning Act 1990, s 78), this would be a mistake. The Examining Authority appears to be very conscious of the additional burden placed upon its shoulders by the inquisitorial nature of the examination system, and will tend to pick up and pursue any apparently well-founded concerns raised by IPs. Applicants should therefore take care to note what is said at OFHs, particularly by members of the Examining Authority in response to concerns that are aired before them.
    - Do the members of the Examining Authority appear to be interested in and/or sympathetic to particular points raised by IPs?
    - What questions do the members of the Examining Authority ask IPs, and what (if any) further details emerge in answer to those questions?
    - Are any reassurances given to IPs that particular issues that are raised will be a focus of later hearings (eg on requirements)?

Meritorious concerns raised by IPs at an OFH will generally be revisited by the Examining Authority at the relevant moment in issue specific hearings later in the examination, and/or in written questions. A well-advised applicant will therefore pay heed to these advanced indications, and prepare its responses accordingly.

Site Inspections

Written by: Gregory Jones QC, ftb
Edited by: Michael Humphries QC, ftb

Introduction

Site inspections are invariably carried out in respect of all planning appeals to the Planning Inspectorate whether the appeals are by way of written representations, hearings or public inquiry conducted under the Town and Country Planning Act 1990 (as amended) (TCPA 1990). Accordingly, whilst there is no direct case authority upon the conduct of site inspections carried out by the Examining Authority under the PA 2008 or of the Infrastructure Planning (Examination Procedure) Rules 2010, SI 2010/103 ('the Examination Procedure Rules') in respect of NSIPs, there is an established body of case law on the conduct of site inspections by planning inspectors, see for example, the Planning Inspectorate Good Practice Note 13 at http://www.planningportal.gov.uk/uploads/pins/gpa_13.pdf which gives general guidance on the conduct of site inspections carried out under the Town and Country Planning Act 1990.

Although strictly speaking, the PINS Guidance Note 13 on site inspections applies only to inspections conducted under the TCPA 1990 its guidance on site inspections for hearings does appear to represent a statement of good practice for the conduct of hearings for DCO applications under the Planning Act 2008. This is helpful because only brief guidance on the conduct of site inspections in respect of NSIPs is given in the DCLG 'Guidance on the examination of applications for development consent' ('the DCLG Examination Guidance').

Unaccompanied site inspections

It is common practice for the persons appointed to examine applications for development consent to make a site visit to familiarise themselves with the proposed development area: see paragraph 99 of the DCLG Examination Guidance.

Rule 16(1) of the Examination Procedure Rules provides that the Examining Authority may make an unaccompanied inspection of an application site before, or during the examination, without giving notice to the persons entitled to take part in the examination.

Such inspections are commonly known as an 'unaccompanied site inspection.' They frequently take place in ordinary planning appeals whether they are conducted by written representations, hearing or public inquiry.

The Examining Authority must ensure that it acts fairly and lawfully in the conduct of any site visits. Accordingly, it is submitted that the Examining Authority should, as matter of good practice, let the parties know what the Examining Authority has seen on the unaccompanied site visit. The best way to do this is to make a written record of the unaccompanied site visit available to the parties – it can be put on the hearing website – describing anything which it saw on the site visit which it considers might be of potential relevance to determination of the application. This allows the parties an opportunity to make representation about anything which the Examining Authority has seen.

In *R (London Borough of Haringey) v The Secretary of State for Communities and Local Government, O.A Kwateng (Ebenezer Community Learning Centre)* [2008] EWHC 1201 (Admin); a planning inspector on a site inspection had observed that neighbouring buildings were being used for educational purposes and relied upon that fact in arriving at his decision to grant planning permission. The High Court quashed his decision, holding not only that it was unfair not to raise this new matter with the parties and allow them a fair opportunity to make representations upon it but also because it subsequently proved that he had made an error of fact in assuming that the educational use was lawful or had been tolerated by the local planning authority. The same principles would appear to apply to a site inspection under the Planning Act 2008.

An unaccompanied site visit might require the Examining Authority to gain access to the site from the owner of the site. The Examining Authority should be wary of engaging in any conversation other than normal pleasantries and certainly not discuss matters relating to the application with, or in the presence of, the owner or his representatives (see *Wilkson Properties Ltd v Royal Borough of Kensington and Chelsea* [2010] EWHC 3274; [2011] JPL 1083).

Accompanied site inspections

Rule 16(2) of the Examination Procedure Rules allows the Examining Authority 'before the completion of its examination of the application or specified matters, inspect any site to which the application or specified matters relate in the company of any interested party or their representative.' This power is more widely drafted than the power to carry out an unaccompanied site visit under rule 16(1). The former is restricted to an inspection of the application site, the latter permits the Examining Authority to conduct an accompanied site inspection to 'any site' to which 'the application or specified matters relate.' This may, for example, allow the Examining Authority, where such issues are relevant, to inspect sites which are said to be comparable sites, or alternatives sites, or sites which are said to be impacted by the proposed development.

It is important to note that rule 16(2) of the Examination Procedure Rules grants a power; it does not impose an obligation. Having said that, where a decision maker has a power, it has a corresponding duty to consider whether to exercise it (see eg *Stovin v Wise* [1996] 3 WLR 388). Thus, an Examining Authority is obliged, at least, to consider any request by an interested party to conduct an accompanied inspection at any such site coming within rule 16(2) of the Examination Procedure Rules. It is for the Examining Authority to determine whether such an inspection is required.

Sometimes landowners are reluctant to allow opposing parties to accompany inspectors on site visits. There are, indeed, instances where planning inspectors considering applications under the TCPA 1990 have gone on site inspections where third parties have been excluded from attending by the land owner. Such approach is said not to be unfair where the local planning authority that has refused to grant planning permission is also present on the site visit to represent the 'opposition side'. This view is open to considerable doubt.

In applications under the PA 2008, however, the role of the local planning authority is quite different and an Examining Authority should be extremely wary of conducting an accompanied site inspection where a particular party has been refused access by the landowner. An Examining Authority could refuse a request for an accompanied site inspection under rule 16(2) of the Examination Procedure Rules. This may not be a significant problem where the site in question is the application site because the Examining Authority has the power to go on an unaccompanied site inspection under rule 16(1) of the Examination Procedure Rules. However, the Examining Authority has no power to go on an unaccompanied site inspection of any site that is not part of the application site. In practice, a landowner who is a party to the proceedings would be well advised not to refuse access to the representatives of an opposing party, since the absence of an accompanied site inspection on their land is likely to tell against the landowner's case whether it be as a promoter or as objector to the NSIP application.

Not surprisingly rule 16 (3) of the Examination Procedure Rules provides that where the Examining Authority intends to make an accompanied site inspection 'it must notify all interested parties of the date, time and place at which it proposes to make the inspection.' However, rule 16(4) of the Examination Procedure Rules provides the Examining authority 'shall not be bound to defer an [accompanied site] inspection ... *where an interested party is neither present nor represented at the time appointed.*' (emphasis added). However, this does not mean that the Examining authority can fix the time of the accompanied site visit without regard for the availability of the interested parties. Like any decision it must be exercised fairly and in a way which would not unfairly cause prejudice to any particular party.

Paragraph 101 of the DCLG Examination Guidance makes clear that 'The Examining Authority will refuse to hear evidence or other submissions during any accompanied visit. It is acceptable, however, for people to draw their attention to particular features of the site and its surroundings.' If something arises at the site inspection which is relevant and which has not been addressed at the hearing, the Examining authority should, depending on the circumstances, either reopen the hearing or invite the matter to be addressed by the parties in writing, rather than discussing the matter with the representatives of the parties who happened to be at the site inspection (see *R (London Borough of Haringey) v The Secretary of State for Communities and Local Government, O.A Kwateng (Ebenezer Community Learning Centre)* (above).

In *Fox v Secretary of State for the Environment* [1993] JPL 448 an inspector who travelled to a site inspection in a car with one of the parties was criticised by the High Court, as was the inspector who went for a drink with both parties and then stayed behind to finish his drink with the local planning authority witness when the applicant had finished up and left (*Cotterell v Secretary of State for the Environment* [1991] JPL 1155). In both cases the decisions were not quashed because the other party had known what had happened and agreed or waived his right to object. Nonetheless, it is not conduct to be encouraged. It is submitted that the distinguished editors of *De Smith's Judicial Review* (6th Edition, Sweet & Maxwell) are correct when they state at 10:058: 'There is little doubt that an inspector who accepts hospitality or a lift on the site visit from one party in the absence of the other would be disqualified for bias, but this would not be the case where the inspector had asked sought and obtained the consent of the parties.'

By contrast, it is respectfully submitted that the courts in England and Wales are unlikely to follow the approach recently adopted by the High Court of Northern Ireland in *Alternative A5 Alliance's Application for Judicial Review* [2013] NIQB 30 which found that there was no apparent bias where inspectors, on more than one occasion, rode in cars with officers employed in the promotion of a road scheme without notifying objectors, still less, getting their consent.

Procedures Following Completion of Examination

Written by: Isabella Tafur, ftb
Edited by: Michael Humphries QC, ftb

Introduction

The timetables for the examination of applications under the PA 2008 are considered in an article entitled 'Timescales for applications'. The examination must be completed within six months, from the day after the preliminary meeting. When the Examining authority has completed its examination, it must inform each of the interested parties of that fact (PA 2008, s 99). The focus of this article is the procedure following completion of the examination.

Reporting to the Secretary of State

Within three months from the deadline for completion of the examination, or, if the examination closed earlier, within three months from the date of its closure, the Examining authority must make a report to the Secretary of State, setting outs its findings and conclusions in respect of the application, and its recommendation as to the decision to be made (PA 2008, s 98(3) and the Infrastructure Planning (Examination Procedure) Rules 2010, SI 2010/103, r 19).

There is no statutory provision governing the form of the Examining Authority's report. However, reports generally provide a file reference at the outset (summarising the dates on which the application was made, received and accepted; the dates on which the examination commenced and closed and a brief summary of the development), followed by a summary of the Examining Authority's recommendation and the main body of the report. With certain minor variations, the main body of the reports often follow a format such as this: introduction, main features of the proposal, legal and policy context, findings and conclusions on main issues, overall conclusion and recommendation on the case for development consent, compulsory acquisition, the development consent order, overall conclusions and recommendation.

Extending the deadline for the report

The period for making the report can be extended by the Secretary of State, who is empowered pursuant to PA 2008, s 98(4) to set a later date for any of the deadlines set out in PA 2008, s 98. The same deadline may be extended more than once, and can be extended even after the deadline has already passed (PA 2008, s 98(5)).

Where the power of extension is exercised, the Secretary of State must notify each interested party of the new deadline, must publicise a new deadline in such a manner as he thinks appropriate and must make a statement (either written or oral) to the House of Parliament of which he is a member, announcing the new deadline.

The Secretary of State's decision

Having received the report from the Examining Authority, the Secretary of State must make a decision on the application within three months of its receipt – or within three months of the deadline under PA 2008, s 98(3) – whichever is the earlier date (PA 2008, s 107(1)).

If the Secretary of State differs from the Examining Authority on any matter of fact mentioned in, or appearing to the Secretary of State to be material to, a conclusion reached by the Examining Authority, or if he takes into account new evidence or new matters of fact, and is for that reason disposed to disagree with a recommendation made by the Examining Authority, he must not come to a decision at variance with the recommendation without first notifying all interested parties of his disagreement with the Examining Authority and the reasons for it, and giving them an opportunity to make representations in writing in respect of any new evidence or new matter of fact (SI 2010/103, r 19(3)). SI 2010/103, r 10 (which makes provisions in respect of written representations, such as empowering the Examining Authority to accept representations by persons who are not interested parties, and ensuring that interested parties are given the opportunity to comment on representations) will apply to any such representation in writing, save that paragraphs (2) and (4) will not apply (which require a minimum period of 21 days to be allowed for the submission of representations and require the representation to identify those parts of the application with which it agrees and disagrees).

Extending the deadline for the decision

Similar to the power of extension under PA 2008, s 98(4), the Secretary of State is also empowered to extend the deadline for making his decision, pursuant to PA 2008, s 107(3). Again, he can extend a deadline more than once, and may extend it even after the date for the deadline has passed. If the deadline is extended, the Secretary of State must make a statement (either written or oral) to the House of Parliament of which he is a member, and must publish that statement in such a form and manner as he considers appropriate.

Experience so far

So far, the power to extend the deadline for the Examining authority to provide a report to the Secretary of State (PA 2008, s 98(4)) has not been exercised in any of the DCO applications submitted to the Planning Inspectorate. In relation to the Thames Tideway Tunnel DCO application, the applicant made an application to extend the length of the examination but this was refused by the Secretary of State.

The power to extend the deadline for making a decision has been exercised once (pursuant to PA 2008, s 107(3)), in respect of the Able Marine Energy Park application. The Secretary of State for Transport issued a statement on 21 May 2013, explaining that he had decided to set a new deadline for the decision to 24 July 2013 (an extension of two months) in order to allow the applicant to negotiate with the Crown Estate the terms of a lease of land that was required for the project and in order to ensure compliance with PA 2008, s 135 and the Crown Estate's statutory duties (https://www.gov.uk/government/speeches/planning-act-2008-application-for-the-proposed-able-marine-energy-park-development-consent-order).

Amendments to a DCO Application

Written by: Isabella Tafur, ftb
Edited by: Michael Humphries QC, ftb

Introduction

Circumstances may arise in which an application for a development consent order requires amendment after it has been accepted by the Secretary of State. There has been some dispute as to the extent to which amendments can be made to the application post-acceptance.

This article examines the extent to which is it possible to amend a DCO application post-acceptance.

PA 2008, s 114

PA 2008, s 114(1) provides that when the Secretary of State has decided an application for an order granting development consent, he or she must either

- make the order granting development consent; or
- refuse development consent.

PA 2008, s 114(1) is not explicit on the point as to whether the Secretary of State can make the order 'with or without modifications', but there is nothing in s.114(1) to limit the Secretary of State's power to make such order he thinks fit.

PA2008, s 114(2) empowers the Secretary of State to make provision regulating the procedure to be followed if he proposes to make an order granting development consent in terms which are materially different from those proposed in the application. No such 'provision' has so far been made by regulation or otherwise, save in relation to compulsory acquisition by the Infrastructure Planning (Compulsory Acquisition) Regulations 2010, SI 2010/104. However, there is nothing in s 114(2) that 'requires' the Secretary of State to make provision for any particular procedure if he proposed to make an order granting development consent on terms materially different from those proposed in the application.

Thus the better view is PA2008, s 114 does allow the Secretary of State to make an order granting development consent on terms materially different from those applied for. This view appears to be entirely consistent with the, so-called, Bob Neill letter.

On 28 November 2011 the then Secretary of State, Bob Neill MP, wrote to Sir Michael Pitt on the scope of s 114 in the context of the Brig y Cwm application. He set out the Government's position as follows:

> 'My Department has received representation questioning whether section 114(1) empowers the decision-maker to make a development consent order in different terms from that applied for. This was the subject of an amendment laid at the Lord Report stage of the Localism Bill, and in response, Earl Attlee confirmed the Government's view, that section 114(1) clearly places

the responsibility for making a development consent order on the decision-maker, and does not limit the terms in which it can be made. If follows from this that the decision-maker has them power under section 114(1) to make a development consent order which is different from that originally applied for, and that no regulations are needed under section 114(2) in order to do so.

The power to make regulations in section 114(2) is unconnected, and has no bearing on the extent of the s 114(1) power. Section 114(2) merely provides the Secretary of State with a power to make regulations about how material changes should be dealt with, if he thinks it appropriate to do so.'

The Examination Procedure Rules

The Infrastructure Planning (Examination Procedure) Rules 2010, SI 2010/103, r 2 provides that amendments can be made to an application post-acceptance, by defining 'application' in the following way:

> 'an application for development consent under section 37 (application for orders granting development consent) and includes –
>
> (a) part of an application;
>
> (b) any accompanying documents and further representations made by the applicant; and
>
> *(c) any amendments made to the application.*' [emphasis added].

The materiality of proposed changes

In the Bob Neill letter, the Secretary of State also commented that:

> 'This power provided by section 114(1) is, of course, limited in a number of ways. If the Examining Authority decides to consider material changes to an application as part of the examination, the Examining Authority will need to act reasonably, and in accordance with the principles of natural justice. In particular the principles arising from the *Wheatcroft* case must be fully addressed, which essentially require that anyone affected by amended proposals must have a fair opportunity to have their views heard and properly taken into account regarding them.
>
> ... Depending on the circumstances, in accordance with the principles set out in *Wheatcroft*, the Examining Authority may need to:
>
> - extend the examination using the power in section 98(4) of the Act to consult interested parties on the effect of the proposed amendments, and allow time to consider any amendments accepted for examination
> - take into account what publicity (if any) the promoter has carried out to ensure people who are not interested parties have an opportunity to make representations
> - use the general power to control the examination of an application in section 87(1) of the 2008 Act to make changes to the timetable to allow for representations to be made regarding any such amendments

- exercise its discretion under rules 10(3) and 14(10) of the Infrastructure Planning (Examination Procedure) Rules 2010 to permit representations to be made by people who are not interested parties in cases where it is appropriate to do so.'

DCLG Guidance for the examination of applications for development consent (2013) (paragraph 105–107) provides as follows on changing a draft development consent order post-submission:

> 'It is expected that applications will be as well prepared as possible prior to submission. However, it may be the case that applicants may need to change a proposal after an application has been accepted for examination. Reasons for this could include, for example, regulatory changes, technical developments or the discovery of previously unknown factors which need to be addressed to preserve the benefit of the proposed development.
>
> When an applicant submits a proposed change to a proposal, the Secretary of State will need to decide on the materiality of the change and whether it is of such a degree that it constitutes a new project or whether it can still be considered under the existing application. If the Secretary of State decides that the change is such that it would result in a materially different project, the applicant will then have to decide whether to withdraw the existing application and restart the pre-application process or whether to continue with the application in its original form.
>
> In accordance with the principles of fairness and reasonableness, and specifically the principles set out in case law7, the Examining Authority may, depending on the circumstances, need to:
>
> - ask the Secretary of State to extend the examination (using the power in section 98(4) of the Planning Act) in order to enable interested parties to be consulted on the effect of the proposed amendments, and allow for time to consider any amendments accepted for examination;
> - take into account what publicity (if any) the applicant has carried out to ensure people have an opportunity to make representations;
> - use the general power to control the examination of an application in section 87(1) of the Planning Act to make changes to the timetable;
> - exercise its discretion under rules 10(3) and 14(10) of the Procedure Rules to permit representations to be made by people who are not interested parties in cases where it is appropriate to do so.'

Some examples in practice

In the Brig y Cwm application for an 'energy from waste' generating station the Examining authority refused to accept changes to the application proposed by the applicant at the Preliminary Meeting. Having allowed time for other parties to make representations about whether the amendments should be allowed, the Examining authority determined not to accept the proposed changes to the application (IPC's letter of 14 July 2011). The reasons given were that:

- 'On the facts and having regard to the effects of the changes, the Examining authority considers that were it minded to grant development consent the proposed development would be substantially different to that proposed in the application accepted for examination on 26 January 2011;
- Applying the approach in the *Wheatcroft* case against the policy background and statutory framework of the PA 2008, the changes are considered substantial because to grant development consent for the changed application might deprive parties entitled to be consulted of the opportunity to express their views and become interested parties.'

The Examining Authority considered that if it were to accept an amended application which was subsequently considered to be 'substantially different' from the application which was made under section 37 of the Act, any decision to grant development consent may be unlawful. It was this decision that led to the Bob Neill letter quoted above. It is important to note that the Bob Neill letter endorsed the Examining Authority's decision in the particular circumstances at Brig y Cwm.

In the Hinkley Point C application for a nuclear power station the Examining Authority accepted amendments to the application proposed at the Preliminary Meeting, concluding that they were not material in the sense that accepting them would be likely to prejudice any party. In reaching this decision the Examining Authority had regard to the fact that the material changes had been advertised by the applicant.

The Examining Authority also permitted post-submission changes to the application in the Preesall Saltfield underground gas storage application; although the application was refused on other grounds. In that case the applicant had discovered various errors in certain plans and had been proactive in notifying interested parties of the errors and proposed amendments and the Examining Authority took into account that fact that those organisations with a principal interest in that aspect of the application were content with the proposed amendments. The Examining Authority accepted that the amendments were not of a sufficient magnitude to constitute a new project or application.

Part 13

Correction of Errors, Changes and Revocation

Correction of Errors in Development Consent Decisions

Written by: Isabella Tafur, ftb
Edited by: Michael Humphries QC, ftb

Introduction

Pursuant to the PA 2008, s 119, Sch 4, the Secretary of State may correct certain errors in development consent decisions. The documents that can be corrected are:

(a) where development consent has been granted, errors in development consent order; and

(b) where development consent has been refused, errors in the refusal letter.

The Act, however, only allows corrections to 'correctable errors'. These are defined as errors or omissions that are part of the document recording the decision, but are *not* part of the statement of reasons for the decision (PA 2008, Sch 4, para 1(3)). Any error in the statement of reasons for the decision cannot, therefore, be corrected. Furthermore, there is no power of correction in relation to DCO provisions included pursuant to PA 2008, Sch 5, paras 30A and 30B which relate to deemed marine licences (see PA 2008, Sch 4, para 1(11)).

Where the development consent order was required to be contained in a statutory instrument, the correction of any error/omission must also be made by an order contained in a statutory instrument (PA 2008, Sch 4, para 1(8)). As soon as possible after the instrument containing the order is made, the Secretary of State must deposit a copy of it in the office of the Clerk of the Parliaments (PA 2008, Sch 4, para 1(10)).

Conditions

The Secretary of State may only correct an error or omission if the following conditions are satisfied:

(a) the Secretary of State has received a written request to correct the error/omission from any person before the end of the relevant period (PA 2008, Sch 4, para 5(a)); or

(b) the Secretary of State has sent a statement in writing to the applicant, explaining the error/omission and stating that the Secretary of State is considering making the correction before the end of the relevant period (PA 2008, Sch 4, para 5(b)).

The 'relevant periods are:

(a) if development consent has been granted, the Secretary of State will only have the power to correct an error if the request is received/statement is sent before the expiry of 6 weeks, beginning with the day on which the order was published, or, if later, the day on which the statement of reasons for making the order was published (PA 2008, Sch 4, para 1(6)(a) and s 118(1)(b)); or

(b) if development consent is refused, the Secretary of State will only have the power to correct an error if the request is received/statement is sent before the expiry of 6 weeks, beginning with the day on which the statement of reasons for refusal is published (PA 2008, Sch 4, para 1(6)(b) and s 118(1)(b)).

Furthermore, the Secretary of State must inform each relevant local planning authority that the request has been made/statement has been sent (PA 2008, Sch 4, para 1(7)).

Correction notices

If a written request has been received or a statement sent, the Secretary of State must issue a correction notice (PA 2008, Sch 4, para 2(1)). The correction notice must be served as soon as practicable after making the correction or deciding not to make the correction (PA 2008, Sch 4, para 2(2)). The notice must specify the correction of the error/omission or give notice of the decision not to correct the error/omission, and it must be given to the applicant, each local planning authority for all (or any part) of the area in which the development is situated, and to the person who requested the correction (PA 2008, Sch 4, para 2(3)). The Secretary of State may also give to the notice to other persons, but is not obliged to do so (PA 2008, Sch 4, para 2(4)).

Effect of a correction

If a correction is made to a decision, the original decision (whether the development consent order or the refusal of development consent) remains in force, but is treated as corrected by the terms specified in the correction notice (PA 2008, Sch 4, para 3(1)). The correction takes effect from the date the correction notice is issued or, if the correction is required to be made by statutory instrument, the date specified in the order.

Where a correction is not made, the original decision continues to have full force and effect (PA 2008, Sch 4, para 2(2)).

Examples of correction notices

An example of a correction notice can be seen in relation to the Galloper Wind Farm Order 2013, SI 2013/1203 (the Order). The Secretary of State's notice and correction order can be downloaded from the following website:

http://infrastructure.planningportal.gov.uk/projects/eastern/galloper-offshore-wind-farm/?document=&ipcsection=search&from=01-07-2013&to=15-09-2013&btnSearch=Search

The notice explains that the Secretary of State has received a request from the applicant to correct certain errors in the Order. It goes on to set out the corrections that the Secretary of State has made as a result of that request. In summary, these are as follows:

(a) corrections to plan references (which had failed to take account of the updated versions which had been submitted before the Order was made);

(b) a correction to the definition, in the interpretation section of the Order, of 'the percentage reduction' as it did not reflect the Secretary of State's conclusions in his decision letter in respect of the maximum number of predicted lesser black-backed gull mortalities which should be attributed to the development;

(c) a correction to the section of the Order dealing with the approval of detailed wind turbine design parameters to correct the fact that it erroneously prevented works commencing onshore until the wind turbine approval process had been completed;

(d) a correction to the section of the Order dealing with aids to navigation to correct the fact that it erroneously prevented works commencing onshore until 14 days after the required notification to Defence Infrastructure Safeguarding.

The notice also sets out those corrections requested by the applicant, which the Secretary of State decided not to make. He declined to amend Article 4 of the Order (which dealt with the maintenance of the authorised project), which the applicant had requested be amended to make clear that maintenance works within the scope of the environmental statement needed no further approval. The Secretary of State considered that the wording of Article 4 properly reflected his intention and that it would not be appropriate to treat the requested change as a 'correctable error'.

The applicant also requested that the words in Article 13 (dealing with street works) be amended by the deletion of the certain words to reflect an agreement the applicant had given to EDF Energy to protect the latter's interests. The Secretary of State considered that as EDF's interests were secured by way of a separate private legal agreement, such a change to the Order was not essential. The notice explained that the wording in the Order had been used in other DCOs and that it would not be appropriate to treat the requested change as a 'correctable error'.

The Galloper Wind Farm (Correction) Order 2013, SI 2013/2086 came into effect on 21 August 2013. The Schedule to SI 2013/2086 contains a table that sets out the relevant provision of the original Development Consent Order which is to be modified (in the first column), the erroneous text (in the second column) and the replacement text (in the third column).

Relationship with other provisions

It is worth noting the relationship between the power to correct errors (in PA 2008, Sch 4) and the power to make changes to, and revocation of, development consent orders (in PA Sch 6, para 3) provides that the Secretary of State may by order make a change to, or revoke, a development consent order without an application being made if he is satisfied that -

(a) the development consent order contains a significant error; and

(b) it would *not* be appropriate for the error to be corrected by means of the power conferred by PA 2008, Sch 4, para 1 (see above) or by PA 2008, Sch 6, para 2 (non-material changes).

It is not entirely clear in what circumstances it would not be 'appropriate' for an error to be corrected under PA 2008, Sch 4, para 1 or Sch 6, para 2, but might still be appropriate to correct such error under PA 2008, Sch 6.

Note also the relationship between PA 2008, Sch 4 and PA 2008, s 161 (breach of terms of order granting development consent). PA 2008, s 161(3) provides that it is a defence for a person charged with an offence under s 161(1) to prove that:

(a) the breach or failure to comply occurred only because of an error or omission in the order; and

(b) a correction notice specifying the correction of the error or omission has been issued under PA 2008, Sch 4, para 2.

Conclusion

Errors and omissions in development consent orders, and in notices refusing development consent can, in certain circumstances, be corrected. Any person may request such a correction, or the Secretary of State may unilaterally decide to make a correction, within the statutory period during which a legal challenge can be made to a decision to grant or refuse an application for development consent. To date this is a power that has only rarely been invoked.

Part 14

Legal Challenges

Legal Challenge to Grant of Development Consent

Written by: Richard Honey, ftb
Edited by: Michael Humphries QC, ftb

Introduction

A legal challenge to the grant of development consent is by way of judicial review. The normal principles and procedures of judicial review generally apply, subject to the provisions of PA 2008, s 118. In particular, there is a six-week time limit for bringing judicial review proceedings.

PA 2008, s 118(1)

PA 2008, s 118 governs legal challenges relating to applications for orders granting development consent. Section 118(1) provides that:

> 'A court may entertain proceedings for questioning an order granting development consent only if
>
> (a) the proceedings are brought by a claim for judicial review, and
>
> (b) the claim form is filed during the period of 6 weeks beginning with
>
> (i) the day on which the order is published, or,
>
> (ii) if later, the day on which the statement of reasons for making the order is published.'

This six-week time limit was unusual when the Act was introduced, but it is now the standard time limit for judicial review of planning decisions given the change made in July 2013 by the Civil Procedure (Amendment No 4) Rules 2013, SI 2013/1412.

The requirement to 'publish' the order is contained in PA 2008, s 117. The order must be published 'in such manner as the Secretary of State thinks appropriate'

(s 117(3)), unless the order:

- makes by-laws,
- introduces offences,
- applies, modifies or excludes a statutory provision, or
- amends, repeals or revokes a statutory provision of local application,

in which case it must be contained in a statutory instrument (s 117(4)). Statutory instruments are officially published by Her Majesty's Stationery Office (HMSO) on the website of The National Archives (www.legislation.gov.uk), where new statutory instruments are listed by publication date.

The requirement to 'publish' a statement of reasons for a decision to grant development consent is contained in PA 2008, s 116. The statement must again be published 'in such manner as the Secretary of State thinks appropriate' (s 116(3)).

Typically an Order granting development consent and the Secretary of State's statement of reasons for making the Order will be published simultaneously on the Planning Inspectorate's website (infrastructure.planningportal.gov.uk).

In the case of Rookery South, where there was the special parliamentary procedure to be followed subsequent to the panel's decision, the Inspectorate advised that 'in cases where special parliamentary procedure applies, the publication of the order, for the purposes of PA 2008, s 118, will follow the special parliamentary procedure' (register of advice, 18 November 2011, Rookery South Energy from Waste Generating Station).

Date from which time runs

It should be noted that in for challenges under s 118 the claim form must be filed during the period of six weeks 'beginning with' the day on which the Order and statement of reasons are published. The words 'beginning with' in s 118 contrast with the word 'from' which is used in r 54.5 of the Civil Procedure Rules (CPR) for judicial review challenges generally. Time for a s 118 challenge begins to run 'on' the date described in the section, and not 'from' the following day: see *Hinde v Rugby BC* [2011] EWHC 3684 (Admin) and *Barker v Hambleton DC* [2012] EWCA Civ 610. Furthermore, the period of six weeks is to be calculated as 6 × 7 days (ie 42 days): see *Okolo v Secretary of State for the Environment* [1997] 4 All ER 242.

For example: if an Order and statement of reasons were published on 1 January, the first day of the six weeks would also be 1 January, and the time for challenge would expire on 12 February.

Accuracy is vital bearing in mind the inability of the court to extend time where there is a statutory time limit (see below).

The time limit of six weeks is set by statute

The time limit of six weeks for challenges to is one set by statute (ie by the terms of s 118 and not by the Civil Procedure Rules) and thus it is important to note that the court has no power or discretion to extend it: see *Mucelli v Government of Albania* [2009] 1 WLR 276.

Procedural issues

Promptness

Apart from the six-week time limit, the requirement for promptness in the CPR r 54.5(1)(a) appears not to apply to judicial reviews within the scope of PA 2008, s 118, because r 54.5(3) states that the rule does not apply when any other enactment specifies a shorter time limit for making a claim for judicial review; s 118 would be such an enactment.

Although the requirement for promptness in the CPR would appear not to apply to judicial reviews brought under PA 2008, s 118, the 'undue delay' provision in s 31(6) of the Senior Courts Act 1981 would still apply. Section 31(6) provides that where the High Court considers that there has been undue delay in making an application for judicial review, the court may refuse to grant permission or relief, if it considers that the granting of the relief sought would be likely to cause substantial hardship to, or substantially prejudice the rights of, any person, or would be detrimental to good administration. Section 31(7) says that this provision is 'without prejudice to any enactment or rule of court which has the effect of limiting the time within which an application for judicial review may be made'. Accordingly, 'undue delay' together with one of the harms identified in s 31(6) (substantial hardship, substantial prejudice of rights, or detriment to good administration) would allow a court to refuse permission or relief, even where a claim was brought within six weeks. It is, however, unlikely that, save in exceptional circumstances, a court would regard six weeks for bringing a claim as representing 'undue delay'. Nonetheless, potential claimants would need to bear this in mind and could not simply wait until the end of the six-week period to bring a claim.

Pre-action protocol for judicial review

The courts will normally expect the Pre-Action Protocol for Judicial Review produced under the CPR to be followed before proceedings are commenced. Given the abridged time limit under PA 2008, s 118 (6 weeks instead of three months) there is likely to be a question as to whether full compliance with the pre-action protocol is practical. In a letter dated 11 November 2011, solicitors for an objector to the Rookery South Energy from Waste Generating Station application said that the pre-action protocol did not apply in light of the timetable (copy published on the register of advice). In a response of the same date, Helen Adlard, the IPC's Director of Legal Services, stated that the pre-action protocol did apply and suggested that in circumstances where the DCO had not yet been made it would be 'highly appropriate' to warn the decision-maker of the grounds of challenge envisaged.

When the new six-week time limit for judicial review of planning decisions was introduced in July 2013 the pre-action protocol was amended to advise that the 'protocol may not be appropriate in cases where one of the shorter time limits … applies. In those cases, the parties should still attempt to comply with this protocol but the court will not apply normal cost sanctions where the court is satisfied that it has not been possible to comply because of the shorter time limits'. In practice claimants and respondents ought to try to comply with the pre-action protocol, although the normal periods for compliance may have to be abridged.

There are two main stages under the pre-action protocol. First, the claimant sends a letter before claim which should identify the issues in dispute and establish whether litigation can be avoided. A standard form letter before claim is included in Annex A to the protocol. The letter should contain the date and details of the decision being challenged and a clear summary of the facts on which the claim is based. It should also contain the details of any relevant information that the claimant is seeking and an explanation of why this is considered relevant. The second stage is the letter of response, sent by the proposed defendant and any interested parties, following the standard form set out in Annex B to the protocol. The letter should be sent within 14 days, or, if this is not possible, then the defendant should send an interim response and propose a reasonable extension of time. If the claim is being conceded in full, in part or not at all, the reply should say so in clear and unambiguous terms. Where appropriate the letter should contain a fuller explanation of the decision being challenged, deal with any points of dispute, and enclose any relevant documents.

Alternative dispute resolution

In applications for judicial review there is generally an encouragement by the courts to consider alternative dispute resolution: see eg *R (Cowl) v Plymouth City Council (Practice Note)* [2002] 1 WLR 803 and the pre-action protocol. However, given the nature of the grant of development consent by means of a DCO the ability to use ADR in this context is almost non-existent.

Standing

To be able to bring a claim for judicial review a claimant must have a sufficient interest in the matter to which the claim relates. Standing is a ground on which both permission and substantive relief may be refused, but the test at the permission stage is lower, essentially to exclude troublemakers. The importance and merits of the claim can alter the degree of standing required. A 'sufficient interest' has been given a wide and flexible interpretation by the courts. In planning and environmental cases, a reasonably low threshold is usually applied, including those with a general interest in the issue to be determined. Representative and campaign groups would usually be regarded as having sufficient standing.

Claim Form

A judicial review claim is commenced using the Part 8 claim procedure. The claim form should be accompanied by a detailed statement of the claimant's grounds, a statement of the facts relied on, and any applications eg for directions. The claim form must be served within seven days from issue, and an acknowledgement of service filed by the defendant and interested parties within 21 days of service, including a statement of grounds for contesting the claim.

Permission to bring an application for judicial review

There is a permission stage in all applications for judicial reviews that will apply also to challenges to the making of a DCOs under PA 2008, s 118(1). It is necessary for a claimant to secure permission from the court to bring an application for judicial review. This is usually considered first by a judge on the papers. At the 'permission stage' the court will consider the merits of the claim against the relevant test: whether the claim discloses an arguable case. Permission should not be granted for judicial review claims that are misguided complaints of administrative error. The purpose of the permission stage is to protect public authorities against weak and vexatious claims. The court will make an order giving or refusing permission, and giving any directions. Permission may be granted with conditions or only on certain of the grounds sought.

If permission is refused it is possible then to renew the application for permission at an oral hearing before a single judge, usually listed for 30 minutes. If permission is refused after an oral hearing then a right of appeal lies to the Court of Appeal. Sometimes, in urgent or complex cases, a judge will order a permission hearing without a paper decision being reached, or that there be a rolled-up hearing, where permission and the substantive case are considered at the same hearing. In July 2013 the CPR were changed to remove the right to reconsideration at a hearing of the refusal of permission in cases where the application was certified as totally without merit by the judge considering the application on the papers.

As far as the costs of the permission stage are concerned, a successful defendant should be entitled to recover the cost for its acknowledgement of service, including the preparation of summary grounds of resistance, but not of any pre-action correspondence (see *R (Mount Cook) v Westminster CC* [2004] 2 P&CR 22 at para 76(1) *and R (Ewing) v Office of the Deputy Prime Minister* [2006] 1 WLR 1260 at 1267A-B). Defendants are not generally entitled to their costs of attending any oral permission hearing, but may be awarded them in certain circumstances as an exception.

Grounds for judicial review

If permission is granted, the defendant and any interested parties must within 35 days serve detailed grounds for contesting the claim and any written evidence. Skeleton arguments must be filed and served before the hearing. The court's permission is required if a claimant seeks to rely on grounds other than those for which he has been given permission to proceed. Where justified by urgency, for example where a development needs to commence, it is possible to seek to have the hearing expedited. If a claim is commenced in, or transferred to, an Administrative Court location outside London it is likely that the claim will be heard more quickly.

The grounds of challenge to the grant of consent are likely often to feature issues of European law, for example arising in connection with the EIA Directive, the Birds Directive or the Habitats Directive. It is also inevitable that some challenges will seek to rely on human rights issues, such as Articles 6 (fair hearing) and 8 (home and family life) and Article 1 of the First Protocol (property). There may also be arguments in relation to statutory duties such as the public sector equality duty in s 149 of the Equality Act 2010, breach of which would give rise to grounds for judicial review.

Otherwise, grounds of judicial review of the grant of development consent will be the same as for any judicial review. These will include: error of law; excess of power, ie going beyond the powers conferred by statute; jurisdictional error; unauthorised delegation; acting as if discretion is fettered; over-rigid adherence to policy or rules; irrelevant considerations taken in to account, or a refusal to take in to account relevant considerations; irrationality; acting in bad faith; failure to observe procedural rules; procedural unfairness; breach of right to a fair hearing; actual or apparent bias; failure to give adequate reasons; misinterpretation of policy; fundamental error of fact; lack of evidence for a conclusion; proportionality; failure properly to consult; and, breach of a substantive or procedural legitimate expectation.

The ambit of judicial review is quite limited and so gives defendants a fair degree of protection from challenges. The merits of the decision cannot be considered. Matters of judgment are the exclusive province of the decision-maker. The assessment of facts and weighing of considerations is in the hands of the decision-maker alone and the court has no power to intervene. A decision-maker is entitled to attach what weight it pleases to relevant considerations, and the courts will not entertain a submission that undue weight was given to one consideration or too little weight was given to another. If a matter would not have caused the decision-maker to reach a different conclusion then it is irrelevant whether it was taken in to account; and, if a judge is uncertain whether a matter would have made a difference to a decision then he cannot conclude that the decision was invalid. Where there is a factual error which is insignificant or insubstantial then the relevant decision will not be quashed. Where it can be shown that notwithstanding any error the decision-maker would have reached the same decision on the other factors stated, the court will not interfere.

Other issues during conduct of proceedings

Orders for disclosure against a respondent can be made, but disclosure is not required. Such orders are fairly rare, since questions of fact play much less part in judicial review proceedings than in other cases and since the decision and the basis for it is usually clearly evidenced (eg by a panel report). However, there has been a trend towards increasing disclosure in judicial review cases. The Secretary of State will normally hold the relevant documents that are not already in the public domain, such as those relating to Ministerial consideration of whether or not to grant a DCO. Traditionally there has been a duty of candour on public authorities voluntarily to provide full and frank disclosure of relevant material to a challenger. Lord Donaldson MR said in *R v Lancashire CC ex p Huddleston* [1986] 2 All ER 941 that judicial review was 'a process which falls to be conducted with all the cards face upwards on the table and the vast majority of the cards will start in the authority's hands'. The courts have made it clear that the duty of candour is a very high and important duty to assist the court with full and accurate explanations of all the facts relevant to the issues the court must decide. An authority should explain fully what it has done and why it has done it, so far as is necessary fairly to meet the challenge made. The duty of candour had perhaps not been working so well in recent years. But following the decisions in *Tweed v Parades Commission* [2007] 1 AC 650, *R (Al-Sweady) v Secretary of State for Defence* [2009] EWHC 2387 (Admin) and *R (Shoesmith) v Ofsted* [2010] EWHC 852 (Admin), it is increasingly common for a defendant to provide something like disclosure.

Cross-examination is unusual in judicial review proceedings (see eg *R (Bancoult) v Foreign Secretary* [2012] EWHC 2115 (Admin)). Cross-examination is exceptional because the primary facts are often not in dispute, or at least those asserted by the defendant are undisputed, and the authority may normally be relied upon to disclose relevant documents pursuant to its duty of candour. But the court retains a discretion to permit cross-examination and should do so if it is necessary for the claim to be, and be seen to be, determined fairly and justly.

Remedies

The remedy sought in judicial review is likely to be the quashing of the DCO. It may also be that a declaration is sought as to what the correct legal position is on some issue. In judicial review all remedies are discretionary, so even where a decision has been held by the court to be unlawful it may be that it is not quashed. However, discretion must be exercised judicially and in most cases in which a decision has been found to be flawed it would not be a proper exercise of discretion to refuse to quash it *(R (Edwards) v Environment Agency* [2008] UKHL 22 at para 63).

Costs

In relation to costs of judicial reviews generally, Part 45 of the CPR now provides a regime of fixed costs in claims to which the Aarhus Convention applies. This is likely to cover most if not all challenges to DCOs, depending on the actual grounds of challenge, as the Aarhus Convention applies to environmental matters generally. CPR rr 45.41 to 45.44 enable a claimant to tick a box on the claim form to seek costs protection, which will apply unless it is successfully challenged by a defendant. The only ground for challenging the application of this fixed costs regime is that the claim is not one within the ambit of the Aarhus Convention. Where the rules apply, the total costs recoverable from a claimant are limited to £5,000 (individual) or £10,000 (others) and the costs recoverable by a claimant are limited to £35,000.

Otherwise there remains an ability for a claimant to apply for a protective costs order in accordance with the principles set out in *R (Corner House Research) v Secretary of State for Trade and Industry* [2005] EWCA Civ 192. The basic guidelines for the award of a PCO are:

- the issues raised are of general public importance;
- the public interest requires that those issues be resolved;
- the claimant has no private interest in the outcome;
- having regard to the financial resources and the costs, it is fair and just to make the order; and
- if the order is not made, the claimant will probably discontinue the proceedings and will be acting reasonably in so doing.

It was also said that if the claimant's lawyers were acting *pro bono* then it would be likely to enhance the merits of the application. These conditions have been applied flexibly in subsequent cases.

Where the grant of development consent is challenged, the promoter will be an interested party. A promoter is entitled to, and in practice is likely to, participate in the judicial review in order to seek to uphold the DCO. The Secretary of State, represented usually by the Treasury Solicitor, will be the defendant. As such, the role of a promoter is somewhat limited. It is unlikely that a third party in such a judicial review would be awarded their costs if the challenge is dismissed (see *Bolton MDC v SSE* [1995] 1 WLR 1176), although two sets of costs are awarded in some cases.

Generally

Given the scale and significance of projects authorised by DCOs, and the limited ability of objectors to probe applications through the PA 2008 process, it is likely that a substantial proportion of DCOs granted will be challenged by judicial review.

Judicial reviews were launched, for example, upon the making of the Rookery South, Hinkley Point and the Heysham to M6 link road DCOs. In relation to Rookery South, the challenge was brought by a waste company who objected to the DCO and petitioned in relation to the special parliamentary procedure. The grounds of challenge include the basis for the decision to include compulsory purchase powers and that the special parliamentary procedure does not provide for an environmental impact assessment process. In relation to Hinkley Point, judicial review proceedings were brought by Greenpeace and An Taisce, the former in relation to the policy effect of the lack of a long-term waste disposal facility and the latter in relation to trans-boundary effects and the failure to consult the Irish government. The Heysham to M6 link road challenge was brought by a campaign group. The grounds included challenges relating to whether the project was properly within the Planning Act 2008 regime, on pre-application consultation, the use of the National Policy Statement, alternatives and ecology.

Judicial reviews will be dealt with by the Administrative Court of the Queen's Bench Division of the High Court. Guidance from the Administrative Court on applying for judicial review is available at: http://www.justice.gov.uk/courts/rcj-rolls-building/administrative-court/applying-for-judicial-review.

Legal Challenge to Refusal of Development Consent

Written by: Richard Honey, ftb
Edited by: Michael Humphries QC, ftb

Introduction

A legal challenge to the refusal of development consent is by way of judicial review. The normal principles and procedures of judicial review generally apply, subject to the provisions of PA 2008, s 118. In particular, there is a six-week time limit for bringing judicial review proceedings.

The main principles and procedural provisions relating to judicial review are considered in another article in this work entitled 'Legal challenge to grant of development consent'. Those principles and procedural provisions, however, also apply to the challenge of a refusal of an application for development consent; subject to some key differences that are considered below.

PA 2008, s 118(2)

PA 2008, s 118 governs legal challenges relating to the refusal of development consent. Section 118(2) provides that:

> 'A court may entertain proceedings for questioning a refusal of development consent only if
>
> (a) the proceedings are brought by a claim for judicial review, and
>
> (b) the claim form is filed during the period of 6 weeks beginning with the day on which the statement of reasons for the refusal is published.'

This six-week time limit was unusual when the Act was introduced, but it is now the standard time limit for judicial review of planning decisions given the change made in July 2013 by the Civil Procedure (Amendment No 4) Rules 2013, SI 2013/1412.

The requirement to 'publish' a statement of reasons for a decision to refuse development consent is contained in PA 2008, s 116. The statement must be published 'in such manner as the Secretary of State thinks appropriate' (s 116(3)).

Procedural issues

Standing

A promoter bringing such a judicial review would have no problem establishing standing. The decision would be defended by the Secretary of State. It is unlikely that an objector to the DCO would actively participate in the judicial review, although that would in practice depend on the circumstances of each case and the grounds of challenge.

Grounds for judicial review

As to grounds of judicial review, a promoter might be arguing that there has been an error of law in the sense that a legal test has been misconstrued and applied more rigorously than it ought to have been. It is, however, more likely that a promoter would be challenging on the grounds for example of: over-rigid adherence to policy or rules; irrelevant considerations taken in to account, or a refusal to take in to account relevant considerations; irrationality; failure to observe procedural rules; procedural unfairness; failure to give adequate reasons; misinterpretation of policy; fundamental error of fact; and, lack of evidence for a conclusion. Other grounds may of course be applicable in particular cases.

Other issues during conduct of proceedings

Where a DCO has been refused contrary to the recommendation of a panel's report, the promoter is likely to wish to secure, by way of disclosure, all documents evidencing the consideration of the application by the Minister and his advisers. This could be secured under the duty of candour or by way of an application for specific disclosure, if necessary.

Remedy

The remedy sought in judicial review is likely to be the quashing of the Secretary of State's decision to refuse consent. If the challenge is successful, the Secretary of State will then have to re-decide the application. Where the error of law lies with the Examining Authority, it may be advisable to seek an order that the report should be quashed as well, but that is unlikely to be necessary. It has been held in relation to comparable decisions that where a decision is quashed then 'the Secretary of State had to start again de novo with a clean sheet' (*Kingswood v SSE* (1989) 57 P&CR 153 at 162). The Judge in *Kingswood* went on to conclude that 'there can be no doubt that the Secretary of State must consider the matter de novo in circumstances where a decision is quashed' (p163). It may also be that a declaration is sought as to what the legal position is.

Costs

In relation to costs it is possible that a promoter would be able to take advantage of the fixed costs regime in Part 45 of the CPR. Although it will depend on the precise grounds of challenge, it is entirely possible that such a challenge would be a claim to which the Aarhus Convention would apply. It is, however, to be doubted that it would be worthwhile to engage this fixed costs regime. First, the costs of the Secretary of State using the Treasury Solicitor and counsel from the Attorney General's panel are not likely to be great, although they will be higher if the defendant goes off-panel and instructs a QC. Secondly, the reciprocal cap of £35,000 is likely to cover only a very small proportion of a claimant promoter's costs.

The availability of the £10,000 cap means however that a promoter would be able to launch a judicial review with limited prospects of success, knowing that costs exposure would be limited if the case were lost. Given how much would have been invested by a promoter in taking a DCO application through examination, some promoters might see the limited further expense of a judicial review as being a worthwhile investment, even if there were only very limited prospects of success.

Generally

The first judicial review by a promoter of a refusal of development consent was in relation to the Preesall Underground Gas Storage DCO. In that case the Secretary of State decided the application contrary to the Examining Authority's recommendation and refused development consent. The promoter in that case, Halite Energy, challenged the Secretary of State's decision on the application.

The Examining Authority was concerned about the adequacy of the geological information provided by the applicant, but concluded that this could be overcome by imposing a requirement that further geological information be provided to the mineral planning authority before the start of development. Halite Energy raised a number of grounds including that it was procedurally unfair for the Examining Authority to reach the conclusion it did without giving the promoter an indication of its concerns, or the opportunity to provide more information, and without holding an issue-specific hearing on the topic. It was said that both PA 2008, s 91 and the Inspectorate's guidance indicated that a hearing should be held in such circumstances. It was also argued that the Secretary of State had misunderstood and misapplied the requirements of policy in NPS EN-4.

In its application for judicial review, Halite Energy referred to cases such as *Dyason v SSE* (1998) 75 P&CR 506 and *LB Croydon v SSETR* [2000] PLCR 171 to show both the inquisitorial duty on the examining authority and the need to alert parties to adverse findings which could be reached against them. It was argued that because the process was inquisitorial, rather than adversarial, there was a heightened burden on the Examining Authority to ensure it made its decision on the correct factual basis. It was also argued that the Examining Authority had a duty to give a party a 'fair crack of the whip' and that that was particularly important in a largely written, inquisitorial system, especially in relation to highly complex infrastructure projects.

The Secretary of State's defence was along the lines that the challenge relied on mis-readings of the panel's report and the decision letter, and that the issues were really ones of expert judgment, and fact and degree, for the decision-maker. On the procedural fairness point the answer given was in essence that the matters were so important that it ought to have been clear to the promoter that they had to be addressed properly. As yet the challenge had not been determined.

Legal Challenge to Decision not to accept Application

Written by: Richard Honey, ftb
Edited by: Michael Humphries QC, ftb

Introduction

A legal challenge to a decision not to accept an application would be by way of judicial review. The normal principles and procedures of judicial review generally apply, subject to the provisions of PA 2008, s 118. In particular, there is a six-week time limit for bringing judicial review proceedings.

The main principles and procedural provisions relating to judicial review are considered in another article in this work entitled 'Legal challenge to grant of development consent'. Those principles and procedural provisions, however, also apply to a challenge to a decision not to accept an application for development consent; subject to some key differences that are considered below.

PA 2008, s 118(3)

PA 2008, s 118 governs legal challenges relating to a decision not to accept an application. Section 118(3) provides that:

> 'A court may entertain proceedings for questioning a decision of the Secretary of State under section 55 not to accept an application for an order granting development consent only if
>
> (a) the proceedings are brought by a claim for judicial review, and
>
> (b) the claim form is filed during the period of 6 weeks beginning with the day on which the Secretary of State notifies the applicant as required by subsection (7) of that section.'

This six-week time limit was unusual when the Act was introduced, but it is now the standard time limit for judicial review of planning decisions given the change made in July 2013 by the Civil Procedure (Amendment No 4) Rules 2013, SI 2013/1412.

PA 2008, s 55 provides that the Secretary of State has 28 days after receipt of what purports to be an application for a development consent order to decide whether or not to accept the application. Section 55(7) provides that if the Secretary of State is of the view that the application cannot be accepted, he must notify the applicant of that and the reasons for it. This is the start date for the six-week period.

Procedural issues

Standing

A promoter bringing such a judicial review would have no problem establishing standing. The decision would be defended by the Secretary of State. It is unlikely that an objector to the DCO would actively participate in the judicial review, although that would in practice depend on the circumstances of each case and the grounds of challenge. If, for example, the applicant was not accepted on grounds relating to adequacy of consultation, it is not inconceivable that a local authority that had given an adverse 'adequacy of consultation representation' (see s 55(4)(b) and (5)) might wish to participate in the judicial review.

Grounds for judicial review

PA 2008, s 55(3) provides that the Secretary of State may accept an application only if he concludes:

(a) that it is an application for an order granting development consent,

(c) that development consent is required for any of the development to which the application relates,

(e) that the applicant has, in relation to a proposed application that has become the application, complied with Chapter 2 of Part 5 (pre-application procedure), and

(f) that the application (including accompaniments) is of a standard that the Secretary of State considers satisfactory.

In relation to PA 2008, s 55(3)(e) above, that is, pre-application procedure, s 55(4) identifies a number of matters to which the Secretary of State must 'have regard' when reaching his conclusion, being:

(a) the consultation report received under PA 2008, s 37(3)(c),

(b) any adequacy of consultation representation received by the Secretary of State from a local authority consultee, and

(c) the extent to which the applicant has had regard to any guidance issued under section 50.

In relation to PA 2008, s 55(3)(f) above, that is, whether the application is of a 'satisfactory' standard, s 55(5A) identifies a number of further matters to which the Secretary of State must 'have regard' when reaching his conclusion, being the extent to which:

(a) the application complies with the requirements in section 37(3) (form and contents of application) and any standards set under section 37(5), and

(b) any applicable guidance given under section 37(4) has been followed in relation to the application.

It can be readily seen, therefore, that inherent in any decision not to accept an application under PA 2008, s 55 are a number of judgments by the Secretary of State that are susceptible to scrutiny in any application judicial review. The Inspectorate could, for example, misunderstand or misinterpret one of the matters in s 55(3), including, for example, whether the pre-application procedures have been properly complied with.

PA 2008, s 55(3)(f) (application of a 'satisfactory' standard) was a matter added to s 55(3) on 1 April 2012 by the Localism Act 2011. This appears to be an additional matter to those in ss 55(3)(a), (c) and (e), rather than a standard against which those other matters should be tested. Thus it would appear that even if an application is of a standard that the Secretary of State considers 'satisfactory' (s 55(3)(f)), he must still be satisfied that it has also 'complied' with Chapter 2 of Part 5 of the Act (s 55(3)(e)). This understanding of how s 55(3) operates has not, however, been tested in the courts.

The reasons given pursuant to PA 2008, s 55(7) could also be inadequate, although reasons challenges often simply result in the reasons being 'corrected'.

Beyond such grounds focused on the requirements of s 55 itself, all the other usual grounds for judicial review would apply. Having said that, however, a challenge alleging that a decision not to accept an application on the basis of 'irrationality' would be likely to struggle to succeed. For a conclusion to be irrational or perverse it must be one that that no reasonable person in the position of the Secretary of State, properly directing himself on the relevant material, could have reached *(Seddon v Secretary of State for the Environment* (1981) 42 P&CR 26). The courts have made it clear that they will require 'something overwhelming' from a claimant before allowing a challenge of this sort (*Associated Provincial Picture Houses v Wednesbury Corporation* [1948] 1 KB 223 at 230; see also 233-234). A claimant alleging that the Inspectorate has reached a *Wednesbury* unreasonable conclusion on a matter of judgment faces a particularly daunting task: see, for example, *R (Newsmith Stainless Ltd) v Secretary of State for the Environment, Transport and the Regions* [2001] EWHC Admin 74 at para 8.

PA 2008, s 55(4)(c) required the Secretary of State to have regard, in reaching the conclusion in s 55(3)(e) (pre-application procedures), to the extent to which the applicant has had regard to any guidance issued by the Secretary of State under s 50. Clearly if an applicant had correctly followed DCLG Guidance on an issue on which its application was later not accepted under s 55, that could raise issues of legitimate expectation: see eg *R v North and East Devon Health Authority, ex parte Coughlan* [2001] QB 213 and *Nadarajah & Abdi v Home Secretary* [2005] EWCA Civ 1363.

Other issues during conduct of proceedings

Where a decision has been made not to accept an application, the promoter is likely to wish to secure by way of disclosure all documents evidencing the consideration of the application by the Inspectorate, including the PA 2008, s 55 application checklist. This is likely to contain more detailed reasons than those set out pursuant to s 55(7). This could be secured under the duty of candour or by way of an application for specific disclosure, if necessary.

Generally

Although PA 2008, s 118(3) applies to a decision not to accept an application it does not apply to a decision to accept an application. Such a challenge would be caught by s 118(7) which applies to 'proceedings for questioning anything else done, or omitted to be done, by the Secretary of State in relation to an application for an order granting development consent'.

As a decision under PA 2008, s 55 is a procedural decision, rather than a substantive decision, and some at least of the impediments to acceptance could be cured by an applicant supplying further or different information, it is a decision which might lead to a different outcome if taken a second time in different circumstances. It is not therefore a final decision in one sense in that the Inspectorate could change its mind in the light of further information. This seems also to be the intention of s 55(8) that provides that 'If in response the applicant modifies (or further modifies) the application, subsections (2) to (7) then apply to the application as modified.'

This is, therefore, one area of judicial review in connection with the PA 2008 where both the pre-action protocol and alternative dispute resolution might have an important role in removing to reducing the need for judicial review. If errors are point out to, and accepted by, the Planning Inspectorate and/or the applicant, then there may be scope to re-submit or modify the application so that the re-submitted or modified application could be accepted.

The position with the Daventry International Rail Freight Terminal application, which was not accepted by the Inspectorate due to non-compliance with PA 2008, s 55(3)(e) and s 55(3)(f), is illustrated by the meeting note published on the register of advice (5 December 2012) and subsequent correspondence (19 December 2012). Following the Planning Inspectorate's decision not to accept, a meeting was held between the Planning Inspectorate and the promoter to agree the way forward; this led to an acceptable re-submission of the application. In the letter dated 28 November 2012 containing the notification of the decision not to accept the application the Inspectorate had stated:

> 'We would also encourage you to meet with us so we can advise how best to address the issues to help facilitate a new application at the earliest opportunity.'

Legal Challenge to other Action of Secretary of State

Written by: Alex Booth, ftb
Edited by: Michael Humphries QC, ftb

Introduction

PA 2008, s 118 deals with legal challenges to applications for orders granting development consent. Its purpose is, in effect, to regulate the timescales within which a challenge by way of judicial review may be brought against a decision of the Secretary of State in relation to an application for an order granting development consent. PA 2008, s 118 identifies six specific 'decisions' to which its provisions relate and then provides a general provision covering anything else done, or omitted to be done, by the Secretary of State. This general provision does not cover challenges to national policy statements, which are specifically dealt with under PA 2008, s 13.

The specific 'decisions' covered by PA 2008, s 118 comprise:

- an order granting development consent (s 118(1));
- a refusal of development consent (s 118(2));
- a decision under s 55 *not* to accept an application for an order granting development (s 118(3));
- a decision under Sch 4 para 1 in relation to an error or omission in a decision document (s 118(4));
- a decision under Sch 6 para 2(1) to make a change to an order granting development consent (s 118(5)); and
- a decision under Sch 6 para 3(1) to make a change to, or revoke, an order granting development consent.

In the case of each of these specific decisions a challenge may *only* be brought by way of judicial review where the claim form is filed within six weeks 'beginning with' the date of an event identified in the individual provision.

The 2008 Act recognises, however, that there could be other decisions of the Secretary of State, or the Examining Authority on behalf of the Secretary of State, which do not fall within the above six cases and where a legal challenge could otherwise be brought under the normal judicial review timescales. As stated above, to deal with this eventuality the Act provides a general provision covering 'anything else done, or omitted to be done, by the Secretary of State' (s 118(7)). This article examines this general provision.

As yet, of the various applications for judicial review that have lodged in respect of the development consent process, none have been brought pursuant to the general provision under s 118(7).

PA 2008, s 118(7)

PA 2008, s 118(7) provides as follows:

> 'A court may entertain proceedings for questioning anything else done, or omitted to be done, by the Secretary of State in relation to an application for an order granting development consent only if –
>
> (a) the proceedings are brought by a claim for judicial review, and
>
> (b) the claim form is filed during the period of 6 weeks beginning with the relevant day.'

It is important to note that a court may entertain proceedings for questions anything else done, or omitted to be done, 'only' if brought by judicial review within six weeks of the 'relevant day'. The effect of s 118(7) is, therefore, to 'oust' any other avenue of legal challenge and impose a strict six-week time limit.

It is also important to note that PA 2008, s 118(7) is directed to anything done, or omitted to be done, 'in relation to an application' for development consent. It is not absolutely clear, therefore, whether it covers an act or omission of the Secretary of State during the pre-application procedures under the 2008 Act. Certainly the point did not appear to have been raised be the defendant in the *Innovia Cellophane Ltd* challenge to the (former) Infrastructure Planning Commission's grant of s 53 authorisation in respect of the then proposed Hinkley Point C application for development consent: see *R (Innovia Cellophane Ltd) v Infrastructure Planning Commission* [2011] EWHC 2883.

Within six weeks 'beginning with' the 'relevant day'

The period within which a claim may be brought is identified as 'beginning with the relevant day' (s 118(7)(b)). The 'relevant day' is itself defined (s 118(8)) as meaning the day on which:

- the application for development consent is withdrawn;
- the order granting development consent or the statement of reasons in respect of that order is 'published', whichever is the later;
- the statement of reasons for refusing to grant development consent is 'published'.

The first of these potential starting dates envisages a scenario in which an applicant for development consent has withdrawn its application, but a person still wishes to challenge a decision of the Secretary of State. Whilst it is not immediately obvious why a person might still wish to challenge a decision of the Secretary of State after an application for a development consent order has been withdrawn, it might be relevant, for example, where the Secretary of State had authorised entry on land by the promoter of a project under PA 2008, s 53 before the application for development consent had been withdrawn. Such a claim would allow a landowner to challenge a 'redundant' s 53 authorisation.

It is worth noting that this 'withdrawn' application scenario provides the only opportunity for a challenge to be brought in respect of a decision of the Secretary of State prior to either the publication of the order or, alternatively, the publication of the statement of reasons for its refusal.

Thus the effect of PA 2008, s 118 in general, and s 118(7) in particular, is to mean that a legal challenge may not be brought in respect of a decision of the Secretary of State from the making of the application until the grant or refusal of consent (subject to the 'withdrawn' application point). Thus a challenge may not be brought to any procedural decision taken during the examination of an application for development consent. The absence of any means of challenge during an examination may, however, mean storing up trouble for later in the process. Indeed, an applicant may even recognise that a particular act or omission by the Examining Authority, on behalf of the Secretary of State, at an early stage in the examination process could afford potential claimants with a fertile ground of challenge, but then be left waiting until the order is granted to see whether a challenge is indeed brought. Thus there is a risk that considerable resources may be expended during the remainder of the examination and ultimately be wasted.

A further point to consider within the context of timing, concerns the second of the start dates identified above, and the fact that the claim form may only be filed during the period of six weeks 'beginning with' the 'publication' of a development consent order.

The requirement to 'publish' the order is contained in PA 2008, s 117. The order must be published 'in such manner as the Secretary of State thinks appropriate' (s 117(3)), unless the order:

- makes by-laws,
- introduces offences,
- applies, modifies or excludes a statutory provision, or
- amends, repeals or revokes a statutory provision of local application,

in which case it must be contained in a statutory instrument (s 117(4). Statutory instruments are officially published by Her Majesty's Stationery Office (HMSO) on the website of The National Archives (www.legislation.gov.uk), where new statutory instruments they are listed by publication date.

The requirement to 'publish' a statement of reasons for a decision to grant development consent is contained in PA 2008, s 116. The statement must again be published 'in such manner as the Secretary of State thinks appropriate' (s 116(3)).

The requirement to 'publish' a statement of reasons for a decision to refuse development consent is contained in PA 2008, s 116. The statement must be published 'in such manner as the Secretary of State thinks appropriate' (s 116(3)).

Typically an Order granting development consent and the Secretary of State's statement of reasons for making the Order will be published simultaneously on the Planning Inspectorate's website (infrastructure.planningportal.gov.uk).

The effect of PA 2008, s 118 delaying legal challenge until the 'publication' of a development consent order can be seen in relation to FCC Environmental Ltd (formerly Waste Recycling Group Ltd) in respect of its s 118(1) claim for judicial review of the development consent order granted to Covanta Rookery South Ltd for a resource recovery facility in Bedfordshire. In that instance, the Infrastructure Planning Commission issued its statement of reasons for the grant of development consent on 13 October 2011 and made a draft DCO on 22 November 2011. The draft was placed before Parliament on 29 November that year, but thereafter underwent special parliamentary procedure. The DCO was then 'published' on 26 March 2013, and it was only at that stage that judicial review proceedings were, or indeed could be, lodged.

Matters for challenge

There are a limited number of matters which might conceivably form the basis of a challenge pursuant to PA 2008, s 118(7), since in most cases proceedings are likely to be brought either pursuant to s 118(1) (challenge to order granting development consent) or s 118(2) (challenge to refusal of development consent). Although as yet there is no legal authority upon the point, such would appear to be the case even if the substance of a complaint related to a procedural decision of the Secretary of State during the examination period. Thus a decision in respect of an application made by an objector that an examination should be suspended pursuant to regulation 17 of the Infrastructure Planning (Environmental Impact Assessment) Regulations 2009, SI 2009/2263, on the basis of the inadequacy of an environmental statement, might well still be made under s 118(1) if development consent were granted; notwithstanding it was a procedural decision on which the claim was founded.

As such, it is only certain discrete actions of the Secretary of State which would fall to be challenged pursuant to PA 2008, s 118(7) such as, by way of example, the decision to issue a certificate pursuant to s 127(2) approving the compulsory acquisition of land held by a statutory undertaker.

In such an instance, the subject-matter of the challenge would not comprise part of the decision reached in respect of the DCO application itself, but would instead comprise an associated but distinct determination. In this example PA 2008, s 118(7) would be relevant as a challenge to the decision to issue/refuse certification for compulsory purchase pursuant to s 127 would not comprise 'proceedings for questioning an order granting development consent' under s 118(1).

It may be that the full scope of PA 2008, s 118(7) will only become apparent as the provision is tested in the courts. For the present, however, it would appear that it will have only limited application.

Part 15

Enforcement

Enforcement under the Planning Act 2008

Written by: Michael Humphries QC, ftb

Introduction

PA 2008, Part 8 sets up the system of 'enforcement' under the Act for: (a) development without development consent; and (b) breach of the terms of an order granting development consent. It is worth noting at the outset that the PA 2008 enforcement system is radically different from that under the Town and Country Planning Act 1990.

In broad terms, PA 2008 creates two criminal offences:

(a) the carrying out of development for which development consent is required without first obtaining without development consent (s 160); and

(b) the carrying out of development in breach of the terms of a DCO or otherwise failing to comply with the terms of a DCO (s 161).

Only where a person has been found guilty of an offence under either of these provisions may a local planning authority serve a 'notice of unauthorised development' requiring 'steps' to be carried out to rectify the position. This is in sharp contrast to the 1990 Act regime where breaches of planning control are first made subject to civil enforcement and on then, in certain circumstances, made the subject-matter of an offence. A local planning authority may, however, apply to the High Court for an injunction to restrain any actual or apprehended activity that would be an offence under PA 2008, s 160 or 161.

This article will consider:

- Offences;
- Notices of unauthorised development; and
- Injunctions.

Offences

PA 2008, ss 160 and 161

PA 2008, Part 8 creates two primary offences, those being under ss 160 and 161.

PA 2008, s 160

PA 2008, s 160 provides that:

> '(1) A person commits an offence if the person carries out, or causes to be carried out, development for which development consent is required at a time when no development consent is in force in respect of the development.'

A person guilty of an offence under this section is liable to a fine not exceeding £50,000 on summary conviction, or an unlimited fine for conviction on indictment: see s 160(2).

The reference in PA 2008, s 160(1) to development for which development consent is 'required' relates directly to s 31 and the requirement for development consent for development to the extent that 'the development is or forms part of a nationally significant infrastructure project.' This again relates back to s 14, which defines the term 'nationally significant infrastructure project', and the various thresholds in ss 15–30.

It seems unlikely that an infrastructure developer would deliberately carry out development requiring development consent without first having obtained a DCO and so offences are likely to fall within two broad categories, being:

- Development thought to be within PA 2008 regime that extends physically or functionally beyond that actually granted by a DCO; or
- Development thought to be outside PA 2008 regime that has breached some NSIP threshold.

In relation to the first of these categories, it is clearly within the power of the promoter to ensure that any DCO is drafted so as to grant the necessary consent to carry out the development. It is for this reason that 'parameters' and the concept of the 'Rochdale envelope' are so important.

In relation to the second category above, it will be particularly important for any developer proposing an infrastructure project to ascertain with some certainty whether such project falls within the scope of PA 2008 as any error of understanding could result in a criminal conviction. Such an error may be made, for example, where what is being proposed is an 'alteration' to an existing infrastructure development, that alteration itself falling above a relevant threshold. An offence will be committed under this section notwithstanding that planning permission, or other consent, may have been granted for the development by a local planning authority or other decision-maker acting under the same error of understanding.

Clearly the criminal law standard of proof (ie beyond reasonable doubt) will apply to any proceedings under PA 2008, s 160.

PA 2008, s 161

PA 2008, s 161 provides that:

> '(1) A person commits an offence if without reasonable excuse the person –
>
> (a) carries out, or causes to be carried out, development in breach of the terms of an order granting development consent, or
>
> (b) otherwise fails to comply with the terms of an order granting development consent.'

Again, a person guilty of an offence under this section is liable to a fine not exceeding £50,000 on summary conviction, or an unlimited fine for conviction on indictment: see PA 2008, s 160(2).

It is important to note that by virtue of s PA 2008, ss 161(2) and 149A(4), a person who fails to comply with a 'condition' under a deemed 'marine licence' does not commit an offence under s 161, although breach of requirement for, or conditions of, a marine licence would be an offence under s 85 of the Marine and Coastal Access Act 2009.

The offence under PA 2008, s 161 may be committed where a person either: (a) carries out development in 'breach' of the terms of an order (s 161(1)(a)); or (b) 'fails to comply with the terms' of an order (s 161(1)(b)). In this context, the expression 'the terms of an order' would appear to comprise the articles in the body of the DCO, the contents of its schedules (including any plans) and, in particular, its 'requirements'.

PA 2008, s 161(1)(a) appears to contemplate the person committing the offence undertaking some positive action in 'carrying out development' in breach of the terms of a DCO which does exist for the project. This offence can be distinguished, therefore, from that under s 160 where the carrying out of development is at a time where there is no DCO for that project. An offence under this provision might comprise, for example, the carrying out of development in breach of a requirement first to submit details for approval by the local planning authority.

By contrast, PA 2008, s 161(1)(b) does not require the person committing the offence to be 'carrying out development' and so would be particularly relevant during the operational stages of any project. An offence under this provision might comprise, for example, operating the project in breach of any requirement relating to hours of operation.

The offence created under PA 2008, s 161 does introduce the potential defence of 'reasonable excuse', which was absent from s 160. The term 'reasonable excuse', which also appears in ss 53(6) and 168, is not defined in PA 2008, although it is a concept that occurs in other legislation. In such circumstances, it would appear that the words should be given their ordinary meaning and that an 'excuse' (in other words, an explanation for not complying with the terms of a DCO) will have to be advanced by a defendant, which will have to be judged 'reasonable' in considering whether an offence has been committed under s 161.

PA 2008, s 161(3) also makes it a defence under s 161 to prove that: (a) the breach or failure to comply occurred only because of 'an error or omission in the order'; and (b) a 'correction notice' specifying the correction of the error or omission has been issued under para 2 of Sch 4 to PA 2008.

Clearly, as with an offence under PA 2008, s 160, the criminal law standard of proof (ie beyond reasonable doubt) will apply to any proceedings under s 161.

Time limits

PA 2008, s 162 sets certain time limits for charging a person with an offence under ss 160 and 161. Section 162(1) provides that a person may not be charged with an offence under s 160 or 161 after the end of:

- the 'relevant four-year period'; or
- in certain circumstances, the 'extended period'.

The four-year period

PA 2008, s 162(2) provides that:

'The 'relevant 4-year period means –

(a) in the case of an offence under section 160, the period of 4 years beginning with the date on which the development was substantially completed;

(b) in the case of an offence under section 161, the period of 4 years beginning with the later of-

  (i) the date on which the development was substantially completed, and

  (ii) the date on which the breach or failure to comply occurred.'

The term 'substantially completed' in s 162(2) reflects the same language s section 171B of the Town and Country Planning Act 1990 and the case law that has developed under that section is likely to be highly material in relation to s 162(2).

The extended period

The 'extended period' applies where an information notice has been served under PA 2008, s 167 (see below) or an injunction applied for under s 171 (see below): see s 162(3). In such circumstances, s 162(4) provides that the four-year period runs from:

- the date of service of any information notice;
- the date of any application for an injunction;
- the later of those dates, if both apply.

The relevant local planning authority

For the purposes of PA 2008, Part 8, the term 'the relevant local planning authority' in relation to any land is defined by s 173 as the local planning authority for the area in which the land is situated.

Where, however, there is both a district planning authority and a county planning authority for an area then:

- if the 'relevant development' (see s 173(6)) is the construction or alteration of a hazardous waste facility within s 14(1)(p), the relevant local planning authority is the county planning authority (s 173(4)); and
- in any other case, the relevant local planning authority is the district planning authority (s 173(5)).

Rights of entry

PA 2008, s 163 provides a right to enter land 'without warrant' if the 'relevant local planning authority' 'has reasonable grounds for suspecting' that an offence under s 160 or 161 'is being, or has been, committed' on or in respect of the land.

The person authorised to enter the land under PA 2008, s 163 may 'at any reasonable hour' enter the land for the purpose of *'ascertaining whether'* an offence under s 160 or 161 has been, or is being, committed on the land: see s 163(2); although the person may only enter a building occupied as a dwelling on the giving of 24 hours' notice to the occupier of the building: see s 163(3).

This power clearly relates to any offence under PA 2008, s 160 or 161 that 'is being, or has been' committed; but not to 'apprehended' future offences. To the extent, therefore, that s 171 allows a local planning authority to apply for an injunction to restrain an 'apprehended' 'prohibited activity' (ie an anticipated future offence under s 160 or 161), s 163 would not give the relevant local planning authority power to enter the land.

PA 2008, s 164 gives the relevant local planning authority power to enter land 'under warrant' where: (a) admission to the land has been refused, or a refusal is reasonably apprehended; or (b) the case is one of urgency.

PA 2008, s 165 set out various supplementary provisions relating to the rights of entry under ss 163 and 164, including in relation to matters such as the wilful obstruction of a person exercising a right of entry as above, and compensation for damage caused to the land and chattels in the exercise of any such right of entry.

Information notices

An 'information notice' may be served under PA 2008, s 167 where it appears to 'the relevant local planning authority' that an offence under s 160 or 161 'may have been committed on or in respect of the land'.

This power clearly relates to offences that 'may have' been committed (ie 'past' offences), rather than anticipated future offences under PA 2008, s 160 or 161. As with the right to enter under s 163, therefore, to the extent that s 171 allows a local planning authority to apply for an injunction to restrain an 'apprehended' 'prohibited activity' (ie an anticipated future offence), section 167 would not allow the relevant local planning authority to require the giving of information to that 'apprehended' activity.

By virtue of PA 2008, s 167(2), such a notice may only be served by 'the relevant local planning authority' and, by s 167(3), may only be served on any person who: (a) is the owner or occupier of the land or has any other interest in it; or (b) is carrying out operations on the land or is using it for any purpose. Thus the power is wide enough to require information from contractors or others carrying out development.

An information notice may require (s 167(4)) the person served to give:

- information about any operations being carried out in, on, over or under the land, any use of the land and any other activities being carried out in, on, over or under the land; and
- information about the provisions of any order granting development consent for development of the land.

Notices of unauthorised development

PA 2008, s 169 provides for the relevant local planning authority to serve a 'notice of unauthorised development' where a person is found guilty of an offence under s 160 or 161.

The first thing to note is that such a notice can only *follow* successful criminal proceedings under PA 2008, s 160 or 161; a notice under s 169 cannot be served in advance of, or in parallel with, such proceedings. This is in sharp contrast with the approach under the Town and Country Planning Act 1990 where civil enforcement precedes any criminal proceedings.

Where the offence in respect of which a person has been found guilty is under PA 2008, s 160, then the relevant local planning authority may serve a notice of unauthorised development on the person by under s 169(2), requiring such 'steps' as may be specified in the notice to be taken:

- to remove the development; and
- to restore the land on which the development has been carried out to its condition before the development was carried out.

The notice of unauthorised development must specify the period within which any 'steps' are required to be taken and may specify different periods for different steps: see s 169(5).

Where the offence in respect of which a person has been found guilty is under PA 2008, s 161, then the relevant local planning authority may serve a notice of unauthorised development on the person by under s 169(4), requiring the person to remedy the breach or failure to comply.

Although PA 2008, s 169(4) does not refer to 'steps' required to be taken to remedy the breach or failure to comply, and therefore it is not clear whether s 169(5) applies, it would appear prudent to set out in the notice any period, or periods, within which the person is to remedy the breach or failure to comply.

PA 2008, s 170 sets out various matters relating to the execution of works required by notice of unauthorised development, including in relation to liability for expenses incurred in complying with any such notice (s 170(2)).

Injunctions

A 'local planning authority' may apply to the High Court for an injunction pursuant to PA 2008, s 171 if it considers it 'necessary or expedient' for any 'actual or apprehended prohibited activity' to be restrained by injunction.

For these purposes a 'prohibited activity' means an activity that constitutes an offence under PA 2008, s 160 or 161 in relation to land in the area of the local planning authority: see s 171(2).

PA 2008, s 171 makes it clear that an application for an injunction may be brought by 'a local planning authority' for the land in respect of which the 'prohibited activity' has taken place; thus the exercise of the power is not restricted to the 'relevant local planning authority' under s 173. Consequently, for land where there is both a district planning authority and a county planning authority, it would appear that either may make an application for an injunction under s 171.

It is important to note that a local planning authority may apply for an injunction under PA 2008, s 171 for any 'actual' or 'apprehended' prohibited activity. An 'actual' prohibited activity is clearly one that has occurred or is occurring. The term 'apprehended' is not one that is defined in PA 2008 but, given its ordinary meaning, an 'apprehended' prohibited activity is clearly one that is reasonably anticipated. Indeed, as injunctions are not granted lightly by the High Court, one might expect a local planning authority to have to demonstrate fairly clear grounds for 'apprehending' that an offence is likely to be committed under s 160 or 161.

On an application under PA 2008, s 171 the court may grant such an injunction as it 'thinks fit' for the purpose of restraining the prohibited activity: see s 171(3).

Part 16

Miscellaneous Issues

Costs in DCO Examinations

Written by: Douglas Edwards QC, ftb
Edited by: Michael Humphries QC, ftb

Introduction

At the conclusion of the examination process it may be that one or more of the interested parties, affected persons or indeed any other person who takes part in an examination wishes to claim the costs, or some of the costs, they incurred in that process from another person. This chapter considers the power to make costs, the procedure for applying for costs, the approach that will be taken to such applications, and also gives some examples of situations were costs awards may be appropriate.

The Department for Communities and Local Government published its guidance on *Award of costs: examination of applications for development consent orders* in July 2013, which replaces the Infrastructure Planning Commission's earlier *Policy on the Award of Costs in Relation to Examinations of Nationally Significant Infrastructure Project Applications.*

It is important to note that the costs guidance in relation to appeals under the Planning Acts, namely Circular 03/2009 on *Costs awards in appeals and other planning proceedings*, expressly does not apply to the development consent process under the PA 2008.

The power to award costs

PA 2008, s 95(4) applies section 250(5) of the Local Government Act 1972 to examinations by the Examining Authority of applications for development consent orders. It consequently gives the Examining Authority the power to award costs in the same way that an Inspector may award costs at a planning inquiry.

Procedure for claiming costs

Who can apply?

Standing to apply for costs is broad; any party who took part in the Examination can apply. That includes interested parties under PA 2008, s 102, affected persons under PA 2008, s 59, additional affected persons and additional interested parties under regulation 2 of the Infrastructure Planning (Compulsory Acquisition) Regulations 2010, and any other person who took part in the examination. The use of the term 'party' in this chapter refers to all such categories of person.

Time limits

An application for costs must be made within 28 days of the Examining Authority giving notice that it has completed its examination. Failure to apply within 28 days will usually result in the Examining Authority refusing to consider the application, unless good reason can be shown for applying late. It is therefore always best practice to apply within the 28 days.

In the event that the examination comes to an early end, perhaps because the application for development consent is withdrawn or because the examination is cancelled, the 28 day period begins to run from the date on which the Examining Authority gives notification of that withdrawal or the cancellation.

Procedure

In either case, the application for costs should be made in writing to the Planning Inspectorate at Temple Quay House, 2 The Square, Temple Quay, Bristol, BS1 6PN. There is no particular format for the application, but it should set out the broad nature of the costs claimed, the basis on which costs are sought (ie the conduct complained of) and should explain how costs have been incurred as a result of that conduct.

The costs application will be assessed by the same Examining Authority which considered the main application for development consent, but as the costs decision is made after the conclusion of the examination it is obviously made separately and a party who, for instance, unsuccessfully opposes development consent, may still be awarded their costs.

Upon receipt of an application for costs, the Examining Authority will first contact the parties against whom costs are sought and require them to respond within a set period of time. It will then invite final comments from the party who applied for costs, again within a set period of time. The Examining Authority will then take all of these submissions into account in reaching a decision.

Assessment of costs

Beyond determining whether an award of costs will be full or partial (see below), the Examining Authority's decision will not settle the amount of costs that should be paid. Therefore, when a party receives a full or partial costs award, the next step will be for that party to contact the paying party and attempt to agree the costs payable.

If the parties cannot agree, then the matter will require detailed assessment by a Costs Officer of the Senior Court Costs Office at Cliffords Inn, Fetter Lane, London, EC4A 1DQ and on 020 7947 7124. Part 47 of the Civil Procedure Rules and its accompanying Practice Direction will apply to any detailed assessment.

Given the various stages in the process it will therefore be appreciated that the final costs decision may come some time after the completion of the examination, and indeed after the initial costs application.

Enforcement

It is to be hoped that matters do not reach this stage, but if after having received a costs award and having the amount of those costs determined by agreement or on detailed assessment, those costs are not then paid, the costs award can be enforced through the courts. Part 70 of the Civil Procedure Rules and its accompanying Practice Direction will apply.

Approach taken to applications for costs

Principles applied

The starting point of any assessment of costs is that, unlike in most litigation, in the ordinary course of events all parties should bear their own costs. An award of costs must therefore be seen as being out of the ordinary, and should be made against this background.

The Examining Authority is most likely to award costs where the following three conditions are satisfied:

- first, the application for costs has been made in a timely manner within 28 days of the completion of the examination;
- secondly, the party from whom costs are sought has acted unreasonably; and
- thirdly, that unreasonable behaviour has caused, in whole or in part, the party seeking their costs to incur wasted or otherwise unnecessary expenditure.

As is therefore apparent, the key issue will be whether the other party acted unreasonably. The courts have been clear that in the context of cost awards, 'unreasonable' is to be given its ordinary English meaning.

Although the costs awarded can only relate to those incurred in the examination itself, the conduct complained of can relate to the pre-examination period or indeed even to the period before the application for development consent was submitted. The key is that the conduct caused costs to be incurred in the examination.

Examples of 'unreasonable' conduct

The list of unreasonable conduct is never closed, but common examples of procedure related behaviour that may be found an award of costs include:

- submitting documents late;
- failing to cooperate or to respond to reasonable requests in a timely fashion;
- submitting new or substantial evidence late, especially where this then requires other parties to submit further evidence in response;
- failing to agree on a statement of common ground or factual matters where this increases the amount of work other parties have to complete on other documents;
- withdrawing evidence at a late stage, especially where other parties have prepared on the basis of the withdrawn documents;
- failing to appear at a hearing or a site visit; and
- withdrawing the development consent application itself where no material change in circumstance can be identified to justify such a course of action, unless other exceptional circumstances can be shown.

Examples of substantive unreasonable behaviour could include:

- submitting a development consent application that is plainly contrary to policy (ie the content of a National Policy Statement);

- making submissions, or acting, contrary to established case law;
- pursuing objections that fail to accord proper weight to policy statements and which fail to provide objective evidence in support of the objection; and
- a local authority requiring the development consent applicant to enter into a obligation which fails to comply with para 204 of the National Planning Policy Framework, or an applicant failing to enter into such an obligation where the Examining Authority consider it necessary.

Compulsory acquisition

An exception to the need to show unreasonable behaviour occurs in development consent applications where the applicant seeks authorisation to compulsorily acquire land. Here an objector will be entitled to costs if they:

(a) maintain their objection throughout the process prior to the Secretary of State's decision (or withdrawal of the application for development consent and/or compulsory acquisition powers);

(b) participate in the examination by way of representations; and

(c) have their objection upheld by the Secretary of State, either through the wholesale refusal of development consent or by way of a development consent order that does not include compulsory acquisition powers (or if the applicant withdraws their request as in (a) above).

If an objector is unsuccessful under (c), they may still be entitled to costs if they can show unreasonable behaviour in the normal way. Partial success in an objection to compulsory acquisition (ie through the exclusion of only some land from the Order) will usually be met with a partial award of costs.

Different time limits also apply in this case. The application for costs should be made within 28 days of notification of the Secretary of State's decision, or withdrawal of the application.

Basis of assessment

Where the Examining Authority decides to make an award of costs it has two options available: a full award, or a partial award.

- A full award will provide for the payment of all of a party's necessary and reasonable costs incurred in its taking part in the examination, including preparation for and involvement in the examination, and the costs of applying for costs.
- A partial award by contrast will award a party its necessary and reasonable costs insofar as they relate to the unreasonable conduct of another, or to a specific part of the examination.

What is included within recoverable costs?

A party may have to incur costs for a number of reasons, including: obtaining professional advice or representation; drafting; document preparation; travel; and accommodation. So long as the unreasonable behaviour can be shown to have caused those costs to be incurred, those costs are in principle, and subject to their being necessary and reasonable, recoverable.

NSIPs and Town or Village Greens

Written by: Gregory Jones QC, ftb
Edited by: Michael Humphries QC, ftb

Introduction

A NSIP just like any other development might be thwarted by the land, or part of the land, being successfully registered as a Town or Village Green (TGV).

Town and village greens developed under customary law as areas of land where local people indulged in lawful sports and pastimes. These might include organised or ad-hoc games, picnics, fetes and similar activities. The court has taken a fairly wide approach and held such activities might include dog walking.

Most greens were registered in the late 1960s under the Commons Registration Act 1965. Provided the right to apply has not been excluded, anyone can apply under section 15(1) of the Commons Act 2006 to register land as a green if it has been used by local people for lawful sports and pastimes 'as of right' – that is without permission, force or secrecy- for at least 20 years (see DEFRA further fact sheet https://www.gov.uk/town-and-village-greens-how-to-register).

Pilot implementation areas

Those promoting NSIPs should check to see whether the site in question is included within any of the pilot implementation areas. In relation to the pilot implementation areas for Part 1 of the Commons Act 2006 (Devon, Kent (but not including unitary authorities in these first two counties), Cornwall, Hertfordshire, Herefordshire, Lancashire (but not Blackpool), and Blackburn with Darwen), the procedures, forms and guidance for applications under section 15 have been revised, and are now contained in the Guidance to Applicants in the pilot implementation areas.

Growth and Infrastructure Act 2013

The new Growth and Infrastructure Act 2013 (GIA 2013) introduces wide ranging implications for landowners and developers, including the introduction of significant changes to the procedure for registering land as a town or village green. The provisions are as yet untested in the courts. They are of great importance to any NSIP promoter who fears that its land may be subject a TVG application.

GIA 2013, s 16 inserted a new s 15C and Sch 1A into the Commons Act 2006. The new Sch 1A prescribes a series of nine occurrences (defined as 'trigger events') which, once triggered, will prevent the commons registration authority from registering the affected land as a town or village green.

Each trigger event is linked to procedures contained in existing planning or infrastructure legislation. Each may be ''terminated' following specified further events. The remainder of this article summarises the nine trigger events and terminating events in the Commons Act 2006, Sch 1A

Trigger Events

Planning applications

This trigger event relates to 'an application for planning permission in relation to the land which would be determined under the Town and Country Planning Act 1990 (TCPA 1990), s 70 is first publicised in accordance with requirements imposed by a development order by virtue of section 65(1) of that Act.' It occurs following receipt of a valid application by the local planning authority – the date of publication of notice of the application in accordance with Article 13 of the Town and Country Planning (Development Management Procedure) (England) Order 2010 (as amended) – namely: publication on the local authority's website site display/serving the notice on any adjoining owner or occupier placing notice in a locally circulating newspaper.

It is lost if the application is withdrawn the local planning authority refuse to determine the application on the basis that it is a 'repeat application' the application is refused and all legal avenues for appeal are exhausted permission is granted but the development is not begun within the period permitted by the permission.

Urgent Crown development

This trigger event arises where there is an application for planning permission made in relation to 'the land under s 293A of the 1990 Act is first publicised in accordance with subsection (8) of that section'. It relates to applications to the Secretary of State by the Crown for urgent developments of national importance. It occurs on the date of publication of notice of the application in accordance with art 13 of the Town and Country Planning (Development Management Procedure) (England) Order 2010, SI 2010/2184 (as amended) – namely:

a publication on the local authority's website site;

b display/serving the notice on any adjoining owner or occupier

c placing notice in a locally circulating newspaper

It is lost if the application is withdrawn or the application is refused and all legal avenues to appeal exhausted or permission is granted but the development is not begun within the period permitted by the permission.

Publication of a draft development plan document (identifying the land for potential development)

This trigger event arises where 'a draft of a development plan document which identifies the land for potential development is published for consultation in accordance with regulations under section 17(7) of the 2004 Act.' It relates to the publication by a local authority of a draft development plan document containing a statement which: encourages the development of use of the land over a specified period allocates the land for a particular type of development or use guides the determination of planning applications in respect of the land. It occurs when the draft development plan document is published by being made available for inspection at the local authority's offices and website notification is sent to relevant consultation bodies.

It is terminated when the draft development plan document is withdrawn the draft development plan document is adopted but this latter event is itself a new trigger (see further below).

Adoption of a development plan document (identifying the land for potential development)

This trigger event arises where 'a development plan document which identifies the land for potential development is adopted under section 23(2) or (3) of the 2004 Act.' It relates to the adoption of a development plan document (identifying the land for potential development – as above) following independent examination.

It occurs on the date of adoption following a resolution by the local planning authority and is terminated if: the development plan document is revoked or the policy relating to the land in question is superseded

Publication of a draft neighbourhood development plan (identifying the land for potential development)

This trigger is 'a proposal for a neighbourhood development plan which identifies the land for potential development is published by a local planning authority for consultation in accordance with regulations under paragraph 4(1) of Schedule 4B of the 1990 Act as it applies by virtue of section 38A(3) of the 2004 Act'.

It occurs upon the publication by a local authority of a draft neighbourhood development plan following submission by a parish council or designated neighbourhood forum when the draft neighbourhood development plan is published by: notice on the local authority's website and in such other manner as the local authority considers is likely to bring the proposal to the attention of people who live, work or carry on business in the neighbourhood area notification is sent to those bodies initially consulted by the parish council or designated neighbourhood forum.

It is terminated if the draft neighbourhood development plan is withdrawn the draft neighbourhood development plan is adopted but this leads to another trigger event, see below.

Making of a neighbourhood development plan (identifying the land for potential development)

This trigger event is where 'a neighbourhood development plan which identifies the land for potential development is made under section 38A of the 2004 Act'. It relates to the making by a local authority of a neighbourhood development plan (identifying the land for potential development – as above) following: independent examination and a local referendum. It occurs upon the publication by the local authority of its 'decision statement' following the making of the neighbourhood development plan.

It terminates where the plan ceases to have effect, is revokes, or where a policy relating to the development on land is superseded by another policy.

Saved structure plans and local plans identifying the land for potential development extant on 25 April 2013

This trigger arises where 'a development plan for the purposes of TCPA 1990, s 27 or 54, or anything treated as contained in such a plan by virtue of Schedule 8 to the

Planning and Compulsory Purchase Act 2004, continues to have effect (by virtue of that Schedule) on the commencement of section 16 of the Growth and Infrastructure Act 2013 and identifies the land for potential development.' It relates to extant structure plans, unitary development plans or local plans identifying the land for potential development and which predate the Planning and Compulsory Purchase Act 2004 which have been saved by the Secretary of State.

It came into force on 25 April 2013 (if the plan was extant on that date) and is terminated when a new policy replacing the saved policy is first published or adopted.

Publication of a proposed application for a nationally significant infrastructure project

This trigger is where 'a proposed planning application for an order granting development consent under section 114 of the 2008 Act in relation to the land is first publicised in accordance with section 48 of that Act ' It relates to proposed applications for nationally significant infrastructure project consent. It occurs upon the publication by the applicant of notice of the proposed application in local and national newspaper.

It is lost on the earlier of: the period of two years following the final newspaper publication the publication by the Secretary of State of an accepted application.

Publication of an accepted application for a nationally significant infrastructure project

This trigger event relates to where 'a proposed planning application for an order granting development consent under section 114 of the 2008 Act in relation to the land is first publicised in accordance with section 48 of that Act.' It is in respect of accepted applications for nationally significant infrastructure project consents. It occurs upon the publication by the applicant of notice of the application in local and national newspapers.

It is lost if the application is withdrawn or the application is refused and all legal avenues to appeal exhausted or consent is granted but the development is not begun within the period permitted by the consent.

Appendix

Planning Act 2008

Planning Act 2008 c 29

An Act to establish the Infrastructure Planning Commission and make provision about its functions; to make provision about, and about matters ancillary to, the authorisation of projects for the development of nationally significant infrastructure; to make provision about town and country planning; to make provision about the imposition of a Community Infrastructure Levy; and for connected purposes.

[26th November 2008]

BE IT ENACTED by the Queen's most Excellent Majesty, by and with the advice and consent of the Lords Spiritual and Temporal, and Commons, in this present Parliament assembled, and by the authority of the same, as follows:—

Part 1 [Infrastructure planning: fees][1]

1–3 …

Repealed by Localism Act 2011, ss 128(2), 237, Sch 13, paras 1, 2, Sch 25, Pt 20 as from 1 April 2012.

1 Words substituted by Localism Act 2011, s 128(2), Sch 13, paras 1, 3(1), (5) (15 January 2012 for the purpose of conferring power on the Secretary of State to make regulations or rules; 1 April 2012 otherwise).

4 Fees

(1) The Secretary of State may make regulations providing for the [charging of fees by the Secretary of State in connection with the performance of any of the Secretary of State's major-infrastructure functions][1].

(2) Regulations under subsection (1) may in particular make provision—

- (a) about when a fee (including a supplementary fee) may, and may not, be charged;
- (b) about the amount which may be charged;
- (c) about what may, and may not, be taken into account in calculating the amount charged;
- (d) about who is liable to pay a fee charged;
- (e) about when a fee charged is payable;
- (f) about the recovery of fees charged;
- (g) about waiver, reduction or repayment of fees;
- (h) about the effect of paying or failing to pay fees charged;
- (i) for the supply of information for any purpose of the regulations.

(3) The regulations may provide for the amounts of fees to be calculated by reference to costs [incurred by the Secretary of State][2]—

- (a) in the performance of any of [the Secretary of State's major-infrastructure functions][3], and
- (b) in doing anything which is calculated to facilitate, or is conducive or incidental to, the performance of any of [the Secretary of State's major-infrastructure functions][3].

[(4) In this section 'the Secretary of State's major-infrastructure functions' means—

(a) the Secretary of State's functions under Parts 2 to 8 and under Part 12 so far as applying for the purposes of those Parts,

(b) the giving of advice to which section 51 applies, and

(c) the Secretary of State's functions, in relation to proposed applications for orders granting development consent, under statutory provisions implementing—

(i) Council Directive 85/337/EC on the assessment of the effects of certain public and private projects on the environment, as amended from time to time, or

(ii) provisions of an EU instrument which from time to time replace provisions of that Directive.

(5) In subsection (4)(c) 'statutory provision' means a provision of an Act or of an instrument made under an Act.][4]

1 Words substituted by Localism Act 2011, s 128(2), Sch 13, paras 1, 3(1), (2) (15 January 2012 for the purpose of conferring power on the Secretary of State to make regulations or rules; 1 April 2012 otherwise).

2 Words substituted by Localism Act 2011, s 128(2), Sch 13, paras 1, 3(1), (3)(a) (15 January 2012 for the purpose of conferring power on the Secretary of State to make regulations or rules; 1 April 2012 otherwise).

3 Words substituted by Localism Act 2011, s 128(2), Sch 13, paras 1, 3(1), (3)(b) (15 January 2012 for the purpose of conferring power on the Secretary of State to make regulations or rules; 1 April 2012 otherwise).

4 Added by Localism Act 2011, s 128(2), Sch 13, paras 1, 3(1), (4) (15 January 2012 for the purpose of conferring power on the Secretary of State to make regulations or rules; 1 April 2012 otherwise).

Part 2 National policy statements

5 National policy statements

(1) The Secretary of State may designate a statement as a national policy statement for the purposes of this Act if the statement—

(a) is issued by the Secretary of State, and

(b) sets out national policy in relation to one or more specified descriptions of development.

(2) In this Act 'national policy statement' means a statement designated under subsection (1) as a national policy statement for the purposes of this Act.

(3) Before designating a statement as a national policy statement for the purposes of this Act the Secretary of State must carry out an appraisal of the sustainability of the policy set out in the statement.

(4) A statement may be designated as a national policy statement for the purposes of this Act only if the consultation and publicity requirements set out in section 7, and the parliamentary requirements set out in section 9, have been complied with in relation to it [and—][1]

[(a) the consideration period for the statement has expired without the House of Commons resolving during that period that the statement should not be proceeded with, or

(b) the statement has been approved by resolution of the House of Commons—

(i) after being laid before Parliament under section 9(8), and

(ii) before the end of the consideration period.][1]

[(4A) In subsection (4) 'the consideration period', in relation to a statement, means the period of 21 sitting days beginning with the first sitting day after the day on which the statement is laid before Parliament under section 9(8), and here 'sitting day' means a day on which the House of Commons sits.][2]

(5) The policy set out in a national policy statement may in particular—

(a) set out, in relation to a specified description of development, the amount, type or size of development of that description which is appropriate nationally or for a specified area;

(b) set out criteria to be applied in deciding whether a location is suitable (or potentially suitable) for a specified description of development;

(c) set out the relative weight to be given to specified criteria;

(d) identify one or more locations as suitable (or potentially suitable) or unsuitable for a specified description of development;

(e) identify one or more statutory undertakers as appropriate persons to carry out a specified description of development;

(f) set out circumstances in which it is appropriate for a specified type of action to be taken to mitigate the impact of a specified description of development.

(6) If a national policy statement sets out policy in relation to a particular description of development, the statement must set out criteria to be taken into account in the design of that description of development.

(7) A national policy statement must give reasons for the policy set out in the statement.

(8) The reasons must (in particular) include an explanation of how the policy set out in the statement takes account of Government policy relating to the mitigation of, and adaptation to, climate change.

(9) The Secretary of State must—

(a) arrange for the publication of a national policy statement[.]

[...][3]

(10) In this section 'statutory undertakers' means persons who are, or are deemed to be, statutory undertakers for the purposes of any provision of Part 11 of TCPA 1990.

1 Added by Localism Act 2011, s 130(1), (2) (1 April 2012).
2 Added by Localism Act 2011, s 130(1), (3) (1 April 2012).
3 Repealed by Localism Act 2011, s 237, Sch 25, Pt 20 (1 April 2012).

6 Review

(1) The Secretary of State must review each national policy statement whenever the Secretary of State thinks it appropriate to do so.

(2) A review may relate to all or part of a national policy statement.

(3) In deciding when to review a national policy statement the Secretary of State must consider whether—

(a) since the time when the statement was first published or (if later) last reviewed, there has been a significant change in any circumstances on the basis of which any of the policy set out in the statement was decided,

(b) the change was not anticipated at that time, and

(c) if the change had been anticipated at that time, any of the policy set out in the statement would have been materially different.

(4) In deciding when to review part of a national policy statement ('the relevant part') the Secretary of State must consider whether—

(a) since the time when the relevant part was first published or (if later) last reviewed, there has been a significant change in any circumstances on the basis of which any of the policy set out in the relevant part was decided,

(b) the change was not anticipated at that time, and

(c) if the change had been anticipated at that time, any of the policy set out in the relevant part would have been materially different.

(5) After completing a review of all or part of a national policy statement the Secretary of State must do one of the following—

(a) amend the statement;

(b) withdraw the statement's designation as a national policy statement;

(c) leave the statement as it is.

(6) Before amending a national policy statement the Secretary of State must carry out an appraisal of the sustainability of the policy set out in the proposed amendment.

(7) The Secretary of State may amend a national policy statement only if the consultation and publicity requirements set out in section 7, and the parliamentary requirements set out in section 9, have been complied with in relation to the proposed amendment [and—][1]

[(a) the consideration period for the amendment has expired without the House of Commons resolving during that period that the amendment should not be proceeded with, or

(b) the amendment has been approved by resolution of the House of Commons—

(i) after being laid before Parliament under section 9(8), and

(ii) before the end of the consideration period.][1]

[(7A) In subsection (7) 'the consideration period', in relation to an amendment, means the period of 21 sitting days beginning with the first sitting day after the day on which the amendment is laid before Parliament under section 9(8), and here 'sitting day' means a day on which the House of Commons sits.][2]

(8) Subsections (6) [to (7A)][3] do not apply if the Secretary of State thinks that the proposed amendment (taken with any other proposed amendments) does not materially affect the policy as set out in the national policy statement.

(9) If the Secretary of State amends a national policy statement, the Secretary of State must—

(a) arrange for the amendment, or the statement as amended, to be published, and

(b) lay the amendment, or the statement as amended, before Parliament.

1 Added by Localism Act 2011, s 130(1), (5) (1 April 2012).
2 Added by Localism Act 2011, s 130(1), (6) (1 April 2012).
3 Words substituted by Localism Act 2011, s 130(1), (7) (1 April 2012).

[6A Interpretation of sections 5(4) and 6(7)

(1) This section applies for the purposes of section 5(4) and 6(7).

(2) The consultation and publicity requirements set out in section 7 are to be treated as having been complied with in relation to a statement or proposed amendment ('the final proposal') if—

(a) they have been complied with in relation to a different statement or proposed amendment ('the earlier proposal'),

(b) the final proposal is a modified version of the earlier proposal, and

(c) the Secretary of State thinks that the modifications do not materially affect the policy as set out in the earlier proposal.

(3) The consultation and publicity requirements set out in section 7 are also to be treated as having been complied with in relation to a statement or proposed amendment ('the final proposal') if—

(a) they have been complied with—

(i) in relation to a different statement or proposed amendment ('the earlier proposal'), and

(ii) in relation to modifications of the earlier proposal ('the main modifications'),

(b) the final proposal is a modified version of the earlier proposal, and

(c) there are no modifications other than the main modifications or, where the modifications include modifications other than the main modifications, the Secretary of State thinks that those other modifications do not materially affect the policy as set out in the earlier proposal modified by the main modifications.

(4) If section 9(8) has been complied with in relation to a statement or proposed amendment ('the final proposal'), the parliamentary requirements set out in section 9(2) to (7) are to be treated as having been complied with in relation to the final proposal where—

(a) the final proposal is not the same as what was laid under section 9(2), but

(b) those requirements have been complied with in relation to what was laid under section 9(2).

(5) Ignore any corrections of clerical or typographical errors in what was laid under section 9(8).][1]

1 Added by Localism Act 2011, s 130(1), (8) (1 April 2012).

[6B Extension of consideration period under section 5(4A) or 6(7A)

(1) The Secretary of State may—

(a) in relation to a proposed national policy statement, extend the period mentioned in section 5(4A), or

(b) in relation to a proposed amendment of a national policy statement, extend the period mentioned in section 6(7A),

by 21 sitting days or less.

(2) The Secretary of State does that by laying before the House of Commons a statement—

(a) indicating that the period is to be extended, and

(b) setting out the length of the extension.

(3) The statement under subsection (2) must be laid before the period would have expired without the extension.

(4) The Secretary of State must publish the statement under subsection (2) in a way the Secretary of State thinks appropriate.

(5) The period may be extended more than once.][1]

1 Added by Localism Act 2011, s 130(1), (8) (1 April 2012).

7 Consultation and publicity

(1) This section sets out the consultation and publicity requirements referred to in sections 5(4) and 6(7).

(2) The Secretary of State must carry out such consultation, and arrange for such publicity, as the Secretary of State thinks appropriate in relation to the proposal.

This is subject to subsections (4) and (5).

(3) In this section 'the proposal' means—

(a) the statement that the Secretary of State proposes to designate as a national policy statement for the purposes of this Act, or

(b) (as the case may be) the proposed amendment.

(4) The Secretary of State must consult such persons, and such descriptions of persons, as may be prescribed.

(5) If the policy set out in the proposal identifies one or more locations as suitable (or potentially suitable) for a specified description of development, the Secretary of State must ensure that appropriate steps are taken to publicise the proposal.

(6) The Secretary of State must have regard to the responses to the consultation and publicity in deciding whether to proceed with the proposal.

8 Consultation on publicity requirements

(1) In deciding what steps are appropriate for the purposes of section 7(5), the Secretary of State must consult—

(a) each local authority that is within subsection (2)[, (3) or (3A)][1], and

(b) the Greater London Authority, if any of the locations concerned is in Greater London.

(2) A local authority is within this subsection if any of the locations concerned is in the authority's area.

(3) A local authority ('A') is within this subsection if—

(a) any of the locations concerned is in the area of another local authority ('B'), [...][2]

[(aa) B is a unitary council or a lower-tier district council, and][2]

(b) any part of the boundary of A's area is also a part of the boundary of B's area.

[(3A) If any of the locations concerned is in the area of an upper-tier county council ('C'), a local authority ('D') is within this subsection if—

(a) D is not a lower-tier district council, and

(b) any part of the boundary of D's area is also part of the boundary of C's area.][3]

(4) In this section 'local authority' means—

(a) a county council, or district council, in England;

(b) a London borough council;

(c) the Common Council of the City of London;

(d) the Council of the Isles of Scilly;

(e) a county council, or county borough council, in Wales;

(f) a council constituted under section 2 of the Local Government etc. (Scotland) Act 1994 (c. 39);

(g) a National Park authority;

(h) the Broads Authority.

[(5) In this section—

'lower-tier district council' means a district council in England for an area for which there is a county council;

'unitary council' means a local authority that is not an upper-tier county council, a lower-tier district council, a National Park authority or the Broads Authority;

'upper-tier county council' means a county council in England for each part of whose area there is a district council.][4]

1 Words substituted by Localism Act 2011, s 130(1), (9) (1 April 2012).
2 Added by Localism Act 2011, s 130(1), (10) (1 April 2012).
3 Added by Localism Act 2011, s 130(1), (11) (1 April 2012).
4 Added by Localism Act 2011, s 130(1), (12) (1 April 2012).

9 Parliamentary requirements

(1) This section sets out the parliamentary requirements referred to in sections 5(4) and 6(7).

(2) The Secretary of State must lay the proposal before Parliament.

(3) In this section 'the proposal' means—

(a) the statement that the Secretary of State proposes to designate as a national policy statement for the purposes of this Act, or

(b) (as the case may be) the proposed amendment.

(4) Subsection (5) applies if, during the relevant period—

(a) either House of Parliament makes a resolution with regard to the proposal, or

(b) a committee of either House of Parliament makes recommendations with regard to the proposal.

(5) The Secretary of State must lay before Parliament a statement setting out the Secretary of State's response to the resolution or recommendations.

(6) The relevant period is the period specified by the Secretary of State in relation to the proposal.

(7) The Secretary of State must specify the relevant period in relation to the proposal on or before the day on which the proposal is laid before Parliament under subsection (2).

[(8) After the end of the relevant period, but not before the Secretary of State complies with subsection (5) if it applies, the Secretary of State must lay the proposal before Parliament.

(9) If after subsection (8) has been complied with—

(a) something other than what was laid under subsection (8) becomes the proposal, or

(b) what was laid under subsection (8) remains the proposal, or again becomes the proposal, despite the condition in section 5(4)(a) not having been met in relation to it,

subsection (8) must be complied with anew.

(10) For the purposes of subsection (9)(a) and (b) ignore any proposal to correct clerical or typographical errors in what was laid under subsection (8).][1]

1 Added by Localism Act 2011, s 130(1), (13) (1 April 2012).

10 Sustainable development

(1) This section applies to the Secretary of State's functions under sections 5 and 6.

(2) The Secretary of State must, in exercising those functions, do so with the objective of contributing to the achievement of sustainable development.

(3) For the purposes of subsection (2) the Secretary of State must (in particular) have regard to the desirability of—

(a) mitigating, and adapting to, climate change;

(b) achieving good design.

11 Suspension pending review

(1) This section applies if the Secretary of State thinks that the condition in subsection (2) or (3) is met.

(2) The condition is that—

(a) since the time when a national policy statement was first published or (if later) last reviewed, there has been a significant change in any circumstances on the basis of which any of the policy set out in the statement was decided,

(b) the change was not anticipated at that time, and

(c) if the change had been anticipated at that time, any of the policy set out in the statement would have been materially different.

(3) The condition is that—

(a) since the time when part of a national policy statement ('the relevant part') was first published or (if later) last reviewed, there has been a significant change in any circumstances on the basis of which any of the policy set out in the relevant part was decided,

(b) the change was not anticipated at that time, and

(c) if the change had been anticipated at that time, any of the policy set out in the relevant part would have been materially different.

(4) The Secretary of State may suspend the operation of all or any part of the national policy statement until a review of the statement or the relevant part has been completed.

(5) If the Secretary of State does so, the designation as a national policy statement of the statement or (as the case may be) the part of the statement that has been suspended is treated as having been withdrawn until the day on which the Secretary of State complies with section 6(5) in relation to the review.

12 ...

Repealed by Localism Act 2011, s 237, Sch 25, Pt 20 as from 1 April 2012.

13 Legal challenges relating to national policy statements

(1) A court may entertain proceedings for questioning a national policy statement or anything done, or omitted to be done, by the Secretary of State in the course of preparing such a statement only if—

(a) the proceedings are brought by a claim for judicial review, and

(b) the claim form is filed during the period of 6 weeks beginning with—

(i) the day on which the statement is designated as a national policy statement for the purposes of this Act, or

(ii) (if later) the day on which the statement is published.

(2) A court may entertain proceedings for questioning a decision of the Secretary of State not to carry out a review of all or part of a national policy statement only if—

(a) the proceedings are brought by a claim for judicial review, and

(b) the claim form is filed during the period of 6 weeks beginning with the day of the decision not to carry out the review.

(3) A court may entertain proceedings for questioning a decision of the Secretary of State to carry out a review of all or part of a national policy statement only if—

(a) the proceedings are brought by a claim for judicial review, and

(b) the claim form is filed during the period of 6 weeks beginning with the day on which the Secretary of State complies with section 6(5) in relation to the review concerned.

(4) A court may entertain proceedings for questioning anything done, or omitted to be done, by the Secretary of State in the course of carrying out a review of all or part of a national policy statement only if—

(a) the proceedings are brought by a claim for judicial review, and

(b) the claim form is filed during the period of 6 weeks beginning with the day on which the Secretary of State complies with section 6(5) in relation to the review concerned.

(5) A court may entertain proceedings for questioning anything done by the Secretary of State under section 6(5) after completing a review of all or part of a national policy statement only if—

(a) the proceedings are brought by a claim for judicial review, and

(b) the claim form is filed during the period of 6 weeks beginning with the day on which the thing concerned is done.

(6) A court may entertain proceedings for questioning a decision of the Secretary of State as to whether or not to suspend the operation of all or part of a national policy statement under section 11 only if—

(a) the proceedings are brought by a claim for judicial review, and

(b) the claim form is filed during the period of 6 weeks beginning with the day of the decision.

Part 3 Nationally significant infrastructure projects

General

14 Nationally significant infrastructure projects: general

(1) In this Act 'nationally significant infrastructure project' means a project which consists of any of the following—

(a) the construction or extension of a generating station;

(b) the installation of an electric line above ground;

(c) development relating to underground gas storage facilities;

(d) the construction or alteration of an LNG facility;

(e) the construction or alteration of a gas reception facility;

(f) the construction of a pipe-line by a gas transporter;

(g) the construction of a pipe-line other than by a gas transporter;

(h) highway-related development;

(i) airport-related development;

(j) the construction or alteration of harbour facilities;

(k) the construction or alteration of a railway;

(l) the construction or alteration of a rail freight interchange;

(m) the construction or alteration of a dam or reservoir;

(n) development relating to the transfer of water resources;

(o) the construction or alteration of a waste water treatment plant [or of infrastructure for the transfer or storage of waste water][1];

(p) the construction or alteration of a hazardous waste facility.

(2) Subsection (1) is subject to sections 15 to 30.

(3) The Secretary of State may by order—

(a) amend subsection (1) to add a new type of project or vary or remove an existing type of project;

(b) make further provision, or amend or repeal existing provision, about the types of project which are, and are not, within subsection (1).

(4) An order under subsection (3)(b) may amend this Act.

(5) The power conferred by subsection (3) may be exercised to add a new type of project to subsection (1) only if—

(a) a project of the new type is a project for the carrying out of works in one or more of the fields specified in subsection (6), and

(b) the works are to be carried out wholly in one or more of the areas specified in subsection (7).

(6) The fields are—

(a) energy;

(b) transport;

(c) water;

(d) waste water;

(e) waste.

(7) The areas are—

(a) England;

(b) waters adjacent to England up to the seaward limits of the territorial sea;

(c) in the case of a project for the carrying out of works in the field of energy, a Renewable Energy Zone, except any part of a Renewable Energy Zone in relation to which the Scottish Ministers have functions.

1 Words added by Infrastructure Planning (Waste Water Transfer and Storage) Order 2012, SI 2012/1645, art 2(1), (2) (23 June 2012: insertion has effect subject to supplementary provision specified in SI 2012/1645, art 3).

Energy

15 Generating stations

(1) The construction or extension of a generating station is within section 14(1)(a) only if the generating station is or (when constructed or extended) is expected to be within subsection (2) or (3).

(2) A generating station is within this subsection if—

(a) it is in England or Wales,

(b) it is not an offshore generating station, and

(c) its capacity is more than 50 megawatts.

(3) A generating station is within this subsection if—

(a) it is an offshore generating station, and

(b) its capacity is more than 100 megawatts.

(4) An 'offshore' generating station is a generating station that is—

(a) in waters in or adjacent to England or Wales up to the seaward limits of the territorial sea, or

(b) in a Renewable Energy Zone, except any part of a Renewable Energy Zone in relation to which the Scottish Ministers have functions.

16 Electric lines

(1) The installation of an electric line above ground is within section 14(1)(b) only if (when installed) the electric line will be—

(a) wholly in England,

(b) wholly in Wales,

(c) partly in England and partly in Wales, or

(d) partly in England and partly in Scotland, subject to subsection (2).

(2) In the case of an electric line falling within subsection (1)(d), the installation of the line above ground is within section 14(1)(b) only to the extent that (when installed) the line will be in England.

(3) The installation of an electric line above ground is not within section 14(1)(b)—

(a) if the nominal voltage of the line is expected to be less than 132 kilovolts, [...][1]

[(aa) if the length of the line (when installed) will be less than two kilometres,

(ab) if—

(i) the line will replace an existing line,

(ii) the nominal voltage of the line is expected to be greater than the nominal voltage of the existing line (but see subsection (3A)),

(iii) the height above the surface of the ground of any support for the line will not exceed the height of the highest existing support or support which is being replaced by more than 10 per cent, and

(iv) where the line is to be installed in a different position from the existing line, the distance between any new support and the existing line will not exceed 60 metres and the existing line will be removed within twelve months from the date on which the installation of the line which replaces it is complete,][2]

(b) to the extent that (when installed) the line will be within premises in the occupation or control of the person responsible for its installation [, or][3]

[(c) if section 37(1) of the Electricity Act 1989 (consent required for overhead lines) does not apply to it by virtue of the Overhead Lines (Exemption) (England and Wales) Regulations 2009 (S.I. 2009/640), as amended by the Overhead Lines (Exempt Installations) (Consequential Provisions) Order 2010.][3]

[(3A) Paragraph (ab)(ii) of subsection (3) (condition that nominal voltage of line expected to be greater than nominal voltage of existing line) does not apply if any part of the line (when installed) will be within a European site or an SSSI.][2]

[(4) In this section—

'European site' has the same meaning as in the Conservation of Habitats and Species Regulations 2010 (S.I. 2010/490);

'existing line' means an electric line which—

(a) has been installed or is kept installed above ground in accordance with a consent granted under section 37(1) of the Electricity Act 1989 or an order granting development consent; or

(b) has been installed above ground and is an electric line to which section 37(1) of the Electricity Act 1989 does not apply by virtue of—

(i) paragraph 5(4) or (5) of Schedule 17 to that Act, or

(ii) the Overhead Lines (Exemption) (England and Wales) Regulations 2009 (S.I. 2009/640), as amended by the Overhead Lines (Exempt Installations) (Consequential Provisions) Order 2010;

'premises' includes any land, building or structure;

'SSSI' means a site of special scientific interest notified under sections 28 to 28D of the Wildlife and Countryside Act 1981.][4]

1 Word repealed by Overhead Lines (Exempt Installations) Order 2010, SI 2010/277, art 2(a) (1 March 2010).
2 Added by Planning Act 2008 (Nationally Significant Infrastructure Projects) (Electric Lines) Order 2013, SI 2013/1479, art 2(a), (b) (18 June 2013).
3 Added by Overhead Lines (Exempt Installations) Order 2010, SI 2010/277, art 2(b) (1 March 2010).
4 Substituted by Planning Act 2008 (Nationally Significant Infrastructure Projects) (Electric Lines) Order 2013, SI 2013/1479, art 2(c) (18 June 2013).

17 Underground gas storage facilities

(1) Development relating to underground gas storage facilities is within section 14(1)(c) only if the development is within subsection (2), (3) or (5).

(2) Development is within this subsection if—

(a) it is the carrying out of operations for the purpose of creating underground gas storage facilities in England, or

(b) it is starting to use underground gas storage facilities in England,

and the condition in subsection (4) is met in relation to the facilities.

(3) Development is within this subsection if—

(a) it is starting to use underground gas storage facilities in Wales,

(b) the facilities are facilities for the storage of gas underground in natural porous strata,

(c) the proposed developer is a gas transporter, and

(d) the condition in subsection (4) is met in relation to the facilities.

(4) The condition is that—

(a) the working capacity of the facilities is expected to be at least 43 million standard cubic metres, or

(b) the maximum flow rate of the facilities is expected to be at least 4.5 million standard cubic metres per day.

(5) Development is within this subsection if—

(a) it is the carrying out of operations for the purpose of altering underground gas storage facilities in England, and

(b) the effect of the alteration is expected to be—

(i) to increase by at least 43 million standard cubic metres the working capacity of the facilities, or

(ii) to increase by at least 4.5 million standard cubic metres per day the maximum flow rate of the facilities.

(6) 'Underground gas storage facilities' means facilities for the storage of gas underground in cavities or in porous strata.

(7) In this section—

'maximum flow rate', in relation to underground gas storage facilities, means the maximum rate at which gas is able to flow out of the facilities, on the assumption that—

(a) the facilities are filled to maximum capacity, and

(b) the rate is measured after any processing of gas required on its recovery from storage;

'working capacity', in relation to underground gas storage facilities, means the capacity of the facilities for storage of gas underground, ignoring any capacity for storage of cushion gas.

(8) In subsection (7) 'cushion gas' means gas which is kept in underground gas storage facilities for the purpose of enabling other gas stored there to be recovered from storage.

18 LNG facilities

(1) The construction of an LNG facility is within section 14(1)(d) only if (when constructed) the facility will be in England and—

(a) the storage capacity of the facility is expected to be at least 43 million standard cubic metres, or

(b) the maximum flow rate of the facility is expected to be at least 4.5 million standard cubic metres per day.

(2) The alteration of an LNG facility is within section 14(1)(d) only if the facility is in England and the effect of the alteration is expected to be—

(a) to increase by at least 43 million standard cubic metres the storage capacity of the facility, or

(b) to increase by at least 4.5 million standard cubic metres per day the maximum flow rate of the facility.

(3) 'LNG facility' means a facility for—

(a) the reception of liquid natural gas from outside England,

(b) the storage of liquid natural gas, and

(c) the regasification of liquid natural gas.

(4) In this section—

'maximum flow rate', in relation to a facility, means the maximum rate at which gas is able to flow out of the facility, on the assumption that—

(a) the facility is filled to maximum capacity, and

(b) the rate is measured after regasification of the liquid natural gas and any other processing required on the recovery of the gas from storage;

'storage capacity' means the capacity of the facility for storage of liquid natural gas.

(5) The storage capacity of an LNG facility is to be measured as if the gas were stored in regasified form.

19 Gas reception facilities

(1) The construction of a gas reception facility is within section 14(1)(e) only if (when constructed)—

(a) the facility will be in England and will be within subsection (4), and

(b) the maximum flow rate of the facility is expected to be at least 4.5 million standard cubic metres per day.

(2) The alteration of a gas reception facility is within section 14(1)(e) only if—

(a) the facility is in England and is within subsection (4), and

(b) the effect of the alteration is expected to be to increase by at least 4.5 million standard cubic metres per day the maximum flow rate of the facility.

(3) 'Gas reception facility' means a facility for—

(a) the reception of natural gas in gaseous form from outside England, and

(b) the handling of natural gas (other than its storage).

(4) A gas reception facility is within this subsection if—

(a) the gas handled by the facility does not originate in England, Wales or Scotland,

(b) the gas does not arrive at the facility from Scotland or Wales, and

(c) the gas has not already been handled at another facility after its arrival in England.

(5) 'Maximum flow rate' means the maximum rate at which gas is able to flow out of the facility.

20 Gas transporter pipe-lines

(1) The construction of a pipe-line by a gas transporter is within section 14(1)(f) only if (when constructed) each of the conditions in subsections (2) to (5) is expected to be met in relation to the pipe-line.

(2) The pipe-line must be wholly or partly in England.

(3) Either—

(a) the pipe-line must be more than 800 millimetres in diameter and more than 40 kilometres in length, or

(b) the construction of the pipe-line must be likely to have a significant effect on the environment.

(4) The pipe-line must have a design operating pressure of more than 7 bar gauge.

(5) The pipe-line must convey gas for supply (directly or indirectly) to at least 50,000 customers, or potential customers, of one or more gas suppliers.

(6) In the case of a pipe-line that (when constructed) will be only partly in England, the construction of the pipe-line is within section 14(1)(f) only to the extent that the pipe-line will (when constructed) be in England.

(7) 'Gas supplier' has the same meaning as in Part 1 of the Gas Act 1986 (c. 44) (see section 7A(11) of that Act).

21 Other pipe-lines

(1) The construction of a pipe-line other than by a gas transporter is within section 14(1)(g) only if (when constructed) the pipe-line is expected to be—

(a) a cross-country pipe-line,

(b) a pipe-line the construction of which would (but for section 33(1) of this Act) require authorisation under section 1(1) of the Pipe-lines Act 1962 (c. 58) (cross-country pipe-lines not to be constructed without authorisation), and

(c) within subsection (2).

(2) A pipe-line is within this subsection if one end of it is in England or Wales and—

(a) the other end of it is in England or Wales, or

(b) it is an oil or gas pipe-line and the other end of it is in Scotland.

(3) For the purposes of section 14(1)(g) and the previous provisions of this section, the construction of a diversion to a pipe-line is treated as the construction of a separate pipe-line.

(4) But if—

(a) the pipe-line to be diverted is itself a nationally significant pipe-line, and

(b) the length of the pipe-line which is to be diverted has not been constructed,

the construction of the diversion is treated as the construction of a cross-country pipe-line, whatever the length of the diversion.

(5) For the purposes of subsection (4), a pipe-line is a nationally significant pipe-line if—

(a) development consent is required for its construction by virtue of section 14(1)(g), and has been granted, or

(b) its construction has been authorised by a pipe-line construction authorisation under section 1(1) of the Pipe-lines Act 1962 (c. 58).

(6) 'Diversion' means a lateral diversion of a length of a pipe-line (whether or not that pipe-line has been constructed) where the diversion is beyond the permitted limits.

(7) The permitted limits are the limits of lateral diversion permitted by any of the following granted in respect of the construction of the pipe-line—

(a) development consent;

(b) authorisation under the Pipe-lines Act 1962;

(c) planning permission.

Transport

[22 Highways

(1) Highway-related development is within section 14(1)(h) only if the development is—

(a) construction of a highway in a case within subsection (2),

(b) alteration of a highway in a case within subsection (3), or

(c) improvement of a highway in a case within subsection (5).

(2) Construction of a highway is within this subsection only if—

(a) the highway will (when constructed) be wholly in England,

(b) the Secretary of State will be the highway authority for the highway, and

(c) the area of development is greater than the relevant limit set out in subsection (4).

(3) Alteration of a highway is within this subsection only if—

(a) the highway is wholly in England,

(b) the Secretary of State is the highway authority for the highway, and

(c) the area of development is greater than the relevant limit set out in subsection (4).

(4) For the purposes of subsections (2)(c) and (3)(c) the relevant limit —

(a) in relation to the construction or alteration of a motorway, is 15 hectares,

(b) in relation to the construction or alteration of a highway, other than a motorway, where the speed limit for any class of vehicle is expected to be 50 miles per hour or greater, is 12.5 hectares, and

(c) in relation to the construction or alteration of any other highway is 7.5 hectares.

(5) Improvement of a highway is within this subsection only if—

(a) the highway is wholly in England,

(b) the Secretary of State is the highway authority for the highway, and

(c) the improvement is likely to have a significant effect on the environment.

(6) Highway-related development does not fall within section 14(1)(h) if—

(a) an order mentioned in section 33(4) has been made in relation to the development before 1 March 2010,

(b) a further order is needed in relation to the development, and

(c) not more than 7 years have elapsed since the making of the earlier order.

(7) Alteration of a highway is not within section 14(1)(h) if

(a) planning permission has been granted for a development,

(b) the alteration is necessary as a result of the development, and

(c) the developer has asked for the alteration to be made to the highway.

(8) Alteration of a highway is not within section 14(1)(h) if—

(a) an order mentioned in section 33(4) has been made in relation to local highway works,

(b) the alteration is necessary as a result of the local highway works, and

(c) the local highway authority responsible for the local highway works has asked for the alteration to be made to the highway.

(9) In this section—

'area of development'—

(a) in relation to construction of a highway, means the land on which the highway is to be constructed and any adjoining land expected to be used in connection with its construction;

(b) in relation to alteration of a highway, means the land on which the part of the highway to be altered is situated and any adjoining land expected to be used in connection with its alteration;

'local highway authority' has the meaning given by section 329(1) of the Highways Act 1980;

'local highway works' means works carried out by or on behalf of a local highway authority in relation to a highway for which it is the highway authority (and the local highway authority is referred to in this section as 'responsible' for those works);

'motorway' means a highway which is a special road in accordance with section 16 of the Highways Act 1980.][1]

1 Substituted by Highway and Railway (Nationally Significant Infrastructure Project) Order 2013, SI 2013/1883, art 3.

23 Airports

(1) Airport-related development is within section 14(1)(i) only if the development is—

(a) the construction of an airport in a case within subsection (2),

(b) the alteration of an airport in a case within subsection (4), or

(c) an increase in the permitted use of an airport in a case within subsection (7).

(2) Construction of an airport is within this subsection only if (when constructed) the airport—

(a) will be in England or in English waters, and

(b) is expected to be capable of providing services which meet the requirements of subsection (3).

(3) Services meet the requirements of this subsection if they are—

(a) air passenger transport services for at least 10 million passengers per year, or

(b) air cargo transport services for at least 10,000 air transport movements of cargo aircraft per year.

(4) Alteration of an airport is within this subsection only if—

(a) the airport is in England or in English waters, and

(b) the alteration is expected to have the effect specified in subsection (5).

(5) The effect is—

(a) to increase by at least 10 million per year the number of passengers for whom the airport is capable of providing air passenger transport services, or

(b) to increase by at least 10,000 per year the number of air transport movements of cargo aircraft for which the airport is capable of providing air cargo transport services.

(6) 'Alteration', in relation to an airport, includes the construction, extension or alteration of—

(a) a runway at the airport,

(b) a building at the airport, or

(c) a radar or radio mast, antenna or other apparatus at the airport.

(7) An increase in the permitted use of an airport is within this subsection only if—

(a) the airport is in England or in English waters, and

(b) the increase is within subsection (8).

(8) An increase is within this subsection if—

(a) it is an increase of at least 10 million per year in the number of passengers for whom the airport is permitted to provide air passenger transport services, or

(b) it is an increase of at least 10,000 per year in the number of air transport movements of cargo aircraft for which the airport is permitted to provide air cargo transport services.

(9) In this section—

'air cargo transport services' means services for the carriage by air of cargo;

'air passenger transport services' means services for the carriage by air of passengers;

'air transport movement' means a landing or take-off of an aircraft;

'cargo' includes mail;

'cargo aircraft' means an aircraft which is—

(a) designed to transport cargo but not passengers, and

(b) engaged in the transport of cargo on commercial terms;

'English waters' means waters adjacent to England up to the seaward limits of the territorial sea;

'permitted' means permitted by planning permission or development consent.

24 Harbour facilities

(1) The construction of harbour facilities is within section 14(1)(j) only if (when constructed) the harbour facilities—

(a) will be in England or Wales or in waters adjacent to England or Wales up to the seaward limits of the territorial sea, and

(b) are expected to be capable of handling the embarkation or disembarkation of at least the relevant quantity of material per year.

(2) The alteration of harbour facilities is within section 14(1)(j) only if—

(a) the harbour facilities are in England or Wales or in waters adjacent to England or Wales up to the seaward limits of the territorial sea, and

(b) the effect of the alteration is expected to be to increase by at least the relevant quantity per year the quantity of material the embarkation or disembarkation of which the facilities are capable of handling.

(3) 'The relevant quantity' is—

(a) in the case of facilities for container ships, 500,000 TEU;

(b) in the case of facilities for ro-ro ships, 250,000 units;

(c) in the case of facilities for cargo ships of any other description, 5 million tonnes;

(d) in the case of facilities for more than one of the types of ships mentioned in paragraphs (a) to (c), an equivalent quantity of material.

(4) For the purposes of subsection (3)(d), facilities are capable of handling an equivalent quantity of material if the sum of the relevant fractions is one or more.

(5) The relevant fractions are—

(a) to the extent that the facilities are for container ships—

x / 500,000

where x is the number of TEU that the facilities are capable of handling;

(b) to the extent that the facilities are for ro-ro ships—

y / 250,000

where y is the number of units that the facilities are capable of handling;

(c) to the extent that the facilities are for cargo ships of any other description—

z / 5,000,000

where z is the number of tonnes of material that the facilities are capable of handling.

(6) In this section—

'cargo ship' means a ship which is used for carrying cargo;

'container ship' means a cargo ship which carries all or most of its cargo in containers;

'ro-ro ship' means a ship which is used for carrying wheeled cargo;

'TEU' means a twenty-foot equivalent unit;

'unit' in relation to a ro-ro ship means any item of wheeled cargo (whether or not self-propelled).

25 Railways

(1) Construction of a railway is within section 14(1)(k) only if—

(a) the railway will (when constructed) be wholly in England,

(b) the railway will (when constructed) be part of a network operated by an approved operator,

[(ba) the railway will (when constructed) include a stretch of track that—

(i) is a continuous length of more than 2 kilometres, and

(ii) is not on land that was operational land of a railway undertaker immediately before the construction work began or is on land that was acquired at an earlier date for the purpose of constructing the railway,][1]

and

(c) the construction of the railway is not permitted development.

(2) Alteration of a railway is within section 14(1)(k) only if—

(a) the part of the railway to be altered is wholly in England,

(b) the railway is part of a network operated by an approved operator,

[(ba) the alteration of the railway will include laying a stretch of track that—

(i) is a continuous length of more than 2 kilometres, and

(ii) is not on land that was operational land of a railway undertaker immediately before the alteration work began or is on land that was acquired at an earlier date for the purpose of the alteration,][1]

and

(c) the alteration of the railway is not permitted development.

[(2A) Construction or alteration of a railway is not within section 14(1)(k) to the extent that it takes place on the operational land of a railway undertaker unless that land was acquired for the purpose of the construction or alteration.][1]

(3) Construction or alteration of a railway is not within section 14(1)(k) to the extent that the railway forms part (or will when constructed form part) of a rail freight interchange.

(4) 'Approved operator' means a person who meets the conditions in subsections (5) and (6).

(5) The condition is that the person must be—

(a) a person who is authorised to be the operator of a network by a licence granted under section 8 of the Railways Act 1993 (c. 43) (licences for operation of railway assets), or

(b) a wholly-owned subsidiary of a company which is such a person.

(6) The condition is that the person is designated, or is of a description designated, in an order made by the Secretary of State.

(7) In this section—

'network' has the meaning given by section 83(1) of the Railways Act 1993 (c. 43);

['operational land' has the same meaning as in the TCPA 1990;][1]

'permitted development' means development in relation to which planning permission is granted by article 3 of the Town and Country Planning (General Permitted Development) Order 1995;

['railway undertaker' has the same meaning as in Part 17 of Schedule 2 to the Town and Country Planning (General Permitted Development) Order 1995;][1]

'wholly-owned subsidiary' has the same meaning as in the Companies Act 2006 (c. 46) (see section 1159 of that Act).

(8) [In the definition of 'permitted development' in subsection (7), the reference][2] to the Town and Country Planning (General Permitted Development) Order 1995 is to that Order as it has effect immediately before the day on which this section comes fully into force.

1 Added by Highway and Railway (Nationally Significant Infrastructure Project) Order 2013, SI 2013/1883, art 4(1)-(5).

2 Substituted by Highway and Railway (Nationally Significant Infrastructure Project) Order 2013, SI 2013/1883, art 4(1), (6).

26 Rail freight interchanges

(1) The construction of a rail freight interchange is within section 14(1)(l) only if (when constructed) each of the conditions in subsections (3) to (7) is expected to be met in relation to it.

(2) The alteration of a rail freight interchange is within section 14(1)(l) only if—

(a) following the alteration, each of the conditions in subsections (3)(a) and (4) to (7) is expected to be met in relation to it, and

(b) the alteration is expected to have the effect specified in subsection (8).

(3) The land on which the rail freight interchange is situated must—

(a) be in England, and

(b) be at least 60 hectares in area.

(4) The rail freight interchange must be capable of handling—

(a) consignments of goods from more than one consignor and to more than one consignee, and

(b) at least 4 goods trains per day.

(5) The rail freight interchange must be part of the railway network in England.

(6) The rail freight interchange must include warehouses to which goods can be delivered from the railway network in England either directly or by means of another form of transport.

(7) The rail freight interchange must not be part of a military establishment.

(8) The effect referred to in subsection (2)(b) is to increase by at least 60 hectares the area of the land on which the rail freight interchange is situated.

(9) In this section—

'goods train' means a train that (ignoring any locomotive) consists of items of rolling stock designed to carry goods;

'military establishment' means an establishment intended for use for naval, military or air force purposes or for the purposes of the Department of the Secretary of State responsible for defence.

(10) The following terms have the meanings given by section 83(1) of the Railways Act 1993—

'network';

'rolling stock';

'train'.

Water

27 Dams and reservoirs

(1) The construction of a dam or reservoir is within section 14(1)(m) only if—

(a) the dam or reservoir (when constructed) will be in England,

(b) the construction will be carried out by one or more water undertakers, and

(c) the volume of water to be held back by the dam or stored in the reservoir is expected to exceed 10 million cubic metres.

(2) The alteration of a dam or reservoir is within section 14(1)(m) only if—

(a) the dam or reservoir is in England,

(b) the alteration will be carried out by one or more water undertakers, and

(c) the additional volume of water to be held back by the dam or stored in the reservoir as a result of the alteration is expected to exceed 10 million cubic metres.

(3) 'Water undertaker' means a company appointed as a water undertaker under the Water Industry Act 1991 (c. 56).

28 Transfer of water resources

(1) Development relating to the transfer of water resources is within section 14(1)(n) only if—

(a) the development will be carried out in England by one or more water undertakers,

(b) the volume of water to be transferred as a result of the development is expected to exceed 100 million cubic metres per year,

(c) the development will enable the transfer of water resources—

(i) between river basins in England,

(ii) between water undertakers' areas in England, or

(iii) between a river basin in England and a water undertaker's area in England, and

(d) the development does not relate to the transfer of drinking water.

(2) In this section—

'river basin' means an area of land drained by a river and its tributaries;

'water undertaker' means a company appointed as a water undertaker under the Water Industry Act 1991;

'water undertaker's area' means the area for which a water undertaker is appointed under that Act.

Waste water

29 Waste water treatment plants

(1) The construction of a waste water treatment plant is within section 14(1)(o) only if the treatment plant (when constructed)—

(a) will be in England, and

(b) is expected to have a capacity exceeding a population equivalent of 500,000.

[(1A) The construction of infrastructure for the transfer or storage of waste water is within section 14(1)(o) only if —

(a) the works will be carried out wholly in England and the infrastructure will (when constructed) be wholly in England,

(b) the main purpose of the infrastructure will be—

(i) the transfer of waste water for treatment, or

(ii) the storage of waste water prior to treatment,

or both, and

(c) the infrastructure is expected to have a capacity for the storage of waste water exceeding 350,000 cubic metres.][1]

(2) The alteration of a waste water treatment plant is within section 14(1)(o) only if—

(a) the treatment plant is in England, and

(b) the effect of the alteration is expected to be to increase by more than a population equivalent of 500,000 the capacity of the plant.

[(2A) The alteration of infrastructure for the transfer or storage of waste water is within section 14(1)(o) only if—

(a) the works will be carried out wholly in England and the part of the infrastructure to be altered is wholly in England,

(b) the main purpose of the infrastructure is —

(i) the transfer of waste water for treatment, or

(ii) the storage of waste water prior to treatment,

or both, and

(c) the effect of the alteration is expected to be to increase the capacity of the infrastructure for the storage of waste water by more than 350,000 cubic metres.][1]

(3) 'Waste water' includes domestic waste water, industrial waste water and urban waste water.

(4) The following terms have the meanings given by regulation 2(1) of the Urban Waste Water Treatment (England and Wales) Regulations 1994 (S.I. 1994/2841)—

'domestic waste water';

'industrial waste water';

'population equivalent';

'urban waste water'.

1 Inserted by Infrastructure Planning (Waste Water Transfer and Storage) Order 2012, SI 2012/1645, art 2(1), (3) (23 June 2012: insertions have effect subject to supplementary provision specified in SI 2012/1645, art 3).

Waste

30 Hazardous waste facilities

(1) The construction of a hazardous waste facility is within section 14(1)(p) only if—

(a) the facility (when constructed) will be in England,

(b) the main purpose of the facility is expected to be the final disposal or recovery of hazardous waste, and

(c) the facility is expected to have the capacity specified in subsection (2).

(2) The capacity is—

(a) in the case of the disposal of hazardous waste by landfill or in a deep storage facility, more than 100,000 tonnes per year;

(b) in any other case, more than 30,000 tonnes per year.

(3) The alteration of a hazardous waste facility is within section 14(1)(p) only if—

(a) the facility is in England,

(b) the main purpose of the facility is the final disposal or recovery of hazardous waste, and

(c) the alteration is expected to have the effect specified in subsection (4).

(4) The effect is—

(a) in the case of the disposal of hazardous waste by landfill or in a deep storage facility, to increase by more than 100,000 tonnes per year the capacity of the facility;

(b) in any other case, to increase by more than 30,000 tonnes per year the capacity of the facility.

(5) The following terms have the same meanings as in the Hazardous Waste (England and Wales) Regulations 2005 (S.I. 2005/894) (see regulation 5 of those regulations)—

'disposal';

'hazardous waste';

'recovery'.

(6) 'Deep storage facility' means a facility for the storage of waste underground in a deep geological cavity.

Part 4 Requirement for development consent

31 When development consent is required

Consent under this Act ('development consent') is required for development to the extent that the development is or forms part of a nationally significant infrastructure project.

32 Meaning of 'development'

(1) In this Act (except in Part 11) 'development' has the same meaning as it has in TCPA 1990.

This is subject to subsections (2) and (3).

(2) For the purposes of this Act (except Part 11)—

(a) the conversion of a generating station with a view to its being fuelled by crude liquid petroleum, a petroleum product or natural gas is treated as a material change in the use of the generating station;

(b) starting to use a cavity or strata for the underground storage of gas is treated as a material change in the use of the cavity or strata;

(c) an increase in the permitted use of an airport is treated as a material change in the use of the airport.

(3) For the purposes of this Act (except Part 11) the following works are taken to be development (to the extent that they would not be otherwise)—

(a) works for the demolition of a listed building or its alteration or extension in a manner which would affect its character as a building of special architectural or historic interest;

(b) demolition of a building in a conservation area;

(c) works resulting in the demolition or destruction of or any damage to a scheduled monument;

(d) works for the purpose of removing or repairing a scheduled monument or any part of it;

(e) works for the purpose of making any alterations or additions to a scheduled monument;

(f) flooding or tipping operations on land in, on or under which there is a scheduled monument.

(4) In this section—

'conservation area' has the meaning given by section 91(1) of the Listed Buildings Act;

'flooding operations' has the meaning given by section 61(1) of the Ancient Monuments and Archaeological Areas Act 1979 (c. 46);

'listed building' has the meaning given by section 1(5) of the Listed Buildings Act;

'permitted' means permitted by planning permission or development consent;

'petroleum products' has the meaning given by section 21 of the Energy Act 1976 (c. 76);

'scheduled monument' has the meaning given by section 1(11) of the Ancient Monuments and Archaeological Areas Act 1979 (c. 46);

'tipping operations' has the meaning given by section 61(1) of that Act.

33 Effect of requirement for development consent on other consent regimes

(1) To the extent that development consent is required for development, none of the following is required to be obtained for the development or given in relation to it—

(a) planning permission;

(b) consent under section 10(1), 11(1) or 12(1) of the Green Belt (London and Home Counties) Act 1938 (c. xciii) (erection of buildings and construction of sewer main pipes, watercourses and electric lines etc. on Green Belt land);

(c) a pipe-line construction authorisation under section 1(1) of the Pipe-lines Act 1962 (c. 58) (authorisation for construction of cross-country pipe-lines);

(d) authorisation by an order under section 4(1) of the Gas Act 1965 (c. 36) (storage of gas in underground strata);

[...][1]

(f) to the extent that the development relates to land in England, consent under section 2(3) or 3 of the Ancient Monuments and Archaeological Areas Act 1979;

(g) to the extent that the development relates to land in England, notice under section 35 of the Ancient Monuments and Archaeological Areas Act 1979;

(h) consent under section 36 or 37 of the Electricity Act 1989 (c. 29) (construction etc. of generating stations and installation of overhead lines);

(i) to the extent that the development relates to land in England, consent under section 8(1), (2) or (3) of the Listed Buildings Act;

(j) to the extent that the development relates to land in England, consent under section 74(1) of the Listed Buildings Act.

(2) To the extent that development consent is required for development, the development may not be authorised by any of the following—

(a) an order under section 14 or 16 of the Harbours Act 1964 (c. 40) (orders in relation to harbours, docks and wharves);

(b) an order under section 4(1) of the Gas Act 1965 (order authorising storage of gas in underground strata);

(c) an order under section 1 or 3 of the Transport and Works Act 1992 (c. 42) (orders as to railways, tramways, inland waterways etc.).

(3) Subsection (2) is subject to section 34.

(4) If development consent is required for the construction, improvement or alteration of a highway, none of the following may be made or confirmed in relation to the highway or in connection with the construction, improvement or alteration of the highway—

(a) an order under section 10 of the Highways Act 1980 (c. 66) (general provisions as to trunk roads) directing that the highway should become a trunk road;

(b) an order under section 14 of that Act (supplementary orders relating to trunk roads and classified roads);

(c) a scheme under section 16 of that Act (schemes authorising the provision of special roads);

(d) an order under section 18 of that Act (supplementary orders relating to special roads);

(e) an order or scheme under section 106 of that Act (orders and schemes providing for construction of bridges over or tunnels under navigable waters);

(f) an order under section 108 or 110 of that Act (orders authorising the diversion of navigable and non-navigable watercourses);

(g) an order under section 6 of the New Roads and Street Works Act 1991 (c. 22) (toll orders).

[(5) The Secretary of State may by order—

(a) amend subsection (1) or (2)—

(i) to add or remove a type of consent, or

(ii) to vary the cases in relation to which a type of consent is within that subsection;

(b) make further provision, or amend or repeal provision, about—

(i) the types of consent that are, and are not, within subsection (1) or (2), or

(ii) the cases in relation to which a type of consent is, or is not, within either of those subsections.

(6) In this section 'consent' means—

(a) a consent or authorisation that is required, under legislation, to be obtained for development,

(b) a consent, or authorisation, that—

(i) may authorise development, and

(ii) is given under legislation, or

(c) a notice that is required by legislation to be given in relation to development.

(7) In subsection (6) 'legislation' means an Act or an instrument made under an Act.

(8) An order under subsection (5) may not affect—

(a) a requirement for a devolved consent to be obtained for, or given in relation to, development, or

(b) whether development may be authorised by a devolved consent.

(9) A consent is 'devolved' for the purposes of subsection (8) if—

(a) provision for the consent would be within the legislative competence of the National Assembly for Wales if the provision were contained in an Act of the Assembly,

(b) provision for the consent is, or could be, made by the Welsh Ministers in an instrument made under an Act,

(c) the consent is not within subsection (6)(c) and the Welsh Ministers have a power or duty—

(i) to decide, or give directions as to how to decide, whether the consent is given,

(ii) to decide, or give directions as to how to decide, some or all of the terms on which the consent is given, or

(iii) to revoke or vary the consent, or

(d) the consent is within subsection (6)(c) and the notice has to be given to the Welsh Ministers or otherwise brought to their attention.

(10) An order under subsection (5)(b) may amend this Act.][2]

1 Repealed by Growth and Infrastructure Act 2013, s 18(3)(a) (25 June 2013).
2 Added by Localism Act 2011, s 131(1), (2) (1 April 2012).

34 Welsh offshore generating stations

(1) Section 33(2) does not prevent an order under section 3 of the Transport and Works Act 1992 (c. 42) from authorising the carrying out of works consisting of the construction or extension of a generating station that is or (when constructed or extended) will be a Welsh offshore generating station.

(2) A 'Welsh offshore generating station' is a generating station that is in waters in or adjacent to Wales up to the seaward limits of the territorial sea.

(3) If, by virtue of subsection (1), an order under section 3 of the Transport and Works Act 1992 authorises the carrying out of any works, development consent is treated as not being required for the carrying out of those works.

[35 Directions in relation to projects of national significance

(1) The Secretary of State may give a direction for development to be treated as development for which development consent is required.

This is subject to the following provisions of this section and section 35ZA.

(2) The Secretary of State may give a direction under subsection (1) only if—

(a) the development is or forms part of—

(i) a project (or proposed project) in the field of energy, transport, water, waste water or waste, or

(ii) a business or commercial project (or proposed project) of a prescribed description,

(b) the development will (when completed) be wholly in one or more of the areas specified in subsection (3), and

(c) the Secretary of State thinks the project (or proposed project) is of national significance, either by itself or when considered with—

(i) in a case within paragraph (a)(i), one or more other projects (or proposed projects) in the same field;

(ii) in a case within paragraph (a)(ii), one or more other business or commercial projects (or proposed projects) of a description prescribed under paragraph (a)(ii).

(3) The areas are—

(a) England or waters adjacent to England up to the seaward limits of the territorial sea;

(b) in the case of a project for the carrying out of works in the field of energy, a Renewable Energy Zone, except any part of a Renewable Energy Zone in relation to which the Scottish Ministers have functions.

(4) The Secretary of State may give a direction under subsection (1) only with the consent of the Mayor of London if—

(a) all or part of the development is or will be in Greater London, and

(b) the development is or forms part of a business or commercial project (or proposed project) of a description prescribed under subsection (2)(a)(ii).

(5) Regulations under subsection (2)(a)(ii) may not prescribe a description of project which includes the construction of one or more dwellings.][1]

1 Sections 35 and 35ZA substituted for s 35 by Growth and Infrastructure Act 2013, s 26(1), (2) (25 April 2013).

[35ZA Directions under sections 35: procedural matters

(1) The power in section 35(1) to give a direction in a case within section 35(2)(a)(i) (projects in the field of energy etc) is exercisable only in response to a qualifying request if no application for a consent or authorisation mentioned in section 33(1) or (2) has been made in relation to the development to which the request relates.

(2) The power in section 35(1) to give a direction in a case within section 35(2)(a)(ii) (business or commercial projects of prescribed description) is exercisable only in response to a qualifying request made by one or more of the following—

(a) a person who proposes to carry out any of the development to which the request relates;

(b) a person who has applied, or proposes to apply, for a consent or authorisation mentioned in section 33(1) or (2) in relation to any of that development;

(c) a person who, if a direction under section 35(1) is given in relation to that development, proposes to apply for an order granting development consent for any of that development.

(3) If the Secretary of State gives a direction under section 35(1) in relation to development, the Secretary of State may—

(a) if an application for a consent or authorisation mentioned in section 33(1) or (2) has been made in relation to the development, direct the application to be treated as an application for an order granting development consent;

(b) if a person proposes to make an application for such a consent or authorisation in relation to the development, direct the proposed application to be treated as a proposed application for development consent.

(4) A direction under section 35(1), or subsection (3) of this section, may be given so as to apply for specified purposes or generally.

(5) A direction under subsection (3) may provide for specified provisions of or made under this or any other Act—

(a) to have effect in relation to the application, or proposed application, with any specified modifications, or

(b) to be treated as having been complied with in relation to the application or proposed application.

(6) If the Secretary of State gives a direction under subsection (3), the relevant authority must refer the application, or proposed application, to the Secretary of State instead of dealing with it themselves.

(7) If the Secretary of State is considering whether to give a direction under subsection (3), the Secretary of State may direct the relevant authority to take no further action in relation to the application, or proposed application, until the Secretary of State has decided whether to give the direction.

(8) The Secretary of State may require an authority within subsection (9) to provide any information required by the Secretary of State for the purpose of enabling the Secretary of State to decide—

(a) whether to give a direction under section 35(1), and

(b) the terms in which such a direction should be given.

(9) An authority is within this subsection if an application for a consent or authorisation mentioned in section 33(1) or (2) in relation to the development has been, or may be, made to it.

(10) If the Secretary of State decides to give a direction under section 35(1), the Secretary of State must give reasons for the decision.

(11) In this section—

'qualifying request' means a written request, for a direction under section 35(1) or subsection (3) of this section, that—

(a) specifies the development to which it relates, and

(b) explains why the conditions in section 35(2)(a) and (b) are met in relation to the development;

'relevant authority'—

(a) in relation to an application for a consent or authorisation mentioned in section 33(1) or (2) that has been made, means the authority to which the application was made, and

(b) in relation to such an application that a person proposes to make, means the authority to which the person proposes to make the application.][1]

1 Sections 35 and 35ZA substituted for s 35 by Growth and Infrastructure Act 2013, s 26(1), (2) (25 April 2013).

[35A Timetable for deciding request for direction under section 35

(1) This section applies if the Secretary of State receives a qualifying request from a person ('R').

(2) The Secretary of State must make a decision on the qualifying request before the primary deadline, subject to subsection (3).

(3) Subsection (2) does not apply if, before the primary deadline, the Secretary of State asks R to provide the Secretary of State with information for the purpose of enabling the Secretary of State to decide—

(a) whether to give the direction requested, and

(b) the terms in which it should be given.

(4) If R—

(a) is asked under subsection (3) to provide information, and

(b) provides the information sought within the period of 14 days beginning with the day on which R is asked to do so,

the Secretary of State must make a decision on the qualifying request before the end of the period of 28 days beginning with the day the Secretary of State receives the information.

(5) In this section—

'the primary deadline' means the end of the period of 28 days beginning with the day on which the Secretary of State receives the qualifying request;

'qualifying request' has the meaning given by [section 35ZA(11)][1].][2]

1 Word substituted by Growth and Infrastructure Act 2013, s 26(1), (3) (25 April 2013).
2 Added by Localism Act 2011, s 132(10) (1 April 2012).

36 Amendments consequential on development consent regime

Schedule 2 makes amendments consequential on the development consent regime.

Part 5 Applications for orders granting development consent

Chapter 1 Applications

37 Applications for orders granting development consent

(1) An order granting development consent may be made only if an application is made for it.

(2) An application for an order granting development consent must be made to the [Secretary of State][1].

(3) An application for an order granting development consent must [, so far as necessary to secure that the application (including accompaniments) is of a standard that the Secretary of State considers satisfactory][2] —

(a) specify the development to which it relates,

(b) be made in the prescribed form,

(c) be accompanied by the consultation report, and

(d) be accompanied by documents and information of a prescribed description.

(4) The [Secretary of State][1] may give guidance about how the requirements under subsection (3) are to be complied with.

(5) The [Secretary of State][1] may set standards for—

(a) the preparation of a document required by subsection (3)(d);

(b) the coverage in such a document of a matter falling to be dealt with in it;

(c) all or any of the collection, sources, verification, processing and presentation of information required by subsection (3)(d).

(6) The [Secretary of State][1] must publish, in such manner as [the Secretary of State][3] thinks appropriate, any guidance given under subsection (4) and any standards set under subsection (5).

(7) In subsection (3)(c) 'the consultation report' means a report giving details of—

(a) what has been done in compliance with sections 42, 47 and 48 in relation to a proposed application that has become the application,

(b) any relevant responses, and

(c) the account taken of any relevant responses.

(8) In subsection (7) 'relevant response' has the meaning given by section 49(3).

1 Word substituted by Localism Act 2011, s 128(2), Sch 13, paras 1, 5(1), (2) (1 April 2012).
2 Words inserted by Localism Act 2011, s 137(1), (5) (1 April 2012).
3 Word substituted by Localism Act 2011, s 128(2), Sch 13, paras 1, 5(1), (3) (1 April 2012).

38 ...

Repealed by Localism Act 2011, ss 128(2), 237, Sch 13, paras 1, 6, Sch 25, Pt 20 as from 1 April 2012.

39 Register of applications

(1) The [Secretary of State][1] is to maintain a register of applications received by [the Secretary of State][2] for orders granting development consent ('the register').

(2) Where the [Secretary of State][1] receives an application for an order granting development consent, [the Secretary of State][2] must cause details of the application to be entered in the register.

(3) The [Secretary of State][1] must publish the register or make arrangements for inspection of the register by the public.

(4) The [Secretary of State][1] must make arrangements for inspection by the public of—

(a) applications received by the [Secretary of State][1] for orders granting development consent,

(b) consultation reports received by the [Secretary of State][1] under section 37(3)(c), and

(c) accompanying documents and information received by the [Secretary of State][1] under section 37(3)(d).

1 Word substituted by Localism Act 2011, s 128(2), Sch 13, paras 1, 7(1), (2) (1 April 2012).
2 Word substituted by Localism Act 2011, s 128(2), Sch 13, paras 1, 7(1), (3) (1 April 2012).

40 Applications by the Crown for orders granting development consent

(1) This section applies to an application for an order granting development consent made by or on behalf of the Crown.

(2) The Secretary of State may by regulations modify or exclude any statutory provision relating to—

(a) the procedure to be followed before such an application is made;

(b) the making of such an application;

(c) the decision-making process for such an application.

(3) A statutory provision is a provision contained in or having effect under this Act or any other enactment.

Chapter 2 Pre-application procedure

41 Chapter applies before application is made

(1) This Chapter applies where a person ('the applicant') proposes to make an application for an order granting development consent.

(2) In the following provisions of this Chapter—

'the proposed application' means the proposed application mentioned in subsection (1);

'the land' means the land to which the proposed application relates or any part of that land;

'the proposed development' means the development for which the proposed application (if made) would seek development consent.

[42 Duty to consult

(1) The applicant must consult the following about the proposed application—

(a) such persons as may be prescribed,

(aa) the Marine Management Organisation, in any case where the proposed development would affect, or would be likely to affect, any of the areas specified in subsection (2),

(b) each local authority that is within section 43,

(c) the Greater London Authority if the land is in Greater London, and

(d) each person who is within one or more of the categories set out in section 44.

(2) The areas are—

(a) waters in or adjacent to England up to the seaward limits of the territorial sea;

(b) an exclusive economic zone, except any part of an exclusive economic zone in relation to which the Scottish Ministers have functions;

(c) a Renewable Energy Zone, except any part of a Renewable Energy Zone in relation to which the Scottish Ministers have functions;

(d) an area designated under section 1(7) of the Continental Shelf Act 1964, except any part of that area which is within a part of an exclusive economic zone or Renewable Energy Zone in relation to which the Scottish Ministers have functions.][1]

1 Existing s 42 renumbered as s 42(1) and s 42(1)(aa) and (2) inserted by Marine and Coastal Access Act 2009, s 23(1), (2) (1 April 2010).

43 [Local authorities for purposes of section 42(1)(b)][1]

(1) A local authority is within this section if the land is in the authority's area.

(2) A local authority ('A') is within this section if—

(a) the land is in the area of another local authority ('B'), [...][2]

[(aa) B is a unitary council or a lower-tier district council, and][2]

(b) any part of the boundary of A's area is also a part of the boundary of B's area.

[(2A) If the land is in the area of an upper-tier county council ('C'), a local authority ('D') is within this section if—

(a) D is not a lower-tier district council, and

(b) any part of the boundary of D's area is also part of the boundary of C's area.][3]

[(3) In this section—

'local authority' means—

(a) a county council, or district council, in England;

(b) a London borough council;

(c) the Common Council of the City of London;

(d) the Council of the Isles of Scilly;

(e) a county council, or county borough council, in Wales;

(f) a council constituted under section 2 of the Local Government etc (Scotland) Act 1994;

(g) a National Park authority;

(h) the Broads Authority;

'lower-tier district council' means a district council in England for an area for which there is a county council;

'unitary council' means a local authority that is not an upper-tier county council, a lower-tier district council, a National Park authority or the Broads Authority;

'upper-tier county council' means a county council in England for each part of whose area there is a district council.][4]

1 Heading substituted by Marine and Coastal Access Act 2009, s 23(1), (3)(a) (1 April 2010).
2 Added by Localism Act 2011, s 133(1), (2) (1 April 2012).
3 Added by Localism Act 2011, s 133(1), (3) (1 April 2012).
4 Substituted by Localism Act 2011, s 133(1), (4) (1 April 2012).

44 [Categories for purposes of section 42(1)(d)][1]

(1) A person is within Category 1 if the applicant, after making diligent inquiry, knows that the person is an owner, lessee, tenant (whatever the tenancy period) or occupier of the land.

(2) A person is within Category 2 if the applicant, after making diligent inquiry, knows that the person—

(a) is interested in the land, or

(b) has power—

(i) to sell and convey the land, or

(ii) to release the land.

(3) An expression, other than 'the land', that appears in subsection (2) of this section and also in section 5(1) of the Compulsory Purchase Act 1965 (c. 56) has in subsection (2) the meaning that it has in section 5(1) of that Act.

(4) A person is within Category 3 if the applicant thinks that, if the order sought by the proposed application were to be made and fully implemented, the person would or might be entitled—

(a) as a result of the implementing of the order,

(b) as a result of the order having been implemented, or

(c) as a result of use of the land once the order has been implemented,

to make a relevant claim.

This is subject to subsection (5).

(5) A person is within Category 3 only if the person is known to the applicant after making diligent inquiry.

(6) In subsection (4) 'relevant claim' means—

(a) a claim under section 10 of the Compulsory Purchase Act 1965 (c. 56) (compensation where satisfaction not made for the taking, or injurious affection, of land subject to compulsory purchase);

(b) a claim under Part 1 of the Land Compensation Act 1973 (c. 26) (compensation for depreciation of land value by physical factors caused by use of public works) [;][2]

[(c) a claim under section 152(3).][2]

1 Heading substituted by Marine and Coastal Access Act 2009, s 23(1), (3)(b) (1 April 2010).
2 Added by Localism Act 2011, s 135(1), (8) (1 April 2012).

45 Timetable for consultation under section 42

(1) The applicant must, when consulting a person under section 42, notify the person of the deadline for the receipt by the applicant of the person's response to the consultation.

(2) A deadline notified under subsection (1) must not be earlier than the end of the period of 28 days that begins with the day after the day on which the person receives the consultation documents.

(3) In subsection (2) 'the consultation documents' means the documents supplied to the person by the applicant for the purpose of consulting the person.

46 Duty to notify [Secretary of State][1] of proposed application

(1) The applicant must supply the [Secretary of State][2] with such information in relation to the proposed application as the applicant would supply to the [Secretary of State][2] for the

purpose of complying with section 42 if the applicant were required by that section to consult the [Secretary of State][2] about the proposed application.

(2) The applicant must comply with subsection (1) on or before commencing consultation under section 42.

1 Word substituted by Localism Act 2011, s 128(2), Sch 13, paras 1, 8(1), (3) (1 April 2012).
2 Word substituted by Localism Act 2011, s 128(2), Sch 13, paras 1, 8(1), (2) (1 April 2012).

47 Duty to consult local community

(1) The applicant must prepare a statement setting out how the applicant proposes to consult, about the proposed application, people living in the vicinity of the land.

(2) Before preparing the statement, the applicant must consult each local authority that is within section 43(1) about what is to be in the statement.

(3) The deadline for the receipt by the applicant of a local authority's response to consultation under subsection (2) is the end of the period of 28 days that begins with the day after the day on which the local authority receives the consultation documents.

(4) In subsection (3) 'the consultation documents' means the documents supplied to the local authority by the applicant for the purpose of consulting the local authority under subsection (2).

(5) In preparing the statement, the applicant must have regard to any response to consultation under subsection (2) that is received by the applicant before the deadline imposed by subsection (3).

(6) Once the applicant has prepared the statement, the applicant [must—][1]

[(za) make the statement available for inspection by the public in a way that is reasonably convenient for people living in the vicinity of the land,][1]

(a) [publish,][2] in a newspaper circulating in the vicinity of the land[, a notice stating where and when the statement can be inspected][3], and

(b) [publish the statement in such manner][4] as may be prescribed.

(7) The applicant must carry out consultation in accordance with the proposals set out in the statement.

1 Words and para (za) substituted for words by Localism Act 2011, s 134(a) (1 April 2012).
2 Word inserted by Localism Act 2011, s 134(b)(i) (1 April 2012).
3 Words inserted by Localism Act 2011, s 134(b)(ii) (1 April 2012).
4 Words substituted by Localism Act 2011, s 134(c) (1 April 2012).

48 Duty to publicise

(1) The applicant must publicise the proposed application in the prescribed manner.

(2) Regulations made for the purposes of subsection (1) must, in particular, make provision for publicity under subsection (1) to include a deadline for receipt by the applicant of responses to the publicity.

49 Duty to take account of responses to consultation and publicity

(1) Subsection (2) applies where the applicant—

(a) has complied with sections 42, 47 and 48, and

(b) proposes to go ahead with making an application for an order granting development consent (whether or not in the same terms as the proposed application).

(2) The applicant must, when deciding whether the application that the applicant is actually to make should be in the same terms as the proposed application, have regard to any relevant responses.

(3) In subsection (2) 'relevant response' means—

(a) a response from a person consulted under section 42 that is received by the applicant before the deadline imposed by section 45 in that person's case,

(b) a response to consultation under section 47(7) that is received by the applicant before any applicable deadline imposed in accordance with the statement prepared under section 47, or

(c) a response to publicity under section 48 that is received by the applicant before the deadline imposed in accordance with section 48(2) in relation to that publicity.

50 Guidance about pre-application procedure

(1) Guidance may be issued about how to comply with the requirements of this Chapter.

(2) Guidance under this section may be issued by [...][1] the Secretary of State.

(3) The applicant must have regard to any guidance under this section.

1 Words repealed by Localism Act 2011, s 237, Sch 25, Pt 20 (1 April 2012).

Chapter 3 Assistance for applicants and others

51 Advice for potential applicants and others

(1) [This section applies to advice][1] about—

(a) applying for an order granting development consent;

(b) making representations about an application, or a proposed application, for such an order.

[(3) The Secretary of State may by regulations make provision about the giving of advice to which this section applies.

(4) In particular, regulations under subsection (3) may make provision that has the effect that—

(a) a request for advice made by an applicant, potential applicant or other person, or

(b) advice given to an applicant, potential applicant or other person,

must be, or may be, disclosed by the Secretary of State to other persons or to the public generally.][2]

1 Words substituted by Localism Act 2011, s 128(2), Sch 13, paras 1, 10(1), (2) (15 January 2012 for the purpose of conferring power on the Secretary of State to make regulations or rules; 1 April 2012 otherwise).

2 Section 51(3)-(4) substituted for s 51(2)-(4) by Localism Act 2011, s 128(2), Sch 13, paras 1, 10(1), (3) (15 January 2012 for the purpose of conferring power on the Secretary of State to make regulations or rules; 1 April 2012 otherwise).

52 Obtaining information about interests in land

(1) Where a person is applying, or proposes to apply, for an order granting development consent, [subsections (2) and (2A) apply][1] for the purpose of enabling the person ('the applicant') to comply with provisions of, or made under, Chapter 2 of this Part or Chapter 1 of Part 6.

(2) The [Secretary of State][2] may authorise the applicant to serve a notice on a person mentioned in subsection (3) requiring the person ('the recipient') to give to the applicant in writing the name and address of any person the recipient believes is one or more of the following—

(a) an owner, lessee, tenant (whatever the tenancy period) or occupier of the land;

(b) a person interested in the land;

(c) a person having power—

(i) to sell and convey the land, or

(ii) to release the land.

[(2A) The Secretary of State may authorise the applicant to serve a notice on a person mentioned in subsection (3) requiring the person ('the recipient') to give to the applicant in writing the name and address of any person the recipient believes is a person who, if the order sought by the application or proposed application were to be made and fully implemented, would or might be entitled—

(a) as a result of the implementing of the order,

(b) as a result of the order having been implemented, or

(c) as a result of the use of the land once the order has been implemented,

to make a relevant claim.][3]

(3) The persons are—

(a) an occupier of the land;

(b) a person who has an interest in the land as freeholder, mortgagee or lessee;

(c) a person who directly or indirectly receives rent for the land;

(d) a person who, in pursuance of an agreement between that person and a person interested in the land, is authorised to manage the land or to arrange for the letting of it.

(4) A notice under subsection (2) [or (2A)][4] must—

(a) be in writing,

(b) state that the [Secretary of State][2] has authorised the applicant to serve the notice,

(c) specify or describe the land to which the application, or proposed application, relates,

(d) specify the deadline by which the recipient must give the required information to the applicant, and

(e) draw attention to the provisions in subsections (6) to (9).

(5) A deadline specified under subsection (4)(d) in a notice must not be earlier than the end of the 14 days beginning with the day after the day on which the notice is served on the recipient of the notice.

[(5A) A notice under subsection (2A) must explain the circumstances in which a person would or might be entitled as mentioned in that subsection.][5]

(6) A person commits an offence if the person fails without reasonable excuse to comply with a notice under subsection (2) [or (2A)][4] served on the person.

(7) A person commits an offence if, in response to a notice under subsection (2) [or (2A)][4] served on the person—

(a) the person gives information which is false in a material particular, and

(b) when the person does so, the person knows or ought reasonably to know that the information is false.

(8) If an offence under this section committed by a body corporate is proved to have been committed with the consent or connivance of, or to be attributable to any neglect on the part of—

(a) a director, manager, secretary or other similar officer of the body,

(b) a person purporting to act in any such capacity, or

(c) in a case where the affairs of the body are managed by its members, a member of the body,

that person, as well as the body, is guilty of that offence and liable to be proceeded against accordingly.

(9) A person guilty of an offence under this section is liable on summary conviction to a fine not exceeding level 5 on the standard scale.

(10) In subsections [(2) to (3)][6] 'the land' means—

(a) the land to which the application, or proposed application, relates, or

(b) any part of that land.

(11) Any other expression that appears in either of paragraphs (b) and (c) of subsection (2) and also in section 5(1) of the Compulsory Purchase Act 1965 (c. 56) has in those paragraphs the meaning that it has in section 5(1) of that Act.

[(12) In subsection (3) as it applies for the purposes of subsection (2A) 'the land' also includes any relevant affected land (see subsection (13)).

(13) Where the applicant believes that, if the order sought by the application or proposed application were to be made and fully implemented, there would or might be persons entitled—

(a) as a result of the implementing of the order,

(b) as a result of the order having been implemented, or

(c) as a result of the use of the land once the order has been implemented,

to make a relevant claim in respect of any land or in respect of an interest in any land, that land is 'relevant affected land' for the purposes of subsection (12).

(14) In this section 'relevant claim' means—

(a) a claim under section 10 of the Compulsory Purchase Act 1965 (compensation where satisfaction not made for compulsory purchase of land or not made for injurious affection resulting from compulsory purchase);

(b) a claim under Part 1 of the Land Compensation Act 1973 (compensation for depreciation of land value by physical factors caused by use of public works);

(c) a claim under section 152(3).][7]

1 Words substituted by Localism Act 2011, s 135(1), (2) (1 April 2012).
2 Word substituted by Localism Act 2011, s 128(2), Sch 13, paras 1, 11 (1 April 2012).
3 Added by Localism Act 2011, s 135(1), (3) (1 April 2012).
4 Words inserted by Localism Act 2011, s 135(1), (4) (1 April 2012).
5 Added by Localism Act 2011, s 135(1), (5) (1 April 2012).
6 Words substituted by Localism Act 2011, s 135(1), (6) (1 April 2012).
7 Added by Localism Act 2011, s 135(1), (7) (1 April 2012).

53 Rights of entry

(1) Any person duly authorised in writing by the [Secretary of State][1] may at any reasonable time enter any land for the purpose of surveying and taking levels of it[, or in order to facilitate compliance with the provisions mentioned in subsection (1A),][2] in connection with—

(a) an application for an order granting development consent, whether in relation to that or any other land, that has been accepted by the [Secretary of State][1],

(b) a proposed application for an order granting development consent, or

(c) an order granting development consent that includes provision authorising the compulsory acquisition of that land or of an interest in it or right over it.

[(1A) Those provisions are any provision of or made under an Act for the purpose of implementing—

(a) Council Directive 85/337/EEC of 27 June 1985 on the assessment of the effects of certain public and private projects on the environment, as amended from time to time,

(b) Council Directive 92/43/EC of 21 May 1992 on the conservation of natural habitats and of wild fauna and flora, as amended from time to time, or

(c) any EU instrument from time to time replacing all or any part of either of those Directives.][3]

(2) Authorisation may be given by the [Secretary of State][1] under subsection (1)(b) in relation to any land only if it appears to the [Secretary of State][1] that—

(a) the proposed applicant is considering a distinct project of real substance genuinely requiring entry onto the land [.][4]

[...][4]

(3) Subject to subsections (9) and (10), power conferred by subsection (1) to survey land includes power to search and bore for the purpose of ascertaining the nature of the subsoil or the presence of minerals or other matter in it.

[(3A) Power conferred by subsection (1) for the purpose of complying with the provisions mentioned in subsection (1A) includes power to take, and process, samples of or from any of the following found on, in or over the land—

(a) water,

(b) air,

(c) soil or rock,

(d) its flora,

(e) bodily excretions, or dead bodies, of non-human creatures, or

(f) any non-living thing present as a result of human action.][5]

(4) A person authorised under subsection (1) to enter any land—

(a) must, if so required, produce evidence of the person's authority, and state the purpose of the person's entry, before so entering,

(b) may not demand admission as of right to any land which is occupied unless 14 days' notice of the intended entry has been given to the occupier, and

(c) must comply with any other conditions subject to which the [Secretary of State's][6] authorisation is given.

(5) A person commits an offence if the person wilfully obstructs a person acting in the exercise of power under subsection (1).

(6) A person guilty of an offence under subsection (5) is liable on summary conviction to a fine not exceeding level 3 on the standard scale.

(7) Where any damage is caused to land or chattels—

(a) in the exercise of a right of entry conferred under subsection (1), or

(b) in the making of any survey for the purpose of which any such right of entry has been conferred,

compensation may be recovered by any person suffering the damage from the person exercising the right of entry.

(8) Any question of disputed compensation under subsection (7) must be referred to and determined by the [Upper Tribunal][7].

(9) No person may carry out under subsection (1) any works authorised by virtue of subsection (3) unless notice of the person's intention to do so was included in the notice required by subsection (4)(b).

(10) The authority of the appropriate Minister is required for the carrying out under subsection (1) of works authorised by virtue of subsection (3) if—

(a) the land in question is held by statutory undertakers, and

(b) they object to the proposed works on the ground that execution of the works would be seriously detrimental to the carrying-on of their undertaking.

(11) In subsection (10)—

'the appropriate Minister' means—

(a) in the case of land in Wales held by water or sewerage undertakers, the Welsh Ministers, and

(b) in any other case, the Secretary of State;

'statutory undertakers' means persons who are, or who are deemed to be, statutory undertakers for the purposes of any provision of Part 11 of TCPA 1990.

1 Word substituted by Localism Act 2011, s 128(2), Sch 13, paras 1, 12(1), (2) (1 April 2012).
2 Words inserted by Localism Act 2011, s 136(1), (2) (1 April 2012).
3 Added by Localism Act 2011, s 136(1), (3) (1 April 2012).
4 Repealed by Localism Act 2011, s 237, Sch 25, Pt 20 (1 April 2012).
5 Added by Localism Act 2011, s 136(1), (5) (1 April 2012).
6 Word substituted by Localism Act 2011, s 128(2), Sch 13, paras 1, 12(1), (3) (1 April 2012).
7 Words substituted by Transfer of Tribunal Functions (Lands Tribunal and Miscellaneous Amendments) Order 2009, SI 2009/1307, art 5(1), (2), Sch 1, paras 291, 292 (1 October 2009: substitution came into force on 1 June 2009 but could not take effect until the commencement of Planning Act 2008, s 53(8) on 1 October 2009).

54 Rights of entry: Crown land

(1) [Subsections (1) to (3A) of section 53][1] apply to Crown land subject to subsections (2) and (3) of this section.

(2) A person must not enter Crown land unless the person ('P') has the permission of—

(a) a person appearing to P to be entitled to give it, or

(b) the appropriate Crown authority.

(3) In section 53(3), the words 'Subject to subsections (9) and (10)' must be ignored.

(4) Subsections (4) to (6) and (9) to (11) of section 53 do not apply to anything done by virtue of subsections (1) to (3) of this section.

1 Words substituted by Localism Act 2011, s 136(1), (6) (1 April 2012).

Part 6 Deciding applications for orders granting development consent

Chapter 1 Handling of application by Commission

55 Acceptance of applications

(1) The following provisions of this section apply where the [Secretary of State][1] receives an application that purports to be an application for an order granting development consent.

(2) The [Secretary of State][1] must, by the end of the period of 28 days beginning with the day after the day on which [the Secretary of State][2] receives the application, decide whether or not to accept the application.

(3) The [Secretary of State][1] may accept the application only if the [Secretary of State][1] concludes—

(a) that it is an application for an order granting development consent,

[...][3]

(c) that development consent is required for any of the development to which the application relates,

[...][3]

(e) that the applicant has, in relation to a proposed application that has become the application, complied with Chapter 2 of Part 5 (pre-application procedure) [, and][4]

[(f) that the application (including accompaniments) is of a standard that the Secretary of State considers satisfactory.][4]

(4) The [Secretary of State][1], when deciding whether [the Secretary of State][2] may reach the conclusion in subsection (3)(e), must have regard to—

(a) the consultation report received under section 37(3)(c),

(b) any adequacy of consultation representation received by [the Secretary of State][2] from a local authority consultee, and

(c) the extent to which the applicant has had regard to any guidance issued under section 50.

(5) In subsection (4)—

'local authority consultee' means—

(a) a local authority consulted under [section 42(1)(b)][5] about a proposed application that has become the application, or

(b) the Greater London Authority if consulted under [section 42(1)(c)][6] about that proposed application;

'adequacy of consultation representation' means a representation about whether the applicant complied, in relation to that proposed application, with the applicant's duties under sections 42, 47 and 48.

[(5A) The Secretary of State, when deciding whether the Secretary of State may reach the conclusion in subsection (3)(f), must have regard to the extent to which—

(a) the application complies with the requirements in section 37(3) (form and contents of application) and any standards set under section 37(5), and

(b) any applicable guidance given under section 37(4) has been followed in relation to the application.][7]

(6) If the [Secretary of State][1] accepts the application, [the Secretary of State][2] must notify the applicant of the acceptance.

(7) If the [Secretary of State][1] is of the view that [the application cannot be accepted, the Secretary of State][8] must—

(a) notify that view to the applicant, and

(b) notify the applicant of [the Secretary of State's][9] reasons for that view.

(8) If in response the applicant modifies (or further modifies) the application, subsections (2) to (7) then apply in relation to the application as modified.

1 Word substituted by Localism Act 2011, s 128(2), Sch 13, paras 1, 13(1), (2) (1 April 2012).
2 Word substituted by Localism Act 2011, s 128(2), Sch 13, paras 1, 13(1), (3) (1 April 2012).
3 Repealed by Localism Act 2011, s 237, Sch 25, Pt 21 (1 April 2012).
4 Added by Localism Act 2011, s 137(1), (3) (1 April 2012).
5 Words substituted by Marine and Coastal Access Act 2009, s 23(1), (4)(a) (1 April 2010).
6 Words substituted by Marine and Coastal Access Act 2009, s 23(1), (4)(b) (1 April 2010).
7 Added by Localism Act 2011, s 137(1), (4) (1 April 2012).
8 Words substituted by Localism Act 2011, s 128(2), Sch 13, paras 1, 13(1), (4)(a) (1 April 2012).
9 Word substituted by Localism Act 2011, s 128(2), Sch 13, paras 1, 13(1), (4)(b) (1 April 2012).

56 Notifying persons of accepted application

(1) Subsections (2), (6) and (7) apply where the [Secretary of State][1] accepts an application for an order granting development consent.

(2) The applicant must give notice of the application to—

(a) such persons as may be prescribed,

[(aa) the Marine Management Organisation, in any case where the development for which the application seeks development consent would involve the carrying on of any activity in one or more of the areas specified in subsection (2A),][2]

[(b) each local authority that is within section 56A,][3]

(c) the Greater London Authority if the land to which the application relates, or any part of it, is in Greater London, and

(d) each person who is within one or more of the categories set out in section 57.

[(2A) The areas are—

(a) waters in or adjacent to England up to the seaward limits of the territorial sea;

(b) an exclusive economic zone, except any part of an exclusive economic zone in relation to which the Scottish Ministers have functions;

(c) a Renewable Energy Zone, except any part of a Renewable Energy Zone in relation to which the Scottish Ministers have functions;

(d) an area designated under section 1(7) of the Continental Shelf Act 1964, except any part of that area which is within a part of an exclusive economic zone or Renewable Energy Zone in relation to which the Scottish Ministers have functions.][4]

(3) Notice under subsection (2) must be in such form and contain such matter, and be given in such manner, as may be prescribed.

(4) The applicant must, when giving notice to a person under subsection (2), notify the person of the deadline for receipt by the [Secretary of State][1] of representations giving notice of the person's interest in, or objection to, the application.

(5) A deadline notified under subsection (4) must not be earlier than the end of the period of 28 days that begins with the day after the day on which the person receives the notice.

(6) The applicant must make available, to each person to whom notice is given under subsection (2), a copy of—

(a) the application, and

(b) the documents and information that were required by section 37(3)(d) to accompany the application.

(7) The applicant must publicise the application in the prescribed manner.

(8) Regulations made for the purposes of subsection (7) must, in particular, make provision for publicity under subsection (7) to include a deadline for receipt by the [Secretary of State][1] of representations giving notice of persons' interests in, or objections to, the application.

(9) A deadline specified in accordance with subsection (8) does not apply to a person to whom notice is given under subsection (2).

1 Word substituted by Localism Act 2011, s 128(2), Sch 13, paras 1, 14 (1 April 2012).
2 Added by Marine and Coastal Access Act 2009, s 23(1), (5)(a) (1 April 2010).
3 Substituted by Localism Act 2011, s 138(1), (2) (1 April 2012).
4 Added by Marine and Coastal Access Act 2009, s 23(1), (5)(b) (1 April 2010).

[56A Local authorities for the purposes of sections 56(2)(b) and 60(2)(a)

(1) A local authority is within this section if the land is in the authority's area.

(2) A local authority ('A') is within this section if—

(a) the land is in the area of another local authority ('B'),

(b) B is a unitary council or a lower-tier district council, and

(c) any part of the boundary of A's area is also a part of the boundary of B's area.

(3) If the land is in the area of an upper-tier county council ('C'), a local authority ('D') is within this section if—

(a) D is not a lower-tier district council, and

(b) any part of the boundary of D's area is also part of the boundary of C's area.

(4) In this section—

'the land' means the land to which the application concerned relates or any part of that land;

'local authority' has the meaning given in section 102(8);

'lower-tier district council' means a district council in England for an area for which there is a county council;

'unitary council' means a local authority that is not an upper-tier county council, a lower-tier district council, a National Park authority or the Broads Authority;

'upper-tier county council' means a county council in England for each part of whose area there is a district council.][1]

1 Added by Localism Act 2011, s 138(1), (3) (1 April 2012).

57 Categories for purposes of section 56(2)(d)

(1) A person is within Category 1 if the applicant, after making diligent inquiry, knows that the person is an owner, lessee, tenant (whatever the tenancy period) or occupier of the land.

(2) A person is within Category 2 if the applicant, after making diligent inquiry, knows that the person—

(a) is interested in the land, or

(b) has power—

(i) to sell and convey the land, or

(ii) to release the land.

(3) An expression, other than 'the land', that appears in subsection (2) of this section and also in section 5(1) of the Compulsory Purchase Act 1965 (c. 56) has in subsection (2) the meaning that it has in section 5(1) of that Act.

(4) A person is within Category 3 if the applicant thinks that, if the order sought by the application were to be made and fully implemented, the person would or might be entitled—

(a) as a result of the implementing of the order,

(b) as a result of the order having been implemented, or

(c) as a result of use of the land once the order has been implemented,

to make a relevant claim.

This is subject to subsection (5).

(5) A person is within Category 3 only if the person is known to the applicant after making diligent inquiry.

(6) In subsection (4) 'relevant claim' means—

(a) a claim under section 10 of the Compulsory Purchase Act 1965 (compensation where satisfaction not made for the taking, or injurious affection, of land subject to compulsory purchase);

(b) a claim under Part 1 of the Land Compensation Act 1973 (c. 26) (compensation for depreciation of land value by physical factors caused by use of public works) [;][1]

[(c) a claim under section 152(3).][1]

(7) In this section 'the land' means the land to which the application relates or any part of that land.

1 Added by Localism Act 2011, s 135(1), (9) (1 April 2012).

58 Certifying compliance with section 56

(1) Subsection (2) applies where—

(a) the [Secretary of State][1] has accepted an application for an order granting development consent, and

(b) the applicant has complied with section 56 in relation to the application.

(2) The applicant must, in such form and manner as may be prescribed, certify to the [Secretary of State][1] that the applicant has complied with section 56 in relation to the application.

(3) A person commits an offence if the person issues a certificate which—

(a) purports to be a certificate under subsection (2), and

(b) contains a statement which the person knows to be false or misleading in a material particular.

(4) A person commits an offence if the person recklessly issues a certificate which—

(a) purports to be a certificate under subsection (2), and

(b) contains a statement which is false or misleading in a material particular.

(5) A person guilty of an offence under this section is liable on summary conviction to a fine not exceeding level 5 on the standard scale.

(6) A magistrates' court may try an information relating to an offence under this section whenever laid.

(7) Section 127 of the Magistrates' Courts Act 1980 (c. 43) has effect subject to subsection (6) of this section.

1 Word substituted by Localism Act 2011, s 128(2), Sch 13, paras 1, 15 (1 April 2012).

59 Notice of persons interested in land to which compulsory acquisition request relates

(1) This section applies where—

(a) the [Secretary of State][1] has accepted an application for an order granting development consent, and

(b) the application includes a request for an order granting development consent to authorise compulsory acquisition of land or of an interest in or right over land (a 'compulsory acquisition request').

(2) The applicant must give to the [Secretary of State][1] a notice specifying the names, and such other information as may be prescribed, of each affected person.

(3) Notice under subsection (2) must be given in such form and manner as may be prescribed.

(4) A person is an 'affected person' for the purposes of this section if the applicant, after making diligent inquiry, knows that the person is interested in the land to which the compulsory acquisition request relates or any part of that land.

1 Word substituted by Localism Act 2011, s 128(2), Sch 13, paras 1, 16 (1 April 2012).

60 Local impact reports

(1) Subsection (2) applies where the [Secretary of State][1] —

(a) has accepted an application for an order granting development consent, and

(b) has received—

(i) a certificate under section 58(2) in relation to the application, and

(ii) where section 59 applies, a notice under that section in relation to the application.

(2) The [Secretary of State][1] must give notice in writing to each of the following, inviting them to submit a local impact report [to the Secretary of State][2] —

[(a) each local authority that is within section 56A, and][3]

(b) the Greater London Authority if the land to which the application relates, or any part of it, is in Greater London.

(3) A 'local impact report' is a report in writing giving details of the likely impact of the proposed development on the authority's area (or any part of that area).

(4) 'The proposed development' is the development for which the application seeks development consent.

(5) A notice under subsection (2) must specify the deadline for receipt by the [Secretary of State][1] of the local impact report.

1 Word substituted by Localism Act 2011, s 128(2), Sch 13, paras 1, 17(1), (2) (1 April 2012).
2 Words substituted by Localism Act 2011, s 128(2), Sch 13, paras 1, 17(1), (3) (1 April 2012).
3 Substituted by Localism Act 2011, s 138(1), (4) (1 April 2012).

61 Initial choice of Panel or single [appointed person][1]

(1) Subsection (2) applies where the [Secretary of State][2] —

(a) has accepted an application for an order granting development consent, and

(b) has received—

(i) a certificate under section 58(2) in relation to the application, and

(ii) where section 59 applies, a notice under that section in relation to the application.

[(2) The Secretary of State must decide whether the application—

(a) is to be handled by a Panel under Chapter 2, or

(b) is to be handled by a single appointed person under Chapter 3.

(3) The Secretary of State must publish the criteria that are to be applied in making decisions under subsection (2).][3]

1 Word substituted by Localism Act 2011, s 128(2), Sch 13, paras 1, 18(1), (4) (1 April 2012).
2 Word substituted by Localism Act 2011, s 128(2), Sch 13, paras 1, 18(1), (2) (1 April 2012).
3 Section 61(2)-(3) substituted for s 61(2)-(5) by Localism Act 2011, s 128(2), Sch 13, paras 1, 18(1), (3) (1 April 2012).

62 Switching from single [appointed person][1] to Panel

(1) Subsection (2) applies where an application for an order granting development consent is being handled by a single [appointed person][1] under Chapter 3.

[(2) The Secretary of State may decide that the application should instead be handled by a Panel under Chapter 2.

(3) The Secretary of State must publish the criteria that are to be applied in making decisions under subsection (2).][2]

1 Word substituted by Localism Act 2011, s 128(2), Sch 13, paras 1, 19(1), (2) (1 April 2012).
2 Section 62(2)-(3) substituted for s 62(2)-(5) by Localism Act 2011, s 128(2), Sch 13, paras 1, 19(1), (3) (1 April 2012).

63 …

Repealed by Localism Act 2011, s 237, Sch 25, Pt 20 (1 April 2012).

Chapter 2 The Panel procedure

Panels

64 Panel for each application to be handled under this Chapter

(1) This Chapter applies where—

(a) the [Secretary of State][1] accepts an application for an order granting development consent, and

(b) under section 61(2) or 62(2), it is decided that the application is to be handled by a Panel under this Chapter.

(2) There is to be a Panel (referred to in this Chapter as 'the Panel') to handle the application.

1 Word substituted by Localism Act 2011, s 128(2), Sch 13, paras 1, 21 (1 April 2012).

65 Appointment of members, and lead member, of Panel

[(1) The Secretary of State must appoint—

(a) three, four or five persons to be members of the Panel, and

(b) one of those persons to chair the Panel.][1]

(2) In this Chapter 'the lead member' means the person who for the time being is appointed to chair the Panel.

[...][2]

1 Substituted by Localism Act 2011, s 128(2), Sch 13, paras 1, 22(1), (2) (1 April 2012).
2 Repealed by Localism Act 2011, ss 128(2), 237, Sch 13, paras 1, 22(1), (3), Sch 25, Pt 20 (1 April 2012).

66 Ceasing to be member, or lead member, of Panel

[...][1]

(2) The person appointed to be the lead member ceases to hold that office if the person ceases to be a member of the Panel.

(3) A person may resign from membership of the Panel by giving notice in writing to the [Secretary of State][2].

(4) The lead member may resign that office, without also resigning from membership of the Panel, by giving notice in writing to the [Secretary of State][2].

(5) The [Secretary of State][3] —

(a) may remove a person ('the Panel member') from membership of the Panel if the [Secretary of State][4] is satisfied that the Panel member is unable, unwilling or unfit to perform the duties of Panel membership;

(b) may remove the lead member from that office, without also removing the lead member from membership of the Panel, if the [Secretary of State][4] is satisfied that the lead member is unable, unwilling or unfit to perform the duties of the office.

1 Repealed by Localism Act 2011, ss 128(2), 237, Sch 13, paras 1, 23(1), (2), Sch 25, Pt 20 (1 April 2012).
2 Word substituted by Localism Act 2011, s 128(2), Sch 13, paras 1, 23(1), (3) (1 April 2012).
3 Words substituted by Localism Act 2011, s 128(2), Sch 13, paras 1, 23(1), (4)(a) (1 April 2012).
4 Word substituted by Localism Act 2011, s 128(2), Sch 13, paras 1, 23(1), (4)(b) (1 April 2012).

67 ...

Repealed by Localism Act 2011, ss 128(2), 237, Sch 13, paras 1, 24, Sch 25, Pt 20 (1 April 2012).

68 Additional appointments to Panel

(1) Subsections (2) and (3) apply at any time after the initial members of the Panel have been appointed under section 65(1)(a).

[(2) The Secretary of State may appoint a person to be a member of the Panel, but this power may not be exercised so as to cause the Panel to have more than five members.][1]

(3) If at any time the Panel has only two members or a single member, it is the duty of the [Secretary of State][2] to ensure that the power under subsection (2) is exercised so as to secure that the Panel again has at least three members.

(4) A person appointed under subsection (2) becomes a member of the Panel in addition to any person who is otherwise a member of the Panel.

[...][3]

1 Substituted by Localism Act 2011, s 128(2), Sch 13, paras 1, 25(1), (2) (1 April 2012).
2 Words substituted by Localism Act 2011, s 128(2), Sch 13, paras 1, 25(1), (3) (1 April 2012).
3 Repealed by Localism Act 2011, ss 128(2), 237, Sch 13, paras 1, 25(1), (4), Sch 25, Pt 20 (1 April 2012).

69 Replacement of lead member of Panel

(1) Subsection (2) applies where a person ceases to hold the office of lead member.

(2) The [Secretary of State][1] must appoint a member of the Panel to chair the Panel.

(3) A person may be appointed under subsection (2) even though that person was not a member of the Panel when the vacancy arose.

[...][2]

1 Words substituted by Localism Act 2011, s 128(2), Sch 13, paras 1, 26(1), (2) (1 April 2012).
2 Repealed by Localism Act 2011, ss 128(2), 237, Sch 13, paras 1, 26(1), (3), Sch 25, Pt 20 (1 April 2012).

70 ...

Repealed by Localism Act 2011, ss 128(2), 237, Sch 13, paras 1, 27, Sch 25, Pt 20 (1 April 2012).

71 Supplementary provision where Panel replaces single [appointed person][1]

(1) Subsections (2) and (3) apply where this Chapter applies as the result of a decision under section 62(2).

(2) [An appointed person][2]—

(a) may be appointed under section 65(1)(a) or 68(2) as a member of the Panel, and

(b) if a member of the Panel, may be appointed under section 65(1)(b) or 69(2) to chair the Panel.

(3) The Panel may, so far as it thinks appropriate, decide to treat things done by or in relation to [an appointed person][3] in proceedings under Chapter 3 on the application as done by or in relation to the Panel.

(4) Where the Panel makes a decision under subsection (3), the lead member is under a duty to ensure that the membership of the Panel has the necessary knowledge of the proceedings under Chapter 3 on the application.

[(5) In this section 'appointed person' means a person appointed to handle the application under Chapter 3.][4]

1 Word substituted by Localism Act 2011, s 128(2), Sch 13, paras 1, 28(1), (5) (1 April 2012).
2 Words substituted by Localism Act 2011, s 128(2), Sch 13, paras 1, 28(1), (2) (1 April 2012).
3 Words substituted by Localism Act 2011, s 128(2), Sch 13, paras 1, 28(1), (3) (1 April 2012).
4 Added by Localism Act 2011, s 128(2), Sch 13, paras 1, 28(1), (4) (1 April 2012).

72 Panel ceasing to have any members

(1) If the Panel ceases to have any members, a new Panel must be constituted under section 65(1).

(2) At times after the new Panel has been constituted (but subject to the further application of this subsection in the event that the new Panel ceases to have any members), references in this Chapter to the Panel are to be read as references to the new Panel.

(3) The new Panel may, so far as it thinks appropriate, decide to treat things—

(a) done by or in relation to a previous Panel appointed to handle the application, or

(b) treated under section 71(3) as done by or in relation to a previous Panel appointed to handle the application,

as done by or in relation to the new Panel.

(4) Where the Panel makes a decision under subsection (3), the lead member is under a duty to ensure that the membership of the Panel has the necessary knowledge of the proceedings on the application up until the reconstitution of the Panel.

(5) The power under section 68(2) is not exercisable at times when the Panel has no members.

73 Consequences of changes in Panel

(1) The Panel's continuing identity is to be taken not to be affected by—

(a) any change in the membership of the Panel;

(b) the Panel's coming to have only two members or a single member;

(c) any change in the lead member;

(d) a vacancy in that office.

(2) When there is a change in the membership of the Panel, the lead member is under a duty to ensure that the membership of the Panel after the change has the necessary knowledge of the proceedings on the application up until the change.

(3) Subsection (2) does not apply where the change occurs as a result of the Panel being reconstituted as required by section 72(1).

Panel's role in relation to application

74 Panel to decide, or make recommendation in respect of, application

[...][1]

(2) [The Panel][2] has the functions of—

(a) examining the application, and

(b) making a report to the Secretary of State on the application setting out—

(i) the Panel's findings and conclusions in respect of the application, and

(ii) the Panel's recommendation as to the decision to be made on the application.

(3) The Panel's functions under this section are to be carried out in accordance with Chapter 4.

[...][1]

1 Repealed by Localism Act 2011, ss 128(2), 237, Sch 13, paras 1, 29(1), (2), (4), Sch 25, Pt 20 (1 April 2012).

2 Words substituted by Localism Act 2011, s 128(2), Sch 13, paras 1, 29(3) (1 April 2012).

75 Decision-making by the Panel

(1) The making of a decision by the Panel requires the agreement of a majority of its members.

(2) The lead member has a second (or casting) vote in the event that the number of members of the Panel agreeing to a proposed decision is the same as the number of members not so agreeing.

76 Allocation within Panel of Panel's functions

(1) This section applies in relation to the Panel's examination of the application.

(2) The Panel, as an alternative to itself undertaking a part of the examination, may allocate the undertaking of that part to any one or more of the members of the Panel.

(3) Where there is an allocation under subsection (2)—

(a) anything that under Chapter 4 is required or authorised to be done by or to the Panel in connection with the allocated part of the examination may be done by or to the member or members concerned (or by or to the Panel), and

(b) findings and conclusions of the member or members concerned in respect of the matters allocated are to be taken to be the Panel's.

(4) Subsection (3)(b) has effect subject to any decision of the Panel, made on the occasion of making the allocation or earlier, as to the status of any such findings or conclusions.

(5) Where there is an allocation under subsection (2) to two or more of the members of the Panel, the making of a decision by the members concerned requires the agreement of all of them.

77 Exercise of Panel's powers for examining application

(1) In this section 'procedural power' means any power conferred on the Panel for the purposes of its examination of the application.

(2) A procedural power, as well as being exercisable by the Panel itself, is also (subject to subsection (3)) exercisable by any one or more of the members of the Panel.

(3) The Panel may decide to restrict or prohibit the exercise of a procedural power otherwise than by the Panel itself.

(4) Subsection (2)—

(a) applies whether or not there is an allocation under section 76(2), and

(b) where there is such an allocation, is in addition to section 76(3)(a).

(5) Subsection (3) does not authorise curtailment of a power conferred by section 76(3)(a).

Chapter 3 The [single appointed person][1] procedure

The single [appointed person][1]

78 Single [appointed person][1] to handle application

(1) This Chapter applies where—

(a) the [Secretary of State][2] accepts an application for an order granting development consent, and

(b) under section 61(2), it is decided that the application is to be handled by a single [appointed person][3] under this Chapter.

(2) In this Chapter ['the single appointed person'][4] means the person who is appointed to handle the application under this Chapter.

1 Word substituted by Localism Act 2011, s 128(2), Sch 13, paras 1, 30(1), (5), (6) (1 April 2012).
2 Word substituted by Localism Act 2011, s 128(2), Sch 13, paras 1, 30(1), (2) (1 April 2012).
3 Word substituted by Localism Act 2011, s 128(2), Sch 13, paras 1, 30(1), (3) (1 April 2012).
4 Word substituted by Localism Act 2011, s 128(2), Sch 13, paras 1, 30(1), (4) (1 April 2012).

[79 Appointment of single appointed person

The Secretary of State must appoint a person to handle the application.][1]

1 Substituted by Localism Act 2011, s 128(2), Sch 13, paras 1, 31 (1 April 2012).

80 Ceasing to be the single [appointed person][1]

[...][2]

(2) A person may resign from being the single [appointed person][3] by giving notice in writing to the [Secretary of State][4].

(3) The [Secretary of State][5] may remove a person ('the appointee') from being the single [appointed person][6] [if the Secretary of State][7] is satisfied that the appointee is unable, unwilling or unfit to perform the duties of the single [appointed person][6].

1 Word substituted by Localism Act 2011, s 128(2), Sch 13, paras 1, 32(1), (5) (1 April 2012).
2 Repealed by Localism Act 2011, ss 128(2), 237, Sch 13, paras 1, 32(1), (2), Sch 25, Pt 20 (1 April 2012).
3 Word substituted by Localism Act 2011, s 128(2), Sch 13, paras 1, 32(1), (3)(a) (1 April 2012).
4 Word substituted by Localism Act 2011, s 128(2), Sch 13, paras 1, 32(1), (3)(b) (1 April 2012).
5 Words substituted by Localism Act 2011, s 128(2), Sch 13, paras 1, 32(1), (4)(a) (1 April 2012).
6 Word substituted by Localism Act 2011, s 128(2), Sch 13, paras 1, 32(1), (4)(b) (1 April 2012).
7 Words substituted by Localism Act 2011, s 128(2), Sch 13, paras 1, 32(1), (4)(c) (1 April 2012).

81 ...

Repealed by Localism Act 2011, ss 128(2), 237, Sch 13, paras 1, 33, Sch 25, Pt 20 (1 April 2012).

82 Appointment of replacement single [appointed person][1]

(1) Where a person ceases to be the single [appointed person][1], a new appointment of a person to handle the application must be made under section 79.

(2) Where that happens, the new single [appointed person][1] may, so far as may be appropriate, decide to treat things done by or in relation to any previous single [appointed person][1] as done by or in relation to the new single [appointed person][1].

(3) Where the single [appointed person][1] makes a decision under subsection (2), the single [appointed person][1] is under a duty to acquire the necessary knowledge of the previous proceedings on the application.

1 Words substituted by Localism Act 2011, s 128(2), Sch 13, paras 1, 34 (1 April 2012).

Single [appointed person][1]'s role in relation to application

83 Single [appointed person][1] to examine and report on application

(1) The single [appointed person][1] has the functions of—

(a) examining the application, and

(b) making a report [to the Secretary of State][2] on the application setting out—

(i) the single [appointed person][1]'s findings and conclusions in respect of the application, and

(ii) the single [appointed person][1]'s recommendation as to the decision to be made on the application.

[...][3]

(3) The single [appointed person][1]'s functions under subsection (1) are to be carried out in accordance with Chapter 4.

[...][3]

1 Words substituted by Localism Act 2011, s 128(2), Sch 13, paras 1, 35(1), (2) (1 April 2012).
2 Words inserted by Localism Act 2011, s 128(2), Sch 13, paras 1, 35(1), (3) (1 April 2012).
3 Repealed by Localism Act 2011, ss 128(2), 237, Sch 13, paras 1, 35(1), (4), (5), Sch 25, Pt 20 (1 April 2012).

Commission's role in respect of application

84–85 ...

Repealed by Localism Act 2011, ss 128(2), 237, Sch 13, paras 1, 36, Sch 25, Pt 20 (1 April 2012).

Chapter 4 Examination of applications under Chapter 2 or 3

86 Chapter applies to examination by Panel or single [appointed person][1]

(1) This Chapter applies—

(a) in relation to the examination of an application by a Panel under Chapter 2, and

(b) in relation to the examination of an application by a single [appointed person][1] under Chapter 3.

(2) In this Chapter as it applies in relation to the examination of an application by a Panel under Chapter 2, 'the Examining authority' means the Panel.

(3) In this Chapter as it applies in relation to the examination of an application by a single [appointed person][1] under Chapter 3, 'the Examining authority' means the single [appointed person][1].

1 Word substituted by Localism Act 2011, s 128(2), Sch 13, paras 1, 37 (1 April 2012).

87 Examining authority to control examination of application

(1) It is for the Examining authority to decide how to examine the application.

(2) The Examining authority, in making any decision about how the application is to be examined, must—

(a) comply with—

(i) the following provisions of this Chapter, and

(ii) any rules made under section 97[.][1]

[...][1]

(3) The Examining authority may in examining the application disregard representations if the Examining authority considers that the representations—

(a) are vexatious or frivolous,

(b) relate to the merits of policy set out in a national policy statement, or

(c) relate to compensation for compulsory acquisition of land or of an interest in or right over land.

1 Repealed by Localism Act 2011, ss 128(2), 237, Sch 13, paras 1, 38, Sch 25, Pt 20 (1 April 2012).

88 Initial assessment of issues, and preliminary meeting

(1) The Examining authority must make such an initial assessment of the principal issues arising on the application as the Examining authority thinks appropriate.

(2) After making that assessment, the Examining authority must hold a meeting.

(3) The Examining authority must invite to the meeting—

(a) the applicant, [...][1]

(b) each other interested party,

[(c) each statutory party, and

(d) each local authority that is within section 88A,][2]

whether or not the Examining authority is required by rules under section 97, or chooses, also to invite other persons.

[(3A) In subsection (3)(c) 'statutory party' means a person specified in, or of a description specified in, regulations made by the Secretary of State.][3]

(4) The purposes of the meeting are—

(a) to enable invitees present at the meeting to make representations to the Examining authority about how the application should be examined,

(b) to discuss any other matter that the Examining authority wishes to discuss, and

(c) any other purpose that may be specified in rules under section 97.

(5) Subsections (2) to (4) do not prevent the Examining authority holding other meetings.

(6) Rules under section 97—

(a) may (in particular) make provision supplementing subsections (1) to (4), and

(b) must make provision as to when the assessment under subsection (1) is to be made and as to when the meeting required by subsection (2) is to be held.

1 Word repealed by Localism Act 2011, s 138(1), (5)(a) (15 January 2012 for the purpose of conferring power on the Secretary of State to make regulations; 1 April 2012 otherwise).
2 Added by Localism Act 2011, s 138(1), (5)(b) (15 January 2012 for the purpose of conferring power on the Secretary of State to make regulations; 1 April 2012 otherwise).
3 Added by Localism Act 2011, s 138(1), (5)(c) (15 January 2012 for the purpose of conferring power on the Secretary of State to make regulations; 1 April 2012 otherwise).

[88A Local authorities for the purposes of section 88(3)(d)

(1) A local authority ('A') is within this section if—

(a) the land is in the area of another local authority ('B'),

(b) B is a unitary council or a lower-tier district council, and

(c) any part of the boundary of A's area is also a part of the boundary of B's area.

(2) If the land is in the area of an upper-tier county council ('C'), a local authority ('D') is within this section if—

(a) D is not a lower-tier district council, and

(b) any part of the boundary of D's area is also part of the boundary of C's area.

(3) In this section—

'the land' means the land to which the application relates or any part of that land;

'local authority' has the meaning given in section 102(8);

'lower-tier district council' means a district council in England for an area for which there is a county council;

'unitary council' means a local authority that is not an upper-tier county council, a lower-tier district council, a National Park authority or the Broads Authority;

'upper-tier county council' means a county council in England for each part of whose area there is a district council.][1]

1 Added by Localism Act 2011, s 138(1), (6) (1 April 2012).

89 Examining authority's decisions about how application is to be examined

(1) The Examining authority must in the light of the discussion at the meeting held under section 88(2) make such procedural decisions as the Examining authority thinks appropriate.

(2) The decisions required by subsection (1) may be made at or after the meeting.

[(2A) Upon making the decisions required by subsection (1), the Examining authority must inform each person mentioned in section 88(3)(c) and (d)—

(a) of those decisions, and

(b) that the person may notify the Examining authority in writing that the person is to become an interested party.][1]

(3) The Examining authority may make procedural decisions otherwise than as required by subsection (1), and may do so at any time before or after the meeting.

(4) The Examining authority must inform each interested party of any procedural decision made by the Examining authority.

(5) In this section 'procedural decision' means a decision about how the application is to be examined.

1 Added by Localism Act 2011, s 138(1), (7) (1 April 2012).

90 Written representations

(1) The Examining authority's examination of the application is to take the form of consideration of written representations about the application.

(2) Subsection (1) has effect subject to—

(a) any requirement under section 91, 92 or 93 to cause a hearing to be held, and

(b) any decision by the Examining authority that any part of the examination is to take a form that is neither—

(i) consideration of written representations, nor

(ii) consideration of oral representations made at a hearing.

(3) Rules under section 97 may (in particular) specify written representations about the application which are to be, or which may be or may not be, considered under subsection (1).

91 Hearings about specific issues

(1) Subsections (2) and (3) apply where the Examining authority decides that it is necessary for the Examining authority's examination of the application to include the consideration of oral representations about a particular issue made at a hearing in order to ensure—

(a) adequate examination of the issue, or

(b) that an interested party has a fair chance to put the party's case.

(2) The Examining authority must cause a hearing to be held for the purpose of receiving oral representations about the issue.

(3) At the hearing, each interested party is entitled (subject to the Examining authority's powers of control over the conduct of the hearing) to make oral representations about the issue.

(4) Where the Examining authority is a Panel acting under Chapter 2, any two or more hearings under subsection (2) may be held concurrently.

92 Compulsory acquisition hearings

(1) This section applies where the application includes a request for an order granting development consent to authorise compulsory acquisition of land or of an interest in or right over land (a 'compulsory acquisition request').

(2) The Examining authority must fix, and cause each affected person to be informed of, the deadline by which an affected person must notify the [Secretary of State][1] that the person wishes a compulsory acquisition hearing to be held.

(3) If the [Secretary of State][1] receives notification from at least one affected person before the deadline, the Examining authority must cause a compulsory acquisition hearing to be held.

(4) At a compulsory acquisition hearing, the following are entitled (subject to the Examining authority's powers of control over the conduct of the hearing) to make oral representations about the compulsory acquisition request—

(a) the applicant;

(b) each affected person.

(5) A person is an 'affected person' for the purposes of this section if the person's name has been given to the [Secretary of State][1] in a notice under section 59.

1 Word substituted by Localism Act 2011, s 128(2), Sch 13, paras 1, 39 (1 April 2012).

93 Open-floor hearings

(1) The Examining authority must fix, and cause the interested parties to be informed of, the deadline by which an interested party must notify the [Secretary of State][1] of the party's wish to be heard at an open-floor hearing.

(2) If the [Secretary of State][1] receives notification from at least one interested party before the deadline, the Examining authority must cause an open-floor hearing to be held.

(3) At an open-floor hearing, each interested party is entitled (subject to the Examining authority's powers of control over the conduct of the hearing) to make oral representations about the application.

1 Word substituted by Localism Act 2011, s 128(2), Sch 13, paras 1, 40 (1 April 2012).

94 Hearings: general provisions

(1) The following provisions of this section apply—

(a) to a hearing under section 91(2),

(b) to a compulsory acquisition hearing (see section 92), and

(c) to an open-floor hearing (see section 93).

(2) The hearing—

(a) must be in public, and

(b) must be presided over by one or more of the members of the Panel or (as the case may be) the single [appointed person][1].

(3) It is for the Examining authority to decide how the hearing is to be conducted.

(4) In particular, it is for the Examining authority to decide—

(a) whether a person making oral representations at the hearing may be questioned at the hearing by another person and, if so, the matters to which the questioning may relate;

(b) the amount of time to be allowed at the hearing—

(i) for the making of a person's representations (including representations made in exercise of an entitlement under section 91(3), 92(4) or 93(3)), or

(ii) for any questioning by another person.

(5) The Examining authority's powers under subsections (3) and (4) are subject to—

(a) subsection (2), and

(b) any rules made under section 97.

(6) Although the Examining authority's powers under subsections (3) and (4) may be exercised for the purpose of controlling exercise of an entitlement under section 91(3), 92(4) or 93(3), those powers may not be exercised so as to deprive the person entitled of all benefit of the entitlement.

(7) In making decisions under subsection (4)(a), the Examining authority must apply the principle that any oral questioning of a person making representations at a hearing (whether the applicant or any other person) should be undertaken by the Examining authority except where the Examining authority thinks that oral questioning by another person is necessary in order to ensure—

(a) adequate testing of any representations, or

(b) that a person has a fair chance to put the person's case.

(8) The Examining authority may refuse to allow representations to be made at the hearing (including representations made in exercise of an entitlement under section 91(3), 92(4) or 93(3)) if the Examining authority considers that the representations—

(a) are irrelevant, vexatious or frivolous,

(b) relate to the merits of policy set out in a national policy statement,

(c) repeat other representations already made (in any form and by any person), or

(d) relate to compensation for compulsory acquisition of land or of an interest in or right over land.

1 Word substituted by Localism Act 2011, s 128(2), Sch 13, paras 1, 41 (1 April 2012).

95 Hearings: disruption, supervision and costs

(1) Where an interested party or any other person behaves in a disruptive manner at a hearing, the Examining authority may decide to do any one or more of the following—

(a) exclude the person from all, or part, of the remainder of the hearing;

(b) allow the person to continue to attend the hearing only if the person complies with conditions specified by the Examining authority;

(c) exclude the person from other hearings;

(d) direct that the person is allowed to attend other hearings only if the person complies with conditions specified by the Examining authority.

(2) In this section 'hearing' means—

(a) a preliminary meeting under section 88,

(b) a hearing under section 91(2),

(c) a compulsory acquisition hearing (see section 92),

(d) an open-floor hearing (see section 93),

(e) any other meeting or hearing that the Examining authority causes to be held for the purposes of the Examining authority's examination of the application, or

(f) a site visit.

[...][1]

(4) Subsection (5) of section 250 of the Local Government Act 1972 (c. 70) (provisions about costs applying where Minister causes a local inquiry to be held) applies in relation to the Examining authority's examination of the application as it applies in relation to an inquiry under that section, but with references to the Minister causing the inquiry to be held being read as references to the Examining authority.

This is subject to subsection (5) of this section.

(5) Subsections (6) to (8) of section 210 of the Local Government (Scotland) Act 1973 (c. 65) (provisions about expenses applying where Minister causes a local inquiry to be held) apply in relation to the Examining authority's examination of the application in so far as relating to a hearing held in Scotland as they apply in relation to an inquiry under that section, but with references to the Minister causing the inquiry to be held being read as references to the Examining authority.

1 Repealed by Public Bodies (Abolition of Administrative Justice and Tribunals Council) Order 2013, SI 2013/2042, art 2(2), Schedule, para 40(a) (19 August 2013).

[95A Hearings: defence and national security

(1) Subsection (2) applies if the Secretary of State is satisfied that if all or part of the Examining Authority's examination of the application takes the form of a meeting or hearing—

(a) the making of particular oral representations at such a meeting or hearing would be likely to result in the disclosure of information as to defence or national security, and

(b) the public disclosure of that information would be contrary to the national interest.

(2) The Secretary of State may direct that representations of a description specified in the direction may be made only to persons of a description so specified (instead of being made in public).

(3) If the Secretary of State gives a direction under subsection (2), the Attorney General or (where the representations are to be made in Scotland) the Advocate General for Scotland may appoint a person (an 'appointed representative') to represent the interests of an interested party who (by virtue of the direction) is prevented from being present when the representations are made.

(4) Rules under section 97 may (in particular) make provision as to the functions of an appointed representative.

(5) The Secretary of State may direct a person (a 'responsible person') to pay the fees and expenses of an appointed representative if the Secretary of State thinks that the responsible person is interested in a meeting or hearing in relation to any representations that are the subject of a direction under subsection (2).

(6) Subsections (7) and (8) apply if the Secretary of State gives a direction under subsection (5).

(7) If the appointed representative and the responsible person are unable to agree the amount of the fees and expenses, the amount must be determined by the Secretary of State.

(8) The Secretary of State must cause the amount agreed between the appointed representative and the responsible person, or determined by the Secretary of State, to be certified.

(9) An amount so certified is recoverable from the responsible person as a civil debt.

(10) In this section 'representations' includes evidence.][1]

1 Added by Localism Act 2011, s 128(2), Sch 13, paras 1, 42 (15 January 2012).

96 Representations not made orally may be made in writing

(1) Subsection (2) applies where—

(a) a person asks the Examining authority to be allowed to make oral representations about the application at a hearing,

(b) the person does not (for whatever reason) make the representations orally at a hearing,

(c) written representations from the person are received by the [Secretary of State][1] before the Examining authority completes the Examining authority's examination of the application, and

(d) the written representations state that they are ones that the person asked to be allowed to, but did not, make orally at a hearing.

(2) The Examining authority must consider the written representations as part of the Examining authority's examination of the application, subject to section 87(3).

1 Word substituted by Localism Act 2011, s 128(2), Sch 13, paras 1, 43 (1 April 2012).

97 Procedure rules

(1) The Lord Chancellor or (if subsection (2) applies) the Secretary of State [...][1] may make rules regulating the procedure to be followed in connection with the Examining authority's examination of the application.

(2) This subsection applies if the development to which the application relates (or part of the development) is the construction (other than by a gas transporter) of an oil or gas cross-country pipe-line—

(a) one end of which is in England or Wales, and

(b) the other end of which is in Scotland.

(3) Rules under subsection (1) may make provision for or in connection with authorising the Examining authority, alone or with others, to enter onto land, including land owned or occupied otherwise than by the applicant, for the purpose of inspecting the land as part of the Examining authority's examination of the application.

(4) Rules under subsection (1) may regulate procedure in connection with matters preparatory to the Examining authority's examination of the application, and in connection with matters subsequent to the examination, as well as in connection with the conduct of the examination.

(5) Power under this section to make rules includes power to make different provision for different purposes.

(6) Power under this section to make rules is exercisable by statutory instrument.

(7) A statutory instrument containing rules under this section is subject to annulment pursuant to a resolution of either House of Parliament.

1 Words repealed by Public Bodies (Abolition of Administrative Justice and Tribunals Council) Order 2013, SI 2013/2042, art 2(2), Schedule, para 40(b) (19 August 2013).

98 Timetable for examining, and reporting on, application

(1) The Examining authority is under a duty to complete the Examining authority's examination of the application by the end of the period of 6 months beginning with the day after the start day.

(2) The start day is the day on which the meeting required by section 88 is held or, if that meeting is held on two or more days, the later or latest of those days.

(3) [[The Examining authority is under a duty to make its report under section 74(2)(b) or 83(1)(b)][2] by the end of the period of 3 months beginning with—

(a) the deadline for completion of its examination of the application, or

(b) (if earlier) the end of the day on which it completes the examination.][1]

(4) The [Secretary of State][3] may set a date for a deadline under this section that is later than the date for the time being set.

(5) The power under subsection (4) may be exercised—

(a) more than once in relation to the same deadline;

(b) after the date for the time being set for the deadline.

[(6) Subsections (7) and (8) apply where the power under subsection (4) is exercised.

(7) The Secretary of State must—

(a) notify each interested party of the new deadline, and

(b) publicise the new deadline in such manner as the Secretary of State thinks appropriate.

(8) The Secretary of State exercising the power must make a statement, to the House of Parliament of which that Secretary of State is a member, announcing the new deadline.

(9) A statement under subsection (8) may be written or oral.][4]

1 Words and (a) and (b) substituted for words by Localism Act 2011, s 139(1), (2) (1 April 2012).
2 Words substituted by Localism Act 2011, s 128(2), Sch 13, paras 1, 44(1), (2) (1 April 2012).
3 Words substituted by Localism Act 2011, s 128(2), Sch 13, paras 1, 44(1), (3) (1 April 2012).
4 Section 98(6)-(9) substituted for s 98(6) by Localism Act 2011, s 128(2), Sch 13, paras 1, 44(1), (4) (1 April 2012).

99 Completion of Examining authority's examination of application

When the Examining authority has completed its examination of the application, it must inform each of the interested parties of that fact.

100 Assessors

(1) The [Secretary of State][1] may, at the request of the Examining authority, appoint a person to act as an assessor to assist the Examining authority in the Examining authority's examination of the application.

(2) A person may be appointed as an assessor only if it appears to the [Secretary of State][2] that the person has expertise that makes the person a suitable person to provide assistance to the Examining authority.

1 Words substituted by Localism Act 2011, s 128(2), Sch 13, paras 1, 45(1), (2) (1 April 2012).
2 Word substituted by Localism Act 2011, s 128(2), Sch 13, paras 1, 45(1), (3) (1 April 2012).

101 Legal advice and assistance

(1) The [Secretary of State][1] may, at the request of the Examining authority, appoint a barrister, solicitor or advocate to provide legal advice and assistance to the Examining authority in connection with its examination of the application.

(2) The assistance that may be given by a person appointed under subsection (1) includes carrying out on behalf of the Examining authority any oral questioning of a person making representations at a hearing.

1 Words substituted by Localism Act 2011, s 128(2), Sch 13, paras 1, 46 (1 April 2012).

102 Interpretation of Chapter 4: 'interested party' and other expressions

(1) For the purposes of this Chapter, a person is an 'interested party' if—

(a) the person is the applicant,

[(aa) the person has been notified of the acceptance of the application in accordance with section 56(2)(d),

(ab) the Examining authority has under section 102A decided that it considers that the person is within one or more of the categories set out in section 102B,][1]

[(ba) the person is the Marine Management Organisation and the development for which the application seeks development consent would involve the carrying on of any activity in one or more of the areas specified in subsection (1A),][2]

[(c) the person is a local authority in whose area the land is located,

(ca) the person—

(i) is mentioned in section 88(3)(c) or (d), and

(ii) has notified the Examining authority as mentioned in section 89(2A)(b),][3]

(d) the person is the Greater London Authority and the land is in Greater London, or

(e) the person has made a relevant representation.

[(1ZA) But a person ceases to be an 'interested party' for the purposes of this Chapter upon notifying the Examining authority in writing that the person no longer wishes to be an interested party.][4]

[(1A) The areas are—

(a) waters in or adjacent to England up to the seaward limits of the territorial sea;

(b) an exclusive economic zone, except any part of an exclusive economic zone in relation to which the Scottish Ministers have functions;

(c) a Renewable Energy Zone, except any part of a Renewable Energy Zone in relation to which the Scottish Ministers have functions;

(d) an area designated under section 1(7) of the Continental Shelf Act 1964, except any part of that area which is within a part of an exclusive economic zone or Renewable Energy Zone in relation to which the Scottish Ministers have functions.][5]

(2) In this Chapter 'representation' includes evidence, and references to the making of a representation include the giving of evidence.

[...][6]

(4) A representation is a relevant representation for the purposes of subsection (1) to the extent that—

(a) it is a representation about the application,

(b) it is made to the [Secretary of State][7] in the prescribed form and manner,

(c) it is received by the [Secretary of State][7] no later than the deadline that applies under section 56 to the person making it,

(d) it contains material of a prescribed description, and

(e) it does not contain—

(i) material about compensation for compulsory acquisition of land or of an interest in or right over land,

(ii) material about the merits of policy set out in a national policy statement, or

(iii) material that is vexatious or frivolous.

[...][6]

(8) In [subsection (1)(c)][8] 'local authority' means—

(a) a county council, or district council, in England;

(b) a London borough council;

(c) the Common Council of the City of London;

(d) the Council of the Isles of Scilly;

(e) a county council, or county borough council, in Wales;

(f) a council constituted under section 2 of the Local Government etc. (Scotland) Act 1994 (c. 39);

(g) a National Park authority;

(h) the Broads Authority.

(9) In this section 'the land' means the land to which the application relates or any part of that land.

1 Section 102(1)(aa) and (ab) substituted for s 102(1)(b) by Localism Act 2011, s 138(1), (8)(a) (1 April 2012).
2 Added by Marine and Coastal Access Act 2009, s 23(1), (6)(a) (1 April 2010).
3 Section 102(1)(c) and (ca) substituted for s 102(1)(c) by Localism Act 2011, s 138(1), (8)(b) (1 April 2012).
4 Added by Localism Act 2011, s 138(1), (8)(c) (1 April 2012).
5 Added by Marine and Coastal Access Act 2009, s 23(1), (6)(b) (1 April 2010).
6 Repealed by Localism Act 2011, ss 138(1), (8)(d), (e), 237, Sch 25, Pt 21 (1 April 2012).
7 Word substituted by Localism Act 2011, s 128(2), Sch 13, paras 1, 47 (1 April 2012).
8 Words substituted by Localism Act 2011, s 138(1), (8)(f) (1 April 2012).

[102A Persons in certain categories may ask to become interested parties etc

(1) Subsection (2) applies if—

(a) a person makes a request to the Examining authority to become an interested party,

(b) the request states that the person claims to be within one or more of the categories set out in section 102B,

(c) the person has not been notified of the acceptance of the application in accordance with section 56(2)(d), and

(d) the applicant has issued a certificate under section 58 in relation to the application.

(2) The Examining authority must decide whether it considers that the person is within one or more of the categories set out in section 102B.

(3) If the Examining authority decides that it considers that the person is within one or more of the categories set out in section 102B, the Examining authority must notify the person, and the applicant, that the person has become an interested party under section 102(1)(ab).

(4) If the Examining authority thinks that a person might successfully make a request mentioned in subsection (1)(a), the Examining authority may inform the person about becoming an interested party under section 102(1)(ab).

But the Examining authority is under no obligation to make enquiries in order to discover persons who might make such a request.][1]

1 Added by Localism Act 2011, s 138(1), (9) (1 April 2012).

[102B Categories for the purposes of section 102A

(1) A person is within Category 1 if the person is an owner, lessee, tenant (whatever the tenancy period) or occupier of the land.

(2) A person is within Category 2 if the person—

(a) is interested in the land, or

(b) has power—

(i) to sell and convey the land, or

(ii) to release the land.

(3) An expression, other than 'the land', that appears in subsection (2) of this section and also in section 5(1) of the Compulsory Purchase Act 1965 has in subsection (2) the meaning that it has in section 5(1) of that Act.

(4) A person is within Category 3 if, should the order sought by the application be made and fully implemented, the person would or might be entitled—

(a) as a result of the implementing of the order,

(b) as a result of the order having been implemented, or

(c) as a result of use of the land once the order has been implemented,

to make a relevant claim.

(5) In subsection (4) 'relevant claim' means—

(a) a claim under section 10 of the Compulsory Purchase Act 1965 (compensation where satisfaction not made for the taking, or injurious affection, of land subject to compulsory purchase);

(b) a claim under Part 1 of the Land Compensation Act 1973 (compensation for depreciation of land value by physical factors caused by use of public works);

(c) a claim under section 152(3).

(6) In this section 'the land' means the land to which the application relates or any part of that land.][1]

1 Added by Localism Act 2011, s 138(1), (9) (1 April 2012).

Chapter 5 Decisions on applications

103 [Secretary of State is to decide applications][1]

(1) The Secretary of State has the function of deciding an application for an order granting development consent [.][2]

[...][2]

[...][3]

1 Heading substituted by Localism Act 2011, s 128(2), Sch 13, paras 1, 48(1), (4) (1 April 2012).
2 Word and s 103(1)(a)-(b) repealed by Localism Act 2011, ss 128(2), 237, Sch 13, paras 1, 48(1), (2), Sch 25, Pt 20 (1 April 2012).
3 Repealed by Localism Act 2011, ss 128(2), 237, Sch 13, paras 1, 48(1), (3), Sch 25, Pt 20 (1 April 2012).

104 [Decisions in cases where national policy statement has effect][1]

(1) This section applies in relation to an application for an order granting development consent if [a national policy statement has effect in relation to development of the description to which the application relates][2].

(2) In deciding the application the [Secretary of State][3] must have regard to—

(a) any national policy statement which has effect in relation to development of the description to which the application relates (a 'relevant national policy statement'), [(aa) the appropriate marine policy documents (if any), determined in accordance with section 59 of the Marine and Coastal Access Act 2009,][4]

(b) any local impact report (within the meaning given by section 60(3)) submitted to the [Secretary of State][5] before the deadline specified in a notice under section 60(2),

(c) any matters prescribed in relation to development of the description to which the application relates, and

(d) any other matters which the [Secretary of State][3] thinks are both important and relevant to [the Secretary of State's][6] decision.

(3) The [Secretary of State][7] must decide the application in accordance with any relevant national policy statement, except to the extent that one or more of subsections (4) to (8) applies.

(4) This subsection applies if the [Secretary of State][7] is satisfied that deciding the application in accordance with any relevant national policy statement would lead to the United Kingdom being in breach of any of its international obligations.

(5) This subsection applies if the [Secretary of State is][8] satisfied that deciding the application in accordance with any relevant national policy statement would lead to the [Secretary of State being in breach of any duty imposed on the Secretary of State][9] by or under any enactment.

(6) This subsection applies if the [Secretary of State][10] is satisfied that deciding the application in accordance with any relevant national policy statement would be unlawful by virtue of any enactment.

(7) This subsection applies if the [Secretary of State][10] is satisfied that the adverse impact of the proposed development would outweigh its benefits.

(8) This subsection applies if the [Secretary of State][10] is satisfied that any condition prescribed for deciding an application otherwise than in accordance with a national policy statement is met.

(9) For the avoidance of doubt, the fact that any relevant national policy statement identifies a location as suitable (or potentially suitable) for a particular description of development does not prevent one or more of subsections (4) to (8) from applying.

1 Heading substituted by Localism Act 2011, s 128(2), Sch 13, paras 1, 49(1), (7) (1 April 2012).
2 Words substituted by Localism Act 2011, s 128(2), Sch 13, paras 1, 49(1), (2) (1 April 2012).
3 Words substituted by Localism Act 2011, s 128(2), Sch 13, paras 1, 49(1), (3)(a) (1 April 2012).
4 Added by Marine and Coastal Access Act 2009, s 58(5) (12 November 2010).
5 Word substituted by Localism Act 2011, s 128(2), Sch 13, paras 1, 49(1), (3)(b) (1 April 2012).
6 Word substituted by Localism Act 2011, s 128(2), Sch 13, paras 1, 49(1), (3)(c) (1 April 2012).
7 Words substituted by Localism Act 2011, s 128(2), Sch 13, paras 1, 49(1), (4) (1 April 2012).
8 Words substituted by Localism Act 2011, s 128(2), Sch 13, paras 1, 49(1), (5)(a) (1 April 2012).
9 Words substituted by Localism Act 2011, s 128(2), Sch 13, paras 1, 49(1), (5)(b) (1 April 2012).
10 Words substituted by Localism Act 2011, s 128(2), Sch 13, paras 1, 49(1), (6) (1 April 2012).

105 [Decisions in cases where no national policy statement has effect][1]

(1) This section applies in relation to an application for an order granting development consent [if section 104 does not apply in relation to the application][2].

(2) In deciding the application the Secretary of State must have regard to—

(a) any local impact report (within the meaning given by section 60(3)) submitted to the [Secretary of State][3] before the deadline specified in a notice under section 60(2),

(b) any matters prescribed in relation to development of the description to which the application relates, and

(c) any other matters which the Secretary of State thinks are both important and relevant to the Secretary of State's decision.

1 Heading substituted by Localism Act 2011, s 128(2), Sch 13, paras 1, 50(1), (4) (1 April 2012).
2 Words substituted by Localism Act 2011, s 128(2), Sch 13, paras 1, 50(1), (2) (1 April 2012).
3 Word substituted by Localism Act 2011, s 128(2), Sch 13, paras 1, 50(1), (3) (1 April 2012).

106 Matters that may be disregarded when deciding application

(1) In deciding an application for an order granting development consent, the [Secretary of State][1] may disregard representations if the [Secretary of State][1] considers that the representations—

(a) are vexatious or frivolous,

(b) relate to the merits of policy set out in a national policy statement, or

(c) relate to compensation for compulsory acquisition of land or of an interest in or right over land.

(2) In this section 'representation' includes evidence.

1 Words substituted by Localism Act 2011, s 128(2), Sch 13, paras 1, 51 (1 April 2012).

107 Timetable for decisions

(1) [The [Secretary of State][2] is under a duty to decide an application for an order granting development consent by the end of the period of 3 months beginning with—

(a) the [deadline under section 98(3)][3], or

(b) (if earlier) the end of the day on which the Secretary of State receives a report on the application under section 74(2)(b) or 83(1)(b).][1]

[...][4]

(3) The [Secretary of State][5] may set a date for the deadline under subsection (1) that is later than the date for the time being set.

[...][4]

(5) The power under subsection (3) may be exercised—

(a) more than once in relation to the same deadline;

(b) after the date for the time being set for the deadline.

[(6) Subsection (7) applies where the power under subsection (3) is exercised.

(7) The Secretary of State exercising the power must make a statement, to the House of Parliament of which that Secretary of State is a member, announcing the new deadline.

(8) A statement under subsection (7) must be published in such form and manner as the Secretary of State considers appropriate.

(8A) A statement under subsection (7) may be written or oral.][6]

1 Words substituted, existing text renumbered as s 107(1)(a), word is inserted and a new s 107(1)(b) inserted by Localism Act 2011, s 139(1), (3) (1 April 2012).
2 Words substituted by Localism Act 2011, s 128(2), Sch 13, paras 1, 52(1), (2)(a) (1 April 2012).
3 Words substituted by Localism Act 2011, s 128(2), Sch 13, paras 1, 52(1), (2)(b) (1 April 2012).
4 Repealed by Localism Act 2011, s 237, Sch 25, Pt 20 (1 April 2012).
5 Words substituted by Localism Act 2011, s 128(2), Sch 13, paras 1, 52(1), (4) (1 April 2012).
6 Section 107(6)-(8A) substituted for s 107(6)-(9) by Localism Act 2011, s 128(2), Sch 13, paras 1, 52(1), (6) (1 April 2012).

Chapter 6 Suspension of decision-making process

108 Suspension during review of national policy statement

(1) This section applies where—

(a) an application is made for an order granting development consent for development of a description in relation to which a national policy statement has effect, and

(b) the Secretary of State thinks that, as a result of a change in circumstances since the national policy statement was first published or (if later) the statement or any part of it was last reviewed, all or part of the statement should be reviewed before the application is decided.

(2) The Secretary of State may direct that, until the review has been completed and the Secretary of State has complied with section 6(5) in relation to the review, [examination of the application by a Panel under Chapter 2, or a single appointed person under Chapter 3, is suspended (if not already completed).][1]

1 Words substituted by Localism Act 2011, s 128(2), Sch 13, paras 1, 53 (1 April 2012).

Chapter 7 Intervention by Secretary of State

109-113 ...

Repealed by Localism Act 2011, ss 128(2), 237, Sch 13, para 54, Sch 25, Pt 20 (1 April 2012).

Chapter 8 Grant or refusal

114 Grant or refusal of development consent

(1) When [the Secretary of State][1] has decided an application for an order granting development consent, the [Secretary of State][2] must either—

(a) make an order granting development consent, or

(b) refuse development consent.

(2) The Secretary of State may by regulations make provision regulating the procedure to be followed if the [Secretary of State][3] proposes to make an order granting development consent on terms which are materially different from those proposed in the application.

1 Word substituted by Localism Act 2011, s 128(2), Sch 13, paras 1, 55(1), (2)(a) (1 April 2012).
2 Words substituted by Localism Act 2011, s 128(2), Sch 13, paras 1, 55(1), (2)(b) (1 April 2012).
3 Words substituted by Localism Act 2011, s 128(2), Sch 13, paras 1, 55(1), (3) (1 April 2012).

115 Development for which development consent may be granted

(1) Development consent may be granted for development which is—

(a) development for which development consent is required, or

(b) associated development.

(2) 'Associated development' means development which—

(a) is associated with the development within subsection (1)(a) (or any part of it),

(b) is not the construction or extension of one or more dwellings, and

(c) is within subsection (3) or (4).

(3) Development is within this subsection if it is to be carried out wholly in one or more of the following areas—

(a) England;

(b) waters adjacent to England up to the seaward limits of the territorial sea;

(c) in the case of development in the field of energy, a Renewable Energy Zone, except any part of a Renewable Energy Zone in relation to which the Scottish Ministers have functions.

(4) Development is within this subsection if—

(a) it is to be carried out wholly in Wales,

(b) it is the carrying out or construction of surface works, boreholes or pipes, and

(c) the development within subsection (1)(a) with which it is associated is development within section 17(3).

(5) To the extent that development consent is granted for associated development, section 33 applies to the development as it applies to development for which development consent is required.

[...][1]

1 Repealed by Localism Act 2011, ss 128(2), 237, Sch 13, paras 1, 56, Sch 25, Pt 20 (1 April 2012).

116 Reasons for decision to grant or refuse development consent

(1) The [Secretary of State][1] must prepare a statement of [the Secretary of State's][2] reasons for deciding to—

(a) make an order granting development consent, or

(b) refuse development consent.

(2) The [Secretary of State][3] must provide a copy of the statement to each person who is an interested party in relation to the application for the purposes of Chapter 4 (see section 102).

(3) The [Secretary of State][4] must publish the statement in such manner as [the Secretary of State][5] thinks appropriate.

[...][6]

1 Words substituted by Localism Act 2011, s 128(2), Sch 13, paras 1, 57(1), (2)(a) (1 April 2012).
2 Word substituted by Localism Act 2011, s 128(2), Sch 13, paras 1, 57(1), (2)(b) (1 April 2012).
3 Words substituted by Localism Act 2011, s 128(2), Sch 13, paras 1, 57(1), (3) (1 April 2012).
4 Words substituted by Localism Act 2011, s 128(2), Sch 13, paras 1, 57(1), (4)(a) (1 April 2012).
5 Words substituted by Localism Act 2011, s 128(2), Sch 13, paras 1, 57(1), (4)(b) (1 April 2012).
6 Repealed by Localism Act 2011, ss 128(2), 237, Sch 13, paras 1, 57(1), (5), Sch 25, Pt 20 (1 April 2012).

117 Orders granting development consent: formalities

(1) This section applies in relation to an order granting development consent.

[...][1]

(3) Except in a case within subsection (4), the [Secretary of State][2] must publish the order in such manner as [the Secretary of State][3] thinks appropriate.

[(4) If the order includes provision—

(a) made under section 120(3) for or relating to any of the matters listed in paragraphs 32A and 32B of Schedule 5, or

(b) made in the exercise of any of the powers conferred by section 120(5)(a) or (b),

the order must be contained in a statutory instrument.][4]

[...][1]

(6) As soon as practicable after the instrument [containing the order is made, the Secretary of State][5] must deposit in the office of the Clerk of the Parliaments a copy of—

(a) the instrument,

(b) the latest version of any plan supplied by the applicant in connection with the application for the order contained in the instrument, and

(c) the statement of reasons prepared under section 116(1).

[...][1]

1 Repealed by Localism Act 2011, ss 128(2), 237, Sch 13, paras 1, 58(1), (2), Sch 25, Pt 20 (1 April 2012).
2 Words substituted by Localism Act 2011, s 128(2), Sch 13, paras 1, 58(1), (3)(a) (1 April 2012).
3 Words substituted by Localism Act 2011, s 128(2), Sch 13, paras 1, 58(1), (3)(b) (1 April 2012).
4 Substituted by Localism Act 2011, s 128(2), Sch 13, paras 1, 58(1), (4) (1 April 2012).
5 Words substituted by Localism Act 2011, s 128(2), Sch 13, paras 1, 58(1), (5) (1 April 2012).

Chapter 9 Legal challenges

118 Legal challenges relating to applications for orders granting development consent

(1) A court may entertain proceedings for questioning an order granting development consent only if—

(a) the proceedings are brought by a claim for judicial review, and

(b) the claim form is filed during the period of 6 weeks beginning with—

(i) the day on which the order is published, or

(ii) if later, the day on which the statement of reasons for making the order is published.

(2) A court may entertain proceedings for questioning a refusal of development consent only if—

(a) the proceedings are brought by a claim for judicial review, and

(b) the claim form is filed during the period of 6 weeks beginning with the day on which the statement of reasons for the refusal is published.

(3) A court may entertain proceedings for questioning a decision of the [Secretary of State][1] under section 55 not to accept an application for an order granting development consent only if—

(a) the proceedings are brought by a claim for judicial review, and

(b) the claim form is filed during the period of 6 weeks beginning with the day on which the [Secretary of State][1] notifies the applicant as required by subsection (7) of that section.

(4) A court may entertain proceedings for questioning a decision under paragraph 1 of Schedule 4 in relation to an error or omission in a decision document only if—

(a) the proceedings are brought by a claim for judicial review, and

(b) the claim form is filed during the period of 6 weeks beginning with the day on which a correction notice in respect of the error or omission is issued under paragraph 2 of that Schedule or, if the correction is required to be made by order contained in a statutory instrument, the day on which the order is published.

(5) A court may entertain proceedings for questioning a decision under paragraph 2(1) of Schedule 6 to make a change to an order granting development consent only if—

(a) the proceedings are brought by a claim for judicial review, and

(b) the claim form is filed during the period of 6 weeks beginning with the day on which notice of the change is given under paragraph 2(12)(b) of that Schedule or, if the change to the order is required to be made by order contained in a statutory instrument, the day on which the order making the change is published.

(6) A court may entertain proceedings for questioning a decision under paragraph 3(1) of Schedule 6 to make a change to, or revoke, an order granting development consent only if—

(a) the proceedings are brought by a claim for judicial review, and

(b) the claim form is filed during the period of 6 weeks beginning with the day on which notice of the change or revocation is given under paragraph 4(6) of that Schedule or, if the change or revocation is required to be made by order contained in a statutory instrument, the day on which the order making the change or revocation is published.

(7) A court may entertain proceedings for questioning anything else done, or omitted to be done, by the Secretary of State […][2] in relation to an application for an order granting development consent only if—

(a) the proceedings are brought by a claim for judicial review, and

(b) the claim form is filed during the period of 6 weeks beginning with the relevant day.

(8) 'The relevant day', in relation to an application for an order granting development consent, means the day on which—

(a) the application is withdrawn,

(b) the order granting development consent is published or (if later) the statement of reasons for making the order is published, or

(c) the statement of reasons for the refusal of development consent is published.

(9) Subsections (7) and (8) do not apply in relation to—

(a) a failure to decide an application for an order granting development consent, or

(b) anything which delays (or is likely to delay) the decision on such an application.

1 Word substituted by Localism Act 2011, s 128(2), Sch 13, paras 1, 59(1), (2) (1 April 2012).
2 Words repealed by Localism Act 2011, ss 128(2), 237, Sch 13, paras 1, 59(1), (3), Sch 25, Pt 20 (1 April 2012).

Chapter 10 Correction of errors

119 Correction of errors in development consent decisions

Schedule 4 (correction of errors in development consent decisions) has effect.

Part 7 Orders granting development consent

Chapter 1 Content of orders

General

120 What may be included in order granting development consent

(1) An order granting development consent may impose requirements in connection with the development for which consent is granted.

(2) The requirements may in particular include[—][1]

[(a) requirements corresponding to conditions which could have been imposed on the grant of any permission, consent or authorisation, or the giving of any notice, which (but for section 33(1)) would have been required for the development;

(b) requirements to obtain the approval of the Secretary of State or any other person, so far as not within paragraph (a).][1]

(3) An order granting development consent may make provision relating to, or to matters ancillary to, the development for which consent is granted.

(4) The provision that may be made under subsection (3) includes in particular provision for or relating to any of the matters listed in Part 1 of Schedule 5.

(5) An order granting development consent may—

(a) apply, modify or exclude a statutory provision which relates to any matter for which provision may be made in the order;

(b) make such amendments, repeals or revocations of statutory provisions of local application as appear to the [Secretary of State][2] to be necessary or expedient in consequence of a provision of the order or in connection with the order;

(c) include any provision that appears to the [Secretary of State][2] to be necessary or expedient for giving full effect to any other provision of the order;

(d) include incidental, consequential, supplementary, transitional or transitory provisions and savings.

(6) In subsection (5) 'statutory provision' means a provision of an Act or of an instrument made under an Act.

(7) Subsections (3) to (6) are subject to subsection (8) and the following provisions of this Chapter.

[(8) With the exception of provision made under subsection (3) for or relating to any of the matters listed in paragraph 32B of Schedule 5, an order granting development consent may not include—

(a) provision creating offences,

(b) provision conferring power to create offences, or

(c) provision changing an existing power to create offences.][3]

(9) To the extent that provision for or relating to a matter may be included in an order granting development consent, none of the following may include any such provision—

(a) an order under section 14 or 16 of the Harbours Act 1964 (c. 40) (orders in relation to harbours, docks and wharves);

(b) an order under section 4(1) of the Gas Act 1965 (c. 36) (order authorising storage of gas in underground strata);

(c) an order under section 1 or 3 of the Transport and Works Act 1992 (c. 42) (orders as to railways, tramways, inland waterways etc.).

1 Existing text renumbered as s 120(2)(a) and s 120(2)(b) inserted by Localism Act 2011, s 140 (1 April 2012).
2 Words substituted by Localism Act 2011, s 128(2), Sch 13, paras 1, 60(1), (2) (1 April 2012).
3 Substituted by Localism Act 2011, s 128(2), Sch 13, paras 1, 60(1), (3) (1 April 2012).

121 ...

Repealed by Localism Act 2011, ss 128(2), 237, Sch 13, paras 1, 61, Sch 25, Pt 20 (1 April 2012).

Compulsory acquisition

122 Purpose for which compulsory acquisition may be authorised

(1) An order granting development consent may include provision authorising the compulsory acquisition of land only if the [Secretary of State][1] is satisfied that the conditions in subsections (2) and (3) are met.

(2) The condition is that the land—

(a) is required for the development to which the development consent relates,

(b) is required to facilitate or is incidental to that development, or

(c) is replacement land which is to be given in exchange for the order land under section 131 or 132.

(3) The condition is that there is a compelling case in the public interest for the land to be acquired compulsorily.

1 Words substituted by Localism Act 2011, s 128(2), Sch 13, paras 1, 62 (1 April 2012).

123 Land to which authorisation of compulsory acquisition can relate

(1) An order granting development consent may include provision authorising the compulsory acquisition of land only if the [Secretary of State][1] is satisfied that one of the conditions in subsections (2) to (4) is met.

(2) The condition is that the application for the order included a request for compulsory acquisition of the land to be authorised.

(3) The condition is that all persons with an interest in the land consent to the inclusion of the provision.

(4) The condition is that the prescribed procedure has been followed in relation to the land.

1 Words substituted by Localism Act 2011, s 128(2), Sch 13, paras 1, 62 (1 April 2012).

124 …

Repealed by Localism Act 2011, ss 128(2), 237, Sch 13, paras 1, 63, Sch 25, Pt 20 (1 April 2012).

125 Application of compulsory acquisition provisions

(1) This section applies if an order granting development consent includes provision authorising the compulsory acquisition of land.

(2) Part 1 of the Compulsory Purchase Act 1965 (c. 56) (procedure for compulsory purchase) applies to the compulsory acquisition of land under the order—

(a) as it applies to a compulsory purchase to which Part 2 of the Acquisition of Land Act 1981 (c. 67) applies, and

(b) as if the order were a compulsory purchase order under that Act.

(3) Part 1 of the Compulsory Purchase Act 1965, as applied by subsection (2), has effect with the omission of the following provisions—

(a) section 4 (time limit for exercise of compulsory purchase powers);

(b) section 10 (compensation for injurious affection);

(c) paragraph 3(3) of Schedule 3 (provision as to giving of bonds).

(4) In so far as the order includes provision authorising the compulsory acquisition of land in Scotland—

(a) subsections (2) and (3) do not apply, and

(b) the Acquisition of Land (Authorisation Procedure) (Scotland) Act 1947 (c. 42) ('the 1947 Act') applies to the compulsory acquisition of that land under the order as if the order were a compulsory purchase order as defined in section 1(1) of that Act.

(5) The 1947 Act, as applied by subsection (4), has effect with the omission of the following provisions—

(a) Parts 2 and 3 of the First Schedule (compulsory purchase by Ministers and special provisions as to certain descriptions of land);

(b) section 116 of the Lands Clauses Consolidation (Scotland) Act 1845 (c. 19) (time limit for exercise of compulsory purchase powers) (that section being incorporated into the 1947 Act by paragraph 1 of the Second Schedule to the 1947 Act).

(6) Subsections (2) to (5) are subject to any contrary provision made by the order granting development consent.

126 Compensation for compulsory acquisition

(1) This section applies in relation to an order granting development consent which includes provision authorising the compulsory acquisition of land.

(2) The order may not include provision the effect of which is to modify the application of a compensation provision, except to the extent necessary to apply the provision to the compulsory acquisition of land authorised by the order.

(3) The order may not include provision the effect of which is to exclude the application of a compensation provision.

(4) A compensation provision is a provision of or made under an Act which relates to compensation for the compulsory acquisition of land.

127 Statutory undertakers' land

(1) This section applies in relation to land ('statutory undertakers' land') if—

(a) the land has been acquired by statutory undertakers for the purposes of their undertaking,

(b) a representation has been made about an application for an order granting development consent before the completion of the examination of the application, and the representation has not been withdrawn, and

(c) as a result of the representation the [Secretary of State][1] is satisfied that—

(i) the land is used for the purposes of carrying on the statutory undertakers' undertaking, or

(ii) an interest in the land is held for those purposes.

(2) An order granting development consent may include provision authorising the compulsory acquisition of statutory undertakers' land only to the extent that the [Secretary of State is satisfied of the matters set out in subsection (3).][2]

(3) The matters are that the nature and situation of the land are such that—

(a) it can be purchased and not replaced without serious detriment to the carrying on of the undertaking, or

(b) if purchased it can be replaced by other land belonging to, or available for acquisition by, the undertakers without serious detriment to the carrying on of the undertaking.

(4) Subsections (2) and (3) do not apply in a case within subsection (5).

(5) An order granting development consent may include provision authorising the compulsory acquisition of a right over statutory undertakers' land by the creation of a new right over land only to the extent that the [Secretary of State is satisfied of the matters set out in subsection (6).][2]

(6) The matters are that the nature and situation of the land are such that—

(a) the right can be purchased without serious detriment to the carrying on of the undertaking, or

(b) any detriment to the carrying on of the undertaking, in consequence of the acquisition of the right, can be made good by the undertakers by the use of other land belonging to or available for acquisition by them.

[...][3]

(8) In this section—

'statutory undertakers' has the meaning given by section 8 of the Acquisition of Land Act 1981 (c. 67) and also includes the undertakers—

(a) which are deemed to be statutory undertakers for the purposes of that Act, by virtue of another enactment;

(b) which are statutory undertakers for the purposes of section 16(1) and (2) of that Act (see section 16(3) of that Act).

(9) In the application of this section to a statutory undertaker which is a health service body (as defined in section 60(7) of the National Health Service and Community Care Act 1990 (c. 19)), references to land acquired or available for acquisition by the statutory undertakers are to be construed as references to land acquired or available for acquisition by the Secretary of State for use or occupation by the body.

1 Words substituted by Localism Act 2011, s 128(2), Sch 13, paras 1, 64(1), (2) (1 April 2012).
2 Words substituted by Growth and Infrastructure Act 2013, s 23(1), (2)(a), (b) (25 June 2013).
3 Repealed by Growth and Infrastructure Act 2013, s 23(1), (2)(c) (25 June 2013).

128, 129 ...

Repealed by Growth and Infrastructure Act 2013, s 24(1) (25 June 2013).

130 National Trust land

(1) This section applies to land belonging to the National Trust which is held by the Trust inalienably.

(2) An order granting development consent is subject to special parliamentary procedure, to the extent that the order authorises the compulsory acquisition of land to which this section applies, if the condition in subsection (3) is met.

(3) The condition is that—

(a) a representation has been made by the National Trust about the application for the order granting development consent before the completion of the examination of the application, [...][1]

[(aa) the representation contains an objection to the compulsory acquisition of the land, and][1]

(b) the [objection][2] has not been withdrawn.

[(3A) In a case to which this section applies and to which section 131 or 132 also applies, special parliamentary procedure—

(a) may be required by subsection (2) whether or not also required by section 131(3) or 132(2), and

(b) may be required by section 131(3) or 132(2) whether or not also required by subsection (2).][3]

(4) In this section 'held inalienably', in relation to land belonging to the National Trust, means that the land is inalienable under section 21 of the National Trust Act 1907 (c. cxxxvi) or section 8 of the National Trust Act 1939 (c. lxxxvi).

(5) In this section 'the National Trust' means the National Trust for Places of Historic Interest or Natural Beauty incorporated by the National Trust Act 1907 (c. cxxxvi).

1 Added by Localism Act 2011, s 141(1), (3)(a) (1 April 2012).
2 Word substituted by Localism Act 2011, s 141(1), (3)(b) (1 April 2012).
3 Added by Growth and Infrastructure Act 2013, s 24(5) (25 June 2013).

131 Commons, open spaces etc: compulsory acquisition of land

(1) This section applies to any land forming part of a common, open space or fuel or field garden allotment.

(2) This section does not apply in a case to which section 132 applies.

(3) An order granting development consent is subject to special parliamentary procedure, to the extent that the order authorises the compulsory acquisition of land to which this section applies, [unless—

(a) the Secretary of State is satisfied that one of subsections (4) to (5) applies, and

(b) that fact, and the subsection concerned, are recorded in the order or otherwise in the instrument or other document containing the order.][1]

(4) This subsection applies if—

(a) replacement land has been or will be given in exchange for the order land, and

(b) the replacement land has been or will be vested in the prospective seller and subject to the same rights, trusts and incidents as attach to the order land.

[(4A) This subsection applies if—

(a) the order land is, or forms part of, an open space,

(b) none of the order land is of any of the other descriptions in subsection (1),

(c) either—

(i) there is no suitable land available to be given in exchange for the order land, or

(ii) any suitable land available to be given in exchange is available only at prohibitive cost, and

(d) it is strongly in the public interest for the development for which the order grants consent to be capable of being begun sooner than is likely to be possible if the order were to be subject (to any extent) to special parliamentary procedure.

(4B) This subsection applies if—

(a) the order land is, or forms part of, an open space,

(b) none of the order land is of any of the other descriptions in subsection (1), and

(c) the order land is being acquired for a temporary (although possibly long-lived) purpose.][2]

(5) This subsection applies if—

(a) the order land does not exceed 200 square metres in extent or is required for the widening or drainage of an existing highway or partly for the widening and partly for the drainage of such a highway, and

(b) the giving in exchange of other land is unnecessary, whether in the interests of the persons, if any, entitled to rights of common or other rights or in the interests of the public.

[...][3]

(11) If an order granting development consent authorises the compulsory acquisition of land to which this section applies, it may include provision—

(a) for vesting replacement land given in exchange as mentioned in subsection (4)(a) in the prospective seller and subject to the rights, trusts and incidents mentioned in subsection (4)(b), and

(b) for discharging the order land from all rights, trusts and incidents to which it is subject.

(12) In this section—

'common', 'fuel or field garden allotment' and 'open space' have the same meanings as in section 19 of the Acquisition of Land Act 1981 (c. 67);

'the order land' means the land authorised to be compulsorily acquired;

'the prospective seller' means the person or persons in whom the order land is vested;

'replacement land' means land which is not less in area than the order land and which is no less advantageous to the persons, if any, entitled to rights of common or other rights, and to the public.

1 Words substituted by Growth and Infrastructure Act 2013, s 24(2)(a) (25 June 2013).
2 Added by Growth and Infrastructure Act 2013, s 24(2)(b) (25 June 2013).
3 Repealed by Growth and Infrastructure Act 2013, s 24(2)(c) (25 June 2013).

132 Commons, open spaces etc: compulsory acquisition of rights over land

(1) This section applies to any land forming part of a common, open space or fuel or field garden allotment.

(2) An order granting development consent is subject to special parliamentary procedure, to the extent that the order authorises the compulsory acquisition of a right over land to which this section applies by the creation of a new right over land, [unless—

(a) the Secretary of State is satisfied that one of subsections (3) to (5) applies, and

(b) that fact, and the subsection concerned, are recorded in the order or otherwise in the instrument or other document containing the order.][1]

(3) This subsection applies if the order land, when burdened with the order right, will be no less advantageous than it was before to the following persons—

(a) the persons in whom it is vested,

(b) other persons, if any, entitled to rights of common or other rights, and

(c) the public.

(4) This subsection applies if—

(a) replacement land has been or will be given in exchange for the order right, and

(b) the replacement land has been or will be vested in the persons in whom the order land is vested and subject to the same rights, trusts and incidents as attach to the order land (ignoring the order granting development consent).

[(4A) This subsection applies if—

(a) the order land is, or forms part of, an open space,

(b) none of the order land is of any of the other descriptions in subsection (1),

(c) either—

(i) there is no suitable land available to be given in exchange for the order right, or

(ii) any suitable land available to be given in exchange is available only at prohibitive cost, and

(d) it is strongly in the public interest for the development for which the order grants consent to be capable of being begun sooner than is likely to be possible if the order were to be subject (to any extent) to special parliamentary procedure.

(4B) This subsection applies if—

(a) the order land is, or forms part of, an open space,

(b) none of the order land is of any of the other descriptions in subsection (1), and

(c) the order right is being acquired for a temporary (although possibly long-lived) purpose.][2]

(5) This subsection applies if—

(a) the order land does not exceed 200 square metres in extent or the order right is required in connection with the widening or drainage of an existing highway or in connection partly with the widening and partly with the drainage of such a highway, and

(b) the giving of other land in exchange for the order right is unnecessary, whether in the interests of the persons, if any, entitled to rights of common or other rights or in the interests of the public.

[...][3]

(11) If an order granting development consent authorises the compulsory acquisition of a right over land to which this section applies by the creation of a new right over land, it may include provision—

(a) for vesting replacement land given in exchange as mentioned in subsection (4)(a) in the persons in whom the order land is vested and subject to the rights, trusts and incidents mentioned in subsection (4)(b), and

(b) for discharging the order land from all rights, trusts and incidents to which it has previously been subject so far as their continuance would be inconsistent with the exercise of the order right.

(12) In this section—

'common', 'fuel or field garden allotment' and 'open space' have the same meanings as in section 19 of the Acquisition of Land Act 1981 (c. 67);

'the order land' means the land to which this section applies over which the order right is to be exercisable;

'the order right' means the right authorised to be compulsorily acquired;

'replacement land' means land which will be adequate to compensate the following persons for the disadvantages which result from the compulsory acquisition of the order right—

(a) the persons in whom the order land is vested,

(b) the persons, if any, entitled to rights of common or other rights over the order land, and

(c) the public.

1 Words substituted by Growth and Infrastructure Act 2013, s 24(3)(a) (25 June 2013).
2 Added by Growth and Infrastructure Act 2013, s 24(3)(b) (25 June 2013).
3 Repealed by Growth and Infrastructure Act 2013, s 24(3)(c) (25 June 2013).

133 Rights in connection with underground gas storage facilities

(1) This section applies if—

(a) the development to which an order granting development consent relates is development within section 14(1)(c), and

(b) the order authorises the compulsory acquisition of one or more rights within subsection (2).

(2) The rights are—

(a) a right to store gas in underground gas storage facilities;

(b) a right to stop up a well, borehole or shaft, or prevent its use by another person;

(c) a right of way over land.

(3) If the right within subsection (2) is an existing right to store gas in underground gas storage facilities, this Act has effect in relation to the compulsory acquisition of the right with the omission of section 131.

(4) If the order authorises the compulsory acquisition of the right by the creation of a new right within subsection (2), this Act has effect in relation to the compulsory acquisition of the right with the omission of sections 127 to 132.

134 Notice of authorisation of compulsory acquisition

(1) This section applies if—

(a) an order is made granting development consent, and

(b) the order includes provision authorising the compulsory acquisition of land.

(2) In this section—

'the order land' means—

(a) in a case where the order granting development consent authorises the compulsory acquisition of a right over land by the creation of a new right, the land over which the right is to be exercisable;

(b) in any other case where the order granting development consent authorises the compulsory acquisition of land, the land authorised to be compulsorily acquired;

'the prospective purchaser' means—

(a) in a case where the order granting development consent authorises the compulsory acquisition of a right over land by the creation of a new right, the person for whose benefit the order authorises the creation of the right;

(b) in any other case where the order granting development consent authorises the compulsory acquisition of land, the person authorised by the order to compulsorily acquire the land.

(3) After the order has been made, the prospective purchaser must—

[(za) make a copy of the order available, at a place in the vicinity of the land, for inspection by the public at all reasonable hours,][1]

(a) serve a compulsory acquisition notice [...][2] on each person to whom subsection (4) applies, and

(b) affix a compulsory acquisition notice to a conspicuous object or objects on or near the order land.

(4) This subsection applies to any person who, if the order granting development consent were a compulsory purchase order, would be a qualifying person for the purposes of section 12(1) of the Acquisition of Land Act 1981 (c. 67) (notice to owners, lessees and occupiers).

(5) A compulsory acquisition notice which is affixed under subsection (3)(b) must—

(a) be addressed to persons occupying or having an interest in the order land, and

(b) so far as practicable, be kept in place by the prospective purchaser until the end of the period of 6 weeks beginning with the date on which the order is published.

(6) The prospective purchaser must also publish a compulsory acquisition notice in one or more local newspapers circulating in the locality in which the order land is situated.

(7) A compulsory acquisition notice is a notice in the prescribed form—

(a) describing the order land,

(b) in a case where the order granting development consent authorises the compulsory acquisition of a right over land by the creation of a new right, describing the right,

(c) stating that the order granting development consent includes provision authorising the compulsory acquisition of a right over the land by the creation of a right over it or (as the case may be) the compulsory acquisition of the land, [...][3]

[(ca) stating where and when a copy of the order is available for inspection in accordance with subsection (3)(za), and][3]

(d) stating that a person aggrieved by the order may challenge the order only in accordance with section 118.

[...][4]

1 Added by Localism Act 2011, s 142(1), (2)(a) (1 April 2012).
2 Words repealed by Localism Act 2011, ss 142(1), (2)(b), 237, Sch 25, Pt 21 (1 April 2012).
3 Added by Localism Act 2011, s 142(1), (3) (15 January 2012 for the purpose of conferring power on the Secretary of State to make regulations; 1 April 2012 otherwise).
4 Repealed by Localism Act 2011, ss 142(1), (4), 237, Sch 25, Pt 21 (1 April 2012).

Miscellaneous

135 Orders: Crown land

(1) An order granting development consent may include provision authorising the compulsory acquisition of an interest in Crown land only if—

(a) it is an interest which is for the time being held otherwise than by or on behalf of the Crown, and

(b) the appropriate Crown authority consents to the acquisition.

(2) An order granting development consent may include any other provision applying in relation to Crown land, or rights benefiting the Crown, only if the appropriate Crown authority consents to the inclusion of the provision.

(3) The reference in subsection (2) to rights benefiting the Crown does not include rights which benefit the general public.

(4) For the purposes of this section 'the Crown' includes—

(a) the Duchy of Lancaster;

(b) the Duchy of Cornwall;

(c) the Speaker of the House of Lords;

(d) the Speaker of the House of Commons;

(e) the Corporate Officer of the House of Lords;

(f) the Corporate Officer of the House of Commons.

136 Public rights of way

(1) An order granting development consent may extinguish a public right of way over land only if the [Secretary of State][1] is satisfied that—

(a) an alternative right of way has been or will be provided, or

(b) the provision of an alternative right of way is not required.

(2) The following provisions of this section apply if—

(a) an order granting development consent makes provision for the acquisition of land, compulsorily or by agreement,

(b) the order extinguishes a public right of way over the land, and

(c) the right of way is not a right enjoyable by vehicular traffic.

(3) The order granting development consent may not provide for the right of way to be extinguished from a date which is earlier than the date on which the order is published.

(4) Subsection (5) applies if—

(a) the order granting development consent extinguishes the right of way from a date ('the extinguishment date') which is earlier than the date on which the acquisition of the land is completed, and

(b) at any time after the extinguishment date it appears to the [Secretary of State][2] that the proposal to acquire the land has been abandoned.

(5) The [Secretary of State][2] must by order direct that the right is to revive.

[...][3]

(7) Nothing in subsection (5) prevents the making of a further order extinguishing the right of way.

1 Words substituted by Localism Act 2011, s 128(2), Sch 13, paras 1, 66(1), (2) (1 April 2012).
2 Words substituted by Localism Act 2011, s 128(2), Sch 13, paras 1, 66(1), (3) (1 April 2012).
3 Repealed by Localism Act 2011, ss 128(2), 237, Sch 13, paras 1, 66(1), (4), Sch 25, Pt 20 (1 April 2012).

137 ...

Repealed by Growth and Infrastructure Act 2013, s 23(3) (25 June 2013).

138 Extinguishment of rights, and removal of apparatus, of statutory undertakers etc.

(1) This section applies if an order granting development consent authorises the acquisition of land (compulsorily or by agreement) and—

(a) there subsists over the land a relevant right, or

(b) there is on, under or over the land relevant apparatus.

(2) 'Relevant right' means a right of way, or a right of laying down, erecting, continuing or maintaining apparatus on, under or over the land, which—

(a) is vested in or belongs to statutory undertakers for the purpose of the carrying on of their undertaking, or

(b) is conferred by or in accordance with the electronic communications code on the operator of an electronic communications code network.

(3) 'Relevant apparatus' means—

(a) apparatus vested in or belonging to statutory undertakers for the purpose of the carrying on of their undertaking, or

(b) electronic communications apparatus kept installed for the purposes of an electronic communications code network.

(4) The order may include provision for the extinguishment of the relevant right, or the removal of the relevant apparatus, [only if the Secretary of State is satisfied that the extinguishment or removal is necessary for the purpose of carrying out the development to which the order relates.][1]

[(4A) In this section 'statutory undertakers' means persons who are, or are deemed to be, statutory undertakers for the purpose of any provision of Part 11 of TCPA 1990.

(4B) In this section the following terms have the meanings given in paragraph 1(1) of Schedule 17 to the Communications Act 2003— 'electronic communications apparatus'; 'electronic communications code'; 'electronic communications code network'; 'operator'.][2]

[...][3]

1 Words substituted by Growth and Infrastructure Act 2013, s 23(4)(a) (25 June 2013).
2 Added by Growth and Infrastructure Act 2013, s 23(4)(b) (25 June 2013).
3 Repealed by Growth and Infrastructure Act 2013, s 23(4)(c) (25 June 2013).

139 Common land and rights of common

(1) An order granting development consent may not include provision the effect of which is to exclude or modify the application of a provision of or made under the Commons Act 2006, except in accordance with section 131 or 132.

(2) For the purposes of section 38(6)(a) of the Commons Act 2006, works carried out under a power conferred by an order granting development consent are not to be taken to be carried out under a power conferred by or under an enactment, except in a case to which section 131 or 132 applies.

(3) An order granting development consent may not authorise the suspension of, or extinguishment or interference with, registered rights of common, except in accordance with section 131 or 132.

(4) 'Registered rights of common' means rights of common registered under—

(a) the Commons Act 2006, or

(b) the Commons Registration Act 1965.

140 Operation of generating stations

An order granting development consent may include provision authorising the operation of a generating station only if the development to which the order relates is or includes the construction or extension of the generating station.

141 Keeping electric lines installed above ground

An order granting development consent may include provision authorising an electric line to be kept installed above ground only if the development to which the order relates is or includes the installation of the line above ground.

142 Use of underground gas storage facilities

An order granting development consent may include provision authorising the use of underground gas storage facilities only if the development to which the order relates is or includes development within section 17(2), (3) or (5).

143 Diversion of watercourses

(1) An order granting development consent may include provision authorising the diversion of any part of a navigable watercourse only if the condition in subsection (2) is met.

(2) The new length of watercourse must be navigable in a reasonably convenient manner by vessels of a kind that are accustomed to using the part of the watercourse which is to be diverted.

(3) In deciding whether the condition in subsection (2) is met, the effect of any bridge or tunnel must be ignored if the construction of the bridge or tunnel is part of the development for which consent is granted by the order granting development consent.

(4) If an order granting development consent includes provision authorising the diversion of any part of a navigable watercourse, the order is also to be taken to authorise the diversion of any tow path or other way adjacent to that part.

144 Highways

(1) An order granting development consent may include provision authorising the charging of tolls in relation to a highway only if a request to that effect has been included in the application for the order.

(2) If an order granting development consent includes provision authorising the charging of tolls in relation to a highway, the order is treated as a toll order for the purposes of sections 7 to 18 of the New Roads and Street Works Act 1991 (c. 22).

[(2A) Subsection (2) does not apply to an order that includes provision authorising other charges in respect of the use or keeping of motor vehicles on roads.

(2B) In subsection (2A)—

'motor vehicle' has the meaning given in section 185(1) of the Road Traffic Act 1988, except that section 189 of that Act (exceptions: certain pedestrian controlled vehicles and electrically assisted pedal cycles) applies as it applies for the purposes of the Road Traffic Acts;

'road' has the meaning given in section 142(1) of the Road Traffic Regulation Act 1984.][1]

[...][2]

1 Added by Growth and Infrastructure Act 2013, s 27(1), (2) (25 June 2013).
2 Repealed by Growth and Infrastructure Act 2013, s 27(1), (3) (25 June 2013).

145 Harbours

(1) An order granting development consent may include provision for the creation of a harbour authority only if—

(a) the development to which the order relates is or includes the construction or alteration of harbour facilities, and

(b) the creation of a harbour authority is necessary or expedient for the purposes of the development.

(2) An order granting development consent may include provision changing the powers or duties of a harbour authority only if—

(a) the development to which the order relates is or includes the construction or alteration of harbour facilities, and

(b) the authority has requested the inclusion of the provision or has consented in writing to its inclusion.

(3) An order granting development consent may include provision authorising the transfer of property, rights or liabilities from one harbour authority to another only if—

(a) the development to which the order relates is or includes the construction or alteration of harbour facilities, and

(b) the order makes provision for the payment of compensation of an amount—

(i) determined in accordance with the order, or

(ii) agreed between the parties to the transfer.

(4) An order granting development consent which includes provision for the creation of a harbour authority, or changing the powers or duties of a harbour authority, may also make other provision in relation to the authority.

This is subject to subsection (6).

(5) Subject to subsection (6), the provision which may be included in relation to a harbour authority includes in particular—

(a) any provision in relation to a harbour authority which could be included in a harbour revision order under section 14 of the Harbours Act 1964 (c. 40) by virtue of any provision of Schedule 2 to that Act;

(b) provision conferring power on the authority to change provision made in relation to it (by the order or by virtue of this paragraph), where the provision is about—

(i) the procedures (including financial procedures) of the authority;

(ii) the power of the authority to impose charges;

(iii) the power of the authority to delegate any of its functions;

(iv) the welfare of officers and employees of the authority and financial and other provision made for them.

(6) The order may not include provision—

(a) which, by virtue of any other provision of this Act, is not permitted to be included in an order granting development consent;

(b) conferring power on a harbour authority to delegate, or makes changes to its powers so as to permit the delegation of, any of the functions mentioned in paragraphs (a) to (f) of paragraph 9B of Schedule 2 to the Harbours Act 1964.

146 Discharge of water

(1) This section applies if—

(a) an order granting development consent includes provision authorising the discharge of water into inland waters or underground strata, and

(b) but for the order, the person to whom development consent is granted would have had no power to take water, or to require discharges to be made, from the inland waters or other source from which the discharges authorised by the order are intended to be made.

(2) The order does not have the effect of conferring any such power on that person.

147 Development of Green Belt land

(1) This section applies if an order granting development consent includes provision—

(a) authorising the acquisition of Green Belt land, compulsorily or by agreement,

(b) authorising the sale, exchange or appropriation of Green Belt land, or

(c) freeing land from any restriction imposed upon it by or under the Green Belt (London and Home Counties) Act 1938 (c. xciii), or by a covenant or other agreement entered into for the purposes of that Act.

(2) The [Secretary of State][1] must notify the relevant local authorities of the provision made by the order.

[…][2]

(4) The relevant local authorities are—

(a) each local authority in whose area all or part of the land is situated,

(b) any local authority in whom all or part of the land is vested, and

(c) each contributing local authority.

(5) In this section 'local authority' and 'contributing local authority' have the same meanings as in the Green Belt (London and Home Counties) Act 1938 (c. xciii) (see section 2(1) of that Act).

1 Words substituted by Localism Act 2011, s 128(2), Sch 13, paras 1, 68(1), (2) (1 April 2012).
2 Repealed by Localism Act 2011, ss 128(2), 237, Sch 13, paras 1, 68(1), (3), Sch 25, Pt 20 (1 April 2012).

148, 149 …

Repealed by Marine and Coastal Access Act 2009, s 321, Sch 22, Pt 2 (6 April 2011).

[149A Deemed consent under a marine licence

(1) An order granting development consent may include provision deeming a marine licence to have been issued under Part 4 of the Marine and Coastal Access Act 2009 (marine licensing) for any activity only if the activity is to be carried out wholly in one or more of the areas specified in subsection (2).

(2) The areas are—

(a) England,

(b) waters adjacent to England up to the seaward limits of the territorial sea,

(c) an exclusive economic zone, except any part of an exclusive economic zone in relation to which the Scottish Ministers have functions,

(d) a Renewable Energy Zone, except any part of a Renewable Energy Zone in relation to which the Scottish Ministers have functions,

(e) an area designated under section 1(7) of the Continental Shelf Act 1964, except any part of that area which is within a part of an exclusive economic zone or Renewable Energy Zone in relation to which the Scottish Ministers have functions.

(3) Subsections (4) and (5) apply if an order granting development consent includes provision—

(a) deeming a marine licence to have been granted under Part 4 of the Marine and Coastal Access Act 2009 subject to specified conditions, and

(b) deeming those conditions to have been attached to the marine licence by the Secretary of State under that Part.

(4) A person who fails to comply with such a condition does not commit an offence under section 161 of this Act.

(5) Sections 68 (notice of applications) and 69(3) and (5) (representations) of the Marine and Coastal Access Act 2009 do not apply in relation to the deemed marine licence.][1]

1 Added by Marine and Coastal Access Act 2009, s 112(1), Sch 8, para 4(1), (2) (6 April 2011).

150 Removal of consent requirements

(1) An order granting development consent may include provision the effect of which is to remove a requirement for a prescribed consent or authorisation to be granted, only if the relevant body has consented to the inclusion of the provision.

(2) 'The relevant body' is the person or body which would otherwise be required to grant the prescribed consent or authorisation.

151 Liability under existing regimes

An order granting development consent may not include provision the effect of which is to exclude or modify the application of—

(a) any provision of the Nuclear Installations Act 1965 (c. 57);

(b) section 28 of, and Schedule 2 to, the Reservoirs Act 1975 (c. 23) (liability for damage and injury due to escape of water from a reservoir constructed after 1930);

(c) section 209 of the Water Industry Act 1991 (c. 56) (civil liability of water undertakers for escapes of water from pipes);

(d) section 48A of the Water Resources Act 1991 (c. 57) (civil remedies for loss or damage due to water abstraction).

152 Compensation in case where no right to claim in nuisance

(1) This section applies if, by virtue of section 158 or an order granting development consent, there is a defence of statutory authority in civil or criminal proceedings for nuisance in respect of any authorised works.

(2) 'Authorised works' are—

(a) development for which consent is granted by an order granting development consent;

(b) anything else authorised by an order granting development consent.

(3) A person by whom or on whose behalf any authorised works are carried out must pay compensation to any person whose land is injuriously affected by the carrying out of the works.

(4) A dispute as to whether compensation under subsection (3) is payable, or as to the amount of the compensation, must be referred to the [Upper Tribunal][1].

(5) Subsection (2) of section 10 of the Compulsory Purchase Act 1965 (c. 56) (limitation on compensation) applies to subsection (3) of this section as it applies to that section.

(6) Any rule or principle applied to the construction of section 10 of that Act must be applied to the construction of subsection (3) of this section (with any necessary modifications).

(7) Part 1 of the Land Compensation Act 1973 (c. 26) (compensation for depreciation of land value by physical factors caused by use of public works) applies in relation to authorised works as if—

(a) references in that Part to any public works were to any authorised works;

(b) references in that Part to the responsible authority were to the person for whose benefit the order granting development consent has effect for the time being;

(c) sections 1(6) and 17 were omitted.

(8) An order granting development consent may not include provision the effect of which is to remove or modify the application of any of subsections (1) to (7).

1 Words substituted by Transfer of Tribunal Functions (Lands Tribunal and Miscellaneous Amendments) Order 2009, SI 2009/1307, art 5(1), (2), Sch 1, paras 291, 293 (1 March 2010: substitution came into force on 1 June 2009 but could not take effect until the commencement of Planning Act 2008, s 152(4) on 1 March 2010).

Chapter 2 Changes to, and revocation of, orders

153 Changes to, and revocation of, orders granting development consent

Schedule 6 (changes to, and revocation of, orders granting development consent) has effect.

Chapter 3 General

154 Duration of order granting development consent

(1) Development for which development consent is granted must be begun before the end of—

(a) the prescribed period, or

(b) such other period (whether longer or shorter than that prescribed) as is specified in the order granting the consent.

(2) If the development is not begun before the end of the period applicable under subsection (1), the order granting development consent ceases to have effect at the end of that period.

(3) Where an order granting development consent authorises the compulsory acquisition of land, steps of a prescribed description must be taken in relation to the compulsory acquisition before the end of—

(a) the prescribed period, or

(b) such other period (whether longer or shorter than that prescribed) as is specified in the order.

(4) If steps of the prescribed description are not taken before the end of the period applicable under subsection (3), the authority to compulsorily acquire the land under the order ceases to have effect.

155 When development begins

(1) For the purposes of this Act (except Part 11) development is taken to begin on the earliest date on which any material operation comprised in, or carried out for the purposes of, the development begins to be carried out.

(2) 'Material operation' means any operation except an operation of a prescribed description.

156 Benefit of order granting development consent

(1) If an order granting development consent is made in respect of any land, the order has effect for the benefit of the land and all persons for the time being interested in the land.

(2) Subsection (1) is subject to subsection (3) and any contrary provision made in the order.

(3) To the extent that the development for which development consent is granted is development within section 17(3), the order granting the consent has effect for the benefit of a person for the time being interested in the land only if the person is a gas transporter.

157 Use of buildings in respect of which development consent granted

(1) If development consent is granted for development which includes the erection, extension, alteration or re-erection of a building, the order granting consent may specify the purposes for which the building is authorised to be used.

(2) If no purpose is so specified, the consent is taken to authorise the use of the building for the purpose for which it is designed.

158 Nuisance: statutory authority

(1) This subsection confers statutory authority for—

(a) carrying out development for which consent is granted by an order granting development consent;

(b) doing anything else authorised by an order granting development consent.

(2) Statutory authority under subsection (1) is conferred only for the purpose of providing a defence in civil or criminal proceedings for nuisance.

(3) Subsections (1) and (2) are subject to any contrary provision made in any particular case by an order granting development consent.

159 Interpretation: land and rights over land

(1) This section applies for the purposes of this Part.

(2) 'Land' includes any interest in or right over land.

(3) Acquiring a right over land includes acquiring it by the creation of a new right as well as by the acquisition of an existing one.

Part 8 Enforcement

Offences

160 Development without development consent

(1) A person commits an offence if the person carries out, or causes to be carried out, development for which development consent is required at a time when no development consent is in force in respect of the development.

(2) A person guilty of an offence under this section is liable—

(a) on summary conviction, to a fine not exceeding £50,000, or

(b) on conviction on indictment, to a fine.

(3) The Secretary of State may by order amend subsection (2)(a) to increase the level of the fine for the time being specified in that provision.

161 Breach of terms of order granting development consent

(1) A person commits an offence if without reasonable excuse the person—

(a) carries out, or causes to be carried out, development in breach of the terms of an order granting development consent, or

(b) otherwise fails to comply with the terms of an order granting development consent.

(2) Subsection (1) is subject to [section 149A(4)][1].

(3) It is a defence for a person charged with an offence under this section to prove that—

(a) the breach or failure to comply occurred only because of an error or omission in the order, and

(b) a correction notice specifying the correction of the error or omission has been issued under paragraph 2 of Schedule 4.

(4) A person guilty of an offence under this section is liable—

(a) on summary conviction, to a fine not exceeding £50,000, or

(b) on conviction on indictment, to a fine.

(5) The Secretary of State may by order amend subsection (4)(a) to increase the level of the fine for the time being specified in that provision.

1 Words substituted by Marine and Coastal Access Act 2009, s 112(1), Sch 8, para 4(1), (3) (6 April 2011).

162 Time limits

(1) A person may not be charged with an offence under section 160 or 161 after the end of—

(a) the relevant 4-year period, or

(b) if subsection (3) applies, the extended period.

(2) The 'relevant 4-year period' means—

(a) in the case of an offence under section 160, the period of 4 years beginning with the date on which the development was substantially completed;

(b) in the case of an offence under section 161, the period of 4 years beginning with the later of—

(i) the date on which the development was substantially completed, and

(ii) the date on which the breach or failure to comply occurred.

(3) This subsection applies if during the relevant 4-year period—

(a) an information notice has been served under section 167, or

(b) an injunction has been applied for under section 171.

(4) The 'extended period' means the period of 4 years beginning with—

(a) the date of service of the information notice, if subsection (3)(a) applies;

(b) the date of the application for the injunction, if subsection (3)(b) applies;

(c) the later (or latest) of those dates, if both paragraphs (a) and (b) of subsection (3) apply.

Rights of entry

163 Right to enter without warrant

(1) This section applies in relation to any land if the relevant local planning authority has reasonable grounds for suspecting that an offence under section 160 or 161 is being, or has been, committed on or in respect of the land.

(2) A person authorised in writing by the relevant local planning authority may at any reasonable hour enter the land for the purpose of ascertaining whether an offence under section 160 or 161 is being, or has been, committed on the land.

(3) A person may enter a building used as a dwelling-house under subsection (2) only if 24 hours' notice of the intended entry has been given to the occupier of the building.

164 Right to enter under warrant

(1) This section applies if it is shown to the satisfaction of a justice of the peace on sworn information in writing—

(a) that there are reasonable grounds for suspecting that an offence under section 160 or 161 is being, or has been, committed on or in respect of any land, and

(b) that the condition in subsection (2) is met.

(2) The condition is that—

(a) admission to the land has been refused, or a refusal is reasonably apprehended, or

(b) the case is one of urgency.

(3) The justice of the peace may issue a warrant authorising any person who is authorised in writing for the purpose by the relevant local planning authority to enter the land.

(4) For the purposes of subsection (2)(a) admission to land is to be regarded as having been refused if no reply is received to a request for admission within a reasonable period.

(5) A warrant authorises entry on one occasion only and that entry must be—

(a) before the end of the period of one month beginning with the date of the issue of the warrant, and

(b) at a reasonable hour, unless the case is one of urgency.

165 Rights of entry: supplementary provisions

(1) A person authorised to enter land in pursuance of a right of entry conferred under or by virtue of section 163 or 164 ('a relevant right of entry')—

(a) must, if so required, produce evidence of the authority and state the purpose of entry before entering the land,

(b) may take on to the land such other persons as may be necessary, and

(c) must, if the person leaves the land at a time when the owner or occupier is not present, leave it as effectively secured against trespassers as it was found.

(2) A person commits an offence if the person wilfully obstructs a person acting in the exercise of a relevant right of entry.

(3) A person guilty of an offence under subsection (2) is liable on summary conviction to a fine not exceeding level 3 on the standard scale.

(4) If any damage is caused to land or chattels in the exercise of a relevant right of entry, compensation may be recovered by any person suffering the damage from the local planning authority that authorised the entry.

(5) Except so far as otherwise provided by regulations, any question of disputed compensation under subsection (4) is to be referred to and determined by the [Upper Tribunal][1].

(6) In relation to the determination of any such question, the provisions of [section 4 of the Land Compensation Act 1961 (c. 33)][2] apply subject to any necessary modifications and to any other prescribed modifications.

1 Words substituted by Transfer of Tribunal Functions (Lands Tribunal and Miscellaneous Amendments) Order 2009, SI 2009/1307, art 5(1), (2), Sch 1, paras 291, 294(a) (1 March 2010: substitution came into force on 1 June 2009 but could not take effect until the commencement of the Planning Act 2008, s 165(5) on 1 March 2010).

2 Words substituted by Transfer of Tribunal Functions (Lands Tribunal and Miscellaneous Amendments) Order 2009, SI 2009/1307, art 5(1), (2), Sch 1, paras 291, 294(b) (1 March 2010: substitution came into force on 1 June 2009 but could not take effect until the commencement of the Planning Act 2008, s 165(5) on 1 March 2010).

166 Rights of entry: Crown land

Sections 163 and 164 do not apply to Crown land.

Information notices

167 Power to require information

(1) This section applies in relation to any land if it appears to the relevant local planning authority that an offence under section 160 or 161 may have been committed on or in respect of the land.

(2) The relevant local planning authority may serve an information notice.

(3) The information notice may be served on any person who—

(a) is the owner or occupier of the land or has any other interest in it, or

(b) is carrying out operations on the land or is using it for any purpose.

(4) The information notice may require the person on whom it is served to give such of the following information as may be specified in the notice—

(a) information about any operations being carried out in, on, over or under the land, any use of the land and any other activities being carried out in, on, over or under the land, and

(b) information about the provisions of any order granting development consent for development of the land.

(5) An information notice must inform the person on whom it is served of the likely consequences of a failure to respond to the notice.

(6) A requirement of an information notice is complied with by giving the required information to the relevant local planning authority in writing.

168 Offences relating to information notices

(1) A person commits an offence if without reasonable excuse the person fails to comply with any requirement of an information notice served under section 167 before the end of the period mentioned in subsection (2)

(2) The period referred to in subsection (1) is the period of 21 days beginning with the day on which the information notice is served.

(3) A person guilty of an offence under subsection (1) is liable on summary conviction to a fine not exceeding level 3 on the standard scale.

(4) A person commits an offence if the person—

(a) makes any statement purporting to comply with a requirement of an information notice which he knows to be false or misleading in a material respect, or

(b) recklessly makes such a statement which is false or misleading in a material respect.

(5) A person guilty of an offence under subsection (4) is liable on summary conviction to a fine not exceeding level 5 on the standard scale.

Notices of unauthorised development

169 Notice of unauthorised development

(1) Subsection (2) applies if a person is found guilty of an offence under section 160 committed on or in respect of any land.

(2) The relevant local planning authority may serve a notice of unauthorised development on the person requiring such steps as may be specified in the notice to be taken—

(a) to remove the development, and

(b) to restore the land on which the development has been carried out to its condition before the development was carried out.

(3) Subsection (4) applies if a person is found guilty of an offence under section 161 committed on or in respect of any land.

(4) The relevant local planning authority may serve a notice of unauthorised development on the person requiring the person to remedy the breach or failure to comply.

(5) A notice of unauthorised development—

(a) must specify the period within which any steps are required to be taken, and

(b) may specify different periods for different steps.

(6) Where different periods apply to different steps, references in this Part to the period for compliance with a notice of unauthorised development, in relation to any step, are to the period within which the step is required to be taken.

(7) A notice of unauthorised development must specify such additional matters as may be prescribed.

170 Execution of works required by notice of unauthorised development

(1) If any of the steps specified in a notice of unauthorised development have not been taken before the end of the period for compliance with the notice, the relevant local planning authority may—

(a) enter the land on which the development has been carried out and take those steps, and

(b) recover from the person who is then the owner of the land any expenses reasonably incurred by it in doing so.

(2) Where a notice of unauthorised development has been served in respect of development—

(a) any expenses incurred by the owner or occupier of the land for the purposes of complying with it, and

(b) any sums paid by the owner of the land under subsection (1) in respect of expenses incurred by the relevant local planning authority in taking steps required by it,

are to be deemed to be incurred or paid for the use and at the request of the person found guilty of the offence under section 160 or 161.

(3) Regulations may provide that all or any of the following sections of the Public Health Act 1936 (c. 49) are to apply, subject to such adaptations and modifications as may be specified in the regulations, in relation to any steps required to be taken by a notice of unauthorised development—

section 276 (power of local authorities to sell materials removed in executing works under that Act subject to accounting for the proceeds of sale);

section 289 (power to require the occupier of any premises to permit works to be executed by the owner of the premises);

section 294 (limit on liability of persons holding premises as agents or trustees in respect of the expenses recoverable under that Act).

(4) Regulations under subsection (3) applying all or any of section 289 of that Act may include adaptations and modifications for the purpose of giving the owner of land to which such a notice relates the right, as against all other persons interested in the land, to comply with the requirements of the notice.

(5) Regulations under subsection (3) may also provide for the charging on the land on which the development is carried out of any expenses recoverable by the relevant local planning authority under subsection (1).

(6) A person commits an offence if the person wilfully obstructs a person acting in the exercise of powers under subsection (1).

(7) A person guilty of an offence under subsection (6) is liable on summary conviction to a fine not exceeding level 3 on the standard scale.

Injunctions

171 Injunctions

(1) A local planning authority may apply to the court for an injunction if it considers it necessary or expedient for any actual or apprehended prohibited activity to be restrained by injunction.

(2) Prohibited activity means activity that constitutes an offence under section 160 or 161 in relation to land in the area of the local planning authority.

(3) On an application under this section the court may grant such an injunction as the court thinks fit for the purpose of restraining the prohibited activity.

(4) In this section 'the court' means the High Court or [the county court][1].

1 Words substituted by Crime and Courts Act 2013, s 17(5), Sch 9, para 52(1)(b), (2) (22 April 2014: subject to transitional provision specified in Crime and Courts Act 2013 (Commencement No. 10 and Transitional Provision) Order 2014, SI 2014/954, art 3).

Isles of Scilly

172 Isles of Scilly

(1) The Secretary of State may by order provide for the exercise by the Council of the Isles of Scilly in relation to land in the Council's area of any functions exercisable by a local planning authority under any provision of this Part.

(2) Before making an order under this section the Secretary of State must consult the Council of the Isles of Scilly.

The relevant local planning authority

173 The relevant local planning authority

(1) This section applies for the purposes of this Part.

(2) The relevant local planning authority in relation to any land is the local planning authority for the area in which the land is situated. This is subject to subsections (3) to (5).

(3) Subsections (4) and (5) apply if the land is in an area for which there is both a district planning authority and a county planning authority.

(4) If any of the relevant development is the construction or alteration of a hazardous waste facility within section 14(1)(p), the relevant local planning authority is the county planning authority.

(5) In any other case, the relevant local planning authority is the district planning authority.

(6) 'The relevant development' is—

  (a) if the relevant offence is an offence under section 160 or 161(1)(a), the development referred to in section 160(1) or 161(1)(a);

  (b) if the relevant offence is an offence under section 161(1)(b), the development to which the order granting development consent mentioned in section 161(1)(b) relates.

(7) 'The relevant offence' is the offence by reference to which a provision of this Part confers a function on a local planning authority.

Part 9 Changes to existing planning regimes

Chapter 1 Changes related to development consent regime

174–177 ...

Amend Town and Country Planning Act 1990 and Town and Country Planning (Scotland) Act 1997.

Grants

178 Grants for advice and assistance: Scotland

(1) The Secretary of State may make grants for the purpose of assisting any person to provide advice and assistance in connection with any matter which is related to the application of this Act to Scotland.

(2) The Secretary of State may, as respects any such grant, provide that it is to be subject to such terms and conditions as the Secretary of State thinks appropriate.

179 ...

Repealed by Local Democracy, Economic Development and Construction Act 2009, s 146(1), Sch 7, Pt 4 (1 April 2010 as SI 2009/3318).

Chapter 2 Other changes to existing planning regimes

180 ...

Amends Planning and Compulsory Purchase Act 2004.

181 ...

Repealed by Local Democracy, Economic Development and Construction Act 2009, s 146(1), Sch 7, Pt 4 (1 April 2010 as SI 2009/3318).

182-186 ...

Amend Planning and Compulsory Purchase Act 2004.

Determination of applications

187 Power to decline to determine applications: amendments

Schedule 7 (power to decline to determine applications: amendments) has effect.

188–192 ...

Amend Town and Country Planning Act 1990.

Trees

193 Existing tree preservation orders: transitional provision

(1) This section applies to a tree preservation order made before the appointed day.

(2) With effect from the beginning of the appointed day, a tree preservation order to which this section applies shall have effect with the omission of all of its provisions other than any that have effect for the purpose of identifying the order or for the purpose of identifying the trees, groups of trees or woodlands in respect of which the order—

(a) is in force, or

(b) may at any later time be in force.

(3) In this section—

'the appointed day'—

(a) in relation to England means the day on which subsection (1) comes fully into force in relation to England, and

(b) in relation to Wales means the day on which subsection (1) comes fully into force in relation to Wales;

'tree preservation order' means an order made under, or an order having effect as if made under, section 198(1) of TCPA 1990.

Use of land

194 Use of land: power to override easements and other rights

(1) Schedule 9 (use of land: power to override easements and other rights when use is in accordance with planning permission) has effect.

(2) The Welsh Ministers may by order amend Schedule 4 to the Welsh Development Agency Act 1975 (c. 70) for the purpose of authorising the use in accordance with planning permission of land acquired under section 21A of that Act, even if the use involves—

(a) interference with an interest or right to which paragraph 6 of that Schedule applies, or

(b) a breach of a restriction as to the user of land arising by virtue of a contract.

(3) The power to make an order under subsection (2) is exercisable by statutory instrument.

(4) The power includes—

(a) power to make different provision for different purposes (including different areas);

(b) power to make incidental, consequential, supplementary, transitional or transitory provision or savings.

(5) No order may be made under subsection (2) unless a draft of the instrument containing the order has been laid before, and approved by resolution of, the National Assembly for Wales.

195–196 ...

Amend Town and Country Planning Act 1990, Planning (Listed Buildings and Conservation Areas) Act 1990 and Planning (Hazardous Substances) Act 1990.

Appeals

197 Appeals: miscellaneous amendments

Schedule 11 (appeals: miscellaneous amendments) has effect.

198–201 ...

Amend Town and Country Planning Act 1990 and Planning and Compensation Act 1991.

Part 10 Wales

202 ...

Amends Government of Wales Act 2006.

203 Power to make provision in relation to Wales

(1) The Welsh Ministers may by order make provision—

(a) which has an effect in relation to Wales that corresponds to the effect an England-only provision has in relation to England;

(b) conferring power on the Welsh Ministers to do anything in relation to Wales that corresponds to anything the Secretary of State has power to do by virtue of an England-only provision.

(2) The England-only provisions are—

section 184 (correction of errors in decisions);

section 189 (compensation where development order or local development order withdrawn);

section 190 (power to make non-material changes to planning permission);

section 194(1) and Schedule 9 (use of land: power to override easements and other rights);

section 195 (applications and appeals by statutory undertakers);

section 196 and Schedule 10 (determination of procedure for certain proceedings);

paragraphs 2(3) and (4) and 3(3) of Schedule 7.

(3) Before an England-only provision is brought into force—

(a) the reference in subsection (1)(a) to the effect an England-only provision has is to be read as a reference to the effect the provision would have, if it were in force;

(b) the reference in subsection (1)(b) to anything the Secretary of State has power to do by virtue of an England-only provision is to be read as a reference to anything the Secretary of State would have power to do by virtue of the provision, if it were in force.

(4) The Welsh Ministers may by order make provision for the purpose of reversing the effect of any provision made in exercise of the power conferred by subsection (1).

(5) The Secretary of State may make an order in consequence of an order under subsection (1) for the purpose of ensuring that an England-only provision continues to have (or will when brought into force have) the effect in relation to England that it would have had if the order under subsection (1) had not been made.

(6) An order under this section may amend, repeal, revoke or otherwise modify a provision of—

(a) an Act, or

(b) an instrument made under an Act.

(7) The powers of the Welsh Ministers to make orders under this section are exercisable by statutory instrument.

(8) Those powers include—

(a) power to make different provision for different purposes (including different areas);

(b) power to make incidental, consequential, supplementary, transitional or transitory provision or savings.

(9) No order may be made by the Welsh Ministers under this section unless a draft of the instrument containing the order has been laid before, and approved by resolution of, the National Assembly for Wales.

204 Wales: transitional provision in relation to blighted land

(1) During the transitional period the repeal by PCPA 2004 of paragraphs 1 to 4 of Schedule 13 to TCPA 1990 in relation to Wales is subject to subsection (2).

(2) That repeal does not affect anything which is required or permitted to be done for the purposes of Chapter 2 of Part 6 of TCPA 1990 (interests affected by planning proposals: blight) in relation to land falling within any of paragraphs 1, 2, 3 and 4 of Schedule 13 to TCPA 1990.

(3) The transitional period is the period during which—

(a) in the case of land falling within paragraph 1 of Schedule 13 to TCPA 1990, a structure plan continues to be or to be comprised in the development plan for an area in Wales by virtue of Part 3 of Schedule 5 to the Local Government (Wales) Act 1994 (c. 19) and Part 1A of Schedule 2 to TCPA 1990;

(b) in the case of land falling within paragraph 2 of Schedule 13 to TCPA 1990, a local plan continues to be or to be comprised in the development plan for an area in Wales by virtue of Part 3 of Schedule 5 to the Local Government (Wales) Act 1994 and Part 1A of Schedule 2 to TCPA 1990;

(c) in the case of land falling within paragraphs 3 or 4 of Schedule 13 to TCPA 1990, a unitary development plan continues to form part of the development plan for an area in Wales by virtue of article 3(1) and (2) of the PCPA No.6 Order 2005.

(4) In this section 'PCPA No.6 Order 2005' means the Planning and Compulsory Purchase Act 2004 (Commencement No.6, Transitional Provisions and Savings) Order 2005 (S.I. 2005/2847).

(5) This section is deemed to have come into force on the same day as the repeal of paragraphs 1 to 4 of Schedule 13 to TCPA 1990 came into force in relation to Wales (see Article 2(e) and (g) of the PCPA No.6 Order 2005).

Part 11 Community Infrastructure Levy

205 The levy

(1) The Secretary of State may with the consent of the Treasury make regulations providing for the imposition of a charge to be known as Community Infrastructure Levy (CIL).

(2) In making the regulations the Secretary of State shall aim to ensure that the overall purpose of CIL is to ensure that costs incurred in [supporting][1] the development of an area can be funded (wholly or partly) by owners or developers of land [in a way that does not make development of the area economically unviable][2].

(3) The Table describes the provisions of this Part.

Section	**Topic**
Section 206	The charge
Section 207	Joint committees
Sections 208 and 209	Liability
Section 210	Charities
Section 211	Amount
Sections 212 to 214	Charging schedule
Section 215	Appeals
[Sections 216 to 216B][3]	Application
Section 217	Collection
Section 218	Enforcement
Section 219	Compensation
Section 220	Procedure
Section 221	Secretary of State
Section 222	CIL regulations and orders: general
Section 223	Relationship with other powers
Section 224	Amendments
Section 225	Repeals

(4) In those sections regulations under this section are referred to as 'CIL regulations'.

1 Words substituted by Localism Act 2011, s 115(1), (2)(a) (15 January 2012 subject to transitional and savings provisions specified in SI 2012/57, arts 6, 7, 9, 10 and 11).
2 Words inserted by Localism Act 2011, s 115(1), (2)(b) (15 January 2012 subject to transitional and savings provisions specified in SI 2012/57, arts 6, 7, 9, 10 and 11).
3 Words substituted by Localism Act 2011, s 115(1), (3) (15 January 2012 subject to transitional and savings provisions specified in SI 2012/57, arts 6, 7, 9, 10 and 11).

206 The charge

(1) A charging authority may charge CIL in respect of development of land in its area.

(2) A local planning authority is the charging authority for its area.

(3) But—

(a) the Mayor of London is a charging authority for Greater London (in addition to the local planning authorities),

(b) the Broads Authority is the only charging authority for the Broads (within the meaning given by section 2(3) of the Norfolk and Suffolk Broads Act 1988 (c. 4)), and

(c) the Council of the Isles of Scilly is the only charging authority for the Isles of Scilly.

(4) CIL regulations may provide for any of the following to be the charging authority for an area, or in the case of Greater London one of the charging authorities, in place of the charging authority under subsection (2), (3)(b) or (c)—

(a) a county council,

(b) a county borough council,

(c) a district council,

(d) a metropolitan district council, and

(e) a London borough council (within the meaning of TCPA 1990).

(5) In this section, 'local planning authority' has the meaning given by—

(a) section 37 of PCPA 2004 in relation to England, [except that a Mayoral development corporation is a local planning authority for the purposes of this section only if it is the local planning authority for all purposes of Part 2 of PCPA 2004 in respect of the whole of its area and all kinds of development,][1] and

(b) section 78 of PCPA 2004 in relation to Wales.

[(6) CIL regulations may make transitional provision in connection with, or in anticipation of, a Mayoral development corporation—

(a) becoming a charging authority as a result of the operation of subsection (2), or

(b) ceasing to be a charging authority as a result of the operation of that subsection.][2]

1 Words inserted by Localism Act 2011, s 222, Sch 22, paras 59, 61(2) (15 January 2012).
2 Added by Localism Act 2011, s 222, Sch 22, paras 59, 61(3) (15 January 2012).

207 Joint committees

(1) This section applies if a joint committee that includes a charging authority is established under section 29 of PCPA 2004.

(2) CIL regulations may provide that the joint committee is to exercise specified functions, in respect of the area specified in the agreement under section 29(1) of PCPA 2004, on behalf of the charging authority.

(3) The regulations may make provision corresponding to provisions relating to joint committees in Part 6 of the Local Government Act 1972 (c. 70) in respect of the discharge of the specified functions.

208 Liability

(1) Where liability to CIL would arise in respect of proposed development (in accordance with provision made by a charging authority under and by virtue of section 206 and CIL regulations) a person may assume liability to pay the levy.

(2) An assumption of liability—

(a) may be made before development commences, and

(b) must be made in accordance with any provision of CIL regulations about the procedure for assuming liability.

(3) A person who assumes liability for CIL before the commencement of development becomes liable when development is commenced in reliance on planning permission.

(4) CIL regulations must make provision for an owner or developer of land to be liable for CIL where development is commenced in reliance on planning permission if—

(a) nobody has assumed liability in accordance with the regulations, or

(b) other specified circumstances arise (such as the insolvency or withdrawal of a person who has assumed liability).

(5) CIL regulations may make provision about—

(a) joint liability (with or without several liability);

(b) liability of partnerships;

(c) assumption of partial liability (and subsection (4)(a) applies where liability has not been wholly assumed);

(d) apportionment of liability (which may—

(i) include provision for referral to a specified person or body for determination, and

(ii) include provision for appeals);

(e) withdrawal of assumption of liability;

(f) cancellation of assumption of liability by a charging authority (in which case subsection (4)(a) applies);

(g) transfer of liability (whether before or after development commences and whether or not liability has been assumed).

(6) The amount of any liability for CIL is to be calculated by reference to the time when planning permission first permits the development as a result of which the levy becomes payable.

(7) CIL regulations may make provision for liability for CIL to arise where development which requires planning permission is commenced without it (and subsection (6) is subject to this subsection).

(8) CIL regulations may provide for liability to CIL to arise in respect of a development where—

(a) the development was exempt from CIL, or subject to a reduced rate of CIL charge, and

(b) the description or purpose of the development changes.

209 Liability: interpretation of key terms

(1) In section 208 'development' means—

(a) anything done by way of or for the purpose of the creation of a new building, or

(b) anything done to or in respect of an existing building.

(2) CIL regulations may provide for—

(a) works or changes in use of a specified kind not to be treated as development;

(b) the creation of, or anything done to or in respect of, a structure of a specified kind to be treated as development.

(3) CIL regulations must include provision for determining when development is treated as commencing.

(4) Regulations under subsection (3) may, in particular, provide for development to be treated as commencing when some specified activity or event is undertaken or occurs, where the activity or event—

(a) is not development within the meaning of subsection (1), but

(b) has a specified kind of connection with a development within the meaning of that subsection.

(5) CIL regulations must define planning permission (which may include planning permission within the meaning of TCPA 1990 and any other kind of permission or consent (however called, and whether general or specific)).

(6) CIL regulations must include provision for determining the time at which planning permission is treated as first permitting development; and the regulations may, in particular, make provision—

(a) about outline planning permission;

(b) for permission to be treated as having been given at a particular time in the case of general consents.

(7) For the purposes of section 208—

(a) 'owner' of land means a person who owns an interest in the land, and

(b) 'developer' means a person who is wholly or partly responsible for carrying out a development.

(8) CIL regulations may make provision for a person to be or not to be treated as an owner or developer of land in specified circumstances.

210 Charities

(1) CIL regulations must provide for an exemption from liability to pay CIL in respect of a development where—

(a) the person who would otherwise be liable to pay CIL in respect of the development is a relevant charity in England and Wales, and

(b) the building or structure in respect of which CIL liability would otherwise arise is to be used wholly or mainly for a charitable purpose of the charity within the meaning of [section 2 of the Charities Act 2011][1].

(2) CIL regulations may—

(a) provide for an exemption from liability to pay CIL where the person who would otherwise be liable to pay CIL in respect of the development is an institution established for a charitable purpose;

(b) require charging authorities to make arrangements for an exemption from, or reduction in, liability to pay CIL where the person who would otherwise be liable to pay CIL in respect of the development is an institution established for a charitable purpose.

(3) Regulations under subsection (1) or (2) may provide that an exemption or reduction does not apply if specified conditions are satisfied.

(4) For the purposes of subsection (1), a relevant charity in England and Wales is an institution which—

(a) is registered in the register of charities kept by the Charity Commission under [section 29 of the Charities Act 2011][2], or

(b) is a charity within the meaning of [section 1(1) of the Charities Act 2011 but is not required to be registered in the register kept under section 29 of that Act][3].

(5) In subsection (2), a charitable purpose is a purpose falling within [section 3(1) of the Charities Act 2011;][4] but CIL regulations may provide for an institution of a specified kind to be, or not to be, treated as an institution established for a charitable purpose.

1 Words substituted by Charities Act 2011, 354(1), Sch 7, para 136(1), (2) (14 March 2012: substitution has effect subject to transitional provisions and savings specified in Charities Act 2011, s 354(1), (2), Sch 7, para 2, Sch 8).
2 Words substituted by Charities Act 2011, 354(1), Sch 7, para 136(1), (3)(a) (14 March 2012: substitution has effect subject to transitional provisions and savings specified in Charities Act 2011, s 354(1), (2), Sch 7, para 2, Sch 8).
3 Words substituted by Charities Act 2011, 354(1), Sch 7, para 136(1), (3)(b) (14 March 2012: substitution has effect subject to transitional provisions and savings specified in Charities Act 2011, s 354(1), (2), Sch 7, para 2, Sch 8).
4 Words substituted by Charities Act 2011, 354(1), Sch 7, para 136(1), (4) (14 March 2012: substitution has effect subject to transitional provisions and savings specified in Charities Act 2011, s 354(1), (2), Sch 7, para 2, Sch 8).

211 Amount

(1) A charging authority which proposes to charge CIL must issue a document (a 'charging schedule') setting rates, or other criteria, by reference to which the amount of CIL chargeable in respect of development in its area is to be determined.

(2) A charging authority, in setting rates or other criteria, must have regard, to the extent and in the manner specified by CIL regulations, to—

(a) actual and expected costs of infrastructure (whether by reference to lists prepared by virtue of section 216(5)(a) or otherwise);

(b) matters specified by CIL regulations relating to the economic viability of development (which may include, in particular, actual or potential economic effects of planning permission or of the imposition of CIL);

(c) other actual and expected sources of funding for infrastructure.

(3) CIL regulations may make other provision about setting rates or other criteria.

(4) The regulations may, in particular, permit or require charging authorities in setting rates or other criteria—

(a) to have regard, to the extent and in the manner specified by the regulations, to actual or expected administrative expenses in connection with CIL;

[(aa) to have regard, to the extent and in the manner specified by the regulations, to actual and expected costs of anything other than infrastructure that is concerned with addressing demands that development places on an area (whether by reference to lists prepared by virtue of section 216(5)(a) or otherwise);

(ab) to have regard, to the extent and in the manner specified by the regulations, to other actual and expected sources of funding for anything other than infrastructure that is concerned with addressing demands that development places on an area;][1]

(b) to have regard, to the extent and in the manner specified by the regulations, to values used or documents produced for other statutory purposes;

(c) to integrate the process, to the extent and in the manner specified by the regulations, with processes undertaken for other statutory purposes;

(d) to produce charging schedules having effect in relation to specified periods (subject to revision).

(5) The regulations may permit or require charging schedules to adopt specified methods of calculation.

(6) In particular, the regulations may—

(a) permit or require charging schedules to operate by reference to descriptions or purposes of development;

(b) permit or require charging schedules to operate by reference to any measurement of the amount or nature of development (whether by reference to measurements of floor space, to numbers or intended uses of buildings, to numbers or intended uses of units within buildings, to allocation of space within buildings or units, to values or expected values or in any other way);

(c) permit or require charging schedules to operate by reference to the nature or existing use of the place where development is undertaken;

(d) permit or require charging schedules to operate by reference to an index used for determining a rate of inflation;

(e) permit or require charging schedules to operate by reference to values used or documents produced for other statutory purposes;

(f) provide, or permit or require provision, for differential rates, which may include provision for supplementary charges, a nil rate, increased rates or reductions.

(7) A charging authority may consult, or take other steps, in connection with the preparation of a charging schedule (subject to CIL regulations).

[(7A) A charging authority must use appropriate available evidence to inform the charging authority's preparation of a charging schedule.

(7B) CIL regulations may make provision about the application of subsection (7A) including, in particular—

(a) provision as to evidence that is to be taken to be appropriate,

(b) provision as to evidence that is to be taken to be not appropriate,

(c) provision as to evidence that is to be taken to be available,

(d) provision as to evidence that is to be taken to be not available,

(e) provision as to how evidence is, and as to how evidence is not, to be used,

(f) provision as to evidence that is, and as to evidence that is not, to be used,

(g) provision as to evidence that may, and as to evidence that need not, be used, and

(h) provision as to how the use of evidence is to inform the preparation of a charging schedule.][2]

(8) The regulations may require a charging authority to provide in specified circumstances an estimate of the amount of CIL chargeable in respect of development of land.

(9) A charging authority may revise a charging schedule.

(10) This section and sections 212, 213 and 214(1) and (2) apply to the revision of a charging schedule as they apply to the preparation of a charging schedule.

1 Added by Localism Act 2011, s 115(1), (4) (15 January 2012 subject to transitional and savings provisions specified in SI 2012/57, arts 6, 7, 9, 10 and 11).

2 Added by Localism Act 2011, s 114(1), (2) (16 November 2011: insertion does not apply in relation to cases where an examiner submits recommendations to a charging authority before the coming into force of Localism Act 2011, s 114, but subject to that the cases in relation to which this amendment applies include a case in which steps in relation to the charging schedule have been taken before then).

212 Charging schedule: examination

(1) Before approving a charging schedule a charging authority must appoint a person ('the examiner') to examine a draft.

(2) The charging authority must appoint someone who, in the opinion of the authority—

(a) is independent of the charging authority, and

(b) has appropriate qualifications and experience.

(3) The charging authority may, with the agreement of the examiner, appoint persons to assist the examiner.

[(4) In this section and sections 212A and 213'the drafting requirements' means the requirements of this Part and CIL regulations (including the requirements to have regard to the matters listed in section 211(2) and (4)), so far as relevant to the drafting of the schedule.

(7) The examiner must consider whether the drafting requirements have been complied with and—

(a) make recommendations in accordance with section 212A, and

(b) give reasons for the recommendations.][1]

(8) The charging authority must publish the recommendations and reasons.

(9) CIL regulations must require a charging authority to allow anyone who makes representations about a draft charging schedule to be heard by the examiner; and the regulations may make provision about timing and procedure.

(10) CIL regulations may make provision for examiners to reconsider their decisions with a view to correcting errors (before or after the approval of a charging schedule).

(11) The charging authority may withdraw a draft.

1 Section 212(4) and (7) substituted for s 212(4)-(7) by Localism Act 2011, s 114(1), (3) (16 November 2011: substitution does not apply in relation to cases where an examiner submits recommendations to a charging authority before the coming into force of Localism Act 2011, s 114, but subject to that the cases in relation to which this amendment applies include a case in which steps in relation to the charging schedule have been taken before then).

[212A Charging schedule: examiner's recommendations

(1) This section applies in relation to the examination, under section 212, of a draft charging schedule.

(2) If the examiner considers—

(a) that there is any respect in which the drafting requirements have not been complied with, and

(b) that the non-compliance with the drafting requirements cannot be remedied by the making of modifications to the draft,

the examiner must recommend that the draft be rejected.

(3) Subsection (4) applies if the examiner considers—

(a) that there is any respect in which the drafting requirements have not been complied with, and

(b) that the non-compliance with the drafting requirements could be remedied by the making of modifications to the draft.

(4) The examiner must—

(a) specify the respects in which the drafting requirements have not been complied with,

(b) recommend modifications that the examiner considers sufficient and necessary to remedy that non-compliance, and

(c) recommend that the draft be approved with—

(i) those modifications, or

(ii) other modifications sufficient and necessary to remedy that non-compliance.

(5) Subject to subsections (2) to (4), the examiner must recommend that the draft be approved.

(6) If the examiner makes recommendations under subsection (4), the examiner may recommend other modifications with which the draft should be approved in the event that it is approved.

(7) If the examiner makes recommendations under subsection (5), the examiner may recommend modifications with which the draft should be approved in the event that it is approved.][1]

1 Added by Localism Act 2011, s 114(1), (4) (16 November 2011: insertion does not apply in relation to cases where an examiner submits recommendations to a charging authority before the coming into force of Localism Act 2011, s 114, but subject to that the cases in relation to which this amendment applies include a case in which steps in relation to the charging schedule have been taken before then).

213 Charging schedule: approval

[(1) A charging authority may approve a charging schedule only if—

(a) the examiner makes recommendations under section 212A(4) or (5), and

(b) the charging authority has had regard to those recommendations and the examiner's reasons for them.

(1A) Accordingly, a charging authority may not approve a charging schedule if, under section 212A(2), the examiner recommends rejection.

(1B) If the examiner makes recommendations under section 212A(4), the charging authority may approve the charging schedule only if it does so with modifications that are sufficient and necessary to remedy the non-compliance specified under section 212A(4)(a) (although those modifications need not be the ones recommended under section 212A(4)(b)).

(1C) If a charging authority approves a charging schedule, it may do so with all or none, or some one or more, of the modifications (if any) recommended under section 212A(6) or (7).

(1D) The modifications with which a charging schedule may be approved include only—

(a) modifications required by subsection (1B), and

(b) modifications allowed by subsection (1C).][1]

(2) A charging authority (other than the Mayor of London) must approve a charging schedule—

(a) at a meeting of the authority, and

(b) by a majority of votes of members present.

(3) The Mayor of London must approve a charging schedule personally.

[(3A) Subsection (3B) applies if—

(a) the examiner makes recommendations under section 212A(4), and

(b) the charging schedule is approved by the charging authority.

(3B) The charging authority must publish a report setting out how the charging schedule as approved remedies the non-compliance specified under section 212A(4)(a).

(3C) CIL regulations may make provision about the form or contents of a report under subsection (3B).][2]

(4) CIL regulations may make provision for the correction of errors in a charging schedule after approval.

[(5) In this section 'examiner' means examiner under section 212.][3]

1 Section 213(1)-(1D) substituted for s 213(1) by Localism Act 2011, s 114(1), (5) (16 November 2011: substtitution does not apply in relation to cases where an examiner submits recommendations to a charging authority before the coming into force of Localism Act 2011, s 114, but subject to that the cases in relation to which this amendment applies include a case in which steps in relation to the charging schedule have been taken before then).

2 Added by Localism Act 2011, s 114(1), (6) (16 November 2011: insertion does not apply in relation to cases where an examiner submits recommendations to a charging authority before the coming into force of Localism Act 2011, s 114, but subject to that the cases in relation to which this amendment applies include a case in which steps in relation to the charging schedule have been taken before then).

3 Added by Localism Act 2011, s 114(1), (7) (16 November 2011: insertion does not apply in relation to cases where an examiner submits recommendations to a charging authority before the coming into force of Localism Act 2011, s 114, but subject to that the cases in relation to which this amendment applies include a case in which steps in relation to the charging schedule have been taken before then).

214 Charging schedule: effect

(1) A charging schedule approved under section 213 may not take effect before it is published by the charging authority.

(2) CIL regulations may make provision about publication of a charging schedule after approval.

(3) A charging authority may determine that a charging schedule is to cease to have effect.

(4) CIL regulations may provide that a charging authority may only make a determination under subsection (3) in circumstances specified by the regulations.

(5) A charging authority (other than the Mayor of London) must make a determination under subsection (3)—

(a) at a meeting of the authority, and

(b) by a majority of votes of members present.

(6) The Mayor of London must make a determination under subsection (3) personally.

215 Appeals

(1) CIL regulations must provide for a right of appeal on a question of fact in relation to the application of methods for calculating CIL to a person appointed by the Commissioners for Her Majesty's Revenue and Customs.

(2) The regulations must require that the person appointed under subsection (1) is—

(a) a valuation officer appointed under section 61 of the Local Government Finance Act 1988 (c. 41), or

(b) a district valuer within the meaning of section 622 of the Housing Act 1985 (c. 68).

(3) Regulations under this section or section 208(5)(d)(ii) may, in particular, make provision about—

(a) the period within which the right of appeal may be exercised,

(b) the procedure on an appeal, and

(c) the payment of fees, and award of costs, in relation to an appeal.

(4) In any proceedings for judicial review of a decision on an appeal, the defendant shall be the Commissioners for Her Majesty's Revenue and Customs and not the person appointed under subsection (1).

216 Application

(1) Subject to [sections 216A(1), 216B(2) and 219(5)][1], CIL regulations must require the authority that charges CIL to apply it, or cause it to be applied, to [supporting development by funding the provision, improvement, replacement, operation or maintenance of infrastructure][2].

(2) In [this section (except subsection (3)) and sections 216A(2) and 216B(2)][3] 'infrastructure' includes—

(a) roads and other transport facilities,

(b) flood defences,

(c) schools and other educational facilities,

(d) medical facilities,

(e) sporting and recreational facilities,[and][4]

(f) open spaces [.][5]

[...][6]

(3) The regulations may amend subsection (2) so as to—

(a) add, remove or vary an entry in the list of matters included within the meaning of 'infrastructure';

(b) list matters excluded from the meaning of 'infrastructure'.

(4) The regulations may specify—

(a) works, installations and other facilities [whose provision, improvement or replacement may or is to be, or may not][7] be, funded by CIL,

[(aa) maintenance activities and operational activities (including operational activities of a promotional kind) in connection with infrastructure that may or are to be, or may not be, funded by CIL,

(ab) things within section 216A(2)(b) that may or are to be, or may not be, funded by CIL passed to a person in discharge of a duty under section 216A(1),

(ac) things within section 216B(2)(b) that may or are to be, or may not be, funded by CIL to which provision under section 216B(2) relates,][8]

(b) criteria for determining the areas [that may benefit from funding][9] by CIL in respect of land, and

(c) what is to be, or not to be, treated as funding.

(5) The regulations may—

(a) require charging authorities to prepare and publish a list of [what is][10] to be, or may be, wholly or partly funded by CIL;

(b) include provision about the procedure to be followed in preparing a list (which may include provision for consultation, for the appointment of an independent person or a combination);

(c) include provision about the circumstances in which a charging authority may and may not apply CIL to [anything][11] not included on the list.

(6) In making provision about funding the regulations may, in particular—

(a) permit CIL to be used to reimburse expenditure already incurred;

(b) permit CIL to be reserved for expenditure that may be incurred [in the future][12] ;

(c) permit CIL to be applied (either generally or subject to limits set by or determined in accordance with the regulations) to administrative expenses in connection with infrastructure [or anything within section 216A(2)(b) or 216B(2)(b)][13] or in connection with CIL;

(d) include provision for the giving of loans, guarantees or indemnities;

(e) make provision about the application of CIL where [anything][14] to which it was to be applied no longer [requires][15] funding.

(7) The regulations may—

(a) require a charging authority to account separately, and in accordance with the regulations, for CIL received or due;

(b) require a charging authority to monitor the use made and to be made of CIL in its area;

(c) require a charging authority to report on actual or expected charging, collection and application of CIL;

(d) permit a charging authority to cause money to be applied in respect of things done outside its area;

(e) permit a charging authority or other body to spend money;

(f) permit a charging authority to pass money to another body (and in paragraphs (a) to (e) a reference to a charging authority includes a reference to a body to which a charging authority passes money in reliance on this paragraph).

1 Word substituted by Localism Act 2011, s 115(1), (5)(a)(i) (15 January 2012 subject to transitional and savings provisions specified in SI 2012/57, arts 6, 7, 9, 10 and 11).
2 Words substituted by Localism Act 2011, s 115(1), (5)(a)(ii) (15 January 2012 subject to transitional and savings provisions specified in SI 2012/57, arts 6, 7, 9, 10 and 11).
3 Words substituted by Localism Act 2011, s 115(1), (5)(b) (15 January 2012 subject to transitional and savings provisions specified in SI 2012/57, arts 6, 7, 9, 10 and 11).
4 Word inserted by Community Infrastructure Levy Regulations 2010, SI 2010/948, reg 63(1), (2) (6 April 2010).
5 Word substituted by Community Infrastructure Levy Regulations 2010, SI 2010/948, reg 63(1), (3) (6 April 2010).
6 Repealed by Community Infrastructure Levy Regulations 2010, SI 2010/948, reg 63(1), (4) (6 April 2010).
7 Words substituted by Localism Act 2011, s 115(1), (5)(c) (15 January 2012 subject to transitional and savings provisions specified in SI 2012/57, arts 6, 7, 9, 10 and 11).
8 Added by Localism Act 2011, s 115(1), (5)(d) (15 January 2012 subject to transitional and savings provisions specified in SI 2012/57, arts 6, 7, 9, 10 and 11).
9 Words substituted by Localism Act 2011, s 115(1), (5)(e) (15 January 2012 subject to transitional and savings provisions specified in SI 2012/57, arts 6, 7, 9, 10 and 11).
10 Words substituted by Localism Act 2011, s 115(1), (5)(f) (15 January 2012 subject to transitional and savings provisions specified in SI 2012/57, arts 6, 7, 9, 10 and 11).
11 Word substituted by Localism Act 2011, s 115(1), (5)(g) (15 January 2012 subject to transitional and savings provisions specified in SI 2012/57, arts 6, 7, 9, 10 and 11).
12 Words substituted by Localism Act 2011, s 115(1), (5)(h) (15 January 2012 subject to transitional and savings provisions specified in SI 2012/57, arts 6, 7, 9, 10 and 11).
13 Words inserted by Localism Act 2011, s 115(1), (5)(i) (15 January 2012 subject to transitional and savings provisions specified in SI 2012/57, arts 6, 7, 9, 10 and 11).

14 Words substituted by Localism Act 2011, s 115(1), (5)(j)(i) (15 January 2012 subject to transitional and savings provisions specified in SI 2012/57, arts 6, 7, 9, 10 and 11).
15 Word substituted by Localism Act 2011, s 115(1), (5)(j)(ii) (15 January 2012 subject to transitional and savings provisions specified in SI 2012/57, arts 6, 7, 9, 10 and 11).

[216A Duty to pass receipts to other persons

(1) CIL regulations may require that CIL received in respect of development of land in an area is to be passed by the charging authority that charged the CIL to a person other than that authority.

(2) CIL regulations must contain provision to secure that money passed to a person in discharge of a duty under subsection (1) is used to support the development of the area to which the duty relates, or of any part of that area, by funding—

(a) the provision, improvement, replacement, operation or maintenance of infrastructure, or

(b) anything else that is concerned with addressing demands that development places on an area.

(3) A duty under subsection (1) may relate to—

(a) the whole of a charging authority's area or the whole of the combined area of two or more charging authorities, or

(b) part only of such an area or combined area.

(4) CIL regulations may make provision about the persons to whom CIL may or must, or may not, be passed in discharge of a duty under subsection (1).

(5) A duty under subsection (1) may relate—

(a) to all CIL (if any) received in respect of the area to which the duty relates, or

(b) such part of that CIL as is specified in, or determined under or in accordance with, CIL regulations.

(6) CIL regulations may make provision in connection with the timing of payments in discharge of a duty under subsection (1).

(7) CIL regulations may, in relation to CIL passed to a person in discharge of a duty under subsection (1), make provision about—

(a) accounting for the CIL,

(b) monitoring its use,

(c) reporting on its use,

(d) responsibilities of charging authorities for things done by the person in connection with the CIL,

(e) recovery of the CIL, and any income or profits accruing in respect of it or from its application, in cases where—

(i) anything to be funded by it has not been provided, or

(ii) it has been misapplied,

including recovery of sums or other assets representing it or any such income or profits, and

(f) use of anything recovered in cases where—

(i) anything to be funded by the CIL has not been provided, or

(ii) the CIL has been misapplied.

(8) This section does not limit section 216(7)(f).][1]

1 Added by Localism Act 2011, s 115(1), (6) (15 January 2012 subject to transitional and savings provisions specified in SI 2012/57, arts 6, 7, 9, 10 and 11).

[216B Use of CIL in an area to which section 216A(1) duty does not relate

(1) Subsection (2) applies where—

(a) there is an area to which a particular duty under section 216A(1) relates, and

(b) there is also an area to which that duty does not relate ('the uncovered area').

(2) CIL regulations may provide that the charging authority that charges CIL received in respect of development of land in the uncovered area may apply the CIL, or cause it to be applied, to—

(a) support development by funding the provision, improvement, replacement, operation or maintenance of infrastructure, or

(b) support development of the uncovered area, or of any part of that area, by funding anything else that is concerned with addressing demands that development places on an area.

(3) Provision under subsection (2) may relate to the whole, or part only, of the uncovered area.

(4) Provision under subsection (2) may relate—

(a) to all CIL (if any) received in respect of the area to which the provision relates, or

(b) such part of that CIL as is specified in, or determined under or in accordance with, CIL regulations.][1]

1 Added by Localism Act 2011, s 115(1), (6) (15 January 2012 subject to transitional and savings provisions specified in SI 2012/57, arts 6, 7, 9, 10 and 11).

217 Collection

(1) CIL regulations must include provision about the collection of CIL.

(2) The regulations may make provision for payment—

(a) on account;

(b) by instalments.

(3) The regulations may make provision about repayment (with or without interest) in cases of overpayment.

(4) The regulations may make provision about payment in forms other than money (such as making land available, carrying out works or providing services).

(5) The regulations may permit or require a charging authority or other public authority to collect CIL charged by another authority; and section 216(7)(a) and (c) apply to a collecting authority in respect of collection as to a charging authority.

(6) Regulations under this section may replicate or apply (with or without modifications) any enactment relating to the collection of a tax.

(7) Regulations under this section may make provision about the source of payments in respect of Crown interests.

218 Enforcement

(1) CIL regulations must include provision about enforcement of CIL.

(2) The regulations must make provision about the consequences of late payment and failure to pay.

(3) The regulations may make provision about the consequences of failure to assume liability, to give a notice or to comply with another procedure under CIL regulations in connection with CIL.

(4) The regulations may, in particular, include provision—

(a) for the payment of interest;

(b) for the imposition of a penalty or surcharge;

(c) for the suspension or cancellation of a decision relating to planning permission;

(d) enabling an authority to prohibit development pending assumption of liability for CIL or pending payment of CIL;

(e) conferring a power of entry onto land;

(f) requiring the provision of information;

(g) creating a criminal offence (including, in particular, offences relating to evasion or attempted evasion or to the provision of false or misleading information or failure to provide information, and offences relating to the prevention or investigation of other offences created by the regulations);

(h) conferring power to prosecute an offence;

(i) for enforcement of sums owed (whether by action on a debt, by distraint against goods or in any other way);

(j) conferring jurisdiction on a court to grant injunctive or other relief to enforce a provision of the regulations (including a provision included in reliance on this section);

(k) for enforcement in the case of death or insolvency of a person liable for CIL.

(5) CIL regulations may include provision (whether or not in the context of late payment or failure to pay) about registration or notification of actual or potential liability to CIL; and the regulations may include provision—

(a) for the creation of local land charges;

(b) for the registration of local land charges;

(c) for enforcement of local land charges (including, in particular, for enforcement—

(i) against successive owners, and

(ii) by way of sale or other disposal with consent of a court);

(d) for making entries in statutory registers;

(e) for the cancellation of charges and entries.

(6) Regulations under this section may—

(a) replicate or apply (with or without modifications) any enactment relating to the enforcement of a tax;

(b) provide for appeals.

(7) Regulations under this section may provide that any interest, penalty or surcharge payable by virtue of the regulations is to be treated for the purposes of sections 216 to 220 as if it were CIL.

(8) The regulations providing for a surcharge or penalty must ensure that no surcharge or penalty in respect of an amount of CIL exceeds the higher of—

(a) 30% of that amount, and

(b) £20,000.

(9) But the regulations may provide for more than one surcharge or penalty to be imposed in relation to a CIL charge.

(10) The regulations may not authorise entry to a private dwelling without a warrant issued by a justice of the peace.

(11) Regulations under this section creating a criminal offence may not provide for—

(a) a maximum fine exceeding £20,000 on summary conviction,

(b) a maximum term of imprisonment exceeding 6 months on summary conviction, or

(c) a maximum term of imprisonment exceeding 2 years on conviction on indictment.

(12) The Secretary of State may by order amend subsection (11) to reflect commencement of section 283 of the Criminal Justice Act 2003 (c. 44).

(13) In this Part a reference to administrative expenses in connection with CIL includes a reference to enforcement expenses.

219 Compensation

(1) CIL regulations may require a charging authority or other public authority to pay compensation in respect of loss or damage suffered as a result of enforcement action.

(2) In this section, 'enforcement action' means action taken under regulations under section 218, including—

(a) the suspension or cancellation of a decision relating to planning permission, and

(b) the prohibition of development pending assumption of liability for CIL or pending payment of CIL.

(3) The regulations shall not require payment of compensation—

(a) to a person who has failed to satisfy a liability to pay CIL, or

(b) in other circumstances specified by the regulations.

(4) Regulations under this section may make provision about—

(a) the time and manner in which a claim for compensation is to be made, and

(b) the sums, or the method of determining the sums, payable by way of compensation.

(5) CIL regulations may permit or require a charging authority to apply CIL (either generally or subject to limits set by or determined in accordance with the regulations) for expenditure incurred under this section.

(6) A dispute about compensation may be referred to and determined by the [Upper Tribunal][1].

(7) In relation to the determination of any such question, the provisions of [section 4 of the Land Compensation Act 1961 (c. 33)][2] apply subject to any necessary modifications and to the provisions of CIL regulations.

1 Words substituted by Transfer of Tribunal Functions (Lands Tribunal and Miscellaneous Amendments) Order 2009, SI 2009/1307, art 5(1), (2), Sch 1, paras 291, 296(a) (1 June 2009).

2 Words substituted by Transfer of Tribunal Functions (Lands Tribunal and Miscellaneous Amendments) Order 2009, SI 2009/1307, art 5(1), (2), Sch 1, paras 291, 296(b) (1 June 2009).

220 Community Infrastructure Levy: procedure

(1) CIL regulations may include provision about procedures to be followed in connection with CIL.

(2) In particular, the regulations may make provision about—

(a) procedures to be followed by a charging authority proposing to begin charging CIL;

(b) procedures to be followed by a charging authority in relation to charging CIL;

(c) procedures to be followed by a charging authority proposing to stop charging CIL;

(d) consultation;

(e) the publication or other treatment of reports;

(f) timing and methods of publication;

(g) making documents available for inspection;

(h) providing copies of documents (with or without charge);

(i) the form and content of documents;

(j) giving notice;

(k) serving notices or other documents;

(l) examinations to be held in public in the course of setting or revising rates or other criteria or of preparing lists;

(m) the terms and conditions of appointment of independent persons;

(n) remuneration and expenses of independent persons (which may be required to be paid by the Secretary of State or by a charging authority);

(o) other costs in connection with examinations;

(p) reimbursement of expenditure incurred by the Secretary of State (including provision for enforcement);

(q) apportionment of costs;

(r) combining procedures in connection with CIL with procedures for another purpose of a charging authority (including a purpose of that authority in another capacity);

(s) procedures to be followed in connection with actual or potential liability for CIL.

(3) CIL regulations may make provision about the procedure to be followed in respect of an exemption from CIL or a reduction of CIL; in particular, the regulations may include provision—

(a) about the procedure for determining whether any conditions are satisfied;

(b) requiring a charging authority or other person to notify specified persons of any exemption or reduction;

(c) requiring a charging authority or other person to keep a record of any exemption or reduction.

(4) A provision of this Part conferring express power to make procedural provision in a specified context includes, in particular, power to make provision about the matters specified in subsection (2).

(5) A power in this Part to make provision about publishing something includes a power to make provision about making it available for inspection.

(6) Sections 229 to 231 do not apply to this Part (but CIL regulations may make similar provision).

221 Secretary of State

The Secretary of State may give guidance to a charging authority or other public authority (including an examiner appointed under section 212) about any matter connected with CIL; and the authority must have regard to the guidance.

222 Regulations and orders: general

(1) CIL regulations—

(a) may make provision that applies generally or only to specified cases, circumstances or areas,

(b) may make different provision for different cases, circumstances or areas,

(c) may provide, or allow a charging schedule to provide, for exceptions,

(d) may confer, or allow a charging schedule to confer, a discretionary power on the Secretary of State, a local authority or another specified person,

(e) may apply an enactment, with or without modifications, and

(f) may include provision of a kind permitted by section 232(3)(b) (and incidental, supplemental or consequential provision may include provision disapplying, modifying the effect of or amending an enactment).

(2) CIL regulations—

(a) shall be made by statutory instrument, and

(b) shall not be made unless a draft has been laid before and approved by resolution of the House of Commons.

(3) An order under section 218(12) or 225(2)—

(a) shall be made by statutory instrument, and

(b) may include provision of a kind permitted by subsection (1)(a), (b) or (f) above, but may not amend an Act of Parliament in reliance on subsection (1)(f).

(4) An order under section 218(12) shall be subject to annulment in pursuance of a resolution of either House of Parliament.

(5) An order under section 225(2) shall be subject to annulment in pursuance of a resolution of the House of Commons.

223 Relationship with other powers

(1) CIL regulations may include provision about how the following powers are to be used, or are not to be used—

(a) section 106 of TCPA 1990 (planning obligations), and

(b) section 278 of the Highways Act 1980 (c. 66) (execution of works).

(2) CIL regulations may include provision about the exercise of any other power relating to planning or development.

(3) The Secretary of State may give guidance to a charging or other authority about how a power relating to planning or development is to be exercised; and authorities must have regard to the guidance.

(4) Provision may be made under subsection (1) or (2), and guidance may be given under subsection (3), only if the Secretary of State thinks it necessary or expedient for—

(a) complementing the main purpose of CIL regulations,

(b) enhancing the effectiveness, or increasing the use, of CIL regulations,

(c) preventing agreements, undertakings or other transactions from being used to undermine or circumvent CIL regulations,

(d) preventing agreements, undertakings or other transactions from being used to achieve a purpose that the Secretary of State thinks would better be achieved through the application of CIL regulations, or

(e) preventing or restricting the imposition of burdens, the making of agreements or the giving of undertakings, in addition to CIL.

(5) CIL regulations may provide that a power to give guidance or directions may not be exercised—

(a) in relation to matters specified in the regulations,

(b) in cases or circumstances specified in the regulations,

(c) for a purpose specified in the regulations, or

(d) to an extent specified in the regulations.

224 ...

Amends Local Government Act 1972, Norfolk and Suffolk Broads Act 1988, Deregulation and Contracting Out Act 1994 and Greater London Authority Act 1999.

225 Community Infrastructure Levy: repeals

(1) The following provisions of PCPA 2004 shall cease to have effect—

(a) sections 46 to 48 (planning contribution), and

(b) paragraph 5 of Schedule 6 (repeal of sections 106 to 106B of TCPA 1990 (planning obligations)).

(2) The Treasury may by order repeal the Planning-gain Supplement (Preparations) Act 2007 (c. 2).

Part 12 Final provisions

The Crown and Parliament

226 The Crown

(1) This Act binds the Crown, subject to subsections (2) and (3).

(2) Sections 40, 54, 135, 166, 228 and 231 make special provision in relation to the application of some provisions of this Act to the Crown.

(3) The amendments made by this Act bind the Crown only to the extent that the provisions amended bind the Crown.

227 'Crown land' and 'the appropriate Crown authority'

(1) In this Act, 'Crown land' and 'the appropriate Crown authority' must be read in accordance with this section.

(2) 'Crown land' is land in which there is a Crown interest or a Duchy interest.

(3) For the purposes of this section, a Crown interest is any of the following—

(a) an interest belonging to Her Majesty in right of the Crown or in right of Her private estates;

(b) an interest belonging to a government department or held in trust for Her Majesty for the purposes of a government department;

(c) an interest belonging to an office-holder in the Scottish Administration or held in trust for Her Majesty for the purposes of the Scottish Administration by such an office-holder;

(d) the interest of the Speaker of the House of Lords in those parts of the Palace of Westminster and its precincts occupied on 23 March 1965 by or on behalf of the House of Lords;

(e) the interest of the Speaker of the House of Commons in those parts of the Palace of Westminster and its precincts occupied on 23 March 1965 by or on behalf of the House of Commons;

(f) the interest in any land of—

(i) the Corporate Officer of the House of Lords;

(ii) the Corporate Officer of the House of Commons;

(iii) those two Corporate Officers acting jointly;

(g) such other interest as the Secretary of State specifies by order.

(4) For the purposes of this section, a Duchy interest is—

(a) an interest belonging to Her Majesty in right of the Duchy of Lancaster, or

(b) an interest belonging to the Duchy of Cornwall.

(5) 'The appropriate Crown authority' in relation to any land is—

(a) in the case of land belonging to Her Majesty in right of the Crown and forming part of the Crown Estate, the Crown Estate Commissioners;

(b) in relation to any other land belonging to Her Majesty in right of the Crown, the government department or, as the case may be, office-holder in the Scottish Administration, having the management of the land;

(c) in relation to land belonging to Her Majesty in right of Her private estates, a person appointed by Her Majesty in writing under the Royal Sign Manual or, if no such appointment is made, the Secretary of State;

(d) in relation to land belonging to Her Majesty in right of the Duchy of Lancaster, the Chancellor of the Duchy;

(e) in relation to land belonging to the Duchy of Cornwall, such person as the Duke of Cornwall, or the possessor for the time being of the Duchy, appoints;

(f) in the case of land belonging to a government department or held in trust for Her Majesty for the purposes of a government department, the department;

(g) in the case of land belonging to an office-holder in the Scottish Administration or held in trust for Her Majesty for the purposes of such an office-holder, the office-holder;

(h) in relation to Westminster Hall and the Chapel of St Mary Undercroft, the Lord Great Chamberlain and the Speakers of the House of Lords and the House of Commons acting jointly;

(i) in relation to Her Majesty's Robing Room in the Palace of Westminster, the adjoining staircase and ante-room and the Royal Gallery, the Lord Great Chamberlain.

(j) in relation to land in which there is a Crown interest by virtue of subsection (3)(d) or (f)(i), the Corporate Officer of the House of Lords;

(k) in relation to land in which there is a Crown interest by virtue of subsection (3)(e) or (f)(ii), the Corporate Officer of the House of Commons;

(l) in relation to land in which there is a Crown interest by virtue of subsection (3)(f)(iii), those two Corporate Officers acting jointly.

(6) If any question arises as to what authority is the appropriate Crown authority in relation to any land it must be referred to the Treasury, whose decision is final.

(7) References to Her Majesty's private estates must be construed in accordance with section 1 of the Crown Private Estates Act 1862 (c. 37).

(8) References to an office-holder in the Scottish Administration are to be construed in accordance with section 126(7) of the Scotland Act 1998 (c. 46).

228 Enforcement in relation to the Crown and Parliament

(1) No act or omission done or suffered by or on behalf of the Crown constitutes an offence under this Act.

(2) For the purposes of this section 'the Crown' includes—

(a) the Duchy of Lancaster;

(b) the Duchy of Cornwall;

(c) the Speaker of the House of Lords;

(d) the Speaker of the House of Commons;

(e) the Corporate Officer of the House of Lords;

(f) the Corporate Officer of the House of Commons.

Service of notices and other documents

229 Service of notices: general

(1) A notice or other document required or authorised to be served, given or supplied under this Act may be served, given or supplied in any of these ways—

(a) by delivering it to the person on whom it is to be served or to whom it is to be given or supplied,

(b) by leaving it at the usual or last known place of abode of that person or, in a case where an address for service has been given by that person, at that address,

(c) by sending it by post, addressed to that person at that person's usual or last known place of abode or, in a case where an address for service has been given by that person, at that address,

(d) by sending it in a prepaid registered letter, or by the recorded delivery service, addressed to that person at that person's usual or last known place of abode or, in a case where an address for service has been given by that person, at that address,

(e) in a case where an address for service using electronic communications has been given by that person, by sending it using electronic communications, in accordance with the condition set out in subsection (2), to that person at that address,

(f) in the case of an incorporated company or body—

(i) by delivering it to the secretary or clerk of the company or body at their registered or principal office,

(ii) by sending it by post, addressed to the secretary or clerk of the company or body at that office,

(iii) by sending it in a prepaid registered letter or, or by the recorded delivery service, addressed to the secretary or clerk of the company or body at that office.

(2) The condition mentioned in subsection (1)(e) is that the notice or other document must be—

(a) capable of being accessed by the person mentioned in that provision,

(b) legible in all material respects, and

(c) in a form sufficiently permanent to be used for subsequent reference.

(3) For the purposes of subsection (2), 'legible in all material respects' means that the information contained in the notice or document is available to that person to no lesser extent than it would be if served, given or supplied by means of a notice or document in printed form.

(4) Subsection (1)(c), (e) and (f)(ii) do not apply to the service, giving or supply of any of the following—

(a) notice under section 53(4)(b);

(b) a compulsory acquisition notice under section 134;

(c) notice under section 163(3);

(d) an information notice under section 167;

(e) a notice of unauthorised development under section 169.

(5) This section is without prejudice to section 233 of the Local Government Act 1972 (c. 70) (general provisions as to service of notices by local authorities).

(6) This section is subject to any contrary provision made by or under this Act.

230 Service of documents to persons interested in or occupying premises

(1) Subsection (2) applies if—

(a) a notice or document is required or authorised to be served on or given or supplied to any person as having an interest in premises, and the name of that person cannot be ascertained after reasonable inquiry, or

(b) a notice or document is required or authorised to be served on or given or supplied to any person as an occupier of premises.

(2) The notice or document is to be taken to be duly served, given or supplied if either the condition in subsection (3) or the condition in subsection (4) is met.

(3) The condition is that the notice or document—

(a) is addressed to the person either by name or by the description of 'the owner' or, as the case may be, 'the occupier' of the premises (describing them), and

(b) is delivered or sent—

(i) in the case of a notice mentioned in section 229(4), in the manner specified in section 229(1)(a), (b) or (d), and

(ii) in any other case, in the manner specified in section 229(1)(a), (b), (c) or (d).

(4) The condition is that the notice or document is so addressed and is marked in such a manner as may be prescribed for securing that it is plainly identifiable as an important communication and—

(a) it is sent to the premises in a prepaid registered letter or by the recorded delivery service and is not returned to the authority sending it, or

(b) it is delivered to a person on those premises, or is affixed conspicuously to an object on those premises.

(5) Subsection (6) applies if—

(a) a notice or other document is required to be served on or given or supplied to all persons who have interests in or are occupiers of premises comprised in any land, and

(b) it appears to the authority required or authorised to serve, give or supply the notice or other document that any part of that land is unoccupied.

(6) The notice or other document is to be taken to be duly served on or given or supplied to all persons having interests in, and on any occupiers of, premises comprised in that part of the land (other than a person who has given to that authority an address for the service of the notice or document on him) if—

(a) it is addressed to 'the owners and any occupiers' of that part of the land (describing it), and

(b) it is affixed conspicuously to an object on the land.

(7) This section is subject to any contrary provision made by or under this Act.

231 Service of notices on the Crown and Parliament

(1) Any notice or other document required under this Act to be served on or given or supplied to the Crown must be served on or given or supplied to the appropriate Crown authority.

(2) Sections 229 and 230 do not apply for the purposes of the service, giving or supply of such a notice or document.

(3) For the purposes of this section 'the Crown' includes—

(a) the Duchy of Lancaster;

(b) the Duchy of Cornwall;

(c) the Speaker of the House of Lords;

(d) the Speaker of the House of Commons;

(e) the Corporate Officer of the House of Lords;

(f) the Corporate Officer of the House of Commons.

General

232 Orders and regulations

(1) Subsections (2) and (3) apply to a power to make an order or regulations conferred on the Secretary of State by this Act, except—

(a) power to make an order granting development consent;

(b) a power conferred by paragraph 1(4) of Schedule 4;

(c) a power to make changes to, or revoke, an order granting development consent;

(d) a power conferred by Part 11 or section 237 or 241.

(2) The power is exercisable by statutory instrument.

(3) The power includes—

(a) power to make different provision for different purposes (including different areas);

(b) power to make incidental, consequential, supplementary, transitional or transitory provision or savings.

(4) A statutory instrument containing an order or regulations under this Act is subject to annulment pursuant to a resolution of either House of Parliament.

This is subject to subsection (5) (and section 222(5)).

(5) Subsection (4) does not apply to a statutory instrument containing—

(a) an order granting development consent;

(b) an order made by virtue of paragraph 1(8) of Schedule 4;

(c) an order changing or revoking an order granting development consent;

(d) an order under [section 14(3), 33(5), 111, 160(3), 161(5), 172(1), 203(5) or 227(3)(g)][1];

(e) regulations under [section 35(2)(a)(ii), 104(2)(c) or 105(2)(b)][2].

(6) No order may be made under [section 14(3), 33(5), 111, 160(3), 161(5), 203(5) or 227(3)(g)][3] unless a draft of the instrument containing the order has been laid before, and approved by resolution of, each House of Parliament.

(7) No regulations may be made under [section 35(2)(a)(ii), 104(2)(c) or 105(2)(b)][4] unless a draft of the instrument containing the regulations has been laid before, and approved by resolution of, each House of Parliament.

1 Word inserted by Localism Act 2011, s 131(1), (3)(a) (1 April 2012).
2 Words inserted by Growth and Infrastructure Act 2013, s 26(1), (4)(a) (25 April 2013).
3 Word inserted by Localism Act 2011, s 131(1), (3)(b) (1 April 2012).
4 Words inserted by Growth and Infrastructure Act 2013, s 26(1), (4)(b) (25 April 2013).

233 Directions

(1) A direction given under this Act must be in writing.

(2) A power conferred by this Act to give a direction includes power to vary or revoke the direction.

234 Abbreviated references to Acts

In this Act—

'the Hazardous Substances Act' means the Planning (Hazardous Substances) Act 1990 (c. 10);

'the Listed Buildings Act' means the Planning (Listed Buildings and Conservation Areas) Act 1990 (c. 9);

'PCPA 2004' means the Planning and Compulsory Purchase Act 2004 (c. 5);

'TCPA 1990' means the Town and Country Planning Act 1990 (c. 8).

235 Interpretation

(1) In this Act (except in Part 11)—

'airport' has the meaning given by section 82(1) of the Airports Act 1986 (c. 31);

'alteration', in relation to an airport, must be read in accordance with section 23(6);

'alteration', in relation to a highway, includes stopping up the highway or diverting, improving, raising or lowering it;

'appropriate Crown authority' has the meaning given by section 227;

'building' has the meaning given by section 336(1) of TCPA 1990;

[...][1]

'construction', in relation to so much of a generating station as comprises or is to comprise renewable energy installations, has the same meaning as in Chapter 2 of Part 2 of the Energy Act 2004 (c. 20) (see section 104 of that Act) (and related expressions must be read accordingly);

'construction', in relation to a pipe-line, includes placing (and related expressions must be read accordingly);

[...][1]

'cross-country pipe-line' has the same meaning as in the Pipe-lines Act 1962 (c. 58) (see section 66 of that Act);

'Crown land' has the meaning given by section 227;

[...][1]

'development' has the meaning given by section 32;

'development consent' has the meaning given by section 31;

'electric line' has the same meaning as in Part 1 of the Electricity Act 1989 (c. 29) (see section 64(1) of that Act);

'extension', in relation to a generating station, has the meaning given by section 36(9) of the Electricity Act 1989 (and 'extend' must be read accordingly);

'gas' includes natural gas;

'gas reception facility' must be read in accordance with section 19(3);

'gas transporter' has the same meaning as in Part 1 of the Gas Act 1986 (c. 44) (see section 7(1) of that Act);

'generating station' has the same meaning as in Part 1 of the Electricity Act 1989 (see section 64(1) of that Act);

'goods' has the meaning given by section 83(1) of the Railways Act 1993 (c. 43);

'Green Belt land' has the meaning given by section 2(1) of the Green Belt (London and Home Counties) Act 1938 (c. xciii);

'harbour' and 'harbour authority' have the meanings given by section 57(1) of the Harbours Act 1964 (c. 40);

'highway' has the meaning given by section 328 of the Highways Act 1980 (c. 66);

'highway authority' has the same meaning as in the Highways Act 1980 (c. 66) (see sections 1 to 3 of that Act);

'improvement', in relation to a highway, has the meaning given by section 329(1) of the Highways Act 1980;

'inland waters' has the same meaning as in the Water Resources Act 1991 (c. 57) (see section 221(1) of that Act);

'land' includes buildings and monuments, and land covered with water, and in relation to Part 7 must be read in accordance with section 159;

'LNG facility' must be read in accordance with section 18(3);

'local planning authority' has the same meaning as in TCPA 1990 (see section 336(1) of that Act);

'monument' has the same meaning as in the Ancient Monuments and Archaeological Areas Act 1979 (c. 46) (see section 61 of that Act);

'nationally significant infrastructure project' has the meaning given by Part 3;

'national policy statement' has the meaning given by section 5(2);

'natural gas' means any gas derived from natural strata (including gas originating outside the United Kingdom);

'navigable watercourse' has the same meaning as in Part 6 of the Highways Act 1980 (see section 111(1) of that Act);

'non-navigable watercourse' means a watercourse that is not a navigable watercourse;

'pipe-line' has the meaning given by section 65 of the Pipe-lines Act 1962 (c. 58);

'planning permission' means permission under Part 3 of TCPA 1990;

'prescribed' means prescribed by regulations made by the Secretary of State (except in relation to matters authorised or required by this Act to be prescribed in another way);

'rail freight interchange' means a facility for the transfer of goods between railway and road, or between railway and another form of transport;

'railway' has the meaning given by section 67(1) of the Transport and Works Act 1992 (c. 42);

'renewable energy installation' has the same meaning as in Chapter 2 of Part 2 of the Energy Act 2004 (c. 20) (see section 104 of that Act);

'Renewable Energy Zone' has the meaning given by section 84(4) of the Energy Act 2004;

'special road' means a highway which is a special road in accordance with section 16 of the Highways Act 1980 or by virtue of an order granting development consent;

'standard', in relation to a volume of gas, means the volume of gas at a pressure of 101.325 kiloPascals and a temperature of 273 Kelvin;

'trunk road' means a highway which is a trunk road by virtue of—

(a) section 10(1) or 19 of the Highways Act 1980,

(b) an order or direction under section 10 of that Act, or

(c) an order granting development consent,

or under any other enactment;

'underground gas storage facilities' must be read in accordance with section 17(6);

'use' has the meaning given by section 336(1) of TCPA 1990.

(2) A reference in this Act to a right over land includes a reference to a right to do, or to place and maintain, anything in, on or under land or in the air-space above its surface.

(3) Subsection (4) applies to the question of which parts of waters up to the seaward limits of the territorial sea—

(a) are adjacent to Wales (and, in consequence, are not adjacent to England), or

(b) are not adjacent to Wales (and, in consequence, are adjacent to England).

(4) The question is to be determined by reference to an order or Order in Council made under or by virtue of section 158(3) or (4) of the Government of Wales Act 2006 (c. 32) (apportionment of sea areas) if, or to the extent that, the order or Order in Council is expressed to apply—

(a) by virtue of this subsection, for the purposes of this Act, or

(b) if no provision has been made by virtue of paragraph (a), for the general or residual purposes of that Act.

(5) Subsection (6) applies to the question of which parts of waters up to the seaward limits of the territorial sea—

(a) are adjacent to Scotland (and, in consequence, are not adjacent to England), or

(b) are not adjacent to Scotland (and, in consequence, are adjacent to England).

(6) The question is to be determined by reference to an Order in Council made under section 126(2) of the Scotland Act 1998 (c. 46) if, or to the extent that, the Order in Council is expressed to apply—

(a) by virtue of this subsection, for the purposes of this Act, or

(b) if no provision has been made by virtue of paragraph (a), for the general or residual purposes of that Act.

1 Definitions repealed by Localism Act 2011, ss 128(2), 237, Sch 13, paras 1, 69, Sch 25, Pt 20 (1 April 2012).

236 Application of Act to Scotland: modifications

The modifications set out in Schedule 12 have effect in the application of this Act to Scotland for the purpose mentioned in section 240(4).

237 Supplementary and consequential provision

(1) The Secretary of State may by order made by statutory instrument make—

(a) such supplementary, incidental or consequential provision, or

(b) such transitory, transitional or saving provision,

as the Secretary of State thinks appropriate for the general purposes, or any particular purpose, of this Act or in consequence of, or for giving full effect to, any provision made by this Act.

(2) The power conferred by subsection (1) includes power to make different provision for different purposes (including different areas).

(3) An order under subsection (1) may amend, repeal, revoke or otherwise modify—

(a) an Act passed on or before the last day of the Session in which this Act is passed, or

(b) an instrument made under an Act before the passing of this Act.

(4) An order under this section which amends or repeals any provision of an Act may not be made unless a draft of the instrument containing the order has been laid before, and approved by resolution of, each House of Parliament.

(5) A statutory instrument containing an order under this section which does not amend or repeal any provision of an Act is subject to annulment pursuant to a resolution of either House of Parliament.

(6) In this section any reference to an Act (other than this Act) includes a reference to an Act of the Scottish Parliament.

[237A Variation and replacement of section 33 consents: transitional provision

(1) This section applies where a section 33 consent ('the original consent') has been granted or made as a result of an application made before Part 4 came into force.

(2) Nothing in section 33 prevents the original consent, or a section 33 consent that replaces it, from being varied or replaced.

(3) If the original consent, or a section 33 consent that replaces it, is varied or replaced, section 31 does not apply to the development to which the consent as varied, or the replacement consent, relates (and so development consent is not required for that development).

(4) A section 33 consent replaces an earlier section 33 consent for the purposes of this section if (but only if)—

(a) it is granted or made on an application for consent for development without complying with conditions subject to which the earlier section 33 consent was granted or made, and

(b) it is granted subject to, or made on, different conditions, or unconditionally.

(5) In this section 'section 33 consent' means a consent, authorisation, order, notice or scheme mentioned in section 33(1), (2) or (4).][1]

1 Added by Growth and Infrastructure Act 2013, s 22(1) (1 March 2010: insertion deemed to have had effect from 1 March 2010).

238 Repeals

Schedule 13 contains repeals (including repeals of spent provisions).

239 Financial provisions

There is to be paid out of money provided by Parliament—

(a) any expenditure incurred under or by virtue of this Act by the Secretary of State, and

(b) any increase attributable to this Act in the sums payable under or by virtue of any other Act out of money so provided.

240 Extent

(1) The following provisions of this Act extend to England and Wales only—

(a) in Part 2, section 13;

(b) in Part 3, sections 15 to 20 and 22 to 30;

(c) in Part 6, section 118;

(d) in Part 7, sections 133 and 139 to 149;

(e) in Part 9, sections 193 and 194;

(f) in Part 10, sections 203 and 204;

(g) Part 11.

(2) Section 178 extends to Scotland only.

(3) The following provisions of this Act extend to England and Wales and (subject to subsection (4)) to Scotland—

(a) Parts 1 to 8 (except the sections listed in paragraphs (a) to (d) of subsection (1));

(b) this Part.

(4) Those provisions extend to Scotland only so far as required for the purpose of the construction (other than by a gas transporter) of an oil or gas cross-country pipe-line—

(a) one end of which is in England or Wales, and

(b) the other end of which is in Scotland.

(5) Subsections (3) and (4) are subject to subsection (6).

(6) So far as it amends or repeals an enactment, this Act has the same extent as the enactment amended or repealed.

(7) An order under section 225(2) extends to each part of the United Kingdom.

241 Commencement

(1) The following provisions of this Act come into force on the day on which this Act is passed—

(a) the provisions of Parts 1 to 9 (except section 194(2) to (5) and paragraph 7 of Schedule 7) which—

(i) confer power to make orders (other than orders granting, or making changes to orders granting, development consent), regulations or rules, or

(ii) make provision about what is (or is not) permitted to be done, or what is required to be done, in the exercise of any such power;

(b) Part 11, except sections 206, 211(7), 224 and 225;

(c) this Part, except section 238.

(2) Nothing in subsection (1)(a) affects the operation of section 13 of the Interpretation Act 1978 (c. 30) in relation to this Act.

(3) Except as provided by subsection (1)(a), the provisions listed in subsection (4) come into force on such day as may be appointed by order made by—

(a) the Welsh Ministers, in relation to Wales;

(b) the Secretary of State, in relation to England.

(4) The provisions are—

(a) sections 183, 185, 187, 188, 191(1) and (3), 192, 193 and 197 to 200;

(b) paragraphs 1, 2(1) and (2), 3(1), (2) and (4) and 4 to 6 of Schedule 7;

(c) Schedules 8 and 11;

(d) the repeals in—

(i) TCPA 1990 (except those in Schedules 1 and 1A to that Act);

(ii) the Environmental Protection Act 1990 (c. 43);

(iii) the Planning and Compensation Act 1991 (c. 34);

(iv) sections 42(3) and 53 of PCPA 2004.

(5) Section 186 and the repeal in Schedule 1A to TCPA 1990 come into force on such day as the Welsh Ministers may by order appoint.

(6) Sections 194(2) to (5), 201, 202, 203 and 225 (together with related entries in Schedule 13), and paragraph 7 of Schedule 7, come into force at the end of two months beginning with the day on which this Act is passed.

(7) Section 204 comes into force in accordance with subsection (5) of that section.

(8) The other provisions of this Act come into force on such day as the Secretary of State may by order appoint.

(9) The powers conferred by this section are exercisable by statutory instrument.

(10) An order under this section may—

(a) appoint different days for different purposes (including different areas);

(b) contain transitional, transitory or saving provision in connection with the coming into force of this Act.

242 Short title

This Act may be cited as the Planning Act 2008.

Schedule 1 ...

Repealed by Localism Act 2011, ss 128(2), 237, Sch 13, paras 1, 2, Sch 25, Pt 20 as from 1 April 2012.

Schedule 2 ...

Amends Green Belt (London and Home Counties) Act 1938, Pipe-lines Act 1962, Harbours Act 1964, Gas Act 1965, Energy Act 1976, Ancient Monuments and Archaeological Areas Act 1979, Highways Act 1980, Electricity Act 1989, Town and Country Planning Act 1990, Planning (Listed Buildings and Conservation Areas) Act 1990, Planning (Hazardous Substances) Act 1990, New Roads and Street Works Act 1991, Water Industry Act 1991, Transport and Works Act 1992, Town and Country Planning (Scotland) Act 1997, Planning (Hazardous Substances) (Scotland) Act 1997, Housing and Regeneration Act 2008, Crossrail Act 2008 (c. 18)

Schedule 3 ...

Repealed by Localism Act 2011, ss 128(2), 237, Sch 13, para 54, Sch 25, Pt 20 (1 April 2012).

Schedule 4 Correction of errors in development consent decisions

1 Correction of errors

(1) This paragraph applies if—

(a) the [Secretary of State][1] makes an order granting development consent, or refuses development consent, and

(b) the decision document contains a correctable error.

(2) The decision document is—

(a) in the case of an order granting development consent, the order;

(b) in the case of a refusal of development consent, the document recording the refusal.

(3) A correctable error is an error or omission which—

(a) is in a part of the decision document which records the decision, and

(b) is not part of the statement of reasons for the decision.

(4) The [Secretary of State][2] may correct the error or omission if (but only if) the conditions in sub-paragraphs (5) and (7) are met.

This is subject to sub-paragraph (11).

(5) The condition is that, before the end of the relevant period—

(a) the [Secretary of State][2] receives a written request to correct the error or omission from any person, or

(b) the [Secretary of State][2] sends a statement in writing to the applicant which explains the error or omission and states that the [Secretary of State][2] is considering making the correction.

(6) The relevant period is—

(a) if the decision document is an order granting development consent, the period specified in section 118(1)(b);

(b) if the decision document is the document recording a refusal of development consent, the period specified in section 118(2)(b).

(7) The condition is that the [Secretary of State][2] informs each relevant local planning authority that the request mentioned in sub-paragraph (5)(a) has been received or the statement mentioned in sub-paragraph (5)(b) has been sent (as the case may be).

(8) If—

(a) the decision document is an order granting development consent, and

(b) the order was required to be contained in a statutory instrument,

the power conferred by sub-paragraph (4) may be exercised only by order contained in a statutory instrument.

[...][3]

(10) As soon as practicable after the instrument [containing the order is made, the Secretary of State][4] must deposit a copy of it in the office of the Clerk of the Parliaments.

(11) The power conferred by sub-paragraph (4) may not be exercised in relation to provision included in an order granting development consent by virtue of [paragraph 30A or 30B of Schedule 5 (deemed marine licence under Marine and Coastal Access Act 2009)][5].

1 Words substituted by Localism Act 2011, s 128(2), Sch 13, paras 1, 70(1), (2) (1 April 2012).
2 Words substituted by Localism Act 2011, s 128(2), Sch 13, paras 1, 70(1), (3) (1 April 2012).
3 Repealed by Localism Act 2011, ss 128(2), 237, Sch 13, paras 1, 70(1), (4), Sch 25, Pt 20 (1 April 2012).
4 Words substituted by Localism Act 2011, s 128(2), Sch 13, paras 1, 70(1), (5) (1 April 2012).
5 Words substituted by Marine and Coastal Access Act 2009, s 112(1), Sch 8, para 4(1), (4) (6 April 2011).

2 Correction notice

(1) If paragraph 1(5)(a) or (b) applies the [Secretary of State][1] must issue a notice in writing (a'correction notice') which—

(a) specifies the correction of the error or omission, or

(b) gives notice of the decision not to correct the error or omission.

(2) The [Secretary of State][1] must issue the correction notice as soon as practicable after making the correction or deciding not to make the correction.

(3) The [Secretary of State][1] must give the correction notice to—

(a) the applicant,

(b) each relevant local planning authority, and

(c) if the correction was requested by any other person, that person.

(4) The Secretary of State may [give the correction notice to persons other than those to whom sub-paragraph (3) requires it to be given.][2]

1 Words substituted by Localism Act 2011, s 128(2), Sch 13, paras 1, 70(1), (6) (1 April 2012).
2 Words substituted by Localism Act 2011, s 128(2), Sch 13, paras 1, 70(1), (7) (1 April 2012).

3 Effect of a correction

(1) If a correction is made in pursuance of paragraph 1—

(a) the original decision and the decision document containing it continue in force, and

(b) the decision document is treated as corrected as specified in the correction notice issued under paragraph 2 with effect from the date the correction notice is issued, or, if the correction is required to be made by order contained in a statutory instrument, the date specified in the order.

(2) If a correction is not made—

(a) the original decision continues to have full force and effect, and

(b) nothing in this Schedule affects anything done in pursuance of or in respect of the original decision.

(3) 'The original decision' means the decision to—

(a) make an order granting development consent, or

(b) refuse development consent.

4 Interpretation

In this Schedule—

'the applicant' means the person who made the application to which the decision relates;

[...][1]

'a relevant local planning authority' means a local planning authority for all or any part of the area in which the land to which the decision relates is situated.

1 Definition repealed by Localism Act 2011, ss 128(2), 237, Sch 13, paras 1, 70(1), (8), Sch 25, Pt 20 (1 April 2012).

Schedule 5 Provision relating to, or to matters ancillary to, development

Part 1 The matters

1

The acquisition of land, compulsorily or by agreement.

2

The creation, suspension or extinguishment of, or interference with, interests in or rights over land (including rights of navigation over water), compulsorily or by agreement.

3

The abrogation or modification of agreements relating to land.

4

Carrying out specified excavation, mining, quarrying or boring operations in a specified area.

5

The operation of a generating station.

6

Keeping electric lines installed above ground.

7

The use of underground gas storage facilities.

8

The sale, exchange or appropriation of Green Belt land.

9

Freeing land from any restriction imposed on it by or under the Green Belt (London and Home Counties) Act 1938 (c. xciii), or by a covenant or other agreement entered into for the purposes of that Act.

10

The protection of the property or interests of any person.

11

The imposition or exclusion of obligations or liability in respect of acts or omissions.

12

Carrying out surveys or taking soil samples.

13

Cutting down, uprooting, topping or lopping trees or shrubs or cutting back their roots.

14

The removal, disposal or re-siting of apparatus.

15

Carrying out civil engineering or other works.

16

The diversion of navigable or non-navigable watercourses.

17

The stopping up or diversion of highways.

18

Charging tolls, fares [(including penalty fares)][1] and other charges.

1 Words inserted by Localism Act 2011, s 128(2), Sch 13, paras 1, 71(1), (2) (1 April 2012).

19

The designation of a highway as a trunk road or special road.

20

The specification of the classes of traffic authorised to use a highway.

21

The appropriation of a highway for which the person proposing to construct or improve a highway is the highway authority.

22

The transfer to the person proposing to construct or improve a highway of a highway for which that person is not the highway authority.

23

The specification of the highway authority for a highway.

24

The operation and maintenance of a transport system.

25

Entering into an agreement for the provision of police services.

26

The discharge of water into inland waters or underground strata.

27–30 …

Repealed by Marine and Coastal Access Act 2009, s 321, Sch 22, Pt 2 (6 April 2011).

[30A

Deeming a marine licence under Part 4 of the Marine and Coastal Access Act 2009 to have been given by the Secretary of State for activities specified in the order and subject to such conditions as may be specified in the order.][1]

1 Added by Marine and Coastal Access Act 2009, s 112(1), Sch 8, para 4(1), (5) (6 April 2011).

[30B

Deeming any such conditions to have been attached to the marine licence by the Secretary of State under that Part.][1]

1 Added by Marine and Coastal Access Act 2009, s 112(1), Sch 8, para 4(1), (5) (6 April 2011).

31

The creation of a harbour authority.

32

Changing the powers and duties of a harbour authority.

[32A

The making of byelaws by any person and their enforcement.][1]

1 Added by Localism Act 2011, s 128(2), Sch 13, paras 1, 71(1), (3) (1 April 2012).

[32B

(1) The creation of offences within sub-paragraph (2) in connection with—

(a) non-payment of tolls, fares or other charges,

(b) a person's failure to give the person's name or address in accordance with provision relating to penalty fares,

(c) enforcement of byelaws, or

(d) construction, improvement, maintenance or management of a harbour.

(2) An offence is within this sub-paragraph if—

(a) it is triable only summarily,

(b) a person guilty of the offence is not liable to imprisonment, and

(c) any fine to which a person guilty of the offence may be liable cannot be higher than level 3 on the standard scale.][1]

1 Added by Localism Act 2011, s 128(2), Sch 13, paras 1, 71(1), (3) (1 April 2012).

33

The transfer of property, rights, liabilities, or functions.

34

The transfer, leasing, suspension, discontinuance and revival of undertakings.

35

The payment of contributions.

36

The payment of compensation.

37

The submission of disputes to arbitration.

38

The alteration of borrowing limits.

Part 2 Interpretation

39

(1) This paragraph applies for the purposes of this Schedule.

(2) 'Transport system' means any of the following—

(a) a railway,

(b) a tramway,

(c) a trolley vehicle system,

(d) a system using a mode of guided transport prescribed by order under section 2 of the Transport and Works Act 1992 (c. 42).

(3) 'Maintenance', in relation to a transport system, includes the inspection, repair, adjustment, alteration, removal, reconstruction or replacement of the system.

(4) The following terms have the meanings given by section 67(1) (interpretation) of the Transport and Works Act 1992 (c. 42)—

'guided transport',

'tramway',

'trolley vehicle system'.

Schedule 6 Changes to, and revocation of, orders granting development consent

Preliminary

1

(1) This paragraph applies for the purposes of this Schedule.

(2) 'The applicant', in relation to a development consent order, means the person who applied for the order.

(3) 'A successor in title of the applicant' means a person who—

(a) derives title to the land from the applicant (whether directly or indirectly), and

(b) has an interest in the land.

[...][1]

(5) 'Development consent order' means an order granting development consent.

(6) 'The land', in relation to a development consent order, means the land to which the order relates or any part of that land.

1 Repealed by Localism Act 2011, ss 128(2), 237, Sch 13, paras 1, 72(1), (2), Sch 25, Pt 20 (1 April 2012).

Non-material changes

2

(1) The [Secretary of State][1] may make a change to a development consent order if [the Secretary of State][2] is satisfied that the change is not material.

This is subject to sub-paragraph (13).

(2) In deciding whether a change is material, the [Secretary of State][1] must have regard to the effect of the change, together with any previous changes made under this paragraph, on the development consent order as originally made.

(3) The power conferred by sub-paragraph (1) includes power—

(a) to impose new requirements in connection with the development for which consent is granted by the development consent order;

(b) to remove or alter existing requirements.

(4) The power conferred by sub-paragraph (1) may be exercised only on an application made to the [Secretary of State][3] by or on behalf of—

(a) the applicant or a successor in title of the applicant,

(b) a person with an interest in the land, or

(c) any other person for whose benefit the development consent order has effect.

(5) An application under sub-paragraph (4) must be made in the prescribed form and manner.

(6) Sub-paragraph (7) applies in relation to an application under sub-paragraph (4) made by or on behalf of a person with an interest in some, but not all, of the land to which the development consent order relates.

(7) The application may be made only in respect of so much of the order as affects the land in which the person has an interest.

(8) The [Secretary of State][1] must comply with such requirements as may be prescribed as to consultation and publicity in relation to the exercise of the power conferred by sub-paragraph (1).

This is subject to sub-paragraphs (9) to (11).

(9) If the development consent order was required to be contained in a statutory instrument, the power conferred by sub-paragraph (1) may be exercised only by order contained in a statutory instrument.

[...][4]

(11) As soon as practicable after the instrument [containing the order][5] is made, the [Secretary of State][1] must deposit a copy of it in the office of the Clerk of the Parliaments.

(12) If a change is made to a development consent order under the power conferred by sub-paragraph (1)—

(a) the order continues in force,

(b) the [Secretary of State][1] must give notice of the change to the order to such persons as may be prescribed, and

(c) the change to the order takes effect from the date on which the notice is issued, or, if the change to the order is required to be made by order contained in a statutory instrument, the date specified in the order making the change.

(13) The power conferred by sub-paragraph (1) may not be exercised in relation to provision included in an order granting development consent by virtue of [paragraph 30A or 30B of Schedule 5 (deemed marine licence under Marine and Coastal Access Act 2009)][6].

1 Words substituted by Localism Act 2011, s 128(2), Sch 13, paras 1, 72(1), (3) (1 April 2012).
2 Word substituted by Localism Act 2011, s 128(2), Sch 13, paras 1, 72(1), (4) (1 April 2012).
3 Word substituted by Localism Act 2011, s 128(2), Sch 13, paras 1, 72(1), (5) (1 April 2012).
4 Repealed by Localism Act 2011, ss 128(2), 237, Sch 13, paras 1, 72(1), (6), Sch 25, Pt 20 (1 April 2012).
5 Words inserted by Localism Act 2011, s 128(2), Sch 13, paras 1, 72(1), (7) (1 April 2012).
6 Words substituted by Marine and Coastal Access Act 2009, s 112(1), Sch 8, para 4(1), (6)(a) (1 October 2011: substitution came into force on 6 April 2011 but cannot take effect until the commencement of Planning Act 2008, Sch 6, para 2 on 1 October 2011).

Changes to, and revocation of, orders granting development consent

3

(1) The [Secretary of State][1] may by order make a change to, or revoke, a development consent order.

(2) The power conferred by sub-paragraph (1) may be exercised only in accordance with—

(a) the following provisions of this paragraph, and

(b) paragraphs 4 and 5.

(3) The power may be exercised without an application being made if the [Secretary of State][1] is satisfied that—

(a) the development consent order contains a significant error, and

(b) it would not be appropriate for the error to be corrected by means of the power conferred by paragraph 1 of Schedule 4 or paragraph 2 of this Schedule.

(4) The power may be exercised on an application made by or on behalf of—

(a) the applicant or a successor in title of the applicant,

(b) a person with an interest in the land, or

(c) any other person for whose benefit the development consent order has effect.

(5) The power may be exercised on an application made by a local planning authority if the [Secretary of State][1] is satisfied that—

(a) the development consent order grants development consent for development on land all or part of which is in the local planning authority's area,

(b) the development has begun but has been abandoned, and

(c) the amenity of other land in the local planning authority's area or an adjoining area is adversely affected by the condition of the land.

[...][2]

(7) [The][3] power may be exercised without an application being made if the Secretary of State is satisfied that—

(a) if the development were carried out in accordance with the development consent order, there would be a contravention of [EU][4] law or any of the Convention rights, or

(b) there are other exceptional circumstances that make it appropriate to exercise the power.

(8) In this paragraph—

['EU law'][4] means—

(a) all the rights, powers, liabilities, obligations and restrictions from time to time created or arising by or under the [EU][5] Treaties, and

(b) all the remedies and procedures from time to time provided for by or under the [EU][5] Treaties;

'the Convention rights' has the same meaning as in the Human Rights Act 1998 (c. 42).

1 Words substituted by Localism Act 2011, s 128(2), Sch 13, paras 1, 72(1), (3) (1 April 2012).
2 Repealed by Localism Act 2011, ss 128(2), 237, Sch 13, para 1, 72(1), (8), Sch 25, Pt 20 (1 April 2012).
3 Words substituted by Localism Act 2011, s 128(2), Sch 13, paras 1, 72(1), (9) (1 April 2012).
4 Word substituted by Treaty of Lisbon (Changes in Terminology) Order 2011, SI 2011/1043, art 6(2)(a) (1 October 2011: substitution came into force on 22 April 2011 but cannot take effect until the commencement of Planning Act 2008, Sch 6, para 3).
5 Word substituted by Treaty of Lisbon (Changes in Terminology) Order 2011, SI 2011/1043, art 6(1)(a) (1 October 2011: substitution came into force on 22 April 2011 but cannot take effect until the commencement of Planning Act 2008, Sch 6, para 3).

Changes to, and revocation of, orders: supplementary

4

(1) An application under paragraph 3 must be—

(a) made in the prescribed form and manner, and

(b) accompanied by information of a prescribed description.

(2) Sub-paragraph (3) applies in relation to an application under paragraph 3(4) made by or on behalf of a person with an interest in some, but not all, of the land to which the development consent order relates.

(3) The application may be made only in respect of so much of the order as affects the land in which the person has an interest.

(4) The Secretary of State may by regulations make provision about—

(a) the procedure to be followed before an application under paragraph 3 is made;

(b) the making of such an application;

(c) the decision-making process in relation to the exercise of the power conferred by paragraph 3(1);

(d) the making of the decision as to whether to exercise that power;

(e) the effect of a decision to exercise that power.

(5) Paragraphs (c) to (e) of sub-paragraph (4) apply in relation to the exercise of the power conferred by paragraph 3(1)—

(a) on an application under paragraph 3, or

(b) on the initiative of the [Secretary of State][1] under paragraph 3(3) or (7).

(6) If a development consent order is changed or revoked in the exercise of the power conferred by paragraph 3(1), the [Secretary of State][1] must give notice of the change or revocation to such persons as may be prescribed.

(7) If a development consent order was required to be contained in a statutory instrument, an order changing or revoking the development consent order made in the exercise of the power conferred by paragraph 3(1) must also be contained in a statutory instrument.

[...][2]

(9) As soon as practicable after the instrument [containing the order][3] is made, the [Secretary of State][1] must deposit a copy of it in the office of the Clerk of the Parliaments.

1 Words substituted by Localism Act 2011, s 128(2), Sch 13, paras 1, 72(1), (3) (1 April 2012).
2 Repealed by Localism Act 2011, ss 128(2), 237, Sch 13, paras 1, 72(1), (10), Sch 25, Pt 20 (1 April 2012).
3 Words inserted by Localism Act 2011, s 128(2), Sch 13, paras 1, 72(1), (11) (1 April 2012).

5

(1) This paragraph applies in relation to the power conferred by paragraph 3(1) to make a change to, or revoke, a development consent order.

(2) The power may not be exercised after the end of the period of 4 years beginning with the date on which the relevant development was substantially completed.

(3) Sub-paragraph (2) does not prevent the exercise of the power—

(a) in relation to requirements imposed by the development consent order in connection with the relevant development, or

(b) to revoke the development consent order.

(4) The power includes power—

(a) to require the removal or alteration of buildings or works;

(b) to require the discontinuance of a use of land;

(c) to impose specified requirements in connection with the continuance of a use of land;

(d) to impose new requirements in connection with the relevant development;

(e) to remove or alter existing requirements.

(5) Subject to sub-paragraph (4)(a), the exercise of the power does not affect any building or other operations carried out in pursuance of the development consent order before the power is exercised.

(6) The power may not be exercised in relation to provision included in an order granting development consent by virtue of [paragraph 30A or 30B of Schedule 5 (deemed marine licence under Marine and Coastal Access Act 2009)][1].

(7) 'The relevant development' is the development for which consent is granted by the development consent order.

1 Words substituted by Marine and Coastal Access Act 2009, s 112(1), Sch 8, para 4(1), (6)(b) (1 October 2011: substitution came into force on 6 April 2011 but cannot take effect until the commencement of Planning Act 2008, Sch 6, para 5 on 1 October 2011).

Compensation

6

(1) This paragraph applies if—

(a) in exercise of the power conferred by paragraph 3, the [Secretary of State][1] makes a change to, or revokes, a development consent order,

(b) the case in which the power is exercised is one falling within sub-paragraph (3) [...][2] or (7) of that paragraph,

(c) on a claim for compensation under this paragraph it is shown that a person with an interest in the land, or for whose benefit the development consent order has effect—

(i) has incurred expenditure in carrying out work which is rendered abortive by the change or revocation, or

(ii) has otherwise sustained loss or damage which is directly attributable to the change or revocation, and

(d) the claim is made to the [Secretary of State][1] in the prescribed manner and before the end of the prescribed period.

(2) Compensation in respect of the expenditure, loss or damage is payable to the person [by the Secretary of State.][3]

(3) The reference in sub-paragraph (1)(c)(i) to expenditure incurred in carrying out any work includes a reference to expenditure incurred—

(a) in the preparation of plans for the purposes of the work, or

(b) on other similar matters preparatory to carrying out the work.

(4) Subject to sub-paragraph (3), no compensation is to be paid under this paragraph—

(a) in respect of any work carried out before the development consent order was made, or

(b) in respect of any other loss or damage arising out of anything done or omitted to be done before the development consent order was made (other than loss or damage consisting of depreciation of the value of an interest in land).

(5) The Secretary of State may by regulations make provision about the assessment of compensation payable under this paragraph.

(6) The regulations may in particular include provision—

(a) for the reference of disputes about compensation for depreciation to, and the determination of such disputes by, [...][4] the Lands Tribunal for Scotland, the First-tier Tribunal or the Upper Tribunal;

(b) applying, with or without modifications, a provision of or made under an Act.

1 Words substituted by Localism Act 2011, s 128(2), Sch 13, paras 1, 72(1), (3) (1 April 2012).
2 Word repealed by Localism Act 2011, s 237, Sch 25, Pt 20 (1 April 2012).
3 Words substituted for para 6(2)(a)-(b) and words by Localism Act 2011, s 128(2), Sch 13, paras 1, 72(1), (12) (1 April 2012).
4 Words repealed by Transfer of Tribunal Functions (Lands Tribunal and Miscellaneous Amendments) Order 2009, SI 2009/1307, art 5(1), (2), Sch 1, paras 291, 297 (1 June 2009).

7

(1) In this paragraph 'compensation for depreciation' means compensation payable under paragraph 6 in respect of loss or damage consisting of depreciation of the value of an interest in land.

(2) The Secretary of State may by regulations make provision about the apportionment of compensation for depreciation between different parts of the land to which the claim for the compensation relates.

(3) The regulations may in particular include provision about—

(a) who is to make an apportionment;

(b) the persons to whom notice of an apportionment is to be given;

(c) how an apportionment is to be made;

(d) the reference of disputes about an apportionment to, and the determination of such disputes by, [...][1] the Lands Tribunal for Scotland, the First-tier Tribunal or the Upper Tribunal.

(4) The Secretary of State may by regulations make provision for, and in connection with, the giving of notice of compensation for depreciation.

(5) The regulations may in particular include provision about—

(a) the persons to whom notice of compensation for depreciation is to be given;

(b) the status of such a notice;

(c) the registration of such a notice.

1 Words repealed by Transfer of Tribunal Functions (Lands Tribunal and Miscellaneous Amendments) Order 2009, SI 2009/1307, art 5(1), (2), Sch 1, paras 291, 297 (1 June 2009).

Schedule 7 ...

Amends Town and Country Planning Act 1990, Planning (Listed Buildings and Conservation Areas) Act 1990 and Planning and Compulsory Purchase Act 2004.

Schedule 8 ...

Amends Forestry Act 1967, Town and Country Planning Act 1990 and Planning and Compensation Act 1991.

Schedule 9 ...

Amends Local Government, Planning and Land Act 1980, New Towns Act 1981, Housing Act 1988, Town and Country Planning Act 1990 and Leasehold Reform, Housing and Urban Development Act 1993.

Schedule 10 ...

Amends Town and Country Planning Act 1990, Planning (Listed Buildings and Conservation Areas) Act 1990 and Planning (Hazardous Substances) Act 1990.

Schedule 11 ...

Amends Town and Country Planning Act 1990, Planning (Listed Buildings and Conservation Areas) Act 1990 and Planning (Hazardous Substances) Act 1990.

Schedule 12 ...

Modifies Town and Country Planning (Scotland) Act 1997,

Schedule 13 ...

Amends Forestry Act 1967, Town and Country Planning Act 1990, Environmental Protection Act 1990, Planning and Compensation Act 1991, Planning and Compulsory Purchase Act 2004 and Greater London Authority Act 2007.

Index

[References are to page numbers]

National Infrastructure Planning

Expert legal opinion, when you need it.

If you find the National Infrastructure Planning ***Handbook*** helpful, then your next stop should be to trial the National Infrastructure Planning ***Service*** – a subscription-based online service. Trials are free and can be arranged by using the contact details below.

"It really is terrific – just what the profession needs"

Quod, Planning consultancy

"Essential as a means of keeping abreast of the legal updates and experiences of the 2008 Planning Act and well as a very useful source for undertaking DCO's."

CgMs Consulting, Planning consultancy

This essential provides searchable, frequently updated, fully hyperlinked access to an entire database devoted to all aspects of the DCO process connected to the Planning Act 2008.

This essential online service help users navigate the Planning Act 2008 as it applies to major planning projects, through expert articles and primary materials relating to NSIPs, that are updated as and when changes occur in the system.

The author team from Francis Taylor Building focuses on problems faced by practitioners on a daily basis and:

- help you access and navigate the infrastructure planning system more effectively;
- share best practice;
- offer advice and solutions in problem areas;
- discuss new ideas and;
- keep you updated with every new development in the field.

Held online, the service gives you instant access from your laptop, tablet or smartphone to commentary and materials connected to every area of national infrastructure planning. It's set out in a logical and highly searchable manner, allowing you to easily locate the opinion and expertise you need to make your projects a reality.

Simple to follow navigational side panels help you find each article and material, while the multi-level search facility allows you to fine-tune the exact terms you are looking for. Whatever you need, you'll find it quickly.

Why should you subscribe to the service?

While textbooks, news sites and material databases provide some insight and guidance about Nationally Significant infrastructure projects, there is no other resource that provides fully-searchable commentary and links through to every piece of legislation, CLG Guidance, Planning Inspectorate Guidance and other relevant material.

When you subscribe to the service you'll have access to:

- Scores of articles relating to nationally significant infrastructure projects
- Frequently updated articles following issues as they arise